Pool & Spa Operator™
Handbook

Artist Statement

"We are shaped and mutated by our physical environment from microbes to ozone. Families provide not only the genetic code but also patterns and mantras that are the foundation of our daily decisions and emotional roots…Today's technology allows us to be in one place mentally, while physically in another. We are constantly manipulated and transformed. I am interested in this state of flux and the effort by which we try to control our individual and social realities.

Water is a lens to see another perspective and is the tool for my latest work. My state of awareness is no more factual than the one distorted by water and processed by the digital camera. The experience of gathering the resource images is about juggling control and abandon, playing with light and buoyancy, training breath and allowing the eye to see, against what the mind believes.

My most recent body of work is called Revelations in the Dark. These paintings embrace contrast. They began as photographs on a night swim in the desert, capturing white flesh suspended in still darkness. At their essence, these pieces are quiet meditations on universal questions of the unknown and personal truth. Like an astronaut floating between celestial bodies or a diver going into blue depths there is an experiential shift that allows us to feel irrelevant and important at once."

Cover Design: © 2015 Abbey Messmer – June Blossoms

Disclaimer

© 1983, 2005, 2006, 2007, 2009, 2012, 2014, 2017, 2017 (2nd ed.) by National Swimming Pool Foundation®
Published by National Swimming Pool Foundation®
4775 Granby Circle
Colorado Springs, CO 80919-3131

The information furnished in this publication is intended to be advisory in nature and is not intended to provide legal advice. The Pool & Spa Operator™ Handbook, the official text for the Certified Pool/Spa Operator® (CPO®) certification program, has been written to provide information and guidelines for the operation of spas and swimming pools used by the public. It is not intended to replace existing laws, regulations, or codes. This publication is not meant to establish standards, but does cite existing standards as published by recognized national and international standards organizations.

A CPO® certification can only be granted upon successful completion of a CPO® certification course. The text material in this book does not constitute comprehensive training. A CPO® certification can be achieved when an individual successfully completes a traditional 14-16 hour CPO® certification class, the Pool Operator Primer™ online course, AND one-day Pool Operator Fusion™ classroom course; or the Advanced Service Technician™ (AST) Fundamentals online course AND one-day Pool Operator Fusion™ classroom course. All in-person courses are administered and taught by NSPF® certified instructors. The individual must also successfully pass the CPO® certification examination.

The CPO® certification holder shall be familiar with, and abide by, all pertinent local, state and federal laws, regulations, codes-of-practice, standards of design and operation, and guidelines. The certified operator shall consult industry publications for current information regarding facility design, equipment, legislative changes, liability concerns, and pool management practices. The operator's responsibility is to be familiar with the common accepted practices, as they would apply to his or her facility, and to have a copy of the appropriate information on file. Several of these references are cited throughout this handbook; however, the certified operator should be aware that these references are under recurring review and changes may have occurred since the printing of this publication.

The Pool & Spa Operator™ Handbook should only be used in concurrence with the applicable, appropriate laws, regulations, and codes, and not as a replacement for those items. Professionals who use this manual should do so in tandem with their own knowledge and experience, and with assistance received from other professionals in the industry. Those with limited knowledge of the spa and pool industry may find this manual informative or useful. However, it is strongly recommended that an attorney or other professional with experience in the specific industry-related matters be consulted for advice as to any particular situation. While the handbook includes many guidelines and recommendations, the handbook cannot meet every need or address every type or kind of situation. It is anticipated and expected that the user will find it necessary to supplement or revise the information to adapt it to apply to a particular situation. Failure to meet reasonable standards for the operation of a pool/spa facility, as it applies to the safe environment for the public and employees, may result in serious legal consequences, even if the guidelines suggested in this publication have been followed.

To the fullest extent not prohibited by applicable law, NSPF®, the authors and editors of this publication disclaim all warranties, express or implied, including, but not limited to, implied warranties of merchantability, accuracy and fitness for a particular purpose. Without limiting the foregoing, NSPF®, the authors and editors do not warrant, and disclaim any warranties, express or implied, that the information contained herein is free from error, applies to every situation, complies with local or federal laws, or is fit for any particular purpose.

Under no circumstances shall NSPF®, the authors or editors be liable for any damages, including direct, incidental, special, consequential or exemplary damages that result from the use of this publication or the information contained therein, even if NSPF®, the authors or editors have been advised of the possibility of such damages. This publication and the information therein, including these legal notices and terms, shall be governed and interpreted in accordance with the substantive law of the State of Colorado of the United States of America, without reference to the principles of conflicts of law.

All rights reserved. Except for the purposes of education and use within the intended environment, no portion of this document should be reproduced, copied or utilized in any form or by any means, electronic or mechanical, including photocopying, recording, or by any information storage and retrieval system, without permission in writing from the National Swimming Pool Foundation®. Inquiries should be made in writing, addressed to NSPF®, 4775 Granby Circle, Colorado Springs, CO 80919-3131. This work is copyrighted and if reproduced in any form, citation must be made as follows: Pool & Spa Operator™ Handbook, National Swimming Pool Foundation®.

Library of Congress Control Number: 2016906350
ISBN 978-1-940345-00-0

© National Swimming Pool Foundation 2017

Preface

Recreational water use at man-made facilities goes back thousands of years. Greek and Roman baths are dated back to 1700 B.C. Today, the swimming pool is a mainstay of healthy activity that spans the world. Several factors contributed to this development. The origination of centrifugal pumps in the late 1800s, broad manufacture of chlorine in the early 1900s, and advances in filter design and heaters in the 1920s played a pivotal role.

The modern Olympic games (1896); sexually-integrated pools; swimmers crossing the English Channel; Hollywood films and media attention given athletes and movie stars like Gertrude Ederle, Johnny Weissmuller, Annette Kellerman, Buster Crabbe, and Ester Williams made swimming and aquatic facilities a focal point for society in the early to mid 1900s. After World War II, prosperity and racial integration of public facilities in the U.S. drove rapid growth in residential pools. Between 1948 and 1960, the number of U.S. residential pools grew from about 2,400 to 300,000. In 2009, there were about 9.4 million residential pools, six million residential spas, and 300,000 public pools in the U.S. alone.[1]

The National Swimming Pool Foundation®

As the number of pools increases, so, too, does the need to prevent injury, illness, drowning, inefficiency, and deterioration. Founded in 1965 as a non-profit foundation, NSPF® has emerged as the leading education and research organization in this field. The NSPF mission is to encourage healthier living through education and research.

Today the NSPF® Pool & Spa Operator™ Handbook and the Certified Pool/Spa Operator® (CPO®) certification program are the most current, comprehensive, and widely accepted resources in our field. Since 1982, over 400,000 people in 98 countries have taken the CPO® certification course. This course has established a baseline of care in the public pool and spa field. These resources are updated annually with references to new technologies and regulations. This handbook and courses are available in English, Spanish, French, Ukrainian, and Russian.

The CPO® certification program is now available in blended formats where students are guided through the Handbook using the Pool Operator Primer™ or Advanced Service Technician™ Fundamentals online courses. Next, students attend the second day of a CPO® certification course to learn from an NSPF® certified instructor and take the certification exam.

It is important to train and certify people who care for aquatic facilities and for those operators and service technicians to remain diligent.[2] It is also important to train managers who supervise pool technicians. Pool Operator Primer™ and Advanced Service Technician™ Fundamentals online courses are available for this purpose.

The Centers for Disease Control and Prevention (CDC) has summarized the violations at public swimming pools and public spas.[3] In the 2013 study, the CDC reported that 12.3% of the pools had "serious violations that threatened the public's health and resulted in immediate pool closure."[3] Serious health violations were at similar levels in 2008,[4] and the latest statistics will be found at www.cdc.gov. To further raise standards, NSPF® offers a spectrum of print and online training materials for aquatic facilities, service companies, retailers, builders, government agencies, academia, and residential pool owners.

NSPF® is unique in its commitment to research that solves today's problems and to refine its spectrum of educational products. Since 2003, NSPF® has funded over $4 million in grants, fellowships, and scholarships. The World Aquatic Health™ Conference brings the latest research findings to professionals in our field. To make advances more accessible, the conference proceedings are also available online (www.thewahc.org).

At the National Swimming Pool Foundation we believe everything we do helps people live healthier lives. We are dedicated to using the investment you make in purchasing each product or program to make pools safer and keep them open. To find more ways to work together, visit www.nspf.org, www.StepIntoSwim.org, or www.HomePoolEssentials.org., or contact us at service@nspf.org or via 719-540-9119.

Thomas M. Lachocki

Thomas M. Lachocki, Ph.D., CEO
National Swimming Pool Foundation®

Ronald L. Ford

Ronald L. Ford - Tropical Aquatics
Author of the 2005 Handbook

1   Source: P.K. Data
2   Lachocki, T.M, Certified Pool Operator Training, Water Conditioning & Purification, Nov. 2006.
3   Hlavsa MC, Gerth TR, Collier SA, et al. Immediate Closures and Violations Identified During Routine Inspections of Public Aquatic Facilities — Network for Aquatic Facility Inspection Surveillance, Five States, 2013. MMWR Surveill Summ 2016;65(No. SS-5):1–26
4   CDC Surveillance Data from Swimming Pool Inspections - Selected States and Counties - U.S. in 2002 (MMWR 2003, 52, 513-6) & in 2008 (MMWR 59(19), 582-7.

© National Swimming Pool Foundation 2017

Acknowledgements

NSPF® Board of Directors

Rob Butcher – Swim Across America
Diane Dahlmann – University of Missouri
G. Bruce Dunn – Mission Pools
Franceen Gonzales – White Water West
D. Scot Hunsaker – Ardent Group
William Kent, Ph.D. – Team Horner
James Mock – Ecolab
John Puetz – Technical Director for Product Development, Retired
Anita Sayed, Ph.D. – Playcore

Past Board of Directors

Peter H. Brown
Donald C. Burns
Joseph Hunsaker
Judy LaKind
Douglas C. Sackett
Phil Sperber
Cory Willis
Don Witte
D.J. Wright, Jr.

NSPF® Instructor Education Committee

Paul Blake – American Pool Consultants
Connie Sue Centrella – Team Horner
Gary Fraser – NSPF® Instructor
Abiezer Gonzalez – Kendar
Wayne Ivusich – Taylor Technologies
Gretchen Julian – Kent State University
Humberto Abaroa Lance – APPAC, México
Steve Lintz – Head Coach, Sierra Nevada Masters
Michael Orr – Foundation for Pool & Spa Industry Education
Fontaine Piper, Ph.D. – NSPF® Instructor Education Committee Chair
Phil Reynolds – NSPF® Instructor
Roy Vore, Ph.D. – Vore & Associates

Expert Contributors and Review Panel

Peter Alexander – SureWater Technologies Inc.
Alex Antoniou, Ph.D. – NSPF® Reviewer
Steve Barnes – Aquastar Pool Products
Michael Beach, Ph.D. – Centers for Disease Control & Prevention
George Belarski – Deceased, October 24, 2011
Kevin Boyer – Aquasol Controllers, Inc.
Robert Burrows – SureWater Technologies Inc.
John Caden – Independent Consultant
Bruce Carney – American Pools & Spas
Sean Connell – IT-Tralee, Co., Kerry, Ireland
Ray Cronise – Pool Genius Network
Tracynda Davis – NSPF® Reviewer
Hugo Díaz – Áreas de Piscinas
M. Robert Edelson, Ph.D. – M. Robert Edelson & Associates
Michael Espino – YMCA of the USA

Richard Falk
Roy Fielding, Ph.D. – University of North Carolina, Charlotte
Ron Ford – Tropical Aquatics
Robert Freligh – NSPF® Instructor
Melissa A. Garvey – Holme Roberts & Owen, LLP
Julie Gilchrist, Ph.D. – Centers for Disease Control & Prevention
Que Hales – Pool Chlor
Beth Hamil – Del Ozone, Inc.
Jim Hunter – Pentair
Ashkahn Jahromi – Float On
Cynthia Jorgensen, Ph.D. – Centers for Disease Control & Prevention
Thomas M. Lachocki, Ph.D. – NSPF® Chief Executive Officer
Cheryl Lee – Editing Consultant
Ed Lightcap – The Chemours Company
Shawn Lin, Ph.D. – All Water Care
R. Neil Lowry, Ph.D. – Deceased, March 28, 2006
Robert Lowry – Lowry Consulting Group
Rose Lyda – NSPF® Product Development Manager
Tom Metzbower – Advisor
Ellen Meyer, Ph.D. – Lonza
James Miller
John Moorman – John Moorman Associates
Alison Osinski, Ph.D. – Aquatic Consulting Services
Barry Rice – Ohio Department of Health
Dennis Ruis – Iwaki America
Steve Scheuer – Tangent Industries
Tom Seechuck – Deceased, January 20, 2010
Lidia Sepeda – APPAC, México
Ellen Sogolow, Ph.D. – Centers for Disease Control & Prevention
Trevor Sherwood – Pool Operation Management
Joseph P. Stone – Jacobs Engineering
Rick Swartz – Jack's Magic
Joe Sweazy – ETS/Hach Company
Graham Talley – Float On
Gwen Taylor – NSPF® Instructor
Christopher Tate – Orangetheory Fitness
Silvia Uribe – NSPF® Reviewer
R. Ann Wieser, Ph.D. – Gateway Educational Center
Maureen Williams – D&D Technologies (USA), Inc.
Cory Willis – Pool & Spa Education/Consulting LLC

Graphic Design and Book Layout

Franklin R.W. King – NSPF® Product Development Specialist

© National Swimming Pool Foundation 2017

Table of Contents

© National Swimming Pool Foundation 2017

Table of Contents

© National Swimming Pool Foundation 2017

1. Pool & Spa Management

2. Regulations & Guidelines

3. Essential Calculations

4. Pool Water Contamination

5. Disinfection

6. Water Balance

7. Pool & Spa Water Problems

8. Chemical Testing

9. Chemical Feed & Control

10. Water Circulation

11. Pool & Spa Filtration

12. Heating & Air Circulation

13. Spa & Therapy Operations

14. Facility Safety

15. Keeping Records

16. Maintenance Systems

17. Troubleshooting

18. Facility Renovation & Design

References

Table of Contents

© National Swimming Pool Foundation 2017

1. Pool & Spa Management
2. Regulations & Guidelines
3. Essential Calculations
4. Pool Water Contamination
5. Disinfection
6. Water Balance
7. Pool & Spa Water Problems
8. Chemical Testing
9. Chemical Feed & Control
10. Water Circulation
11. Pool & Spa Filtration
12. Heating & Air Circulation
13. Spa & Therapy Operations
14. Facility Safety
15. Keeping Records
16. Maintenance Systems
17. Troubleshooting
18. Facility Renovation & Design

References

© National Swimming Pool Foundation 2017

ix

© National Swimming Pool Foundation 2017

© National Swimming Pool Foundation 2017

Table of Contents

© National Swimming Pool Foundation 2017

1. Pool & Spa Management

2. Regulations & Guidelines

3. Essential Calculations

4. Pool Water Contamination

5. Disinfection

6. Water Balance

7. Pool & Spa Water Problems

8. Chemical Testing

9. Chemical Feed & Control

10. Water Circulation

11. Pool & Spa Filtration

12. Heating & Air Circulation

13. Spa & Therapy Operations

14. Facility Safety

15. Keeping Records

16. Maintenance Systems

17. Troubleshooting

18. Facility Renovation & Design

References

© National Swimming Pool Foundation 2017

Notes

© National Swimming Pool Foundation 2017

Chapter 1:
Pool & Spa Management

"A Professional is a person who can do his best at a time when he doesn't particularly feel like it."

—Alistair Cooke

Swimming pool and spa facilities exist in all sizes and vary greatly as to the activity or programs provided. Regardless of feature size or programs offered, a pool or spa is a large investment, benefit, and potential liability. There must be trained support staff that understands the proper management of water and facility operation. In every case, the individual responsible for operating the facility should be a trained professional. This is true even if the care of the pool is contracted to an outside service company.

Some facilities are large municipal or resort operations with multi-pool installations. The smaller the facility, the more likely that the staff must be multi-skilled and able to perform several tasks in a reasonable manner. These facilities may offer programs that range from infant swim instruction to competitive swim meets. Included may be curricula involving water aerobics, water walking, simple open swimming sessions, or water sports like water polo and synchronized swimming. Often there are diving programs, slides for children, and interactive water features.

Other facilities are single pool operations that may be an amenity to a closed community, such as a condominium, apartment complex, hotel, or campground. There are no added attractions and the only program is that the pool is open for use.

The management organizations can be as varied as the facilities. As facilities become larger and more complex, the requirements of the staff become equally more diverse and specialized.

Understanding water quality is only the first step. The responsible individuals should also have a good understanding of the system

Photo 1-1. *As facilities become larger and more complex, the requirements of the staff become equally more diverse and specialized.*

© National Swimming Pool Foundation 2017

components, their operational limits, the hazards, and the required routine and preventative maintenance. This is true even if the care of the pool is contracted to an outside service company.

Many facilities use a third party service company. This does not relieve the facility management of the duty to understand the basics of proper pool management. Several state administrative codes recognize this need. An example of a common regulatory statement is, "All owners, managers, lifeguards, swim coaches, instructors, or pool operators, etc. shall be responsible for the supervision and safety of the pool and its users."

Owners and managers should ensure that the delegated staff who are responsible for water quality control and system component maintenance have the necessary training and competency to perform these duties.

The National Swimming Pool Foundation® provides training programs to improve operations, reduce risks, and comply with government regulations through the Certified Pool/Spa Operator® certification program.

Types of Pools

Pool classifications are under constant review. There will be some variation in classification definition within local regulations. Pool operators who receive the Certified Pool/Spa Operator® certification should be aware of the regulations and definitions which cover their facility. How a facility is classified will often determine the regulations that govern that facility.

Recreational water facilities have two basic categories—commercial (sometimes called public) and residential (sometimes called private). State regulations define private pools as those that service a residential home or sometimes a group home. Commercial pools are defined as any pool other than a private pool.

Public pools are further classified in the following manner as commonly accepted practice:

Class A: Any pool intended for use by accredited competitive aquatic events. The use of the pool is not limited to competitive events and may be used for recreational purposes. This type of pool is sometimes referred to in codes as a Competition Pool.

Class B: Any pool intended for public recreational use. This type of pool is sometimes referred to in codes as a Public Pool.

Class C: Any pool intended for use by apartments, condominiums, property owners associations, multi-family owned pools, etc. Included in this group are pools operated solely for, and in conjunction with, lodgings such as hotels and motels. This type of pool is sometimes referred to in codes as a Semi-Public Pool.

Class D: Any pool operated for special purposes such as, but not limited to, vortex pools, sand bottom pools, splash pools, float tanks, and interactive water attractions. This type of pool is sometimes referred to in codes as an Other Pool, Aquatic Playground, or Aquatic Recreational Facilities. Local code development may lag industry innovation, however, and therefore may not recognize or regulate new pool configurations.

Class E: Any pool used for physical therapy and operated above 86°F (30°C). This type of pool is sometimes referred to in codes as a Therapy Pool.

Class F: Any pool used for wading purposes. These are sometimes referred to as a Kiddie Pool or Wading Pool.

Health Agencies

The primary concern of the health inspector is the health and safety of the community of pool users. Without enforcement, codes and regulations have little value. Enforcement begins with the approval of the original construction design. This oversight continues with regular on-site inspections of the facility operation. Pool operators who achieve

Photo 1-2. *The health inspector should be considered an ally by the certified operator.*

© National Swimming Pool Foundation 2017

the Certified Pool/Spa Operator® certification recognize the value of these inspections and should consider the inspector an ally.

Certified operators will find it helpful to use the health inspector's checklist as a starting point for the opening procedure for a facility. Many health agency checklists will include the following issues:

- Pool/spa is free of floating material, visible dirt, and algae
- Deck has a minimum of a four-foot (1.22 m) clearance around the pool/spa
- The pool/spa finish is intact and in good repair
- Depth markings are intact and in proper locations
- Handrails, grab-rails and ladders are secure
- Gutter drains are covered with a fully intact grate, and no protrusions are present
- Skimmers have an intact weir in place. Deck covers are in place and properly secured
- Underwater lights are in working order and properly in place with no crevices between the niche and light fixture
- Diving boards are secure and slip resistant
- The shepherd's hook(s) attached to a 16-foot (4.88 m) non-extendable pole is fully accessible and easily seen
- The 18-inch (45.72 cm) diameter lifesaving ring with sufficient rope attached to reach all parts of the pool is fully accessible and easily seen
- A floating safety line is in place two feet (0.61 meters) toward the shallow end before the slope break
- The required pool/spa rules are posted in the mandatory locations
- Sanitary facilities have the appropriate supplies and are properly maintained

Photo 1-3. *The certified operator must maintain safe water conditions at all times.*

Failure to comply with the following items should result in immediate pool or spa closure:

- Self-closing, self-latching gates and fencing to prevent access to unsupervised children
- Free available chlorine levels should not fall below 1 ppm (mg/L). Ideal levels in pools range from 2-4 ppm (mg/L) and in spas from 3-5 ppm (mg/L). Total bromine should fall between 4-6 ppm (mg/L) for pools and spas. The maximum level of chlorine should not exceed 4 ppm (mg/L) [10 ppm (mg/L) bromine] unless allowed by local code
- The pH shall be between 7.2 and 7.8
- The water circulation/filtration system must be operating and circulating water at the proper rate
- Pool/spa main drains must be visible, properly attached, and fully intact
- All drain covers must be VGB compliant and comply with ANSI/APSP-16 or successor standard
- Pools or spas with single drains must be VGB compliant and have an additional level of protection against entrapment
- Water temperature should not exceed 104°F (40°C)

- There is an approved test kit at the site, capable of testing chlorine or bromine, pH, calcium hardness and total alkalinity. If necessary, other testing capability should be available, such as cyanuric acid tests, salt tests, and tests for metals such as copper
- Cyanuric acid, if used, shall not exceed levels required by the local health code. In many cases the limit is 100 ppm. In some cases, lower, higher, or no limits exist, although most codes prohibit the use of cyanuric acid at indoor facilities
- Disinfection feeders are in place and are properly operational. If electrical feed pumps are used, they are electrically interlocked with the circulation pump

The above list is only meant to be a representative sample. To learn more about health official inspections, NSPF offers the Certified Pool/Spa Inspector™ handbook and online course.

The health inspector will review many items other than those listed above. They will require that a daily log of pool operations be maintained. Proper storage of chemicals will be

© National Swimming Pool Foundation 2017

noted. Chemical solution containers and feed mechanisms will be evaluated. Pool-side showers and changing rooms will be assessed.

The inspector is usually limited by the regulations as to what areas may be evaluated. The area most often overlooked is the preventative maintenance of equipment. Thus, preventative maintenance generally becomes the responsibility of the owner.

There is a positive side to an inspection that has many written-up items. Certified operators may use a negative inspection report as a guide to develop an improvement plan and to help secure funding for needed equipment. Additional training in the Aquatic Facility Audits™ program may help operators perform effective self-audits.

Management

A pool operator may have management responsibilities over the facility or staff members. A manager's primary responsibility is to make sure that the team understands what is expected of them and that they have the tools they need to get their jobs done. Therefore, everyone's roles and responsibilities need to be defined. For example, some activities involve action, such as backwashing the filter. Other activities involve management, such as planning when to backwash a filter. The manager specifies who is responsible to perform each of these tasks. Successful managers must continue to develop their communication skills since many of the activities they carry out involve communication.

There are four management work functions (see illustration 1-1):
- **Planning:** deciding the course of action before the work is started
- **Organizing:** defining and connecting the work to be done so it can be executed effectively
- **Leading:** encouraging people to take proper action
- **Controlling:** measuring and regulating all work in progress and evaluating the results

Many of the manager's work functions rely on keeping records documenting that these management tasks were, in fact, carried out. See the Keeping Records chapter for more information on this subject.

Planning

The planning function requires a clear understanding of the facility's objectives. The goals and objectives at a condominium pool are quite different than those at a major resort facility. A competition pool at a YMCA facility will have different objectives than those of a therapy pool at a hospital.

The planning process involves several activities related to the people, the facility, and the equipment:
- Forecasting (estimating future conditions)
- Developing objectives (desired results)
- Programming (action steps)
- Scheduling (time sequence)
- Budgeting (planning and allocating resources)
- Developing policies (establishing standing decisions)
- Developing procedures (standardizing repetitive work)

Some daily records, such as the amount of chemical used, can be compiled into monthly reports for management use. Injury reports can be used to develop new objectives such as training, necessary facility renovations, and equipment replacement. Gauge readings can be analyzed to schedule filter backwashing. Equipment failure dates can be used to revise the schedule for preventative maintenance.

Organizing

A properly organized facility is more efficient because work can proceed in a manner consistent with the understood objectives. Good organization prevents overlap and duplication. Work can be grouped logically. This allows the staff to understand their individual duties and their roles in the success of the facility.

Illustration 1-1. *The combination of planning, organizing, leading, and controlling is the basis of successful management.*

© National Swimming Pool Foundation 2017

The key functions of organization are
- Organizational structure: identify and arrange work
- Delegation: define responsibilities and create accountability
- Define relationships: create management structure

An organizational chart is an important record that should be developed based on the facility's objectives. While creating the organizational chart, the operator should consider only the needs of the facility and not the current staff. Once completed, the new, optimal chart can be compared to the current organization. Managers may need to develop an interim strategy as the organization moves away from the current structure and staff toward the new structure. A good manager will always involve the people who will be affected when changes are made.

Written procedures and policies are an important tool to help employees know what is expected of them. People understand better if management's expectations are communicated in a variety of ways. Therefore, people understand better if they are told verbally, they read a written procedure, and they are shown how to perform a task. The written procedures help staff members understand what they are supposed to do. The procedures also help managers communicate and understand how different operations are performed.

The roles and responsibilities of each team member must be defined. Once defined, decision making is easier and quicker. For example, if there is a written procedure that the pool should be closed if the circulation pump fails, an operator can instruct a lifeguard to close the pool without fear that the decision will be second-guessed. Job responsibilities are normally defined in a job description. Job descriptions help team members understand what is expected of them.

Leading

The pool/spa facility manager must at all times influence the staff to take effective actions. A good manager is one who is able to make decisions and delegate tasks. Once a course of action has been decided, then the manager is able to encourage and compel the necessary action on the part of the staff. This is accomplished by creating an understanding of the required action through effective communication.

Photo 1-4. *Roles and responsibilities of each team member must be defined.*

A good manager will be careful in the selection and hiring process. Managers must act in ways that set good examples for their staff. In addition, managers must develop the staff's skills and abilities to satisfy their career and leadership interests. Staff will have a feeling of pride and improved motivation when given the opportunity for further training. The key functions of leading are
- Decision making: reach conclusions and make judgments
- Motivating: inspire and encourage people
- Communicating: allow people to understand
- Hiring: screen, select, place people
- Staff development: training to improve knowledge, skills, and attitudes

It is important to maintain the required employee records in hiring, discipline, training, awards, promotions, and routine evaluations. Employee records help a manager understand their staff's skills, capabilities, and potential. The records also help prevent misunderstandings or miscommunications between managers and staff. Misunderstandings can impair productivity, motivation, and the success of management, staff, and the facility.

Controlling

The existence of a plan, objectives, organization documents, and a well-trained staff is no guarantee that work will be accomplished when necessary. There must be a method of tracking and evaluating performance.

For proper control to take place there must be a way to measure and report how well performance matches the established standards or policies. For instance, if the pool or spa has a pH that exceeds the maximum allowed by code, immediate corrective action is necessary. This may require closing the facility. Written procedures should name the staff position responsible for making these decisions. Notations of the variance should be recorded along with the corrective action taken and the results. Records play a very important role in this management function. The key functions of controlling are

- Standards: develop measurement standards of performance
- Measuring: record and report performance
- Evaluating: compare performance to standards
- Correction: eliminate any difference between performance and standards

How a manager sets objectives when planning and organizing has an impact on how well those objectives can be tracked. Effective objectives should be Specific, Measurable, Achievable, Relevant, and Time-based. In other words, they should be SMART. An objective that is specific means that it is an observable action or behavior. An objective that is measurable means there has to be a way to track and record the behavior. Achievable means the person is capable of achieving the objective, not that the objective is easy. An objective that is relevant means the objective is important to the organization. If people understand why something is important, they are almost always more willing to help accomplish the goal. An objective that is time-based simply means that it defines exactly when the goal will be completed.

Here is an example of a SMART objective:

Measure the free chlorine reading using a commercial DPD test kit (specific) at 9:00 am, 12:00 noon, 2:00 pm, and 4:00 pm every day (time) and record (measurable) the readings in the daily log book (achievable) located in the pump room just beneath the CPO® certifications for the staff; this ensures we protect our customers from recreational water illnesses (relevant).

Risk Management

Aquatic facility management bears the responsibility of ensuring not only the health and safety of patrons using the swimming pool or spa, but also the staff working at the facility. This is accomplished through risk management.

Aquatic facility risk management encompasses the prevention of injuries to patrons and staff, the protection of facility assets, and the minimizing of legal liability. In order to manage risk, hazards in the facility environment must be identified and evaluated, and strategies developed to manage, reduce or eliminate exposure.

When developing a risk management plan, operators should take several key factors into consideration. They are

- Negligence
- Standard of Care
- Duty of Care
- Record Keeping

Negligence

Most legal matters involving aquatic facilities center around the concept of negligence. Negligence is concerned with unintentional fault or carelessness resulting in injury. In other words, negligence deals with avoidable accidents that should have been anticipated and prevented by taking reasonable precautions. Even if no harm was intended, a person may still be negligent if the individual failed to take reasonable measures to prevent a foreseeable accident. Negligence is the failure to act in accordance with the corresponding standard of care.

Standard of Care

How does the law determine the amount of reasonable care to judge whether a person is negligent or not? There has to be some consistent standard against which one's actions are compared. In the aquatic industry, this standard is that of an individual who uses due care and acts prudently under the circumstances. Of course this person does not exist, but it is the standard to which all is compared.

The public expects a certain standard of care when using an aquatic facility. The standard of care for the pool operator includes, but is not limited to

- Good disinfectant level in the water
- No broken glass on the deck

© National Swimming Pool Foundation 2017

- Main drain covers intact and in place
- Adequate signage
- Operators trained and certified

In a lawsuit, a court may determine whether the facility was negligent by not following the standards of care.

Duty of Care

The standard of care is a measure used to establish a standard against which actual conduct is judged. This standard is called the duty of care. The duty of care is that amount of reasonable care owed to individuals using the aquatic facility.

The pool operator has a duty to act with reasonable care towards patrons and staff so as not to create an unreasonable risk of harm. For example, the pool operator has a duty to act by ensuring the chemical storage room remains locked at all times.

In becoming a pool operator, there is a legal relationship between you and the patrons using the facility. This type of duty has specific standards of care. There are particular duties of care owed by the operator with respect to the water and equipment used by patrons.

Record Keeping

Keeping records is essential in order to protect the facility against possible lawsuits. Record keeping is discussed in greater detail in the Keeping Records chapter. Documentation that shows a facility meets a standard of care is very helpful in defending a facility and its staff.

For more information on risk management and legal issues in the aquatic industry, operators should consult the Aquatic Safety Compendium™, National Swimming Pool Foundation, 2005, and the NSPF® Aquatic Risk Management booklet and online training course at www.nspf.org. In addition operators should consult with a local attorney to address any questions on issues.

Who Should Become a Certified Operator?

There should be a trained and certified operator at every pool facility. If the routine maintenance is provided by a third-party service company, the outside service technician should have a Certified Pool/Spa Operator® (CPO®) certification. The owner or manager of the facility serviced by an outside company should also be certified so that he/she can evaluate the performance of the service technician.

The owner or manager is also responsible for the safety of the pool, which is another reason to be certified. The owners, managers, and pool operators should all have a comprehensive knowledge of statutes, administrative codes, regulations, and commonly accepted practices. The CPO® certification program provides this education base.

Any individual who makes changes to the water quality, or performs routine maintenance of swimming pool system components, should obtain CPO® certification. The following statement is taken from the ANSI/APSP American National Standards for Public Swimming Pools and is considered to be commonly accepted practice:

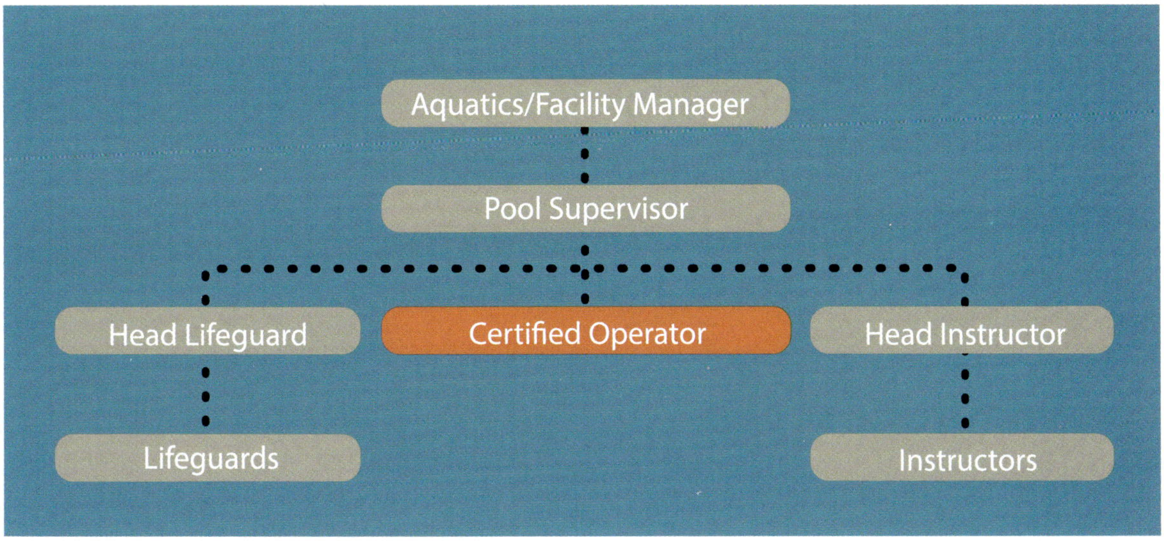

Illustration 1-2. *The relationship of the certified operator to other aquatic staff members.*

7

© National Swimming Pool Foundation 2017

"Both existing and new public swimming pools (and spas) shall be maintained under the supervision and direction of a properly trained operator who shall be responsible for the sanitation, safety, and proper maintenance of the pool and all physical and mechanical equipment. The operator shall be certified in accordance with state/local codes or comparable certifying organizations."

Many organizations also require head lifeguards or head instructors to be trained and certified as operators. This helps ensure other managers are familiar with risks and prevention. This is important since these managers are closely involved with pool activities.

All repair and maintenance work should be performed by a qualified person. In some cases a contractor or licensed professional must be used. In other cases it must be a certified operator.

Hotels, Motels, Apartments, and Condominium Pools

There is very little delegation with smaller Class C pools. The owner quite often could be the manager. The maintenance person may spend some time operating the pool. The part time pool operator should obtain CPO® certification.

The owner/manager of a small Class C pool still has responsibility for the safety and supervision of the pool. This individual may or may not have hands-on capability. Even so, the manager should have a good understanding of basic pool operations and have CPO® certification. This provides continuity throughout the frequent turnover of maintenance personnel.

This small pool operation may have a spa facility as an added amenity. The additional responsibility of a hot water feature places more emphasis on the need for proper training.

An engineering department may manage larger Class C pools. The pool operator's position may be a full-time job. In many instances, the pool may be open for use up to 24 hours a day. To provide continuity, the department manager should have a CPO® certification. Any individual who evaluates and adjusts the pool water chemistry should have a CPO® certification. There should be a pool operator on-site at any time the pool is open for use. It is particularly important to consider coverage on weekends when facilities are more crowded.

Photo 1-5. *The facility is maintained in a clean manner, and informational signs and safety equipment are in place, functional, and easily seen.*

© National Swimming Pool Foundation 2017

Therapy Facility Pools

Class E pools (medical treatment, therapy, exercise and other special purpose) usually have a very small, specialized staff. The pool operation is only one of many staff responsibilities. Often, the routine maintenance is contracted to an outside third-party technician. This technician should have a CPO® certification. The facility manager should also be trained and certified.

Kiddie or Wading Pools

Class F pools are usually associated with pools of other classifications. The same certification requirements would apply.

Competition, Park Pools and Water Parks

Classes A, B, and D pools usually have a highly trained and professional aquatics staff. There will be several layers of management structure. At the head will be the facility director. There will also be aquatics coordinators, swim coaches, lifeguards, a pool supervisor, and maintenance personnel. Every level of this management team has the responsibility of supervision and safety of the aquatics facility.

Written job descriptions at these large pool facilities should require training and certification at each level for maintenance personnel, head lifeguard, pool supervisor, and facility director. Only in this way can the facility be assured that management is familiar with and reducing risk.

Lifeguarding

The main responsibility of a lifeguard is to prevent and respond to aquatic emergencies. This is accomplished by enforcing facility policies, rules, and regulations. It is the responsibility of the lifeguard to inspect the aquatic facility for unsafe conditions and equipment, and to inform management of any concerns.

The lifeguard is charged with the duty to administer first aid and provide CPR in an emergency. There are secondary duties for a lifeguard. These include education, assisting patrons, and record keeping.

The lifeguard may also be assigned the duty of water quality testing, but generally a lifeguard is not responsible for water quality management.

Photo 1-6. *Risk Management includes identifying and evaluating hazards and strategizing to reduce or eliminate risk of exposure.*

This is an area that requires training beyond lifeguard certification.

Secondary duties, including water testing, can only be performed when the lifeguard is not responsible for surveillance of swim patrons. Surveillance is the primary job of a lifeguard. This may be a legal responsibility in that a lifeguard generally is considered a professional rescuer. There are standards to be met, and failure to do so could be considered a negligent act.

Owners or managers of facilities that have lifeguard supervision, should never expect the lifeguard to perform the duties of an operator while on surveillance duty. It is possible that a lifeguard may be a certified operator. However, it is never possible to perform these duties concurrently. If the lifeguard needs to cease surveillance, and there is no certified lifeguard replacement, the pool should be closed to patrons. For more information on this subject consult NSPF® Emergency Response Planning™.

The Certified Operator

The employer's job description defines the operator's responsibilities. Typically, operators must have a CPO® certification as a minimum training requirement. Operators seeking contractor licensure will need a pre-licensure certification, of which CPO® certification may be a component. Pool operators servicing residential pools and spas should consider NSPF® Advanced Service Technician™ certification, a comprehensive pre-licensure certification program for pool and spa service professionals. Operators should be familiar with all pertinent legislation, regulations, codes-of-practice, standards of design and operation, and guidelines, as they apply to their facility. It is the operator's responsibility to have a copy of the relevant information on file.

The operator consults industry publications for current information regarding facility design, equipment, legislative changes, liability concerns, and manangement practices. Many publications are free or inexpensive. Operators who are service professionals join service-focused associations that provide professional benefit and growth opportunities.

The operator has a good understanding of the facility's mechanical system and all of its components. The pool operator understands how to troubleshoot system components to ensure minimum downtime.

Pool operators who achieve certification are responsible for the maintenance of water quality and are knowledgeable about providing proper disinfection as well as water balance.

Pool operators who graduate from the CPO® certification program minimize hazards to the patrons as well as the staff by understanding the requirements of proper chemical storage, usage, and handling. The facility will be maintained in a clean manner and informational signs and safety equipment are in place, functional, and easily seen. Risk management is part of pool operators' responsibilities. They need to be able to identify and evaluate risks at the aquatic facility and then determine the strategy to minimize those risks. For more information about risk management operators may consult the NSPF® Aquatic Risk Management training.

The manager and operator never stop learning. There is a continuing effort to attend classes and seminars related to swimming pool/spa operations. The pool operator attends trade shows, vendor training programs, or provides on-site education to staff. The pool operator should be trained at least to the level of all subordinates in matters such as CPR, lifeguarding, first aid, and chemical safety.

The operator should also have management skills to the level of his or her job assignment. These may include the setting of contracts, establishing budgets, personnel decisions, record keeping, and replacement of equipment. The operator understands the need for proper insurance at all levels. Individual insurance coverage may be necessary, as well as insurance covering the facility.

A pool operator might be a maintenance person with part-time pool responsibility. A pool operator could have a position on an engineering staff, with full-time pool operations responsibility. The pool operator could be a manager without hands-on responsibility or who has management authority over other operators in staff positions.

The pool operator could be an outside service technician, providing third party support to a pool operation. The pool operator might be a lifeguard, providing pool operations management when not surveilling.

© National Swimming Pool Foundation 2017

Photo 1-7. *The pool operator might be a lifeguard, providing pool operations management when not surveilling.*

And finally, a pool operator could be a facility owner, who recognizes that the ultimate responsibility for the supervision of any aquatic facility resides at this level.

Whether owner or technician, manager or lifeguard, the certified operator embodies an Aquatic Facility Professional.

© National Swimming Pool Foundation 2017

Chapter 2:
Regulations & Guidelines

"For every action there is an equal and opposite government program."

–Bob Wells

A swimming pool or spa facility is a complex system made up of many mechanical components, as well as the water. The surrounding environment, the community of pool users, and the workforce are also part of the system.

The owner/manager of an aquatic facility must understand the duty to provide a safe recreational environment for the community being served. An aquatic-related death or injury could be an extreme financial and emotional hardship on all of the individuals involved.

The facility owner or manager must ensure that staff members know and comply with all regulations, standards, and guidelines. Proper training as it applies to all aspects of the facility must be provided, as well.

This chapter largely focuses on U.S. organizations. Certified NSPF® Instructors teaching in other countries around the world will address regulatory agencies that apply.

This chapter provides a general overview of the regulations and standards that may apply to swimming pool and spa facilities and their operators. This chapter is not intended to provide legal advice. The manager/owner of an aquatic facility should consult with legal counsel for specific advice to ensure compliance with all applicable laws and regulations.

There are some basic matters that apply to the health, safety, and welfare of those who use public pools or spas. They are
- Human and environmental contamination of the water
- Facility design and construction
- Facility operation and management

Hazards include physical situations which could result in fatal or non-fatal drowning, entrapment, or spinal injuries. Hazards could also be micro-biological, physical, or chemical. Any of these factors could become a risk to health. For this reason, regulations and guidelines for proper pool/spa operations have been developed.

There are several public regulatory agencies at each level of government in the U.S. At the federal level there are
- Environmental Protection Agency (EPA)
- Occupational Safety & Health Administration (OSHA)
- Consumer Product Safety Commission (CPSC)
- Department of Transportation (DOT)
- Department of Justice (DOJ)
- Centers for Disease Control & Prevention (CDC)

The CDC is also a U.S. federal agency; however, its role is advisory and investigative rather than regulatory. Besides regulations, there are also standards. These have been developed by various national and international organizations. These standards serve as guidelines to the pool operator. Organizations that create standards include:
- American National Standards Institute (ANSI)
- ASTM International (ASTM)
- Chlorine Institute
- Council for the Model Aquatic Health Code (CMAHC)
- International Code Council (ICC)
- NSF International (NSF)
- National Fire Protection Agency (NFPA)
- Underwriters Laboratories (UL)
- World Health Organization (WHO)

Photo 2-1. *Improper storage of chemicals could result in dangerous chemical reactions.*

© National Swimming Pool Foundation 2017

13

Other organizations, including the YMCA and the American Red Cross, also set standards.

Many states, provinces, counties, and cities have regulations for both public and private pools. These statutes often allow for the creation of administrative codes. A government department is then given the duty to apply the administrative codes. Examples would be a Department of Health or Bureau of Recreation and Conservation.

Quite often local laws cover items such as barriers, accessibility, and hours of operation. There may also be a need to consider whether the facility complies with the Americans with Disabilities Act.

The Environmental Protection Agency (EPA)

The mission of the U.S. Environmental Protection Agency is to protect human health and to safeguard the natural environment. Listed among the purposes of the EPA is all Americans are protected from significant risks to human health and the environment where they live, learn, and work. The EPA has many regulations that can affect and guide pool operators.

Labels

The EPA controls pesticide product registration and labeling. This is done under the authority of the Federal Insecticide, Fungicide, Rodenticide Act (Title 7, Chapter 6). A pesticide is a chemical used to prevent, destroy, repel, or mitigate pests. In an aquatic facility, pests can be pool algae, fungi, or microorganisms, such as bacteria and viruses. Most pesticides contain chemicals that can be harmful to people.

Labels use signal words to show how toxic or unsafe a product can be. They are **Caution, Warning, and Danger.**

Danger

Danger is the strongest signal word. If a label has the word Danger on it, the user must be extremely careful handling the product. If it is used the wrong way, medical problems or injury such as blindness or death could occur. Danger is also used on products that could explode if they become heated.

Warning

Warning is less strong than Danger, but it still

SAMPLE STORAGE AND DISPOSAL LABEL:

Store in original container in areas inaccessible to children. Do not reuse empty container. Wrap container and put in trash.
PRECAUTIONARY STATEMENTS
HAZARDS TO HUMANS AND DOMESTIC ANIMALS
DANGER: Corrosive. Causes irreversible eye damage and skin burns. May be fatal if swallowed. Do not get in eyes, on skin or on clothing. Wear safety glasses, rubber gloves and protective clothing. Wash thoroughly with soap and water after handling and before eating, drinking, or using tobacco. Remove contaminated clothing and wash clothing before reuse.

Illustration 2-1. *The signal word on this label is Danger. Courtesy of BioLab, Inc. – A KIK Company*

SAMPLE PRODUCT LABEL:

This algicide is compatible with most chemicals normally used in swimming pool maintenance; however, in its concentrated form, this chemical should not come in contact with high concentrations of chlorine. **DO NOT MIX THIS ALGICIDE AND CHLORINE TOGETHER** before adding to the pool. These chemicals should be handled separately. **DIRECTIONS FOR USE:** It is a violation of Federal Law to use this product in a manner inconsistent with its labeling.

1. For an initial application or when pool water is changed, use one quart per 25,000 gallons of water.
2. For maintenance, use one ounce per week per 5,000 gallons of water. After each rain of consequence, add one ounce per 5,000 gallons of water in addition to the above amounts.
3. The appropriate amount of this algicide should be added by pouring directly into the pool. More rapid distribution will be achieved by pouring a little of the specified amount into several areas of the pool. Circulation or swimming activity will assure rapid dispersion.

Illustration 2-2. *Labels give directions as to proper use and dosage amounts. Courtesy of BioLab, Inc. – A KIK Company*

© National Swimming Pool Foundation 2017

means that the user could become very ill or badly injured by exposure. Warning is also used to identify products that can easily catch on fire.

Caution

Caution shows that the product could be harmful, but less harmful than products with a Danger or Warning signal word. Caution is used for products that could cause skin irritation, illness if the fumes are breathed, or trauma if the product contacts the eyes.

Labels also provide information about proper chemical dosage, storage, disposal, and proper methods of empty container disposal. The pool operator must be aware of the safety data provided on labels and follow the label's instructions.

Chlorine Gas

The FQPA (Food Quality Protection Act of 1996) governs the use of chlorine gas as it is applied to swimming pools (7 U.S.C. Sec. 136w-5 "Minimum Requirements for Training of Maintenance Applicators and Service Technicians"). Each state may establish minimum requirements for training.

To reduce the risks of poisoning from chlorine's high acute toxicity, the EPA requires that use in nonresidential swimming pools be restricted to certified pesticide applicators, or to those under their direct control.

California has a system designed to track pesticide illnesses. Over the years, most of the accidents with gas chlorine occurred at swimming pools and food processing plants.

Problems at pools involved pool operator error in switching cylinders, resulting in the release of chlorine gas. A large number of these problems involved untrained workers or resulted from lack of proper safety measures.

Aquatic facility staff and other people in the area can be exposed to gas chlorine released when metering equipment fails. Human error in working with the tank and equipment, or contamination of a chlorine-containing disinfectant, may cause chlorine gas to be released. Accidents involving chlorine gas create hazardous exposure to the skin, eyes, and respiratory tract.

The EPA has determined that the chlorine gas used for nonresidential swimming pools should be reclassified from General Use to Restricted Use. Based chiefly on California incident reports, the EPA determined that many applicators of chlorine gas lacked proper training. This greatly added to the potential for accidents.

The EPA has left the certification for gas chlorine applicators up to the states. Operators who have gone through the Certified Pool/Spa Operator® certification program must be aware of the detailed state requirements as they apply to their facilities.

Photo 2-2. *Gas chlorine use requires proper training concerning handling and storage. Cylinders must be individually chained to the wall and the regulator flow must be slow enough to prevent ice formation on the cylinder.*

For non-residential application, the EPA has classified elemental gas chlorine as a Restricted Use Pesticide. For residential application of chlorine gas, the EPA does not enforce restriction of use to specially authorized applicators. However, in addition to EPA, OSHA, and DOT regulation of chlorine gas, in 2007 the Department of Homeland Security (DHS) named chlorine gas a Chemical of Interest (COI). The subsequent layers of security and regulation have significantly reduced use of chlorine gas in residential settings.

Photo 2-3. *Incompatible chemicals could release chlorine gas. The surrounding community should be protected by having an emergency response plan in place.*

SARA Title III

The Emergency Planning & Community Right-to-Know Act (EPCRA) was passed by Congress as part of the Superfund Amendments and Reauthorization Act of 1986 (SARA). As a result, EPCRA is also referred to as SARA Title III.

SARA Title III exists to encourage emergency planning efforts at the state and local level, regarding the release or spill of hazardous or toxic chemicals. More information on the Emergency Planning and Community Right-to-Know Act (EPCRA) can be found in the online training module at www.nspf.org.

A pool operator who has earned Certified Pool/Spa Operator® certification should be aware that SARA Title III requires that a plan be made for responding to accidental chemical release.

Common pool facility chemicals covered under SARA Title III include:

- Aluminum Sulfate
- Ammonia
- Calcium Hypochlorite
- Chlorine Gas
- Hydrogen Peroxide
- Muriatic Acid
- Sodium Bisulfate
- Sodium Hypochlorite

In some cases, the limit for chemical storage on site could be as low as 100 pounds (45 kg) for a certain chemical. The facility manager should confer with legal counsel and the facility's insurance carrier to determine whether the aquatic facility complies, or should comply, with SARA Title III.

The Occupational Safety & Health Administration (OSHA)

The mission of the Occupational Safety & Health Administration (OSHA) is to save lives, prevent injuries, and protect the health of America's workers.

OSHA has estimated that more than 32 million workers are exposed to 650,000 hazardous chemical products in more than three million American workplaces. This exposure may be a grave problem for workers and their employers. A key protective measure includes a Hazard Communication Program and Safety Data Sheets (SDS).

Safety Data Sheets (SDS)

The basic goal of a Hazard Communication Program is to ensure that employers and workers know about work hazards and how to protect themselves. This should help reduce the rate of chemical source illness and injuries.

Chemicals pose a wide range of health hazards (irritation, sensitization, and carcinogenicity) and physical hazards (flammability, corrosion, and reactivity).

OSHA's Hazard Communication Standard (HCS) is designed to ensure that the facts about these hazards and protective measures are distributed to workers and employers. Chemical manufacturers and importers are required to evaluate the hazards of the chemicals they produce or import and provide details about them. This information is provided on labels attached to shipping containers as well as the SDS.

The HCS provides workers the right to know the names of the chemicals they are exposed to in the workplace and the associated hazards.

Photo 2-4. *SDS must be available to all employees at the job location where the chemical is used.*

© National Swimming Pool Foundation 2017

When workers have this information, they can better take part in their employer's protective programs and take steps to protect their own safety and the safety of others. The standard also gives employers the information they need to design and apply a protective program for workers who might come in contact with the chemical.

The SDS must be available to all workers at the job site where the chemical is used. A copy of the SDS should also be filed in a secure place for a period of 30 years after the last use of the chemical.

The Consumer Product Safety Commission (CPSC)

The U.S. Consumer Product Safety Commission protects the public from unreasonable risk of serious injury or death from more than 15,000 types of consumer products under the agency's control. The CPSC is committed to protecting consumers and families from products that pose a fire, electrical, chemical, or mechanical hazard, or that can injure children. The CPSC's work includes products used with swimming pools and spas.

The pool operator should be aware of product recalls involving the safety of facility users or staff. Recent recalls include items such as dive sticks, flotation training devices, chemicals, swim masks, and suction covers. Operators with Certified Pool/Spa Operator® certification or someone on the facility staff should visit the CPSC web site on a regular basis to stay current with regard to recalled products.

The U.S. Consumer Product Safety Commission has plans to develop safety guidelines for retrofitting older swimming pools and spas to remove likely entrapment hazards (see information on the Virginia Graeme Baker Pool & Spa Safety Act in the Facility Safety chapter). The CPSC recognizes the need for guidelines to help industry, health officials, inspectors, and maintenance personnel prevent deaths and injuries in spas and pools. The pool operator should obtain a copy of these guidelines to assist in any renovation project.

CPSC guidelines, which the pool operator should have on file and have knowledge of, include:

- Safety Barrier Guidelines for Home Pools
- Guidelines for Entrapment Hazards

Illustration 2-3. *SDS provide important information to the employee concerning chemical handling and storage, exposure, personal protection, chemical disposal, fire fighting, and first aid. Courtesy of Church & Dwight Co., Inc.*

- An Evaluation of Swimming Pool Alarms
  Even though the word Home is used in the first article, many governments incorporate this Home guideline in their regulations for commercial or public facilities.

Photo 2-5. *A small child can open this gate. The CPSC provides guidelines covering gates and latches for proper installation.*

The Department of Transportation (DOT)

Hazardous materials are those that pose a threat to public safety or the environment during transport because of their physical, chemical, or nuclear properties. The pool operator should be aware of national and local transportation rules. The U.S. Department of Transportation (DOT) classifies many chemicals on site. This is most easily learned by reading the SDS for each chemical.

The pool operator must know and follow the transport regulations if he or she is involved in the transport of chemicals. The pool staff should be well-informed and have the needed means to control a chemical spill.

A few of the chemicals classified as hazardous by the DOT are

Class 2 **Compressed, flammable, nonflammable, and poison gases**
    Chlorine Gas

Class 5 **Oxidizers and organic peroxides**
    Calcium Hypochlorite
    Chlorine Gas
    Lithium Hypochlorite
    Trichlor
    Dichlor

Class 8 **Corrosive materials**
    Muriatic Acid
    Sodium Hypochlorite

If the facility owner/manager has an outside third party either using pool chemicals or delivering chemicals, this person must comply with DOT regulations.

The Department of Justice (DOJ)

The Americans with Disabilities Act (ADA) is administered by the Department of Justice (DOJ). Facility management must have expert advice from the facility's legal council and insurance carrier on matters concerning the ADA. These rules are under constant review, and court rulings affect enforcement on a regular basis. Here is a finding from a recent settlement at a public pool:

1. There is no accessible route connecting the swimming pool with the bathhouse. Provide at least one accessible route connecting the swimming pool with the bathhouse. Standards §§ 4.1.2(2), 4.3.
2. The entrance gate to the fence surrounding the pool is 23 inches (58.42 cm) wide. Provide an entrance gate with a clear opening at least 32 inches (81.28 cm) with the gate open 90 degrees. Standards §§ 4.1.3(7), 4.13.5.

In another ruling the following settlement was reached with a university: XYZ University will obtain a mobile lift for the Aquatic Center swimming pool that will be available and in place at all times that the pool is available for public use (Standard § 4.1.3(1)).

Photo 2-6. *A pool lift may be a requirement for your facility.*

© National Swimming Pool Foundation 2017

The owner/manager of an aquatic facility should be aware that the ADA applies to new pool construction as well as renovations. Expert help should be obtained from an outside source early in the planning phase to assure compliance. See Appendix C-2 for information about the 2010 ADA regulations.

The Center for Disease Control & Prevention (CDC)

The mission of the Centers for Disease Control and Prevention (CDC) is to promote health and quality of life by preventing and controlling disease, injury, and disability. The CDC has a prime concern with regard to aquatic facilities due to Recreational Water Illnesses (RWIs).

RWIs spread by swallowing, breathing, or having contact with contaminated water from swimming pools, spas, lakes, rivers, or oceans. These RWIs can cause a wide range of symptoms, including skin, ear, respiratory, eye, and wound infections. The most commonly reported symptom for a RWI is diarrhea. Germs such as Crypto (short for *Cryptosporidium*), *Giardia*, *Shigella*, and *E. coli* O157:H7 can cause diarrheal illnesses.

The CDC provides many publications that can be downloaded from the NSPF web site. They are
- Vomit and Blood Contamination of Pool Water
- Cleaning Up Body Fluid Spills on Pool Surfaces
- Fecal Incident Response Recommendations for Pool Staff

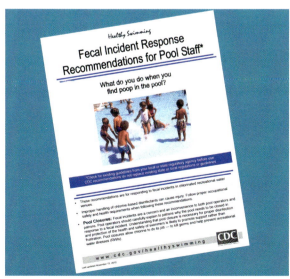

Illustration 2-4. *Centers for Disease Control Fecal Incident Guidelines*

The pool operator is urged to secure a copy of each of these guidelines. The suggested actions should be incorporated into the aquatic facility's operating procedures.

Through an initial grant from NSPF, the CDC worked with public health and industry representatives to build a Model Aquatic Health Code (MAHC). The MAHC 1st Edition Code and Annex were posted on August 29, 2014, followed by the second edition in August 2016. The MAHC serves as a model and guide for local and state agencies needing guidance to update or implement standards. The Council for the Model Aquatic Health Code (CMAHC) advocates for implementation and organizes research in support of the MAHC. See Appendix C-3 for more information.

International Code Council (ICC)

The International Code Council (ICC) was formed in 1994 to develop codes that have no regional limitations. Under the ICC, the International Building Code (IBC) was created for use in the design, build, and compliance process to construct safe, sustainable, affordable and resilient structures. These codes are used throughout the U.S. and many global markets.

Internationally, code officials recognized the need for a modern, up-to-date code governing the design, construction, alteration, repair, and maintenance of swimming pools, spas, hot tubs and aquatic facilities. The International Code Council's International Swimming Pool & Spa Code (ISPSC) 2015 coordinates and enhances the provisions previously found in the International Codes and Association of Pool & Spa Professionals standards (covered in the following section) and upgrades pool and spa safety to meet the requirements of the Virginia Graeme Baker Pool & Spa Safety Act.

Association of Pool & Spa Professionals (APSP)

The Association of Pool & Spa Professionals is a trade association for manufacturers, distributors, retailers, service companies and builders in the pool/spa and hot tub industry. APSP has developed standards relevant to private and public swimming pools and spas. These standards may have in the title or body the word residential; many jurisdictions may add residential code into their regulations for commercial or public facilities.

Most of the APSP standards are now held by the ICC (above). These standards have been formed in accordance with the requirements of the American National Standards Institute (ANSI), a private, non-profit organization that directs and coordinates the U.S. voluntary standardization and conformity assessment system. ANSI/APSP standards are developed under review by public health officials, architects, building code officials, academia, regulatory agencies, and safety experts. Pool operators should ensure compliance with ANSI/APSP-16 2011 "Suction Fittings for Use in Swimming Pools, Wading Pools, Spas, & Hot Tubs," and all other standards relevant to their facilities.

The World Health Organization (WHO)

The World Health Organization has developed Guidelines for Safe Recreational Water Environments: Volume 2 Swimming Pools, Spas and Similar Recreational Water Environments. The main goal of these guidelines is to ensure that aquatic facilities are operated as safely as possible. In this fashion, the largest possible group of users gets the greatest possible benefit. The WHO guidelines focus on three main groups of hazards:

- Those concerning injuries and physical hazards which have the potential to contribute to drowning or spinal injury
- Microbiological hazards
- Those concerning exposure to chemicals

The WHO knows that pool users are influenced by social, cultural, environmental and economic conditions. The pool operator must understand the makeup of the pool users that use his or her facility. The facility must satisfy the needs of the public that the aquatic facility serves.

The Chlorine Institute

The Chlorine Institute, Inc., exists to support the chlor-alkali industry and serve the public. The Institute promotes the constant evaluation of and improvements to the safety and protection

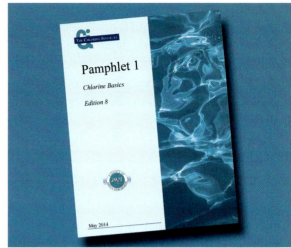

Illustration 2-5. *The Chlorine Institute has several publications that are useful to the pool operator.*

of human health and the environment. This applies to the production, distribution, and use of chlorine, sodium and potassium hydroxides, and sodium hypochlorite. The Institute works with the government to promote the use of current science and technology to create rules that improve the industry.

The pool operator should refer to any applicable Chlorine Institute publications and add those suggested guidelines to the aquatic facility's operating procedures. Examples of the Chlorine Institute's publications that may have an impact on the pool operator are

- Pamphlet 1, Chlorine Basics
- Pamphlet 63, First Aid, Medical Management/Surveillance & Occupational Hygiene Monitoring Practices for Chlorine
- Pamphlet 82, Recommendations for Using 100 & 150 Pound Cylinders at Swimming Pools
- Pamphlet 96, Sodium Hypochlorite Manual

NSF International (NSF)

NSF International (NSF) has a pool and spa equipment program that works with a voluntary standard (NSF/ANSI Standard 50) that represents a consensus of manufacturers, users, and regulatory authorities. NSF also offers a voluntary conformity assessment program—testing, certification, and production facility audits—to show compliance with the standard.

The registered NSF certification mark on a pool, spa, or hot tub system part confirms that NSF has assessed—and certified—its conformity with the relevant section of NSF/ANSI standard 50.

© National Swimming Pool Foundation 2017

NSF/ANSI Standard 50

The NSF/ANSI Standard 50 covers equipment for swimming pools, spas, hot tubs, and other recreational water facilities. This includes:
- Diatomaceous earth filters
- Sand filters
- Cartridge filters
- Recessed automatic surface skimmers
- Centrifugal pumps
- Adjustable output rate chemical feeding equipment
- Multi-port valves
- Flow-through chemical feeding equipment and process equipment, including in-line and brine type electrolytic chlorinators
- Copper/silver and copper ion generators
- UV-hydrogen peroxide and ozone generators

NSF also audits each authorized production facility to assure that certified products continue to comply with the appropriate requirements of the standard. The pool operator should be aware of NSF certification of pool-related equipment and piping and insist that all equipment conform to these standards or their equal.

As part of the Standard 50 registration, equipment manufacturers are required to create equipment installation, operating, and maintenance manuals. The pool operator should always have these manuals on file.

Photo 2-7. *Pool circulation equipment should bear the proper regulatory certification markings.*

ASTM International (ASTM)

The American Society for Testing & Materials, International (ASTM International) is a not-for-profit organization that provides a global forum for the development and publication of voluntary consensus standards for materials, products, systems, and services. ASTM standards serve as the basis for manufacturing, procurement, and regulatory activities. ASTM International provides standards that are accepted and used in research and development, product testing, and quality systems.

Illustration 2-6. *ASTM International has several publications of importance available at www.astm.org. Extracted from the copyrighted standard ASTM F2461-09 and reprinted with permission.*

The pool operator should be aware of the following ASTM publications:
- F2049-03 Standard Guide for Fences/Barriers for Public, Commercial, and Multi-Family Residential Use Outdoor Play Areas
- F2409-10 Standard Guide for Fences for Non-Residential Outdoor Swimming Pools, Hot Tubs, and Spas
- F1346-91 (2003) Standard Performance Specification for Safety Covers and Labeling Requirements for All Covers for Swimming Pools, Spas and Hot Tubs
- F2518-06 Standard Guide for Use of a Residential Swimming Pool, Spa, and Hot Tub Safety Audit to Prevent Unintentional Drowning
- F2208-08 Standard Safety Specification for Residential Pool Alarms
- F2387-04 Standard Specification for Manufactured Safety Vacuum Release Systems (SVRS) for Swimming Pools, Spas and Hot Tubs
- F2461-09 Standard Practice for Manufacture, Construction, Operation, and Maintenance of Aquatic Play Equipment

Underwriters Laboratories (UL)

Underwriters Laboratories Inc. (UL) is an independent, not-for-profit product-safety testing and certification organization. UL has tested products for public safety for more than a century.

If the pool operator uses equipment that is not certified by NSF International, then a UL or equivalent certification should be in place, for example: certificates for installed alarm systems are available only from UL-listed alarm service companies. UL qualifies alarm service companies for listing and for certificate service by reviewing examples of their work. After the alarm company becomes listed, they can then issue certificates for each system they install.

National Fire Protection Association (NFPA)

The mission of the international nonprofit NFPA is to reduce fire and other hazards by providing and advocating consensus codes and standards, research, training, and education.

Photo 2-8. *The NFPA 704 ratings are displayed in markings that are commonly referred to as the NFPA hazard diamond. The red number represents the flammability rating, the blue represents the health hazard rating, and the yellow represents the instability hazard rating. The lettering in the white area represents any special hazards; in this example the material is corrosive.*

Some codes that are of particular importance to the pool operator include:
- NFPA 400 code for storage of liquid and solid oxidizers applies to the storage of oxidizers that are liquid or solid at ambient conditions
- NFPA 704 presents a system to simplify determining the degree of health, flammability and instability hazards of

chemicals. The system also provides for the recognition of unusual water reactivity and oxidizers. The NFPA 704 ratings are displayed in markings that are commonly referred to as the NFPA hazard diamond.
- The National Electrical Code (NEC) NFPA 70 addresses electrical equipment and safe installation and use by consumers. Article 680 deals specifically with swimming pools. Training on the NFPA 70 Electrical Code is available at www.nspf.org.

American Red Cross

For a century, the American Red Cross has been preparing people to save lives through health and safety education and training. The American Red Cross provides training in first aid, CPR, and lifeguarding. Additionally, education is provided for swimming, HIV/AIDS education, and babysitting and child care training.

The American Red Cross strives to respond to the health and safety concerns of Americans at home, in school, and in the workplace. American Red Cross programs also include teaching the public and professionals how to use defibrillators to save victims of sudden cardiac arrest.

The pool operator should be trained at least to the level of any subordinate staff member. American Red Cross certification for lifeguarding and CPR for the Professional Rescuer may be among the programs that the pool operator should pursue.

Illustration 2-7. *The American Red Cross, can provide guidelines on specific safety devices necessary for your pool.*

Water Safety USA

Water Safety USA was established in February 2014 by governmental and nongovernmental organizations with the mission of empowering people with resources, information, and tools to safely enjoy and benefit from U.S. aquatic

© National Swimming Pool Foundation 2017

Illustration 2-8. *Water Safety USA members collaborate to enhance individual organizational efforts to promote water safety and prevent drowning.*

environments. While not specifically a standards-setting organization, the organization is comprised of longstanding national organizations with a strong record of providing drowning prevention and water safety programs, including public education. Member organizations include:

- American Academy of Pediatrics
- American Red Cross
- Boy Scouts of America
- Centers for Disease Control & Prevention
- National Park Service
- National Safe Boating Council
- National Swimming Pool Foundation
- Safe Kids Worldwide
- U.S. Coast Guard
- U.S. Consumer Product Safety Commission
- United States Lifesaving Association
- USA Swimming Foundation
- YMCA of the USA

To achieve its mission, the approach of Water Safety USA is to engage in ongoing dialogue aimed at improving cohesive and consistent delivery of water safety information, tools, and resources that are as effective as possible. Each year, the members of Water Safety USA select a single water safety topic that all members agree upon to promote collaboratively throughout the year. For more information and to learn about this year's topic visit http://www.watersafetyusa.org/.

Resource Contact List

An aquatic facility that has specific programs should abide by the guidelines set by the national or international organizations that are the commonly accepted leaders for an activity. The following list is provided to assist the pool operator in finding the most current information. Web sites for each organization are available on the NSPF® web site at www.nspf.org.

- American Academy of Pediatrics (AAP)
- American Alliance for Health, Physical Education, Recreation & Dance (AAHPERD)
- American Chemistry Council
- Aquatic Exercise Association (AEA)
- American National Standards Institute (ANSI)
- American Red Cross
- American Swimming Coaches Association (ASCA)
- Aquatic Therapy & Rehab Institute (ATRI)
- Association of Pool & Spa Professionals (APSP)
- ASTM International (ASTM)
- Boy Scouts of America (BSA)
- Centers for Disease Control & Prevention Foundation (CDC)
- The Chlorine Institute, Inc.
- Consumer Product Safety Commission (CPSC)
- College Swimming Coaches Association of America (CSCAA)
- Department of Justice (DOJ)
- Department of Transportation (DOT)
- Environmental Protection Agency (EPA)
- Federation Internationale de Natation Amateur (FINA)
- International Academy of Aquatic Art (IAAA)
- International Association of Amusement Parks and Attractions (IAAPA)
- International Association of Plumbing and Mechanical Officials (IAPMO)
- International Code Council (ICC)
- Jeff Ellis & Associates
- Jewish Community Center Association (JCCA)
- National Drowning Prevention Alliance (NDPA)
- National Fire Protection Association (NFPA)
- National Intramural-Recreational Sports Association (NIRSA)
- National Interscholastic Swimming Coaches Association (NISCA)
- National Park Service (NPS)
- National Recreation & Park Association (NRPA)
- NSF International (NSF)
- National Safe Boating Council (NSBC)
- National Swimming Pool Foundation (NSPF)
- Occupational Health and Safety Administration (OSHA)

© National Swimming Pool Foundation 2017

Photo 2-9. *Guidelines for operating an aquatic facility are available from numerous training and standards organizations.*

- Safe Kids Worldwide (SKW)
- Swim Today
- USA Swimming
- U.S. Coast Guard
- U.S. Consumer Product Safety Commission
- U.S. Department of Labor
- U.S. Diving
- U.S. Lifesaving Association (USLA)
- U.S. Masters Swimming (USMS)
- U.S. Swim School Association (USSSA)
- U.S. Synchronized Swimming (USSS)
- U.S. Water Fitness Association (USWFA)
- U.S. Water Polo
- Underwriters Laboratory (UL)
- Water Safety USA
- World Health Organization (WHO)
- World Waterpark Association (WWA)
- YMCA/YWCA of the USA

© National Swimming Pool Foundation 2017

Chapter 3:
Essential Calculations

"Do not worry about your difficulties in mathematics. I can assure you mine are still greater."

–Albert Einstein

A fundamental understanding of aquatic facility calculations is necessary for the successful pool operator. Water quality management, facility planning, renovation, and equipment replacement require that the pool operator be competent in basic calculations. Failure to perform calculations correctly can result in hazardous conditions and threaten the health, safety, and welfare of the facility users and staff. The original construction drawings contain basic information, such as dimensions and volume in gallons.

Basic Arithmetic

The certified operator must possess basic math skills and the ability to use a hand-held calculator. The professional pool manager must be able to evaluate water quality test results and take corrective action. Liquid and dry quantity conversions, and chemical dosages are examples of the type of daily computations required of the pool operator.

The daily care of an aquatic facility requires the use of common terms, such as pounds, gallons, feet, square feet, meters, and liters. Calculations must be converted to common pool industry terminology to insure proper understanding between staff members. Figure 3-1 Useful Conversions and Constants may be helpful to the operator on a routine basis.

Example 3-1: Amount Conversion

You determine from the results of your pool water test that you need to add 36 ounces of soda ash to your pool. How many pounds is this?

Ounces ÷ 16 = pounds

36 ounces ÷ 16 ounces/pound = 2.25 pounds

Example 3-1: Metric

You determine from the results of your water test that you need to add 2500 grams of soda ash to your pool. How many kilograms is this?

Grams ÷ 1000 = kilograms

2500 ÷ 1000 = 2.5 kilograms

Example 3-2: Distance Conversion

Your pool is 25 meters long and 25 yards wide. What are the dimensions in feet?

Yards x 3 = feet

Meters x 3.28 = feet

25 yards x 3 = 75 feet

25 meters x 3.28 = 82 feet

82 feet long and 75 feet wide

(Note: 1 meter is actually 3.28084 feet. Rounding to 3.28 is done to simplify the calculations.)

Example 3-3: Distance Conversion

Your pool is 50 meters long and 32 meters wide. What are the dimensions in feet?

Meters x 3.28 = feet

50 meters x 3.28 = 164 feet

32 meters x 3.28 = 105 feet

164 feet long and 105 feet wide

Example 3-3: Metric

Your pool is 50 meters long and 32 meters wide. Measurements remain in meters.

Example 3-4: Filter Surface Area

Your D.E. filter has 8 grids measuring 18 inches by 24 inches each. Each grid filters from both sides. What is the filter area?

sq. in. ÷ 144 sq. in./sq. ft. = sq. ft.

18 inches x 24 inches = 432 sq. in.

432 sq. in. x 2 sides = 864 sq. in./grid

864 sq. in./ grid x 8 grids = 6,912 sq. in.

6,912 sq. in. ÷ 144 sq. in./sq. ft. = 48 sq. ft.

© National Swimming Pool Foundation 2017

Example 3-4: Metric

Your D.E. filter has 8 grids measuring 0.5 by 0.75 meters each. Each grid filters from both sides. What is the filter area?

$$0.5m \times 0.75m = 0.375 \ m^2$$
$$0.375 \ m^2 \times 2 \ sides = 0.75 \ m^2 \ /grid$$
$$0.75 \ m^2/grid \times 8 \ grids = 6 \ m^2$$

Example 3-5: Metric

You determine from the results of your pool water test that you need to add 950 milliliters of muriatic acid to your pool. How many liters is this?

$$Milliliters \div 1000 = liters$$
$$950 \div 1000 = 0.95 \ liters$$

Example 3-5: Volume Conversion

You determine from the results of your pool water test that you need to add 32 fluid ounces of muriatic acid to your pool. How many cups is this?

$$Fluid \ ounces \div 8 = cups$$
$$32 \ fluid \ ounces \div 8 = 4 \ cups$$

Example 3-6: Volume Conversion

You determine from the results of your pool water test that you need to add 640 fluid ounces of sodium hypochlorite to breakpoint chlorinate your pool. How many gallons is this?

$$Fluid \ ounces \div 128 = gallons$$
$$640 \ fluid \ ounces \div 128 = 5 \ gallons$$

Useful Conversions and Constants

Ounces to Pounds Ounces ÷ 16 = Pounds	**Grams or Milliliters to Kilos or Liters** Grams or Milliliters ÷ 1000 = Kilos or Liters
Fluid Ounces to Gallons Fluid Ounces ÷ 128 = Gallons	**1 Micron = 1 Millionth of a Meter** 25.4 microns per 1/1000 inch
Liters to Gallons Liters ÷ 3.785 = Gallons	**Meters to Feet** Meters x 3.28 = Feet
Fluid Ounces to Cups Fluid Ounces ÷ 8 = Cups	**Cubic Meters to Liters** Cubic Meters x 1000 = Liters
Yards to Feet Yards x 3 = Feet	**Fluid Ounces to Milliliters** Fluid Ounces x 29.57 = Milliliters
Cubic Feet to Gallons Cubic Feet x 7.5 = Gallons	**Parts per Million and Milligrams per Liter** 1 ppm = 1 mg/L
Quarts to Gallons Quarts ÷ 4 = Gallons	**1 ppm = 8.33 Pounds of Chemical in One Million Gallons of Water**
Pints to Quarts Pints ÷ 2 = Quarts	**Celsius (°C) to Fahrenheit (°F)** °F = (9/5 x °C) + 32
Gallons to Pounds Gallons x 8.33 = Pounds	**Fahrenheit (°F) to Celsius (°C)** °C = 5/9 x (°F - 32)
Square Inches to Square Feet Square Inches ÷ 144 = Square Feet	**1 Pound per Square Inch (psi) is the pressure created by a column of water 2.31 feet high**
British Thermal Units vs. Temperature Rise BTUs = Gallons x 8.33 x °F (Temp Rise)	**Kilojoules vs. Temperature Rise** Kilojoules = Liters x 4.18 x °C (Temp. Rise)
Pounds per Square Inch (psi) to Bar 1 psi = 0.069 bar	**Bars to Pounds per Square Inch (psi)** 1 Bar = 14.51 psi
Pounds per Square Inch (psi) to Kilo Pascals (kPa) 1 psi = 6.89 kPa	**Kilo Pascals (kPa) to Pounds per Square Inch (psi)** 1 kPa = 0.145 psi

Figure 3-1: *Useful conversions.*

© National Swimming Pool Foundation 2017

Example 3-6: Metric

You determine from the results of your pool water test that you need to add 19,000 milliliters of sodium hypochlorite to breakpoint chlorinate your pool. How many liters is this?

Milliliters ÷ 1000 = liters
19,000 ÷ 1000 = 19 liters

Pool Volume (Capacity)

Knowing the volume (gallons or liters) of water in any aquatic feature is critical for the proper management of operating equipment, chemical dosing, and patron use.

Usually the design engineer who prepared the original specifications includes this information on the technical drawings. If the drawing specifications are not available, local health officials may have the necessary technical information on file. The pool operator should have a copy of the facility's technical specifications on file at all times. The design calculations and the actual as-built water volume may be different due to construction deviations.

Pool floors do not have uniform slopes. Pool walls usually have a slight variation from vertical. Walls and floors are joined by a radius, or blend. These fluctuations result in a pool volume that is at best only an approximation. For this reason, calculations concerning swimming pool volumes are considered reasonable if a ± 5% deviation from the actual volume is obtained.

Surface Area

To find a pool or spa's approximate volume, calculate the water's surface area first. The surface area of any aquatic facility is that area of the pool water exposed to the air. This area is also used to determine pool cover sizing, user load (in some codes), and for calculating water temperature losses. In the simplest terms, area corresponds to the length of the pool multiplied by the width. The formula for calculating surface area is

Surface area = length x width

Irregularly shaped pools pose a problem. Figure 3-3 has several of the most common shapes. Other surface areas of concern include the pool wall surface (for resurfacing) and deck (for pool-related leisure activities). Calculating filter area is important for water quality management. Filter surface area is discussed in the Pool & Spa Filtration chapter.

Volume

To calculate pool volume in gallons, multiply the surface area by the average depth and a conversion factor of 7.5. This factor requires the length, width, and depth to be measured in feet.

Conversions
- For every cubic foot of water there are 7.5 gallons of water.
- For every cubic meter of water there are 1000 liters of water.

Photo 3-1. *Calculate the volume of a multi-shaped pool by dividing the pool into sections.*

Volume = surface area x average depth x 7.5

The factor 7.5 is an approximation. The actual value is 7.48 gallons per cubic foot. In a pool of 60,000 gallons, the error is only 160.5 gallons. This deviation is only 0.25%. The ease of using 7.5 rather than 7.48 in calculations far exceeds the value of the error. Additionally, volume calculations are typically rounded up, (e.g. 49,850 gallons is rounded up to 50,000 gallons).

Average depth is not always easy to determine. For a simple constant-slope pool, it is the average of the two depths, the shallow and deep ends (see Figure 3-2). For more complex pools, divide the pool into multiple sections, and determine each section's volume separately. Then, add the volumes of all the sections together for the total volume in gallons. Refer to Figure 3-4.

Metric Volume

To calculate pool volume in liters, all measurements remain in meters. Multiply the surface area by the average depth in meters. The resulting value is in meters cubed (m^3). Multiply the m^3 by a conversion factor of 1000, since there are 1000 liters in a cubic meter of water.

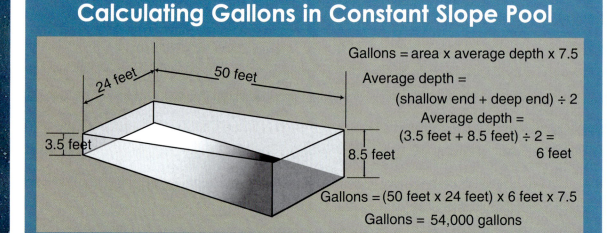

Calculating Gallons in Constant Slope Pool

Gallons = area x average depth x 7.5

Average depth = (shallow end + deep end) ÷ 2

Average depth = (3.5 feet + 8.5 feet) ÷ 2 = 6 feet

Gallons = (50 feet x 24 feet) x 6 feet x 7.5

Gallons = 54,000 gallons

Figure 3-2a

Calculating Liters in Constant Slope Pool

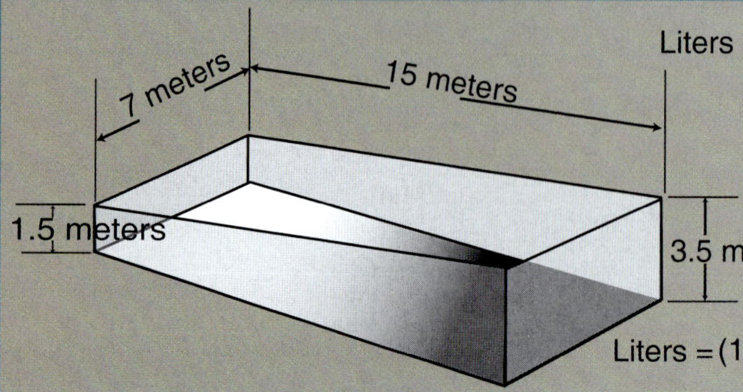

Liters = Area x Average depth x 1000

Average depth = (shallow end + deep end) ÷ 2

Average depth = (1.5 m + 3.5 m) ÷ 2 = 2.5 meters

Liters = (15 m x 7 m) x 2.5 meters x 1000

Liters = 262,500 liters

Figure 3-2b

© National Swimming Pool Foundation 2017

Essential Calculations

Calculating Surface Area and Gallons and Liters
(for liters, measurements are in meters)

To determine the approximate number of gallons or liters in a pool or spa, first determine the surface area. Then multiply the area by the average depth and the constant conversion factor of 7.5 to convert cubic feet to gallons, or 1000 to convert from cubic meters to liters. To find the average depth for a more complex shaped pool, divide the complex shape into several simple shapes, calculate each one separately, and add them back together. For circular pools, R stands for radius.

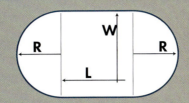

OBLONG

Area = R x R x 3.14 + (L x W)

Gallons = area x average depth x 7.5

Liters = area x average depth x 1000

RECTANGLE

Area = L x W

Gallons = area x average depth x 7.5

Liters = area x average depth x 1000

CIRCULAR

Area = R x R x 3.14

Gallons = area x average depth x 7.5

Liters = area x average depth x 1000

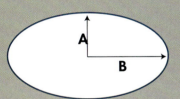

OVAL

Area = A x B x 3.14

Gallons = area x average depth x 7.5

Liters = area x average depth x 1000

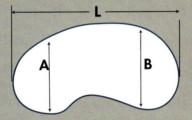

KIDNEY

Area (approx.) = (A + B) x L x 0.45

Gallons = area x average depth x 7.5

Liters = area x average depth x 1000

Figure 3-3

Photo 3-2. *The volume of a kidney-shaped pool is calculated using the area x average depth x 7.5.*

© National Swimming Pool Foundation 2017

Calculating Gallons in a Multi-depth Pool

Your pool is 50 feet long and 25 feet wide. The shallow end varies in depth from 3 feet - 6 inches to 5 feet deep. The main drain is at a depth of 10 feet, and the deep end wall is 8 feet - 6 inches deep. How many gallons are in your pool?

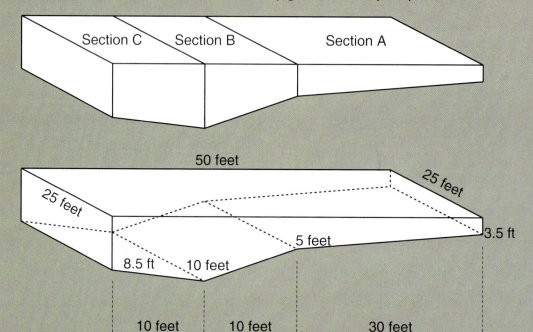

Section A - Section A is 30 feet long, with a width of 25 feet. The depth varies from 3.5 feet to 5 feet deep.

Section B - Section B is 10 feet long, with a width of 25 feet. The depth varies from 5 feet to 10 feet deep.

Section C - Section C is 10 feet long, with a width of 25 feet. The depth varies from 10 feet to 8.5 feet deep.

Section A

Gallons$_A$ = area x average depth x 7.5

Area = length x width

Average depth = (3.5 feet + 5 feet) ÷ 2
          = 8.5 feet ÷ 2 = 4.25 feet

Gallons$_A$
    = (30 feet x 25 feet) x 4.25 feet x 7.5

Gallons$_A$ = 23,906 gallons

Section B

Gallons$_B$ = area x average depth x 7.5

Area = length x width

Average depth = (5 feet + 10 feet) ÷ 2
          = 15 feet ÷ 2 = 7.5 feet

Gallons$_B$ = (10 feet x 25 feet) x 7.5 feet x 7.5

Gallons$_B$ = 14,063 gallons

Section C

Gallons$_C$ = area x average depth x 7.5

Area = length x width

Average depth = (10 feet + 8.5 feet) ÷ 2
          = 18.5 feet ÷ 2 = 9.25 feet

Gallons$_C$
    = (10 feet x 25 feet) x 9.25 feet x 7.5

Gallons$_C$ = 17,344 gallons

Total Pool

Total Pool = Gallons$_A$ + Gallons$_B$ + Gallons$_C$

Total Pool
    = 23,906 gal + 14,063 gal + 17,344 gal

Total Pool = 55,313 gallons

or rounded off to 55,500 gallons

Figure 3-4a

© National Swimming Pool Foundation 2017

Essential Calculations

Calculating Liters in a Multi-depth Pool

Your pool is 25 meters long and 15 meters wide. The shallow end varies in depth from 1 meter to 1.5 meters. The main drain is at a depth of 3 meters, and the deep end wall is 2.5 meters. How many liters are in your pool?

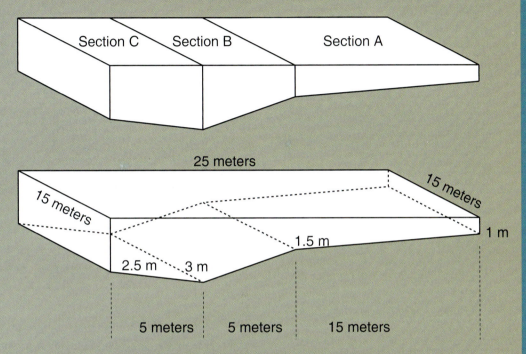

Section A - Section A is 15 meters long, with a width of 15 meters.
The depth varies from 1 m to 1.5 m deep.

Section B - Section B is 5 meters long, with a width of 15 meters.
The depth varies from 1.5 m to 3 m deep.

Section C - Section C is 5 meters long, with a width of 15 meters.
The depth varies from 3 m to 2.5 m deep.

Section A

$Liters_A$ = area x average depth x 1000

Area = length x width

Average depth = (1 m + 1.5 m) ÷ 2
= 2.5 m ÷ 2 = 1.25 m

$Liters_A$ = (15 m x 15 m) x 1.25 m x 1000

$Liters_A$ = 281,250 liters

Section B

$Liters_B$ = area x average depth x 1000

Area = length x width

Average depth = (1.5 m + 3 m) ÷ 2
= 4.5 m ÷ 2 = 2.25 m

$Liters_B$ = (5 m x 15 m) x 2.25 m x 1000

$Liters_B$ = 168,750 liters

Section C

$Liters_C$ = area x average depth x 1000

Area = length x width

Average depth = (3 m + 2.5 m) ÷ 2
= 5.5 m ÷ 2 = 2.75 m

$Liters_C$ = (5 m x 15 m) x 2.75 m x 1000

$Liters_C$ = 206,250 liters

Total Pool

Total Pool = $Liters_A$ + $Liters_B$ + $Liters_C$

Total Pool = 281,250 + 168,750 + 206,250

Total Pool = 656,250 Liters

or rounded off to 657,000 Liters

Figure 3-4b

Calculating Gallons in 1 Inch of Depth

Use the previous pool for this example. You return to the pool on a Monday and find that the auto-fill failed to operate. Your pool water level is 3 inches too low. How many gallons must be added?

Gallons = area x average depth x 7.5
Area = length x width
Average depth for 1 inch = 1 foot ÷ 12 = 0.0833 feet
Gallons for 1 inch = (50 feet x 25 feet) x 0.0833 feet x 7.5
Gallons for 1 inch = 781 gallons
Gallons for 3 inches = 781 gallons x 3 = 2,343 gallons

Calculating Liters in 1 Centimeter of Depth

Your 25 m x 15 m pool water level is 7.6 centimeters too low. How many liters must be added?

Liters = area x average depth x 1000
Area = length x width (measured in meters)
7.6 centimeters = (7.6 ÷ 100) = 0.076 meters
Liters for 7.6 centimeters = 25 meter x 15 meters x 0.076 meters x 1000
Liters for 7.6 centimeters = 28,500 liters

Figure 3-5: *Replacement water calculation*

Makeup Water

Aquatic facilities lose water in a number of ways:
- Evaporation
- User splash-out and drag-out
- Plumbing and shell leaks
- Planned dilution

For operational and planning purposes, the pool operator needs to understand how much water is in one inch of depth. It's the same formula used tp calculate the volume for a constant slope pool. The difference is that there is no slope; the depth is constant. Refer to Figure 3-5.

Other Useful Calculations

The calculations covered in this chapter apply to several chapters throughout this handbook. There are other calculations that a pool operator is likely to perform or need to understand. Rather than cover them in this general chapter, they are reviewed in the chapter where they apply. For example, the following calculations will be discussed in later chapters:
- Chemical dosing - Pool & Spa Water Problems chapter
- Filter area - Pool & Spa Filtration chapter
- Flow rate - Pool & Spa Filtration chapter
- Turnover rate - Water Circulation chapter
- Heater sizing - Heating & Air Circulation chapter
- User loads - Facility Safety chapter

More useful calculations and sample problems also can be found in the Pool Math™ Workbook.

Photo 3-3. *Evaporation, splash out, and leaks contribute to water loss that must be replaced.*

© National Swimming Pool Foundation 2017

Calculating Gallons in a Multi-Depth Circular Spa

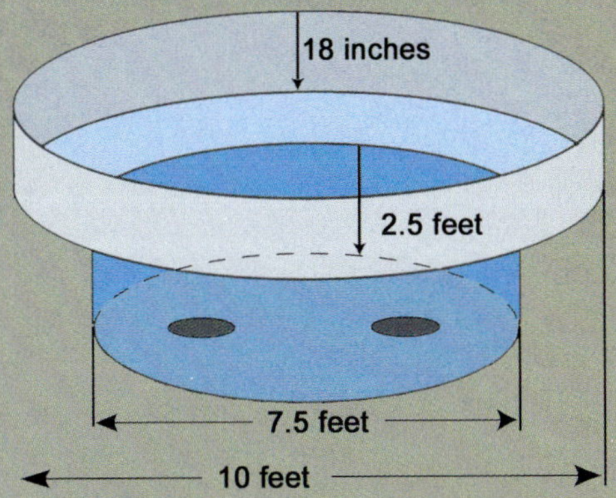

18 inches

2.5 feet

7.5 feet

10 feet

The pool must first be separated into its component parts. Each part must be calculated and then added back together.

Radius (R) = Diameter ÷ 2

Section A
Section A is the top of the spa down to the seat. The depth is 18 inches (1.5 feet) and the diameter is 10 feet

Area = R x R x 3.14
Area = 5 feet x 5 feet x 3.14
    = 78.5 square feet
    the average depth is 18 inches, or 1.5 feet
Gallons = area x average depth x 7.5
Gallons = 78.5 square feet x 1.5 feet x 7.5
Gallons$_A$ = 883.13

Section B
Section B is the foot well of the spa from the seat down to the main drain floor. The depth is 2.5 feet and the diameter is 7.5 feet

Area = R x R x 3.14
Area = 3.75 feet x 3.75 feet x 3.14
    = 44.16 square feet
    the average depth is 2.5 feet
Gallons = area x average depth x 7.5
Gallons = 44.16 square feet x 2.5 feet x 7.5
Gallons$_B$ = 828

Total Pool = Gallons$_A$ + Gallons$_B$
Total Pool = 883.13 gallons + 828 gallons
Total Pool = 1,711.13 gallons or rounded off to 1,712 gallons

Figure 3-6a

Photo 3-4. *Multi-depth spa*

Calculating Liters in a Multi-Depth Circular Spa

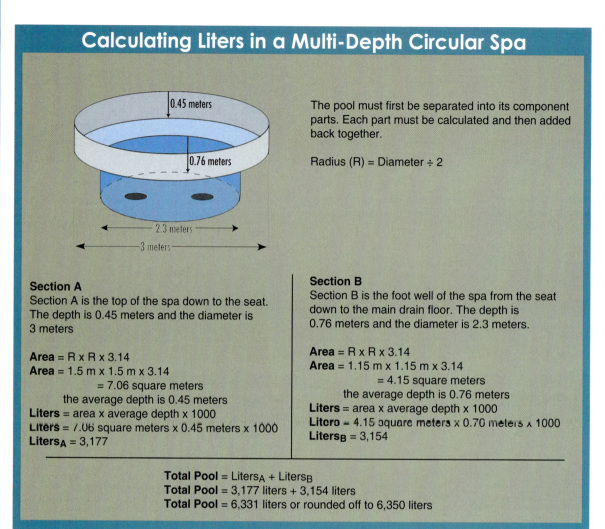

The pool must first be separated into its component parts. Each part must be calculated and then added back together.

Radius (R) = Diameter ÷ 2

Section A
Section A is the top of the spa down to the seat. The depth is 0.45 meters and the diameter is 3 meters

Area = R x R x 3.14
Area = 1.5 m x 1.5 m x 3.14
            = 7.06 square meters
        the average depth is 0.45 meters
Liters = area x average depth x 1000
Liters = 7.06 square meters x 0.45 meters x 1000
Liters$_A$ = 3,177

Section B
Section B is the foot well of the spa from the seat down to the main drain floor. The depth is 0.76 meters and the diameter is 2.3 meters.

Area = R x R x 3.14
Area = 1.15 m x 1.15 m x 3.14
            = 4.15 square meters
        the average depth is 0.76 meters
Liters = area x average depth x 1000
Liters = 4.15 square meters x 0.76 meters x 1000
Liters$_B$ = 3,154

Total Pool = Liters$_A$ + Liters$_B$
Total Pool = 3,177 liters + 3,154 liters
Total Pool = 6,331 liters or rounded off to 6,350 liters

Figure 3-6b

© National Swimming Pool Foundation 2017

Essential Calculations

34

Chapter 4:
Pool Water Contamination

"First the doctor told me the good news: I was going to have a disease named after me."

–Steve Martin

Swimming has historically been associated with exercise and health. Exercise that people receive from swimming and other aquatic activities provides a tremendous public health benefit for society. The ability to swim builds self-confidence and leads to a wide variety of other aquatic-related activities. However, the water, and sometimes the air above the water, can contribute to unhealthy conditions for the user unless proper water quality management is maintained.

Preventing people from getting sick due to contact with or ingestion of water or inhalation of water vapor is the primary reason pools are constantly treated with disinfectant. Disinfectants kill germs that make people sick. Protecting people from disease-causing germs is also one of the biggest reasons that public health departments often require operators or health officials to attend and demonstrate competency in Certified Pool/Spa Operator® certification classes. The Certified Pool/Spa Inspector™ (CPI™) program is an additional training program for pool inspections and audits, which are important health initiatives.

The pool operator plays an important role in reducing the spread of Recreational Water Illnesses (RWI). The challenge of this role is real and requires constant attention. The Centers for Disease Control and Prevention's (CDC) Model Aquatic Health Code Annex states that operators and health officials who receive standardized training better prevent health code violations. The NSPF Recreational Water Illness™ course provides more detailed analysis of risk related to particular illnesses.

About one-fourth of the disease outbreaks are due to germs that are easily killed by chlorine or other disinfectants. In many instances, no disinfectant (like chlorine) was present to protect

Photo 4-1. *The ability to swim builds self-confidence and leads to a wide variety of other aquatic related activities.*

© National Swimming Pool Foundation 2017

Photo 4-2. *Swim pants are required at many facilities. Some pools and spas even require that rubber pants be worn over the swim pants.*

the users. This shows that many pools are being inadequately treated and reinforces the need for educated pool operators in the field.

An important aspect of health codes is to prevent disease in people who use pools and spas. Yet many health inspections continue to find that pools and spas are not in compliance with the codes. The CDC reported on 84,187 pool inspections that were carried out in 2013 in 16 state and local agencies (Morbidity and Mortality Weekly Report [MMWR] 65 (5); 2016). There were 66,098 identified violations leading to immediate closures documented during these inspections. 8,118 (12.3%) of the inspections resulted in immediate closures of the pools due to serious violations, such as the lack of an appropriate disinfectant level required to kill bacteria to safe levels.

During inspections, environmental health officials serve as illness-and-injury-prevention advisors to aquatic facility operators. Immediate closures and identified violations offer an opportunity to educate operators about how to properly operate and maintain aquatic facilities and why these measures are necessary. Currently, no public pool code exists at the national level: pool and spa rules are created at the state and local levels. The variation in codes throughout the country creates a potential barrier to prevention and control of disease associated with recreational water. As mentioned in the Regulations & Guidelines chapter, the CDC's Model Aquatic Health Code can provide guidance (not regulatory authority) for states or countries when updating codes.

Recreational Water Illness

Illnesses spread by water used for recreating (swimming, soaking, playing) are called Recreational Water Illnesses (RWI). RWIs are spread by swallowing, breathing, or having contact with contaminated water from swimming pools, spas, hot tubs, water parks, interactive fountains, and other recreational water.

Water can be contaminated by microscopic organisms such as bacteria, viruses, or protozoa. Microorganisms causing illness in humans are said to be pathogens. These organisms can end up in the water from the environment (air, soil, water, animals) or from users. Showering before entering the pool and structuring programming to include regular bathroom breaks will help reduce the risk of contamination from human bacteria and other contaminants that negatively impact water quality—including, but not limited to, perspiration, urine, skin, body oils, lotions, deodorants, etc.

RWIs can cause a wide variety of symptoms, including gastrointestinal, skin, ear, respiratory, eye, neurologic, and wound infections. The most commonly reported RWI symptom is diarrhea caused by pathogens such as *Cryptosporidium* (Crypto), Norovirus, *Shigella*, *Escherichia coli* 0157:H7, and *Giardia*. Gastroenteritis refers to an inflammation of the stomach and intestinal tract. Symptoms associated with gastroenteritis are diarrhea, nausea, vomiting, and abdominal cramping. Large outbreaks occur more frequently in the summer.

The CDC issues reports on disease outbreaks every two years. State and local jurisdictions report their illnesses and outbreaks to the CDC. However, many illnesses from recreational facilities are not identified, investigated or reported to the CDC. Therefore, the true number of illnesses is underreported. It is important to notice that since the 1980's the number of reported RWI outbreaks has increased steadily.

If a user or employee working in the water is ill with diarrhea, the germs they carry can contaminate the water if they have an accident in the pool. On average, people have about 0.14 grams of feces on their buttocks, which, when rinsed off, can contaminate the water. When people are ill with diarrhea, their stool can contain millions of germs. Therefore, swimming

© National Swimming Pool Foundation 2017

when ill with diarrhea can easily contaminate water. If someone swallows water that has been contaminated with feces, he or she may become sick. Many of these diarrhea-causing germs do not have to be swallowed in large amounts to cause illness. This route of exposure is called the fecal-oral route of transmission. Standing water is not necessary for RWIs to spread, so even spray decks (interactive spray attractions) can become contaminated (the water is just in a collection tank underground) and spread illness. To ensure that most germs are killed, proper disinfectant levels and pH must be maintained at all times.

Fecal contamination may come from sources other than users. Feces from warm blooded animals can be tracked into the pool area from contaminated soil. Animals that enter the pool area can contaminate the water. Birds, ducks, or geese can contaminate water with their droppings (J. Environ. Health, 2004, 66(7), 34–37).

> More advanced training on RWIs is available at **www.nspf.org**. and **www.thewahc.org**

Fecal Related Illnesses

When organisms such as Crypto, *Giardia*, *E. coli* O157:H7 and *Shigella* find their way into the water, it is most often through an Accidental Fecal Release (AFR). These pathogens may be the reason why a person has diarrhea. When people infected with these diseases have a fecal release in the water and there is insufficient disinfectant to inactivate the pathogen, then users who ingest water will swallow some of these germs and may become ill. Therefore, people who have diarrhea should not use recreational water since they could contaminate the water with pathogens.

Not all of these organisms are easily controlled by chlorine or other disinfectants. These chlorine resistant organisms have become very prevalent in recent years in recreational water. Prevention of fecal related illness and treatment of pool and spa water is very different if you are dealing with inactivation of these chlorine-resistant microorganisms.

Photo 4-3. *Someone who swallows water that has been contaminated with feces may become sick.*

Protozoa

Protozoa are single cell microscopic organisms that can be transmitted through food and water, and cause disease in humans. Once the protozoa are ingested, they live in the intestine, where they make their host ill, and are passed in the stool. Protozoa are larger than bacteria and viruses, though none of these can be seen by the naked eye. The two protozoan parasites most commonly involved in recreational water illnesses are Crypto and *Giardia*. In 2011–2012, Crypto and *Giardia* were responsible for 94% of the gastroenteritis outbreaks associated with treated swimming venues in the U.S. In fact, parasites were responsible for almost 12 times more illness cases than bacteria (MMWR 2015;64(24):668-672).

Cryptosporidium

Crypto is protected by an outer shell that allows it to survive harsh conditions, including chlorine disinfection. It can remain active at normal operating disinfectant levels for days. Ordinary water treatment methods cannot destroy Crypto. Even the best filters may allow Crypto to pass through them. There is a growing body of evidence that filter enhancers can help existing filters remove most of the Crypto. Ultraviolet light, ozone, and chlorine dioxide effectively inactivate Crypto.

If ingested, there is an incubation period lasting as long as seven days before symptoms of cryptosporidiosis (the disease caused by Crypto) appear. Individuals whose immune systems are compromised have more severe reactions, which may be life-threatening. In healthy users, the illness typically lasts about 10 to 14 days and the symptoms include diarrhea, vomiting, fever, and abdominal cramps. Infected persons have been reported to shed one billion organisms in a single bowel movement and can excrete organisms for up to 50 days after diarrhea has ceased. The CDC recommends people who have been diagnosed with cryptosporidiosis not enter recreational water for two weeks after symptoms cease. Data suggests that ingestion of fewer than 10 organisms can result in cryptosporidiosis (MMWR 2007 (56)07;1–10).

In 2005, an effective drug (Nitazoxanide) was approved for the treatment of cryptosporidiosis for children and adults with healthy immune systems. The availability of this new drug may have increased how often health care providers test for Crypto in patients with diarrhea. This could be one of the reasons the number of cases of cryptosporidiosis has risen. Since 1998, the number of recreational water outbreaks caused by infectious pathogens has consistently and significantly increased. In 2011–2012, the CDC reports that Crypto was responsible for 36 treated recreational water-associated outbreaks (MMWR 2015;64(24):668-672).

One of the largest waterborne outbreaks reported in a treated recreational water venue involved approximately 2,300 persons following exposure at a spray park (an interactive play attraction) in New York. The investigation revealed that recycled water was not adequately filtered and disinfected. Reports of investigations from three other outbreaks indicated that filters with diatomaceous earth might be more effective at removing these small parasites than sand or cartridge filters (MMWR 57(SS-9) 2008).

NSPF® has funded research to help understand how effective various disinfectants are at controlling Crypto. In addition, NSPF-funded projects have explored ways to use UV light, ozone, and filters to better remove Crypto from water. Recreational water illness prevention is a subject addressed every year at the World Aquatic Health™ Conference. Conference proceedings can be viewed on the NSPF® YouTube channel. Follow the YouTube icon link at www.nspf.org. NSPF-funded research has also led to the CDC's Fecal Indent Recommendations, discussed later in this chapter.

Giardia

Giardia has an outer shell that allows it to survive in harsh conditions, though it is not as resistant to chlorine disinfection as Crypto. The symptoms, illness duration, and infectious dose are very similar to Crypto. However, because of the availability of several prescription drugs to treat *Giardia*, the incidence of death is low compared to Crypto. Unlike Crypto, *Giardia* is not as resistant to normal pool and spa operating disinfectant levels and can be destroyed within 45 minutes at 1 ppm (mg/L) of free chlorine at pH of 7.5 or less.

Bacteria

Bacteria are single cell microorganisms, less complex and smaller than protozoa. Bacteria can multiply in water with the proper nutrients. Bacteria such as *E. coli* O157:H7 and *Shigella* are sensitive to chlorine, so outbreaks appear to be a rare occurrence in chlorinated pools. However, outbreaks caused by lack of disinfection and heavy use of diaper-aged children still occur, highlighting the importance of proper operation and maintenance.

Shigella

Shigella is present in the diarrheal stools of infected persons while they are sick and for up to two weeks after the diarrhea ceases. Most *Shigella* infections are the result of the fecal-oral route of transmission. Children, especially toddlers aged 2 to 4, are the most likely to get shigellosis. Many cases are related to the spread of illness in child care settings, and many are the result of the spread of the illness in families with small children, due to poor hand-washing and hygiene habits.

Most that are infected with *Shigella* develop diarrhea, fever, and stomach cramps starting a day or two after they are exposed to the bacterium. The diarrhea is often bloody.

> ### Shigella
> When there is little water movement in a small body of water, a single AFR provides a sufficient infectious dose for nearby users. *Shigella* is readily controlled by chlorine.

© National Swimming Pool Foundation 2017

Shigellosis usually runs its course in five to seven days. Persons with shigellosis in the United States rarely require hospitalization. Some persons who are infected may have no symptoms at all, but may still pass the *Shigella* bacteria to others.

Fortunately, *Shigella* is quickly inactivated by the disinfectants used in swimming pools and spas. The latest documented outbreaks have occurred in pools that were drained and filled with untreated water.

Escherichia coli O157:H7

E. coli O157:H7 is one of hundreds of strains of the bacterium *Escherichia coli*. Although most strains are harmless and live in the intestines of healthy humans and animals, the 0157:H7 strain produces a powerful toxin and can cause severe illness. Investigations have documented transmission by consumption of under-cooked beef, unpasteurized milk and cider, contaminated water used to wash vegetables, consumption of contaminated water, and person-to-person transmission. When the news reports about outbreaks of *E. coli* infections, reports are usually addressing *E. coli* O157:H7.

> ### *E. coli* O157:H7
> This bacteria is easily controlled by chlorine at normal pool treatment levels. However, if an AFR occurs in a swimming pool, this organism will not be instantly eliminated in all cases. Time must be provided to allow for total disinfection.

The symptoms vary for each person but often include severe stomach cramps, diarrhea (often bloody), and vomiting, usually three to four days after exposure. The symptoms often begin slowly, with mild stomach pain or non-bloody diarrhea that worsens over several days. Most people get better within five to seven days. Some infections are very mild, but others are severe or even life-threatening. Very young children and the elderly are more likely to develop severe illness, but even healthy older children and young adults can become seriously ill.

Outbreaks still occur in untreated recreational water, such as lakes. However, the CDC did not document outbreaks in treated waters during 2011–2012. Work from the U.S. EPA demonstrates that these bacteria are quickly inactivated by chlorine in water (Emerging Infectious Disease 5(3), May–June 1999).

Viruses

Viruses are smaller than protozoa and bacteria, and, unlike bacteria, cannot grow outside of a person's body. Viruses do not respond to antibiotics as bacteria do, though some vaccines are available.

Norovirus

Noroviruses are a group of viruses that cause gastroenteritis and are found in the stool or vomit of infected people. Symptoms of norovirus illness usually begin about 24 to 48 hours after ingestion of the virus, but they can appear as early as 12 hours after exposure.

The symptoms of norovirus illness usually include nausea, vomiting, diarrhea, and some stomach cramping. Sometimes people additionally have a low-grade fever, chills, headache, muscle aches, and a general sense of tiredness. The illness often begins suddenly, and the infected person may feel very sick. In most people the illness is self-limiting, with symptoms lasting for about one or two days. In general, children experience more vomiting than adults.

Noroviruses are very contagious and can spread easily from person-to-person, or from a person to an object to a person. As few as 10 viral particles may be sufficient to infect an individual. The CDC estimates that 23 million cases of acute gastroenteritis are due to norovirus infection, and it is now thought that at least 50% of all foodborne outbreaks of gastroenteritis can be attributed to noroviruses. During 2011–2012, two outbreaks resulting in 122 cases of norovirus were documented (MMWR 2015;64(24):668-672).

Because of the many different strains of norovirus, it is difficult for a person's body to develop long-lasting immunity. Therefore, norovirus illness can recur throughout a person's lifetime. In addition, because of differences in genetic factors, some people are more likely to become infected and develop more severe illnesses than others. Currently, there is no antiviral medication that works against norovirus, nor is there a vaccine to prevent infection.

Adenovirus

Adenoviruses most commonly cause respiratory illness; however, they may also cause various other illnesses, such as gastroenteritis, conjunctivitis (eye infection), and skin rashes. Patients with compromised immune systems are especially susceptible to severe complications of adenovirus infection. Adenoviruses are unusually resistant to chemical or physical agents and adverse pH conditions, allowing for prolonged survival outside of the body. Adenoviruses are transmitted by direct contact, fecal-oral transmission, and occasionally waterborne transmission.

An outbreak in Greece occurred among athletes participating in a swim event. At least 80 persons displayed symptoms of the illness, with the predominant symptoms being high fever, sore throat, conjunctivitis, headache, and abdominal pain. Poor chlorination was probably the cause of the outbreak (residual chlorine <0.2 mg/L), since after hyperchlorination the outbreak of adenoviruses stopped (J. Infection 36 (1) 1999 p.101–103). Maintaining adequate levels of chlorination is necessary for preventing swimming pool and spa-associated outbreaks of adenovirus.

Hepatitis A

The word *hepatitis* means inflammation of the liver. Hepatitis is also the name of a family of viral infections that affect the liver, with three prevalent Hepatitis virus strains: A, B, C. Only Hepatitis A has the potential to contaminate a pool, because it is transmitted through the feces. Hepatitis B and C are transmitted through blood.

Infection with the Hepatitis A virus leads to a contagious liver disease. The most common symptoms are nausea, vomiting, diarrhea, low grade fever, rash, fatigue, jaundice, dark urine, and liver pain. Jaundice is a condition characterized by yellowing of the skin and eyes. Many people, especially children, have no symptoms. If symptoms occur, they usually appear from two to six weeks after exposure. Symptoms usually last less than two months, although some people can be ill for as long as six months. While Hepatitis A causes liver inflammation, most people's livers can fully recover without any long-term damage.

Studies have shown that Hepatitis A can be easily inactivated in a properly maintained pool with free chlorine levels of 1 ppm (mg/L) within 16 minutes (see Table 4-1). The best way to prevent Hepatitis A is by getting vaccinated.

Fecal Incident Response Recommendations for Pool Staff

It is important that a facility have a plan and the pool staff properly trained for response to accidental fecal releases (AFRs).

All AFRs are not equal with regard to disease potential. The fully formed stool, while easily seen, does not contain Crypto, based on a study by the CDC on 300 stool samples that were obtained from pools (MMWR 2001; 50 (20):410-2). Only a small portion of the formed stool samples contained *Giardia*. The diarrheal AFR presents a much more serious problem and is less easily noticed. The staff response will vary depending upon the form of the AFR. Therefore, NSPF® recommends facilities follow the CDC fecal response procedure that is summarized below.

Fecal Response

- For any type of AFR, direct all users to leave the pool. If the filtration system services more than one body of water, all of the affected pools must be closed. The pool(s) must remain closed until all of the following procedures have been completed.
- For any type of AFR, manually remove as much of the material as possible. If the AFR is formed, remove it from the pool without breaking it apart. It is less likely that RWIs will spread if this action is taken in promptly. Use a scoop or net, and dispose of the material using the sanitary facilities. Vacuuming is not recommended; however, if performed, vacuum the immediate area to waste.
- Clean and disinfect the scoop, net and vacuum hose that were used in the removal and disposal process
- Pools that contain chlorine stabilizers, such as cyanuric acid, dichlor, and trichlor may require higher free chlorine levels.

Formed Stool

- Raise the free available chlorine level to 2 ppm (mg/L) and ensure the pH is 7.5 or less and the temperature is 77°F (25°C) or higher.

© National Swimming Pool Foundation 2017

- Maintain the chlorine concentration for at least 25 minutes before opening the pool. Local and state codes may vary on this requirement and should be consulted.
- Ensure the filtration system is operating while the pool reaches and maintains the proper free chlorine concentration during the disinfection process

Diarrheal Discharge

- Raise the free available chlorine level to 20 ppm (mg/L). Maintain the pH of 7.5 or less and a temperature of 77°F (25°C) or higher. Maintain the pH and chlorine level for 12.75 hours.
- The filtration system should be operating the entire disinfection time
- Backwash the filter after the full disinfection time. The filter effluent should be directed to waste, and not back to the pool. Follow any state or local regulations that may apply.
- Return the chlorine level to normal levels, as required by state or local regulations

Germ Inactivation Time (CT Value) for Chlorinated Water
1 ppm (1 mg/L) chlorine at pH 7.5 and 77°F (25°C)

GERM		TIME
E. coli O157:H7	Bacterium	Less than 1 minute
Hepatitis A	Virus	about 16 minutes
Giardia	Parasite	about 45 minutes
Cryptosporidium	Parasite	about 15,300 minutes (10.6 days)

Giardia Inactivation Time for Formed Incident

Chlorine Levels (ppm or mg/L)	Disinfection Time
1.0	45 minutes
2.0	25 minutes
3.0	19 minutes

Crypto Inactivation Time for Diarrheal Incident

Chlorine Levels (ppm or mg/L)	Disinfection Time
1.0	255 hours
10	25.5 hours
20	12.75 hours

Table 4-1. Germ inactivation times with no cyanuric acid present in the water.

Control of Fecal Viruses
Maintaining proper levels of chlorine disinfectant at all times is most important. However, high concentrations of organic matter as a result of excessive user load can result in an inadequate amount of free available chlorine to control the viruses. An AFR or vomitus will allow for the transfer of the viruses, even if acceptable levels of chlorine are maintained. The best method for control of these pathogens is education regarding good hygienic behavior in recreational waters.

- Open the pool to normal user activities CDC has extrapolated current data and has proposed the following remediation procedures for pools that contain stabilized chlorine or cyanuric acid: if the cyanuric acid concentration is 1–15 ppm, raise the free chlorine concentration to 20 ppm and maintain it for 28 hours; or raise the free chlorine concentration to 30 ppm and maintain it for 18 hours; or raise the free chlorine concentration to 40 ppm and maintain it for 8.5 hours. If the cyanuric acid concentration is more than 15 ppm, lower the concentration to 1–15 ppm by draining partially and adding fresh water without chlorine stabilizer before attempting to hyperchlorinate. Another method is dilution— draining the pool of enough water to reach 50 mg/L stabilizer—and then following the procedure above. If that cannot be accomplished, the pool could also be drained completely and scrubbed. Aquatic venues with secondary disinfection systems could simply be closed and allowed to circulate to achieve a 3-log reduction in the level of Cryptosporidium below one oocyst/100mL.

For any type of fecal release, an AFR Incident Log should be established. Record the date, time, AFR type, and chlorine and pH levels at the time of the event. Note the response taken to the event, and the total time taken for disinfection. Record the time the pool is reopened for use.

Germ Inactivation Times (CT Values)
To effectively disinfect the pool after some form of pathogen is known to be present, it is required that the pathogen be 99.9% inactivated. To achieve this level of germ inactivation for any pathogen the Contamination Time (CT) value for that pathogen must be achieved. The CT

© National Swimming Pool Foundation 2017

inactivation value is the concentration (C) of free chlorine in ppm (mg/L) multiplied by time (T) in minutes.

$$CT\ value = C \times T$$

The CT value for *Giardia* is 45 and the CT value for Crypto is 15,300: both at about pH 7.5, 77°F (25°C). If you choose to use a different chlorine concentration or inactivation time, you must ensure that the CT values remain the same.

For example, to determine the length of time needed to disinfect a pool after a diarrheal accident at 15 ppm (mg/L), use the following formula:

Time = 15,300 ÷ 15 ppm (mg/L) = 1,020 minutes or 17 hours.

It would take 17 hours to inactivate Crypto at 15 ppm (mg/L). You can do the same for *Giardia* by using the CT inactivation value of 45.

Time = 45 ÷ 15 ppm (mg/L) = 3 minutes

Vomit and Blood Contamination in Pool Water

The most common germs spread through recreational water are germs that cause diarrheal illnesses and skin rashes. These are spread by swallowing water contaminated with feces or by the user's skin exposure to contaminated water. Pool water is unlikely to spread illness via vomit or blood.

Vomiting while swimming is a common event. Often, vomiting is a result of swallowing too much water. In these cases, the vomit is probably not infectious. However, if the full contents of the stomach are vomited, respond to the vomit accident as you would respond to a formed fecal accident, using CDC's recommendations.

Noroviruses are the most likely germs to be spread by vomit. The time and chlorine level combinations needed to kill noroviruses and *Giardia* are similar. Since killing *Giardia* is the basis of CDC's formed fecal accident response recommendations, this protocol should be adequate for disinfecting a potentially infectious vomit accident.

Germs (e.g., Hepatitis B virus or HIV) found in blood are spread when infected blood or certain body fluids get into the body and bloodstream (e.g., by sharing needles and by sexual contact). There is no evidence that these germs have ever been transmitted from a blood spill in a pool.

Non-Fecal Illnesses

There are several diseases that can be transmitted or contracted in the recreational water environment that are not associated with feces and do not cause gastrointestinal illness, but can still cause disease.

Pseudomonas aeruginosa

Pseudomonas aeruginosa is the most common bacteria isolated from skin rashes and ear infections. It is commonly found on skin and hair, and is common throughout the environment in soil, water, plants and leaves.

Common infections include dermatitis and folliculitis (infection of hair follicle), which are usually seen in armpits, groin, abdomen, and areas covered by swim suits. Rashes range from itchy small red bumps like flea bites, to larger pus-filled blisters like poison ivy. The rash usually occurs within two to eight days after contact and can last a week.

Pseudomonas grows in warm water and is more commonly associated with rashes from poorly maintained spas than swimming pools. The Spa & Therapy Operations chapter reviews the challenges operators face when maintaining proper water chemistry in a spa. If the concentration of disinfection dips below proper operating levels, the environment becomes perfect for *Pseudomonas* growth. This is why it is sometimes referred to as hot tub rash. Surrounding damp areas, such as decks, benches, and drains, can also provide optimum growth conditions. Normal disinfectant levels are sufficient to control *Pseudomonas*.

Risk factors associated with *Pseudomonas* outbreaks include the length of time in contact with the bacterium, type of swim suit (those with liners trap water up against your skin), exceeding of the maximum user load, and individual susceptibility differences.

The rash does not usually prompt persons to seek medical treatment, and, even when seen, patients are frequently misdiagnosed, especially when they forget to mention the use of a spa. Rashes usually clear up over time without treatment.

In 2011–2012, there were two documented outbreaks involving spas and heated pools, accounting for 16 illnesses. The long time it takes

© National Swimming Pool Foundation 2017

Photo 4-4. *Infected users can contaminate the water and pool area by contact.*

for the rash to develop and the limited need for medical treatment contribute to under-reporting of *Pseudomonas* outbreaks.

Swimmer's Ear

Otitus externa, or swimmer's ear, is a *Pseudomonas* infection of the outer ear canal causing the ear to become sensitive and inflamed. It may be painful to move the head or touch the ear. Pus may also drain from the ear. This disease is more common with children and young adults. Doctor prescribed antibiotics are normally used to treat the ear infection.

To protect against swimmer's ear, dry your ears after swimming. If it is difficult to get water out of your ear, apply a few drops of an alcohol-based ear product into the ear. These products are available over the counter at stores that sell basic medicines.

Legionella pneumophila

Legionellosis (Legionnaires' disease) is a very severe form of pneumonia, caused by the *Legionella pneumophila* bacteria. The bacteria can exist in poorly maintained pools and spas and is transmitted by the mists (breathable droplets) produced by spa aeration or by spray features. *Legionella pneumophila* causes two different diseases. The more severe form of infection, which includes pneumonia, is called Legionnaires' disease. Symptoms usually begin two to 14 days after being exposed to the bacteria. Legionnaires' disease can have symptoms like many other forms of pneumonia, so it can be hard to diagnose at first. Signs of the disease can include a high fever, chills, and a cough. Some people may also suffer from muscle aches and headaches.

Legionnaires' disease can be very serious and can cause death in up to 5% to 30% of cases. Most cases can be treated successfully with antibiotics, and healthy people usually recover from infection. Those with weak immune systems, predisposing lung conditions, and the elderly are more likely to get sick from *Legionella* bacteria. Fortunately, the bacteria are not spread from one person to another.

A milder infection caused by the same type of *Legionella* bacteria is called Pontiac fever. The flu-like symptoms of Pontiac fever usually last for two to five days and may include fever, headaches, and muscle aches; however, there is no pneumonia. Symptoms go away on their own without treatment and without causing further problems.

The *Legionella* bacteria are found naturally in the environment, usually in water. The bacteria grow best in warm water, like the kind found in hot tubs/spas, cooling towers, hot water tanks, large plumbing systems, or parts of the air conditioning systems of large buildings. They do not seem to grow in car or window air conditioners.

Normal disinfectant levels and frequent filter maintenance are necessary to control these bacteria. This is true even for spas that are used only for display purposes. An individual does not have to be immersed in the water to become infected; they only need to breathe contaminated air near the spa.

Outbreaks have been linked to aerosol sources in the community, such as poorly managed spas, showers, spray/mist features, and ornamental fountains in community settings, such as hotels, restaurants, and office buildings. Nine outbreaks with treated recreational water (both pool and spa water) caused by *Legionella* were documented during 2011–2012, causing 33 cases of Legionellosis (MMWR 2015;64(24):668-672).

Hypersensitivity Pneumonitis (HP)

There have been rare reports of people having shortness of breath, coughing, fever and/or weight loss in indoor environments that have either spas or water features. Most cases of this disease occur in the agricultural and metal working industries. The symptoms go away when the individual leaves the environment. When the individual returns, the symptoms return within four to six hours. This disease is called hypersensitivity pneumonitis. The disease has also been called hot tub lung in some accounts.

HP occurs when people inhale small water droplets created by mist or aerosol, that contain bacteria or parts of dead bacteria. The exact cause is being debated. However, a group of bacteria called *Mycobacterium avium* Complex (MAC) are the likely contributor. MAC has been isolated from victims' lungs and from spas in some of the investigations. Some scientists suggest that parts of dead bacteria (endotoxins) inhaled into the lung are a contributing factor in HP. In either case, the body has a response to the inhaled particles that cause the symptoms.

This medical condition can be avoided by maintaining disinfectant residual and good ventilation. MAC does form biofilm. As a result, it is important to maintain a disinfectant residual in all parts of the pool and spa including the plumbing lines that feed water features. Eliminating locations that have stagnant water will reduce the risk of HP since disinfectant can be used up in stagnant water and not replenished.

The absence of any documented HP outbreak in outdoor spas or water features reinforces that good ventilation is important. Indoor environments are also likely to have chloramines, which can be irritating and can cause some of the same symptoms of HP. As a result, good ventilation helps prevent HP and irritation due to chloramines. See the Pool & Spa Water Problems chapter for more information on chloramines and the Heating & Air Circulation chapter for more information on ventilation.

Methicillin-Resistant Staphylococcus Aureus (MRSA)

MRSA is a type of *Staphylococcus*, or staph bacterium that has developed resistance to methicillin, the antibiotic usually used to treat persons with staph infections. It is inactivated in water by normal disinfectant levels and is normally transmitted by contact with infected people or surfaces like towels, razor blades, etc.

Molluscum Contagiosum

Molluscum contagiosum is a relatively common viral infection of the skin that most often affects children. It results in firm bumps (papules) that are painless and usually disappear within a year without treatment. If the papules are scratched or injured, the infection can spread to surrounding skin.

Molluscum contagiosum spreads through direct person-to-person contact and through contact with contaminated objects. It is not well understood how long the *molluscum* virus can live in swimming pool water and if such water can infect users.

Open sores and breaks in the skin can become infected by many different germs. Therefore, people with open sores or breaks in the skin from any cause should not go into recreational water. If a person has *molluscum* bumps, the following recommendations should be followed when swimming: cover all visible

© National Swimming Pool Foundation 2017

growths with watertight bandages, dispose of all used bandages at home, and do not share towels, kick boards or other equipment, or toys.

Plantar Warts

The technical name for this foot infection is verrucas. It is acquired by contact with deck or locker room floor surfaces contaminated by skin fragments infected with causative papillomavirus. Barring individuals who are infected from using the aquatic facility is not a feasible plan, since verrucas is common. Immunity to the infection usually develops in adults. Regular cleaning and disinfection of decks and locker room floors will reduce the chance of infection.

Athlete's Foot

The ringworm (Tinea pedis) infection caused by dermatophyte fungi produces itchy scale between the toes. It is spread by contact with pool decks and locker rooms contaminated with skin fragments infected with the fungus.

Users with severe cases of athlete's foot should not be allowed to use the aquatic facility. However, this is very difficult to enforce. This infection is more common in adults than in children. Regular cleaning and disinfection of decks and locker room floors will reduce the chance of infection.

Other Pool Areas

Infected users and pool/spa visitors can contaminate the water and pool area by contact. Humans can harbor germs themselves, even when they are not showing signs of illness. This is also why many state and local regulations do not allow people with open sores in the pool, and require showers prior to entering the pool area. Showering with soap removes biological contaminants and also other contaminants including sweat, urine, hair products, lotion, make-up, cologne, and deodorant. Showering reminds patrons that the pool is shared with others, and everyone should do their own part to reduce the number of contaminants brought into the pool area.

Hygiene Facilities

A minimum standard of hygiene must be maintained for all locker rooms, toilet, and shower areas. The barefoot rule should apply: if the area is not clean enough for the staff to walk barefoot, then it is not clean enough.

Provide diaper changing areas at a location away from the pool deck, preferably in bathrooms. Diaper changing stations should be cleaned daily, stocked with soap, and maintained properly. Dirty or damaged stations will not be used by parents. Using pool-side furniture as a changing table must be prohibited.

Regular diapers disintegrate in chlorinated water. Swim diapers are made to withstand the water and may hold some feces; however, scientific evidence exists on how poorly they are able to keep feces from leaking into the pool. Swim diapers are not a solution for a child with diarrhea or a substitute for frequent diaper changing. Encourage all children to visit the restroom before entering the pool and often during their use of the pool.

The use of swim diapers and swim pants may give many parents a false sense of security regarding fecal contamination. The operator must make sure they understand the importance of NOT swimming when ill with diarrhea or within two weeks after the symptoms have gone.

Pool Basin

The pool bottom should be vacuumed daily, or more often if debris is visible. The Water Circulation chapter discusses the need for adequate water circulation to eliminate dead spots and stagnant areas.

Aquatic Play Features

Aquatic play features are becoming more popular. The NSPF® Aquatic Play Feature™ Handbook and online training course describe different features and information about water quality, management and operations. These features create some unique risks. Research has been shown that play features (ropes, padding materials, handrails, toddler swings) can also harbor disease-causing microorganisms when not properly cleaned and maintained (J. Water and Health, Vol. 7, 2009). Pool operators should review and follow manufacturer's instructions on cleaning these materials. If no cleaning protocol is available, operators should contact the manufacturer directly to select disinfectants that are compatible with the materials.

Photo 4-5. *Pool equipment such as kickboards, fins, and toys should be thoroughly disinfected.*

Contaminated Surfaces

Pool decks with standing water or puddles created in areas that may not slope to drain have also been shown to harbor microorganisms. (J. Water and Health, Vol. 7, 2009). It is good practice to wash the decks with chlorinated water as part of the closing procedure. During construction or deck renovation it is important to slope floors to drains to prevent puddles. Additionally, pool equipment such as kickboards, fins, and toys should be thoroughly disinfected and dried to kill any microorganisms and prevent biofilms from forming.

Clean up of Bodily Fluids on Pool Decks

Pool decks, walkways, and pool-side furniture can become contaminated as a result of contact with blood, vomit or other body fluids. Usually an EPA registered hard-surface disinfectant or a dilute solution of sodium hypochlorite (solution consisting of 1 part sodium hypochlorite and 10 parts water) is sufficient for dealing with these situations. A fresh hypochlorite solution should be made before a clean up, since chlorine will degrade over time.

Follow these tips for dealing with contaminated surfaces:

- Block off area from patrons until spill is cleaned up
- Wear rubber gloves
- Remove excess contaminant material with paper towels or other disposable wipes
- Gently add disinfectant solution to surface; let solution remain for 20 minutes
- Wipe up solution
- Deposit all towels, gloves, rags, and paper towels into a biohazard bag and then dispose of the bag according to local regulations
- All non-disposable materials, such as mops and brushes, should be soaked in a bleach solution and hung up to air dry
- Cleanse all non-porous surfaces with disinfectant and rinse with hot water Never flush any contaminant into the pool or spa water or circulation system
- Never flush any contaminant into the pool or spa water or circulation system
- Thoroughly wash hands with hot soapy water and dry using disposable towels

Additional training for handling bloodborne pathogens to prevent the spread of disease may be required by OSHA, depending on job responsibilities. Online bloodborne pathogen training is available at www.nspf.org.

Ventilation Systems

Bacteria can survive in aquatic facility areas, such as air conditioning, ventilation, and heating equipment. Wet surfaces can also allow for the growth of these organisms. The risks include respiratory, dermal, or central nervous system infections or diseases.

Air contamination can have a harmful effect on people in an indoor environment. In facilities that house pools and spas, good water treatment helps ensure good air quality, minimizing exposure to potentially harmful chemicals or bacteria. Depending on the size and number of staff at a facility, personnel who operate the pool and those who operate the air handling should coordinate efforts to maintain an ideal environment. For more information on indoor air quality, see the Heating & Air Circulation chapter. Additional training specific to indoor air quality is available at www.nspf.org.

Summary of Illness Prevention

- Make pool patrons aware that they should avoid swimming if they currently have or recently had (within two weeks) diarrhea
- Shower with soap and warm water before swimming
- Parents should ensure that children use the restroom before going swimming and that they take regular bathroom breaks
- Diapers should be changed frequently in a bathroom and never be changed pool-side

© National Swimming Pool Foundation 2017

- Pool operators should ensure diaper changing areas are always clean and usable
- Hands should be washed with warm water and soap after using the bathroom
- Pool water should not be swallowed
- Operators and staff should develop and practice a contaminant response plan
- Operators and staff must maintain effective levels of disinfection, circulation and water balance during all times that the pools, water features, spray features and spas are open for use

Other Pool Water Health Concerns

Disinfection By-Products

When disinfectants like bromine, chlorine, UV, or ozone are used to keep the water sanitary, they react with contaminants in the water. The use of chlorine to disinfect water was the biggest public health advance in the 20th century. As a result, average life span has increased dramatically. Diseases like cholera, typhoid, dysentery, polio, malaria, and others thankfully are no longer prevalent.

Despite the great benefits of chlorine, it has long been recognized that chlorine and bromine react with contaminants in water to produce disinfection by-products (DBPs). In fact, drinking water is regulated to minimize many DBPs. The most common DBPs are chloramines and bromamines. The Pool & Spa Water Problems chapter discusses these and ways to minimize them.

Some DBPs can cause chronic illness after years of exposure. For example, some cause cancer or harm people in other ways when they are exposed to the products for extended periods of time. Exposure to DBPs can occur through ingestion, inhalation, and skin contact. Much less water is ingested through recreational water than drinking water. Regardless, operators and management should work to minimize the causes of DBPs. Although, many countries wish to minimize DBPs, most do not have regulations in place. Understanding how to minimize DBPs remains an active topic among researchers. It is widely acknowledged that minimizing contaminants in water reduces DBPs.

Chemical Rashes

Some users can develop skin irritations or rashes not associated with pathogens. These ailments can come about as a result of exposure to disinfection chemicals or their by-products. Scientific literature has documented rashes that resulted from exposure to pools treated with bromine or chlorine. Some individuals are more sensitive than others and may develop contact dermatitis (rash/itchy skin), or eczema. In swimming pools, a variety of contaminants are present that can react with chlorine or bromine to produce chemicals that may be irritating. These by-products are likely the cause of chemical rashes. See the Pool & Spa Water Problem chapter for a discussion on reducing combined chlorine or chloramines.

Rashes due to exposure to chemicals are different than those due to bacterial exposure. Rashes of this type are medically classified as contact dermatitis rather than infections. Chemical rashes usually occur within 12 hours of exposure, which is much quicker than bacterial infections. The development of this condition varies substantially between individuals and is greatly influenced by the amount of exposure to the water. Some individuals that swim or use a spa on a daily basis may develop a reaction after a few months. In other cases, it may take years of repeated exposure to show any reaction.

Bromine Itch

Bromine itch is the most commonly reported type of chemical rash. As discussed in the Disinfection chapter, there are two general types of bromine-based disinfectants: organic brominating agents like BCDMH or DBDMH, and bromine generated by adding bromide ions and an oxidizer in the water.

Most cases of bromine itch seem to be due to irritation and not an allergy. However, it is likely that there are different causes. For example, in one case, a patch test showed the victim was allergic to BCDMH. In others, an allergic response was ruled out. In some cases, the rash persisted for weeks. In others, the rash developed after exposure and diminished after leaving the water. In some cases, children were more sensitive.

Since the exact cause is not clear, it is impossible to create a definitive prevention

Photo 4-6. *Good ventilation helps remove any contaminants that evaporate into the air.*

strategy. Some good practices are likely to help. Follow label directions by maintaining bromine levels within the proper ranges. One Australian study suggests that frequent oxidation will reduce the number of rashes due to bromine and chlorine disinfectants. In the cases where rashes are caused by disinfection by-products, water replacement can help reduce irritating contaminants in the water.

Trihalomethanes (THMs)

The most widely recognized DBPs regulated in drinking water are trihalomethanes (THMs). Disinfectant and organic contaminants which contain carbon react and produce THMs. The contaminants come from urine, perspiration, personal hygiene products, and/or the environment.

Chlorine compounds will react with the contaminants in the water forming trichloromethane, which is also called chloroform. If a product containing bromine or bromide is used in the water, then bromochloromethane chemicals or bromomethane chemicals can form, like tribromomethane, which is also called bromoform.

Trihalomethanes can form in the water and can be present in the air above the water. Research on DBPs in drinking water has been an active field of scientific research for several decades. There has been some research on DBP's in recreational water, as well. Currently, the risk to human health due to trihalomethanes in swimming pool water is relatively low. As more research is undertaken, efforts should be made to reduce THM formation.

In Europe, The Federation Internationale De Natation (FINA) recommended standard for THMs is 20 parts per billion (20 ug/L). The testing for THMs in North America is rare, and many of the principles taught in this manual can help minimize the occurrence of DBPs. Any practice that reduces the amount of contaminants in the water can help reduce their by-products.

Good filtration, good circulation, minimizing the dirt and contaminants that can come from users or the environment, and using products that help remove contaminants from water are just a few of the ways to minimize DBPs. In addition, good ventilation helps remove any contaminants that evaporate into the air, reducing inhalation. Users can minimize contaminants by showering before entering the water. Water clarifiers help remove contaminants from the water, too. This topic area remains an area of interest for NSPF® and public health policy makers.

© National Swimming Pool Foundation 2017

Chapter 5:
Disinfection

"For a community to be whole and healthy, it must be based on people's love and concern for each other."

–Millard Fuller

Disinfection is accomplished when the transmission of infections between persons or from the water is kept to a minimum and algae and other nuisance organisms are controlled. Disinfection is the process of destroying microorganisms that might cause human disease.

Many factors affect the disinfection process in swimming pools and spas: the pH of the water, temperature, environmental wastes, and user contamination. As the level of waste and contamination increases, the proper level of disinfection becomes harder to maintain.

Throughout this chapter, recommendations are made on chemical levels. These recommendations are made with the express caution that there is a legal requirement to follow each chemical's labeled instructions. Disinfectants discussed in this chapter are registered by the U.S. Environmental Protection Agency, pursuant to the Federal Insecticide, Fungicide and Rodenticide Act (FIFRA) unless noted otherwise.

FIFRA requires that registered chemicals have labels that instruct end users on the proper use, storage and disposal of the material. Product labels have specific directions for use for swimming pool and spa water treatment. They include the proper range of concentration, frequency of treatment, methods of application, treatment procedures for newly filled pools, and essential water quality conditions necessary for the effective use of the product. It is unlawful to use registered chemicals in a manner that does not comply with the label instructions. The operator should always consult and comply with any labeled instructions, as well as any other applicable federal, or local laws and regulations.

The term disinfectant is sometimes called sanitizer, while disinfection is called sanitization. In this handbook, the term disinfectant will be used. In some cases, the handbook will call

the water sanitary, which would be a condition achieved by proper use of a disinfectant. Disinfectants eliminate nearly all pathogens. Sanitary water is free of almost all pathogens.

The most common disinfectants, chlorine and bromine, used in pools and spas are also oxidizers. The disinfectants react with and kill or inactivate microorganisms and oxidize contaminants. These two properties help eliminate microorganisms and contaminants. Oxidation plays an important role in maintaining a sanitary condition. Besides the ability to kill pathogens and oxidize contaminants, a disinfectant must also maintain a concentration in the water for extended periods of time (a residual). The disinfectant residual inactivates or kills microorganisms and oxidizes contaminants as they enter the water to protect users from pathogens brought into the water by people or from the environment. Disinfectants that either do not maintain a residual concentration or do

Photo 5-1. *Chlorine, the most common disinfectant used in commercial pools, is also an oxidizer.*

not act quickly against pathogens can only be considered a supplement and should always be used with a disinfectant.

The most common processes to prevent disease contraction are disinfection and filtration. Now, more facilities are using supplemental systems such as, ozone, UV, or chlorine dioxide to oxidize or disinfect or improve water quality. When choosing a disinfectant, there are many factors to consider:

- Water temperature
- Bathing loads
- Location of the vessel: indoor or outdoor
- Type of facility: pool, spa, therapy, waterpark
- Source water chemistry
- Chemical storage and safety concerns
- Supervision and maintenance concerns
- Codes and regulations

Chlorine Chemistry

The most common disinfectants used to treat swimming pool water release chlorine, also known as hypochlorous acid. Hypochlorous acid effectively kills or inactivates pathogens and algae. It also oxidizes, or chemically destroys, other materials from the environment or users. The terms hypochlorous acid and chlorine are often used interchangeably. Hypochlorous acid is stable enough to maintain a residual concentration in the water over hours or even days if there is no exposure to sunlight or high bather load. It also quickly inactivates almost all pathogens.

There are two basic categories of chemicals/chlorinating agents that release hypochlorous acid into water: unstabilized, also called inorganic, and stabilized, also called organic because they contain some carbon atoms. The unstabilized chlorines are sodium hypochlorite (NaOCl), calcium hypochlorite (Ca[OCl]$_2$), lithium hypochlorite (LiOCl), and chlorine gas (Cl$_2$). There are two stabilized or organic chlorines. The first is trichloro-s-triazinetrione (C$_3$N$_3$O$_3$Cl$_3$), also known as trichlor or trichloroisocyanuric acid. The second is sodium dichloro-s-triazinetrione (C$_3$N$_3$O$_3$Cl$_2$Na), also known as dichlor or dichloroisocyanurate.

When added to water, chlorine produces hypochlorous acid (HOCl), the hypochlorite ion (OCl$^-$), the hydrogen ion (H$^+$), and a by-product specific to the type of chlorinating agent.

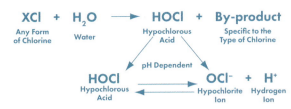

The hypochlorous acid and the hypochlorite ion, together, are called free chlorine (FC). Free chlorine is the chlorine in the water that is available for disinfection. The HOCl is between 60 to 100 times more effective than the OCl$^-$ at killing microorganisms. Chlorine testing measures FC and does not distinguish between the HOCl and the OCl$^-$.

Hypochlorous Acid

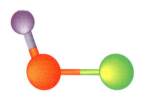

Hypochlorous acid (HOCl) is the active killing form of chlorine in water. As discussed in the previous section, hypochlorous acid is constantly dissociating into and reforming from hypochlorite ion (OCl$^-$) and free hydrogen (H$^+$) as shown by the following equation:

% Active HOCl	pH	% Less Active OCl$^-$
97	6.0	3
91	6.5	9
76	7.0	24
66	7.2	34
50	7.5	50
33	7.8	67
24	8.0	76
9	8.5	91

Table 5-1. *Active Chlorine vs. pH at 86°F (30°C) (reference R.W. Lowry, Pool Chlorination Facts)*

Hypochlorous acid and hypochlorite ion are in equilibrium with each other, which means a hydrogen ion attaches to make HOCl and detaches to make OCl$^-$ many times every

© National Swimming Pool Foundation 2017

second. If some HOCl molecules are consumed, in an instant OCl⁻ ions attach to H⁺ ions to maintain the same ratio of HOCl to OCl⁻ ions. As the pH goes down, the water becomes more acidic, there are more H^+ ions in the water, and more HOCl is formed on average. The relative concentration of HOCl versus OCl⁻ ions is shown in Table 5-1.

As HOCl is used, OCl⁻ immediately converts back to HOCl to maintain the equilibrium according to the pH. If a pool contained 3 ppm (mg/L) free chlorine at a pH of 7.5, there would be about 1.5 ppm (mg/L) HOCl and 1.5 ppm (mg/L) OCl⁻. If 1 ppm (mg/L) is consumed, the free chlorine would drop to 2 ppm (mg/L), 1 ppm or mg/L as HOCl and 1 ppm or mg/L as OCl⁻. If the pH rises to 7.8 and the free chlorine remains at 2 ppm (mg/L), the HOCl would be 0.66 ppm (mg/L), and the OCl⁻ would be 1.34 ppm (mg/L) (0.66 + 1.34 = 2.0 ppm or mg/L). The shift is virtually instantaneous. It is important for chlorine efficiency and user comfort to control the water pH as discussed in the Water Balance chapter.

Free Chlorine

Free chlorine (FC) is the active available disinfectant in the water. It is the sum of the HOCl and OCl⁻ and is determined by the DPD test as discussed in the Chemical Testing chapter.

$$FC = HOCl + OCl^-$$

| Free Chlorine | Hypochlorous Acid | Hypochlorite Ion |

The common practice in pools is to maintain the free chlorine at 2.0 to 4.0 ppm (mg/L). The accepted minimum is 1.0 ppm (mg/L) in the U.S., and the maximum is subject to debate. Minimum levels may vary in other regions around the world. Product labels approved by the U.S. Environmental Protection Agency set the maximum at 4.0 ppm (mg/L). However, many health codes set the maximum at 5.0 ppm (mg/L) or even higher.

Combined Chlorine

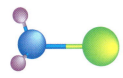

Combined chlorine (CC) forms when free chlorine (FC) reacts with two types of contaminants in the

water. When free chlorine reacts with ammonia, inorganic chloramines, those which do not contain carbon, are produced as shown in the following equation:

$$HOCl + R\text{-}NH_2 \longrightarrow R\text{-}NHCl + H_2O$$

| Hypochlorous Acid | Organic Amine | Organic Chloramine | Water |

"R" may be a variety of different structures.

When FC reacts with organic, or carbon-containing, nitrogen compounds, organic chloramines form as shown in the following equation:

$$HOCl + NH_3 \longrightarrow NH_2Cl + H_2O$$

| Hypochlorous Acid | Ammonia | Inorganic Chloramine | Water |

Both inorganic and organic chloramines show up in a DPD test as combined chlorine. Both are generically called chloramines. Urine, sweat, and the environment are sources of ammonia and organic nitrogen-containing chemicals. It is important to know how much of the total chlorine is due to CC because CC is not an effective disinfectant.

The presence of combined chlorine poses several challenges that the facility staff must work to address. Chloramines evaporate and are the cause of the chlorine-like smell often experienced in indoor pools. Chloramines are also more irritating to skin and mucous membranes. Thus, removal or destruction of combined chlorine is a common problem operators must work to solve. Several options to minimize CC are presented in the Pool & Spa Water Problems chapter.

Disinfectants

Disinfectants inactivate or kill the vast majority (greater than 99.9%) of microorganisms that can cause disease (pathogens). Pathogens include bacteria, fungi, viruses, and protozoan parasites. In addition, disinfectants are effective at killing

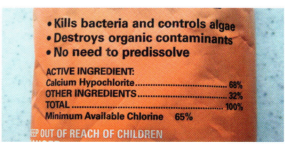

Photo 5-2. *Disinfectants inactivate or kill the vast majority of microorganisms that can cause disease.*

Characteristics of Disinfectants

	Sodium Hypochlorite	Calcium Hypochlorite	Lithium Hypochlorite	Gas Chlorine	Trichlor	Dichlor	BCDMH (Bromine)
% Available Chlorine Content	10 - 12%	47 - 78%	35%	100%	90%	56 - 63%	27%
% Active Strength	10 - 12%	47 - 78%	29%	100%	> 99%	> 99%	95.5%
pH in 1% Solution	9 - 14	8.5 - 11	10.8	0	2.8 - 3.5	6.5 - 6.8	4.8
pH Effect in Water	Raises	Raises	Raises	Lowers	Lowers	Neutral	Lowers
Physical Appearance	Liquid	Granular, Tabs, Briquet	Granular	Gas	Granular, Tabs	Granular	Granular, Tabs

Table 5-2. *Characteristics of different forms of disinfectants.*

algae. The reason we use the word inactivate in addition to kill is that some pathogens, like viruses or microscopic cysts, are not alive and cannot be killed. Fortunately, they can be inactivated so they are not infectious. Some parasites such as *Giardia* and *Cryptosporidium* are not easily controlled by pool water chemical disinfectants such as chlorine (see Pool Water Contamination chapter); however, both parasites are readily inactivated with supplemental disinfectants like ozone or ultraviolet (UV). Chlorine dioxide is also effective, but it is not registered for use in the U.S. There is a growing body of data showing how to use filter enhancers, also known as water clarifiers, to allow the filters to remove crypto from water.

The pool operator has many chemical tools available for the disinfection process. Chlorine and bromine are the most commonly used. These two disinfectants are highly reactive and provide residual properties that ensure continuous, efficient control of microorganisms.

Available Versus Active Chlorine

It is important to understand the difference between the terms available chlorine content and active chlorine percentage.

Available Chlorine Content (ACC) is a comparison of the relative amount of chlorine released into water for different chlorine disinfectants. ACC is developed using chlorine gas as the standard reference of 100%. Table 5-2 provides information concerning the ACC of each of the chlorine disinfectants.

Active Chlorine Percentage is the percentage by weight of the technical grade active ingredient in the product. As an example, a 100 pound container of trichlor would contain essentially 100 pounds of actual trichlor in the container, since the active ingredient percentage is usually greater than 99%.

When you consider the available chlorine content, pure trichlor has an ACC equal to 90%. The trichlor in this container can release 90% as much chlorine as 100 lbs of chlorine gas (Cl_2) could release when dissolved in water. In other words, on a pound-per-pound basis, trichlor releases only about 10% less chlorine than a pound of gas chlorine. In contrast, a pound of sodium hypochlorite releases 88-90% less chlorine compared to a pound of gas chlorine. Table 5-2 compares most major disinfectants.

In some cases, a disinfectant may contain other ingredients that show up on a label as Inert, or Other Ingredients. The presence of these ingredients reduces the amount of active ingredient and the available chlorine content. Inert ingredients may be formed in the manufacturing process of the active ingredient or they may be intentionally added by the

© National Swimming Pool Foundation 2017

manufacturer. In some cases the inert provides other benefits, but are listed as inert because they do not provide disinfection.

Unstabilized Disinfectants

Unstabilized disinfectants do not contain the carbon atom, which is why they are sometimes referred to as inorganic disinfectants. Unstabilized disinfectants with no spearately added cyanuric acid in the water are very sensitive to the UV radiation in sunlight. Inorganic disinfectants are more easily automated and controlled by an oxidation reduction potential (ORP) system. Following is a discussion of each of the unstabilized disinfectants that release chlorine.

Sodium Hypochlorite (NaOCl)

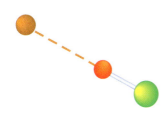

Active Strength 10 – 12%
ACC 10 – 12%
pH 9 – 14

Sodium hypochlorite is a liquid chlorine-releasing disinfectant that is the most common disinfectant used to treat commercial pools. The convenience of liquid chemical feeding, as well as the relatively low cost, play an important role in the popularity of sodium hypochlorite. Its reaction when introduced into pool or spa water is as follows:

$$NaOCl + H_2O \rightarrow HOCl + Na^+ + OH^-$$

The hydroxide ion (OH^-) reacts with the pool or spa water to raise the pH. The strength when used at the pool or spa facility is 10% to 12% available chlorine content (ACC) with a pH between 9 and 14. The pH must be corrected by the addition of an acidic material. The amount of acid needed to control pH depends on the pH of the sodium hypochlorite. Sodium hypochlorite raises the water's total dissolved solids (TDS) by adding sodium (Na^+) and chloride (Cl^-) ions to the water. Sodium chloride does not have any negative effect on disinfection. Unfortunately,

there is no easy way to differentiate between TDS due to salt/sodium and TDS due to less desirable contaminants. Therefore, dilution to lower TDS is recommended.

Sodium hypochlorite is not stable in storage and gradually loses its strength, especially at higher temperatures. This fact may reduce sodium hypochlorite's economic benefit to operators. Therefore, sodium hypochlorite should be stored in a cool, dark environment. Unfortunately, test kits are not commonly available to confirm sodium hypochlorite is at label concentrations. Sodium hypochlorite has substantial shipping cost since it contains about 88-90% water and inert salt.

Sodium hypochlorite is usually introduced into commercial pools and spas by the use of positive displacement feeder pumps (see Chemical Feed & Control chapter). Manual addition of sodium hypochlorite is common in residential applications and some small pools when the facility is closed to users. The usual pH correction with muriatic acid (31%) involves using between 10 and 16 fluid ounces (295.7 and 473.12 milliliters) for every one gallon (3.785 liters) of sodium hypochlorite.

Calcium Hypochlorite (Ca[OCl]₂)

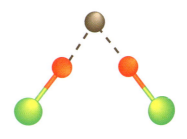

Active Strength 47% – 78%
ACC 47% – 78%
pH 8.5 – 11 (1% solution)

Calcium hypochlorite is a dry form of chlorine often called cal-hypo. It is available in granular, tablet, or briquette form. Depending on how cal-hypo is manufactured, the ACC can vary from 47% to 78%. The amount of active ingredient and the ACC are the same with cal-hypo. Cal-hypo's reaction when introduced into pool or spa water is as follows:

$$Ca(OCl)_2 + 2H_2O \rightarrow 2HOCl + Ca^{+2} + 2OH^-$$

Calcium hypochlorite is commonly used to superchlorinate water because of its high ACC

(47–78%) and moderate solubility. Maintaining good circulation and brushing granules from the bottom can help prevent bleaching of vinyl liners if cal-hypo is added directly to the pool or spa. It is also commonly used in erosion feeders as the primary disinfectant. The calcium hydroxide $(Ca[OH]_2)$ by-product is responsible for the increase in the water's pH when using cal-hypo. The pH of cal-hypo is between 8.5 and 11.

One pound of cal-hypo that has from 47% to 78% ACC, when dissolved into 10,000 gallons of water will deliver from 5.6 ppm (mg/L) to 9.4 ppm (mg/L) of chlorine, respectively. Formulated cal-hypo products have different properties based on what is added to the formula. When the formulation is composed of less than 65% cal-hypo, other products will have been formulated into the product to make up the difference. The product label and SDS will provide information on dosages, benefits, hazards, etc.

Continuous use of cal-hypo may result in high calcium levels in the water, affecting water balance (see Water Balance chapter). In areas where the source water is hard, the build-up of calcium may result in scale on the pool/spa wall surfaces, filter, and heating components. In soft-water regions, cal-hypo has the benefit of adding calcium hardness to soft water.

The National Fire Protection Association (NFPA) classifies cal-hypo as a Class 3 oxidizer, meaning it "causes a severe increase in the burning rate of a combustible material with which it comes into contact." Oxidizers can ignite if contaminated or heated. It is incompatible with organic compounds, and great care should be taken when storing and handling this disinfectant. Manufacturers have formulated cal-hypo with inert ingredients to create a NFPA Class 1 oxidizer, a less hazardous form. Formulated products are more commonly sold in residential applications. Refer to the SDS and label provided by the supplier for proper safety, storage, and handling information.

Lithium Hypochlorite (LiOCl)

Active Strength 29%
ACC 35%
pH 10.8 (1% solution)

Lithium hypochlorite is a dry, granular compound of chlorine. It is rapidly and completely soluble, making it a good choice for superchlorination. Lithium hypochlorite reacts when introduced into pool or spa water as follows:

$$LiOCl + H_2O \longrightarrow HOCl + Li^+ + OH^-$$

Lithium hypochlorite is not widely used in commercial pool facilities due to the relatively low active strength of 29% (ACC of 35%) and the relatively high cost. It dissolves very quickly, making it ideal for use in vinyl-lined, fiberglass, or painted pools and in hard-water regions and spas. Lithium hypochlorite is a NFPA Class 1 oxidizer, meaning it is an oxidizer "that does not moderately increase the burning rate of combustible materials with which it comes into contact."

Chlorine Generation

Chlorine can be produced on-site utilizing a mixture of sodium chloride, salt, and water. Electricity is passed through the salt solution and chlorine gas is produced. Permanent, specially fabricated and treated rare-metal electrodes are used to supply the electrical energy (⚡) to the solution.

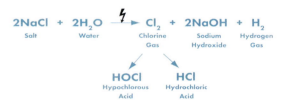

$$2NaCl + 2H_2O \xrightarrow{\;\;} Cl_2 + 2NaOH + H_2$$
$$HOCl \qquad HCl$$

There are two basic styles or types of chlorine generation systems. The first, called in-line, produces chlorine utilizing salt that is dissolved in the pool or spa water. The second, called brine method, uses an off-line system to produce chlorine from a solution of salt and water.

In-line generation systems require salt to be added to the pool or spa water. The circulation system passes the salt water thorough a device that contains electrochemical cells. These cells convert the sodium chloride into free chlorine. The Chemical Feed & Control chapter has more information about in-line chlorine generators.

The brine method has a separate tank containing solid salt. The system mixes salt and water. The salt water, or brine, is then converted to free chlorine with an electrochemical cell. The

© **National Swimming Pool Foundation** 2017

Photo 5-3. *When chlorine is generated, the chlorine and sodium hydroxide dissolve into the water and the hydrogen gas escapes to the atmosphere.*

brine method is discussed in greater detail in the Chemical Feed & Control chapter.

Chlorine Gas (Cl₂)

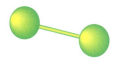

Active Strength 100%
ACC 100%
pH 0 (1% solution)

Elemental chlorine gas has both 100% active chlorine strength and 100% ACC. The reaction of chlorine gas when introduced into pool or spa water is as follows:

$$Cl_2 + H_2O \longrightarrow HOCl + HCl$$

| Chlorine Gas | Water | Hypochlorous Acid | Hydrochloric Acid |

The formation of hydrochloric acid (HCl), also known as muriatic acid, rapidly lowers the pH of the water and destroys its buffering capability. Approximately one-half pound of HCl is formed for every pound of chlorine gas used. For this reason, pools using chlorine gas usually have an automated addition of sodium carbonate (Na_2CO_3), known as soda ash, or sodium hydroxide (NaOH), known as caustic soda.

Chlorine gas is an effective disinfectant and some new facilities are built to use this disinfectant. The relative numbers of facilities that use chlorine gas have dropped over the last few decades, despite its low cost and efficacy. The cost of maintaining and repairing the feed equipment, insurance costs, high operator training requirements, high toxicity of chlorine gas, and the effects a leak has on the facility, staff, and surrounding community have contributed to the reduced use of chlorine gas.

Cyanuric Acid (C₃N₃O₃H₃)

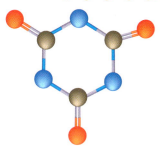

Cyanuric Acid (CyA), sometimes called stabilizer or conditioner, is a compound that is either added directly or added indirectly via stabilized chlorine products (to be described later in the section on Disinfectants) and is typically used to protect chlorine from the effects of UV light in sunlight. Half of the chlorine in water can be destroyed by sunlight in less than one hour. As a result, free chlorine (FC) concentrations can drop below the recommended minimum, risking disease transmission between people. When CyA is present in the water in sufficient concentrations, the FC residuals remain three to ten times longer than in water without CyA.

Cyanuric acid has no disinfection properties. For optimum chlorine protection, the CyA level should be maintained between 30 and 50 ppm (mg/L). Many jurisdictional codes limit the use of CyA, especially at indoor facilities. In the event a diarrheal fecal accident occurs in water that contains CyA, higher chlorine concentrations or longer contact times may be needed to inactivate *Cryptosporidium*, a common cause of recreational water illness. The Pool Water Contamination chapter has more information.

CyA functions as a stabilizer for free chlorine and does not stabilize bromine. Excessive levels of CyA may lead to an increased risk of algae. The most common method of reducing CyA concentration is to partially drain and replace water with fresh potable water.

Depending on the size of the CyA granule,

it may dissolve slowly, taking as long as two days to go into full solution. Suspending CyA in a perforated plastic container into the surge or atmospheric tank allows for dissolution without closing the facility to users. Broadcasting cyanuric acid directly into the pool may cause a delay in reopening the pool to users, in order to allow the CyA to dissolve completely.

Stabilized Disinfectants

There are two chlorinated isocyanurate, commonly called iso, disinfectants available. They are called trichloro-s-triazinetrione (trichloroisocyanuric acid), commonly called trichlor, and sodium dichloro-s-triazinetrione (sodium dichloroiso-cyanurate), commonly called dichlor. These two disinfectants contain cyanuric acid as part of their molecular structure. It is important to remember that once the chlorine portion of the iso has been depleted, the cyanuric acid remains and will increase in concentration as more iso is added to the water.

Trichlor ($C_3N_3O_3Cl_3$)

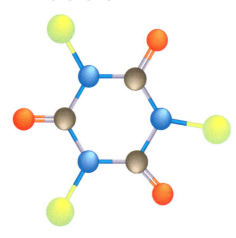

Active Strength >99%
ACC 90%
Chlorine Content 46%
pH 2.8 – 3.5 (1% solution)

Trichlor is a dry compound most commonly available in tablet (one and three-inch diameter) or stick form. These tablets are usually fed into the water by means of an erosion feeder (see Chemical Feed & Control chapter). Granular products are less common. There are two types of granular products. Pure trichlor granules are commonly used for treating pool surface algae such as black algae. Formulated trichlor products have lower available chlorine content and ingredients added by the manufacturer

to provide other properties, such as faster dissolution, clarification, etc. Trichlor is a National Fire Protection Agency (NFPA) Class 1 oxidizer, meaning it does not moderately increase the burning rate of combustible materials with which it comes into contact.

Trichlor has a relatively low solubility. It has an ACC of about 90%. This may vary depending upon the inert ingredient content used by the manufacturer that created and packaged the product. Trichlor's reaction when introduced into pool or spa water is as follows:

$$C_3N_3O_3Cl_3 + 3H_2O \longrightarrow 3HOCl + C_3H_3N_3O_3$$
Trichlor　　　Water　　　Hypochlorous　Cyanuric
　　　　　　　　　　　　　　Acid　　　　Acid

The pH of trichlor is 2.8–3.5 and will lower the total alkalinity and pH over time. To correct for this, a chemical feeder can be used to increase pH with either sodium carbonate ($NaCO_3$) or sodium sesquicarbonate ($Na_2CO_3 \bullet NaHCO_3 \bullet 2H_2O$). By testing and maintaining the proper total alkalinity, the need for pH adjustment may be minimal.

The convenient slow dissolution properties and availability of suitable erosion feeders has resulted in this disinfectant's becoming popular with pool service companies and in residential pools. The stabilizing effect that trichlor offers makes it ideal for use in outdoor situations. Trichlor is less commonly used in commercial pools since it releases cyanuric acid into the water, and many local and state codes limit how much CyA can be present in the water.

Dichlor ($NaCl_2C_3N_3O_3$)

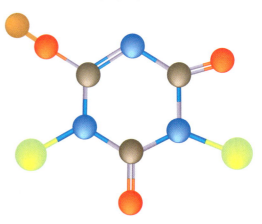

Active Strength >99%
ACC 56% – 63%
Chlorine Content 33%
pH 6.5 – 6.8 (1% solution)

© National Swimming Pool Foundation 2017

Disinfection

Sodium dichlor is unique among the disinfectants because its pH is almost neutral, being about 6.7. There are two common forms of dichlor available. The first form is called anhydrous, meaning no water is bound to the dichlor molecule. As a result, anhydrous dichlor has a higher ACC of 62%. Anhydrous dichlor is more hazardous for storage and handling and is an NFPA Class 3 oxidizer, indicating "that it can cause a severe increase in the burning rate of combustible materials with which it comes into contact." The second type of dichlor available is called dichlor dihydrate, which means that the dichlor molecule has two molecules of water (di-hydrate) bound to it. Because some of the weight in dichlor dihydrate is due to water, it has a lower ACC content of 56% and is a NFPA Class 1 oxidizer. When dichlor is dissolved in water, the following reaction takes place:

$$NaC_3N_3O_3Cl_2 + 2H_2O \rightarrow HOCl + NaOCl + C_3H_3N_3O_3$$

Dichlor   Water   Hypochlorous   Sodium   Cyanuric
                   Acid   Hypochlorite Acid

Dichlor is a salt and is very soluble. It is often used to superchlorinate vinyl-lined pools. It is also used in spas when pH control is a concern. Dichlor may be used to superchlorinate pool water and raise the stabilizer level at the same time. One pound (454 grams) of anhydrous dichlor or dichlor dihydrate per 10,000 gallons (37,843 liters) will provide about 7.4 ppm (mg/L) or 6.7 ppm (mg/L) of chlorine, respectively. This dosage will add about 7 ppm (mg/L) or 6 ppm (mg/L) of stabilizer, respectively, for these two products. Manufacturers have formulated dichlor with inert ingredients. Formulated dichlor products are more commonly distributed through locations that focus on residential pools. Refer to the SDS and label provided by the supplier for use, safety, storage, and handling information.

Bromine

Bromine belongs to the same chemical family as chlorine; they are both halogens. It is a disinfectant, has good algicidal properties, and is an oxidizer. Unlike chlorine (Cl_2), which is a gas, elemental bromine (Br_2) is a heavy reddish-brown liquid. The elemental form of bromine is not available for use as a disinfectant, but several compounds that release bromine, or hypobromous acid, are currently used.

There are two methods of providing hypobromous acid (HOBr) to pools and spas other than elemental bromine. The first is sodium bromide activated by the oxidizer, potassium monopersulfate. This method is called the two-part system, it is limited in use to small volumes of water, and is not used for commercial pools. The second is a solid form of bromine bound to an organic molecule. This solid is dissolved in a soaking or erosion type feeder to deliver hypobromous acid. Organic bromine compounds are used in commercial pools and spas.

Hypobromous Acid (HOBr)

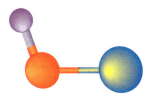

The chemistry of hypobromous acid is very similar to that of hypochlorous acid (HOCl). When dissolved in water, bromine-releasing chemicals form hypobromous acid, hypobromite ion, and hydrogen ion. Hypobromous acid partly dissociates to form hydrogen ions (H^+) and hypobromite ions (OBr^-).

As with chlorine, the relative percentage of hypobromous acid and hypobromite ions is dependent on the pH value of the water. When the pH value is between 6.5 and 9, both hypobromous acid and hypobromite ions are present in water.

Like with chlorine, if water contains ammonia (NH_3), then monobromamine (NH_2Br), dibromamine ($NHBr_2$), and nitrogen tribromide (NBr_3) form. Similarly, organic amines will produce organic bromamines. Bromamines are excellent disinfectants, have less odor, and are less irritating to eyes and mucous membranes than chloramines. As a result, bromine-releasing chemicals have gained wider acceptance in high-use applications like spas.

Bromine-releasing chemicals are oxidizers but are not as strong as chlorine. It is common practice to periodically oxidize pools or spas that use bromine with a chlorine or non-chlorine oxidizer. As a result of the disinfection process, bromide ions (Br^-) are formed. Oxidizers like HOCl, potassium monopersulfate, or ozone will react with bromide to form a new molecule of hypobromous acid.

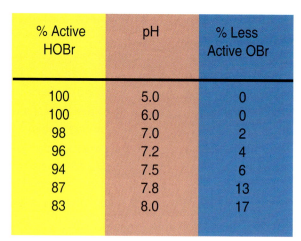

% Active HOBr	pH	% Less Active OBr
100	5.0	0
100	6.0	0
98	7.0	2
96	7.2	4
94	7.5	6
87	7.8	13
83	8.0	17

Table 5-3. *The relationship of pH to active HOBr*

Bromine, like chlorine, creates equilibrium between hypobromous acid (HOBr) and hypobromite ion (OBr⁻). HOBr is more effective at inactivating and killing microorganisms. Hypobromous acid is a weaker acid than hypochlorous acid. As a result, at a similar pH, there is more hypobromous acid and less hypobromite. For example, at a pH of 7.5, about 94% of the total bromine in the water is present as HOBr and only 6% is present as hypobromite (see Table 5-3). Based on this difference in chemistry, bromine-releasing disinfectants have gained wider acceptance in treating spas that tend to have a higher pH (see Spa & Therapy Operations chapter).

The HOBr is destroyed by sunlight much like HOCl. About half of bromine can be destroyed by sunlight in 60 to 90 minutes. Cyanuric acid does not protect HOBr from ultraviolet sunlight destruction. Once a brominating product is used, bromide will remain in the water. Adding a stronger oxidizer like a chlorinating chemical will cause the bromide to be oxidized to hypobromous acid, consuming the hypochlorous acid. Therefore, cyanuric acid no longer stabilizes the chlorine once bromine has been used, since hypobromous acid will be present in place of hypochlorous acid as follows:

$$HOCl + Br^- \dashrightarrow HOBr + Cl^-$$

Hypochlorous Acid   Bromide Ion   Hypobromous Acid   Chloride Ion

Bromine Tablets (BCDMH)

1-Bromo-3-chloro-5,5-dimethylhydantoin (BCDMH, $C_5H_6N_2O_2ClBr$) is an organic substance with chlorine and bromine attached to the organic carrier molecule, dimethylhydantoin (DMH). As BCDMH is dissolved into water, HOCl

and HOBr are formed along with the organic DMH. BCDMH is available as sticks, tablets, or granules. BCDMH is an NFPA Class 2 oxidizer, indicating that it "causes a moderate increase in burning rate of combustible materials with which it comes into contact."

When BCDMH is dissolved in water, hypobromous acid and hypochlorous acid are released. As the HOBr reacts with the organic matter in the water, the bromide ion (Br-) is formed. This is sometimes referred to as the bromide bank. The HOCl releases as BCDMH dissolves. The HOCl reacts with this bromide ion already in the water, producing additional hypobromous acid.

Two additional types of organic brominating disinfectants are available commercially with similar chemical structures as BCDMH. The first contains a mixture of DMH and a similar molecule EMH (ethylmethylhydantoin) with bromine and chlorine bound to them. The result is a mixture that has three chemicals:

BCDMH, 1-bromo-3-chloro-5,5-dimethylhydantoin;

DCDMH, 1,3-dichloro-5,5-dimethylhydantoin; and DCEMH, 1,3-dichloro-5-ethyl-5-methylhydantoin.

The second type of organic brominating disinfectant is DBDMH (1,3-dibromo-5,5-dimethylhydantoin). It has the same DMH organic carrier as BCDMH. The difference is that DBDMH has two bromine atoms bound to the DMH and no chlorine atoms. Therefore, when it dissolves it does not release any hypochlorous acid.

Secondary Disinfectant Systems

The use of chlorine-based disinfectants remains one of the biggest public-health advances of the last century. No one chemical class, however, can be expected to perform every function necessary to protect public health. Thus innovations like bromine disinfection—now almost a half century old—and biguanide disinfection (PHMB)—now used for decades—have been identified as chlorine alternatives.

© National Swimming Pool Foundation 2017

In addition, physical purification methods like filtration continue to play a vital role in making disinfection more effective and improving water clarity.

Over the last two decades, supplemental disinfectant systems have become more common in public pools and in some residential pools and hot tubs. These systems are called supplemental since they are used in conjunction with a primary disinfectant—most commonly chlorine. These supplemental disinfection systems have unique features that inactivate chlorine-resistant pathogens and improve water and air quality. Information about three supplemental systems are presented in this section: ozone, ultraviolet light, and chlorine dioxide.

Ozone (O3)

Ozone is a gaseous molecule with three oxygen atoms and is slightly soluble in water. It is considered a supplemental oxidizer and disinfectant since it does not create a disinfectant residual in the water. It must be used in conjunction with a disinfectant that maintains a residual in the water. It cannot be transported and must be generated on-site for pool and spa use.

Ozonators are sized and installed in the circulation system. Ozone systems are designed to treat a portion of the total flow through the system. The systems allow the ozone to dissolve and react with contaminants. Ozone is largely consumed before the water is returned to the pool or spa. This helps minimize any potential exposure to ozone, which is a hazardous gas. Ozone acts as a disinfectant by killing or inactivating bacteria, viruses, and parasites like *Cryptosporidium* and *Giardia*. Once the side stream is treated, the water is returned to the circulation system. Traces of ozone can inactivate pathogens in the main flow of the water.

When the water is returned to the pool or spa, ozone is present at a very low concentration, or is not present at all. Thus, a disinfectant must be maintained to protect users from pathogens introduced by the users or from the environment. Ozone also oxidizes inorganic and organic chloramines to help reduce combined chlorine and improve air quality in indoor aquatic facilities.

There are two methods for the generation of ozone, and they are discussed in detail in the Chemical Feed & Control chapter. An efficient method to introduce ozone into the water is important. Venturi injection is the most common way to dissolve ozone into water.

Ozone partially oxidizes organics and minerals resulting in ionic molecules. Some of these molecules are attracted to each other, agglomerate (group together), and are then removed by the filter. Removing contaminants helps reduce demand on the chlorine disinfectant.

As mentioned earlier, ozone can be used to regenerate the bromide ion, creating another disinfectant in the water. This process is shown as

$$Br^- + O_3 + H_2O \longrightarrow HOBr + OH^- + O_2$$

Bromide Ion · Ozone · Water · Hypobromous Acid · Hydroxide Ion · Oxygen

Ultraviolet (UV) Light

Ultraviolet light (UV) is a high-energy, low-wavelength light that provides a non-chemical method to disinfect water. UV is considered a supplemental oxidizer and disinfectant since it does not create a disinfectant residual in the water. It must be used in conjunction with a disinfectant that provides a residual. UV light cannot be stored or transported. It must be generated on site for pool use.

UV acts as a disinfectant by killing or inactivating bacteria, viruses, and parasites like *Cryptosporidium* and *Giardia*. Unlike chemical systems, UV inactivates pathogens with high energy. If the intensity of light is high enough and the exposure is long enough, UV stops reproduction by damaging the DNA of the pathogens.

The effectiveness of UV as a disinfectant is based on the applied energy within the given area of the treatment chamber where the UV bulb is located. The energy level is expressed as follows:

Dose = Lamp Intensity x Exposure Time

For more on UV see the Chemical Feed & Control chapter.

Photo 5-4. *This cut-out unit shows the UV lamp that the pool water continuously flows by.*

Photo 5-5. *Proper disinfectant levels help to achieve clear water conditions.*

Chlorine Dioxide (ClO$_2$)

Chlorine dioxide is a selective oxidizing agent and disinfectant. Chlorine dioxide is used to kill bacteria, algae, viruses, and microscopic cysts like *Cryptosporidium* or *Giardia*. The systems sold in Europe and Canada use a chemical that releases chlorine dioxide disinfectant in water. Commercial systems also use water clarifiers. At this time it is not registered as a disinfectant in the U.S. Chlorine dioxide reacts only with reduced sulfur compounds, secondary and tertiary amines, and some other highly reduced and reactive organics. Chlorine dioxide does not react with ammonia. It has been used in the U.S. to combat mildew and biofilm in the plumbing of PHMB treated pools.

Polyhexamethylene Biguanide (PHMB)

PHMB is an organic polymeric disinfectant that has been registered by the U.S. EPA to treat swimming pools and spas. This disinfectant is used in conjunction with hydrogen peroxide (H$_2$O$_2$), which is an oxidizer, and with a quat, or quaternary ammonium compound, algicide. This disinfection system is largely marketed to residential applications. Before it is used in commercial pools or spas, it is important to check with the local health department to ensure that PHMB is approved.

PHMB is not compatible with common products like chlorine-releasing chemicals, copper algicides, potassium monopersulfate. Chlorine dioxide (ClO$_2$) has been registered for use with PHMB to kill mildew and slime that can build up in plumbing. Some systems use ozone as a supplemental oxidizer. If PHMB is used, it is important to consult with the manufacturer for compatible problem-solving chemicals.

© National Swimming Pool Foundation 2017

Chapter 6:
Water Balance

"The meek shall inherit the Earth, but not its mineral rights."

–J. Paul Getty

Water is commonly called the universal solvent, and pool or spa water is no exception. Water containing no dissolved material will be very aggressive, and there will be a natural attempt to balance this condition by causing surface materials that contact the water to go into solution. The materials most commonly attacked are tile-line grout, cement pool wall material, and iron and copper materials found in pumps, heaters, piping, and valves. When water is satisfied and the proper mineral balance is achieved, water is no longer aggressive. Iron or copper dissolved from the system to achieve balance have the potential to cause future stains.

On the other hand, water that contains too much dissolved material becomes balanced by dropping calcium carbonate out of solution. The resulting deposit is a hard, rough-surfaced precipitate called calcium carbonate or scale. Scale can collect dirt and becomes an unsightly gray or dark deposit on the surfaces of the pool or spa and can plug the filtration, heater, and circulation piping.

Balance Factors

Properly balanced water creates an environment that optimizes the disinfection process. It also protects the pool/spa system components from chemical corrosion, thus increasing the useful operating life of equipment. Properly balanced water provides a more enjoyable swimming experience for the pool/spa users.

The factors that contribute to the balance of water are pH, total alkalinity, calcium hardness, temperature, and total dissolved solids.

pH

pH stands for *potens hydrogen*, which is Latin for the power of hydrogen (ion). As a water balance factor, pH has the most impact on properly balanced water and user comfort.

Water is a weak electrolyte, a solution that

Photo 6-1. *Properly balanced water creates an environment that optimizes the disinfection process.*

conducts electricity; and that is easily ionized, or converted to ions. Water is in equilibrium and the ionization equation is represented by

Under all conditions in water, when you multiply the H^+ ion concentration by the OH^- ion concentration, the product is always the same: 1×10^{-14} (or 0.00000000000001). For example, if the H^+ concentration is 1×10^{-7} (0.0000001) and the OH^- ion concentration is 1×10^{-7} (0.0000001), the product is 1×10^{-14} (0.00000000000001), which is a very small number. Similarly, if the H^+ concentration is 1×10^{-6} (0.000001), then the OH^- ion concentration has to be 1×10^{-8} (0.00000001) so that the product remains 1×10^{-14}. To avoid the use of such small numbers, the acidity or alkalinity of a solution is commonly expressed in pH units. pH is a measurement of the hydrogen ion concentration in water.

The technical definition for the pH of a solution is the negative logarithm of the hydrogen ion concentration shown as

pH = − log (concentration of H⁺ ion)

An easier way to remember this is if the H^+ ion concentration is 1×10^{-1} (0.1), then the pH is 1; if the concentration is 1×10^{-2} (0.01), then the pH is 2; if the concentration is 1×10^{-7} (0.0000001), then the pH is 7, etc.

As the H^+ ions increase, the OH^- ions decrease so that the product remains constant. As the H^+ ion concentration increases, the solution is said to be acidic. The smaller the pH unit, the more acidic the solution. Likewise, as the OH^- ions increase, the H^+ ions decrease, and the solution is said to be basic, or alkaline. Because the scale is logarithmic, a small change in pH actually represents a large change in acidity. Water that has a pH equal to six is 10 times more acidic than water that has a pH equal to seven. A pH of zero, close to the pH of muriatic acid, is

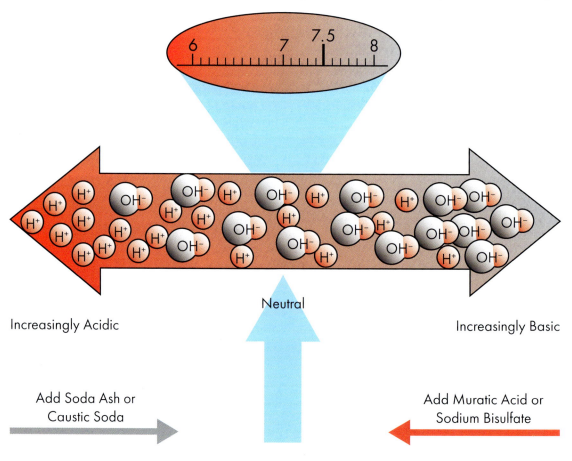

pH Scale

Illustration 6-1.

© National Swimming Pool Foundation 2017

10,000,000 times more acidic than water with a pH equal to 7.

The acceptable pH of pool/spa water is slightly alkaline (7.2 - 7.8). The pH of tears from a human eye is about 7.5. To assist in user comfort, the ideal range for pH is 7.4 to 7.6. There are many influencing factors that affect the pH of pool or spa water, including:

- User waste
- Disinfectants
- Source water
- Air-borne debris
- Water balance chemicals
- Aeration
- Evaporation

Control of pH

Control of pH is important for the comfort of users, the efficiency of the disinfectant, and the protection of the pool system components.

The method used to control pH is to maintain the proper level of total alkalinity, as discussed later in this chapter. Before making any pH change, test, and, if necessary, correct the total alkalinity. When the alkalinity is correct, it is often found that the pH will be correct as well.

To lower the pH, acids or acid salts such as sodium bisulfate ($NaHSO_4$) are added to the pool or spa water. This causes an increase in the H^+ ion, lowering the pH. The most common liquid acid used in the pool/spa environment is muriatic acid (a.k.a. HCl or hydrochloric acid). If muriatic acid is used to lower the pH, it is typically diluted with 50% water before it is fed into the pool or spa water. It should be added slowly over a return flow, preferably at the deep end of the pool. To prevent pooling, the sides and bottom of the pool where the acid was added may be lightly brushed. This prevents the potential of corrosion in pool or spa equipment. Full-strength muriatic acid (31.45% Hydrochloric Acid) can fume, so add the acid downwind or use half-strength that may fume less. To prevent corrosion, a 50/50 dilution is recommended. If you prepare your own dilution, remember: always add acid to water.

For pools using sodium hypochlorite or calcium hypochlorite as a disinfectant, carbon dioxide gas (CO_2) may be used as an alternative to any of the above listed acids. Carbon dioxide when dissolved into water produces carbonic acid, a weak acid that acts to reduce the pH of pool water. One by-product of the use of CO_2 to lower pH is the production of bicarbonates which raise the total alkalinity. Typically, operators will use muriatic acid to lower alkalinity to the lower end of the acceptable range. Pools using calcium hypochlorite as the primary disinfectant and pools with source water high in total alkalinity or calcium hardness may have problems with scale formation when using CO_2.

To increase the pH, a basic material is added, the most common being sodium carbonate, known as soda ash (Na_2CO_3). Other bases for raising pH could be sodium hydroxide (NaOH), sodium sesquicarbonate ($Na_2CO_3 \bullet NaHCO_3$

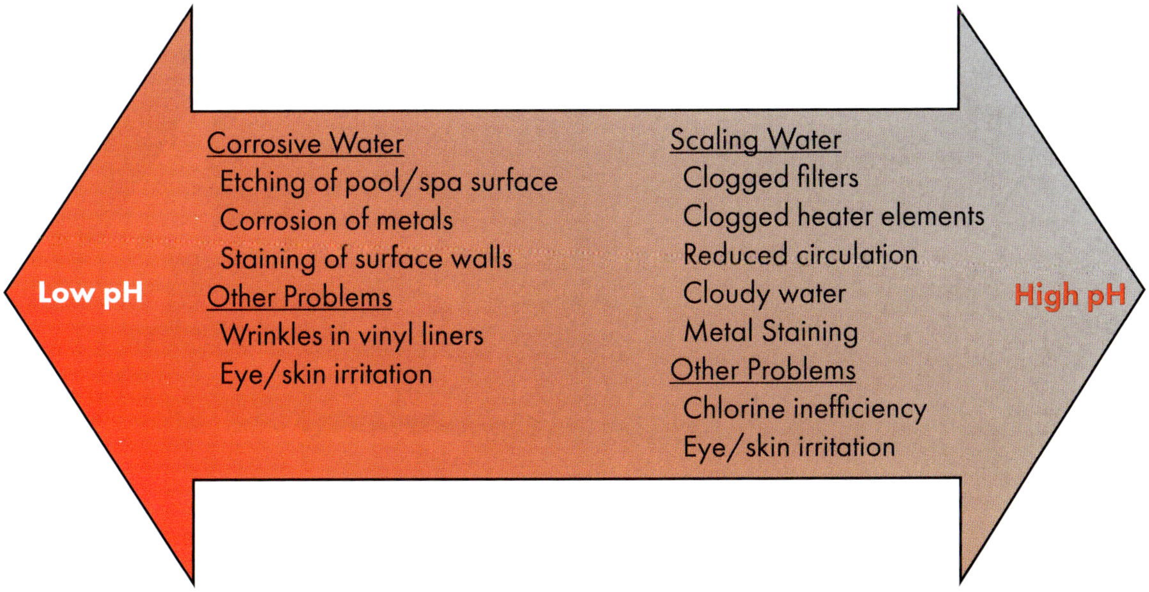

Corrosive Water
  Etching of pool/spa surface
  Corrosion of metals
  Staining of surface walls
Other Problems
  Wrinkles in vinyl liners
  Eye/skin irritation

Low pH

Scaling Water
  Clogged filters
  Clogged heater elements
  Reduced circulation
  Cloudy water
  Metal Staining
Other Problems
  Chlorine inefficiency
  Eye/skin irritation

High pH

pH Related Pool Problems

Illustration 6-2.

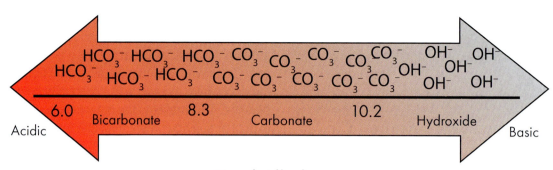

Total Alkalinity

Illustration 6-3.

• 2H$_2$O), and sodium bicarbonate (NaHCO$_3$). When a base is added, there is an increase in the OH$^-$ ions and the pH.

Sodium bicarbonate should not be used to raise pH on a regular basis. The correct method is to use sodium bicarbonate to achieve the desired total alkalinity, and then if further correction is necessary, use soda ash.

Acids and bases may be directly added to the pool or spa water as per label directions. There must be no people in the water, and the facility must remain closed until the chemicals are completely dissolved and dispersed.

Total Alkalinity

Total alkalinity is the measure of the ability of water to resist changes in pH. It is a buffer. A buffer is ionic compounds that resist change in the water's pH. The total alkalinity of the pool/spa water is the water's resistance to a change in pH. Total alkalinity is like an anchor for keeping pH where it should be.

As mentioned earlier, pH is affected by many things. Without proper buffering, the pH may swing dramatically from highs to lows. This is called pH bounce. A rapid movement of pH up and down with the addition of even small amounts of chemicals. When this happens, the water can become out of balance, affecting chlorine's ability to kill bacteria and causing corrosion, staining, scaling, or eye/skin irritation.

Total alkalinity is made up of bicarbonate (HCO$_3^-$), carbonate (CO$_3^-$), and hydroxide (OH$^-$) ions. In addition, there may be interferences from borates, phosphates, cyanurates, and silicates. When pools are operated in the acceptable range of 7.2 to 7.8 pH, the greatest contributor to total alkalinity is the bicarbonate ion.

In some cases the contribution that cyanuric acid makes to the total alkalinity is substantial. When cyanuric acid is high, the interference to total alkalinity due to cyanuric acid should be subtracted from total alkalinity before the saturation index is calculated (Saturation Index is discussed later in this chapter).

The ideal level for total alkalinity depends

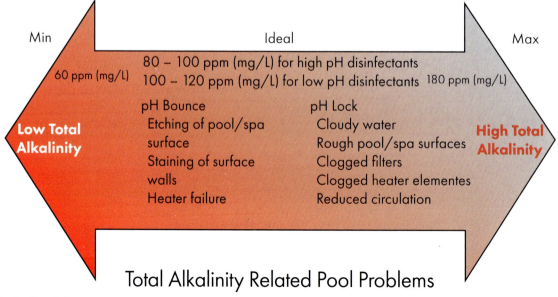

Total Alkalinity Related Pool Problems

Illustration 6-4.

© National Swimming Pool Foundation 2017

on the source of chlorine that is used and is generally 80 to 120 ppm (mg/L). High pH disinfectants/hypochlorites will usually require a total alkalinity in the lower part of this range. Low pH disinfectants, such as dichlor, trichlor, BCDMH bromine, and gas chlorine, require a total alkalinity in the higher part of this range.

Low Total Alkalinity

When there are not enough bicarbonate ions to provide buffering of the pH, the pool or spa water will exhibit pH bounce. Small amounts of chemical additions can make this occur. Acid rains or high user loads may cause the pH to fluctuate. Low alkalinity may result in water with a green tint if iron or copper are in the water. Low alkalinity may also cause corrosion/etching of the pool/spa wall surfaces. To increase total alkalinity, labels typically recommend adding sodium bicarbonate at the rate of 1.4 pounds per 10,000 gallons (670g per 40,000 liters) of water for a 10 ppm (mg/L) increase.

High Total Alkalinity

At higher levels of total alkalinity, the pH is usually higher than ideal and becomes very difficult to change, referred to as pH lock. Cloudy water due to calcium carbonate suspended in the water is a very real possibility with high total alkalinity conditions.

The total alkalinity can be lowered by the addition of acid, either muriatic acid or sodium bisulfate.

Calcium Hardness

The calcium content of the water is present naturally, due to the leaching process that occurs in nature. As ground water comes in contact with rocks and soils containing calcium and magnesium, water, the universal solvent, dissolves these minerals into the water. Included in this process are bicarbonate, carbonate, and sulfate.

Total hardness and calcium hardness are two different but related entities. Total hardness is the sum of calcium and magnesium and is sometimes expressed in grains of hardness (1 grain = 17.1 ppm or mg/L). The terms soft water and hard water are an indication of the water's total hardness. In pools and spas, it is the calcium hardness, not total hardness, that is important to achieve a balanced saturation index so that calcium carbonate is neither dissolved from plaster/gunite/grout nor deposited as scale. Low calcium hardness is a contributor to foaming in spas.

In pool water, it is easier to lower the pH or total alkalinity than the calcium hardness. In spas, calcium is easier to lower by replacing water. In areas where the source water has a high calcium hardness, pH and total alkalinity are the water properties that need to be adjusted to maintain a balanced saturation index.

The calcium hardness of pool/spa water is measured as calcium carbonate ($CaCO_3$), which, when not in solution, is called scale.

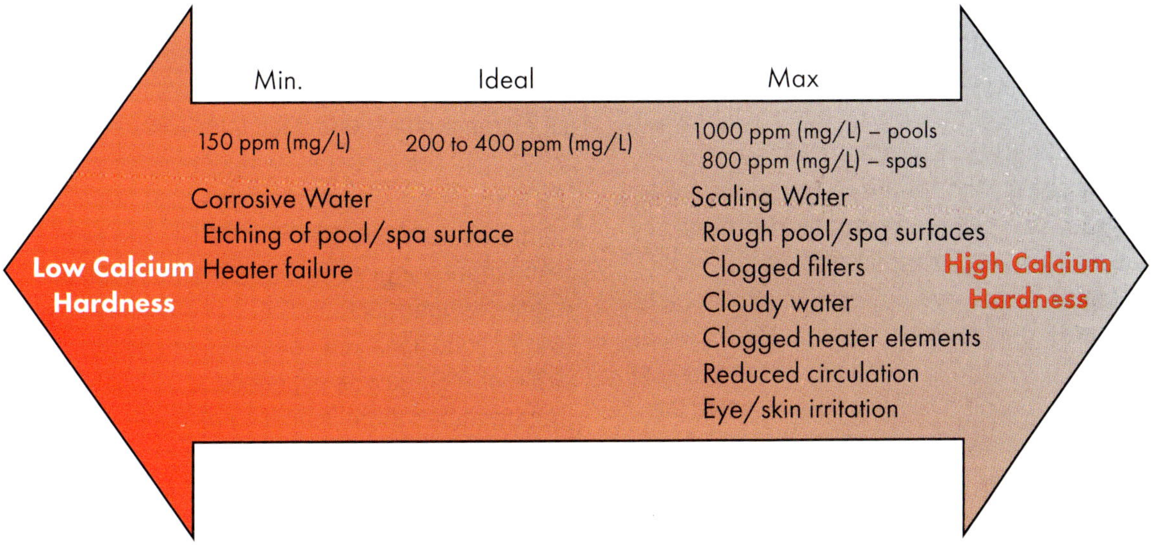

	Min.	Ideal	Max
	150 ppm (mg/L)	200 to 400 ppm (mg/L)	1000 ppm (mg/L) – pools / 800 ppm (mg/L) – spas

Low Calcium Hardness

Corrosive Water
Etching of pool/spa surface
Heater failure

Scaling Water
Rough pool/spa surfaces
Clogged filters
Cloudy water
Clogged heater elements
Reduced circulation
Eye/skin irritation

High Calcium Hardness

Calcium Hardness Related Pool Problems

Illustration 6-5.

© National Swimming Pool Foundation 2017

Calcium carbonate is a salt found in nature as chalk, calcite, aragonite, or limestone. Calcium carbonate is not very soluble and easily drops out of solution unless water balance is maintained. At low pH and alkalinity, a low calcium hardness level disrupts the equilibrium of calcium carbonate, and the water becomes more corrosive.

Another concern is the behavior of calcium in water. Unlike most chemicals, calcium becomes less soluble as the temperature rises. This further complicates the management of hot water systems.

The ideal level for calcium hardness (as measured by $CaCO_3$) is 200 to 400 ppm (mg/L). When the calcium hardness approaches 1,000 ppm (mg/L), it is essentially impossible to maintain water balance, pH, and total alkalinity in the proper ranges. As calcium hardness exceeds 500 ppm (mg/L), extreme care must be taken to maintain lower total alkalinity and pH levels to avoid scale, especially in hot water environments.

Low Calcium Hardness

Pool/spa water will become increasingly more aggressive or corrosive to plaster or concrete surfaces with low calcium hardness when combined with low pH or total alkalinity. When water has low calcium content, it has more capacity to dissolve calcium carbonate. Many pool finishes are made of cement or plaster products. Calcium carbonate is a main constituent of these surfaces. Corrosive water may cause etching of these surfaces in a very short period of time. In pools or spas that have surfaces made from polymeric resins/fiberglass or plastic/vinyl, low calcium hardness is less important since low calcium does not affect the corrosion of these surfaces.

Calcium chloride ($CaCl_2$) is used to increase calcium hardness. There are two forms of calcium chloride: hydrated calcium chloride (77% strength), and anhydrous calcium chloride (100% strength). Both forms generate a significant amount of heat when added to water. It is generally a good practice to pre-dissolve the calcium chloride into a bucket of water, mix, and then slowly add to the pool or spa in the deepest area.

The 77% strength hydrated calcium chloride is added at the rate of 1.2 pounds per 10,000 gallons (575 g per 40,000 liters) to achieve an increase of 10 ppm (mg/L). 100% strength anhydrous calcium chloride is added at the rate of 0.9 pounds per 10,000 gallons to achieve an increase of 10 ppm (mg/L) (402 g per 40,000 liters). It is important to follow label directions and remember to never add water to chemicals, especially with calcium chloride, because the water may boil, projecting steam and chemical.

High Calcium Hardness

As shown in Illustration 6-5, high levels of calcium hardness can result in several problems: rough pool/spa surfaces that can harbor bacteria or scratch skin, clogged filters, cloudy water, clogged heater elements, and reduced circulation.

Lowering calcium hardness is very difficult, except in spas due to the smaller volume of water. It generally involves partially draining and replacing the existing water with source water containing lower levels of hardness. Fill water can be passed through a water softener to reduce calcium hardness.

To maintain a balanced saturation index, the pH and total alkalinity can be lowered to compensate for higher calcium hardness levels. The lower alkalinity level will allow the pH to change more, and corrosive or scale conditions may quickly develop.

A sequestering agent may be used to keep calcium in solution. This method helps to prevent scale by interfering with the development of calcium carbonate crystal formation.

Temperature

Temperature is the one water balance factor that is not chemical—it is a physical factor. Only at extreme conditions does temperature play a big role. For example, temperature should be considered in spas that have high water temperature (up to 104°F or 40°C). The heat-exchanger surfaces within heaters can have even higher temperatures (>104°F or 40°C). During winter conditions, low temperatures (as low as 32°F or 0°C) can be experienced. At higher temperatures there is an increasing tendency for scaling conditions. At lower temperatures there is an increasing tendency for corrosive conditions.

Total Dissolved Solids

Total Dissolved Solids (TDS) is the total weight of all soluble matter in the water. The TDS

© National Swimming Pool Foundation 2017

concentration can be approximately derived by measuring the electrical conductivity of the water. Dissolved charged ions add to the water's conductivity. Contaminants that are neutral are not measured using the conductivity method. The lower the water's conductance, the more pure the water.

All dissolved matter added to pool/spa water contributes to TDS, including salt, user waste, algicides, metal and stain control chemicals, clarifiers, defoamers, enzymes, wind-borne debris, and water balance chemicals.

Disinfection chemicals added to pool/spa water contribute to the increase in TDS, mostly as salt. As an example, when sodium hypochlorite is added to water, inert ingredients, including a substantial amount of salt (NaCl) and some amount of sodium hydroxide, which is caustic, are present as a result of the bleach manufacturing process. These inert ingredients are introduced into the water with the bleach. In addition, the bleach (NaOCl) disinfectant is introduced into the water and the pH rises as a result of the following reaction:

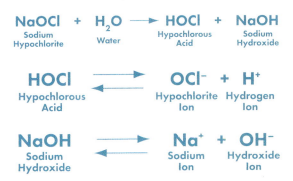

$$NaOCl + H_2O \rightarrow HOCl + NaOH$$
Sodium Hypochlorite + Water → Hypochlorous Acid + Sodium Hydroxide

$$HOCl \rightleftharpoons OCl^- + H^+$$
Hypochlorous Acid ⇌ Hypochlorite Ion + Hydrogen Ion

$$NaOH \rightleftharpoons Na^+ + OH^-$$
Sodium Hydroxide ⇌ Sodium Ion + Hydroxide Ion

After the hypochlorite reacts with contaminants in the water, it leaves a chloride ion (Cl^-) and sodium ion (Na^+) as shown in the reaction below:

$$Na^+ + OCl^- + Contaminants \rightarrow Na^+\ Cl^- + Oxidized\ Contaminants$$

The ions from the bleach and the inert ingredients do not evaporate and are only removed when water is removed from the pool, through back washing, splash out, carry out, etc. The ions build up as TDS as more disinfectant is added over time. Similarly, other disinfectants introduce salts and inert ingredients.

Chemical additions are not the only factor in increasing TDS. Evaporation removes pure water, leaving the dissolved solids behind. Replacement source water may contain as much as 400 ppm (mg/L) or more TDS. Over time, TDS climbs higher as a result of the replacement of evaporative losses.

TDS is in some manner a measurement of the age of the water. As TDS increases, the amount of partially oxidized and unoxidized organic contaminants also increases. Included in this would be nitrogenous contaminants from user waste. Much of this material is uncharged or neutral and therefore does not contribute to TDS as measured by conductivity. This added material may increase the consumption of disinfectant by fueling the growth rates of algae and bacteria. There are expensive and time-consuming methods of testing for these items, but TDS is generally accepted as a good indicator of tired water. When TDS is high, the organic contamination may also be high.

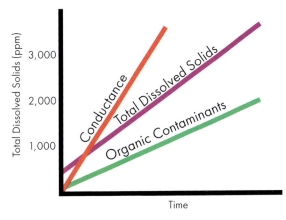

Relationship Between TDS and Organic Contaminants/Conductance

Illustration 6-6.

Galvanic Corrosion

As TDS increases, there is a greater probability of galvanic corrosion when there are dissimilar metals within the system. For example, if a pool has a copper heat exchanger and other metals in the plumbing, light fixtures, or metal pump impellers, then galvanic corrosion can occur. Galvanic corrosion would be observed by the discoloration of metal parts in the water.

It is commonly recommended that the TDS should not exceed 1,500 ppm (mg/L) higher than the TDS when the pool or spa was started up. There is no minimum or maximum. The start-up level includes the TDS of the source water as well as any inorganic salt used by chlorine generation systems.

1. Pool & Spa Management
2. Regulations & Guidelines
3. Essential Calculations
4. Pool Water Contamination
5. Disinfection
6. Water Balance
7. Pool & Spa Water Problems
8. Chemical Testing
9. Chemical Feed & Control
10. Water Circulation
11. Pool & Spa Filtration
12. Heating & Air Circulation
13. Spa & Therapy Operations
14. Facility Safety
15. Keeping Records
16. Maintenance Systems
17. Troubleshooting
18. Facility Renovation & Design
References

Photo 6-2. *An example of galvanic corrosion. Copper staining on a stainless steel surface as a result of high TDS and improper bonding and grounding.*

TDS Summary

Excessively high levels of TDS will cause the water to look dull or tired and may exhibit a bad or salty taste. Hot water facilities such as spas develop high TDS as a result of evaporation, excessive user load, and chemical use. A program of planned water replacement is a good management tool to use to maintain proper TDS levels in pools and spas. Some facilities develop a daily water replacement based on average user load. See the Spa & Therapy Operations chapter for more discussion concerning the water replacement interval.

Saturation Index

Wilfred F. Langelier, a professor of Civil Engineering at the University of California–Berkeley, developed a method of coating water distribution piping with a thin layer of scale. His published paper "The Analytical Control of Anti-Corrosive Water Treatment" quantified the corrosive potential of water. The index developed in this paper is called the Langelier Index.

The Langelier Index has been adopted by many industries and has spread to industrial water treatment as well as domestic drinking water treatment. The swimming pool industry developed a modified version of the Langelier Index in the 1970s. This index was adjusted for pool/spa water conditions and provides a method for determining whether the water is balanced with regard to calcium carbonate equilibrium.

The Saturation Index (SI) is a method of determining whether water will deposit calcium carbonate or maintain it in solution. The SI incorporates the five balance factors discussed in this chapter: pH, total alkalinity, calcium hardness, temperature, and total dissolved solids. Sequestering agents used to prevent scale, staining, or discoloration in water can improve the solubility characteristics of calcium carbonate, reducing the formation of scale. As a result, the balance point (0) of the SI can shift to a more positive number.

When higher cyanuric acid levels are present in water, the contribution of cyanuric acid should be removed from the total alkalinity since the saturation index uses the alkalinity due to carbonate, or total carbonate alkalinity, to determine the water balance. The cyanuric acid concentration should be divided by 3 to give the contribution to total alkalinity. For example, if the total alkalinity reading was 90 ppm (mg/L) and the cyanuric acid level is 60 ppm (mg/L), the total carbonate alkalinity would be 70 ppm (mg/L), since 20 ppm (mg/L) of the total alkalinity reading was due to the cyanuric acid interference (60 ppm (mg/L) ÷ 3 = 20 ppm (mg/L)).

Temperature, calcium hardness, total alkalinity, and total dissolved solids are expressed in the SI as factors Tf, Cf, Af, and TDSf respectively, as shown in Illustration 6-7. The pH of the water is substituted directly into the index.

For pool and spa waters, the ideal result of performing this index is to have a result of zero, i.e., SI = 0. Balanced water is between − 0.3 and + 0.3. Corrosive water is − 0.4 and lower. Scaling water is + 0.4 and higher.

Calculating the Saturation Index

To determine whether pool or spa water is properly balanced, a full water chemistry analysis is necessary. When calculating the SI, use the factors in Illustration 6-7. If an actual measurement is not found in the chart, use the next greatest value. The measured pH value is used directly in the formula. The Saturation Index formula is as follows:

$$SI = pH + Tf + Cf + Af - TDSf$$

SI	pH	Tf	Cf	Af	TDSf
Saturation Index	pH as tested	Temperature factor	Calcium factor	Alkalinity factor	TDS factor

If the water is not balanced, adjustments must be made to bring the water back into balance. The sequence of adding chemicals to make the adjustment should be total alkalinity first, followed by pH, and calcium hardness third. Temperature is not normally adjusted for water balance as most of the time it is not a controllable factor.

Example 6.1

Your pool water test readings are as follows:

pH	7.2
Temperature	84°F (28.9°C)
Calcium Hardness	200 ppm or mg/L
Total Alkalinity	100 ppm or mg/L
TDS	2,250 ppm or mg/L

Using the Saturation Index formula, the following results are obtained:

SI = pH + Tf + Cf + Af - TDSf
SI = 7.2 + 0.7 + 1.9 + 2.0 - 12.2
SI = - 0.4

The water is slightly corrosive.

Example 6.2

Your spa water test readings are as follows:

pH	7.7
Temperature	104°F (40°C)
Calcium Hardness	400 ppm or mg/L
Total Alkalinity	100 ppm or mg/L
TDS	3,500 ppm or mg/L

Using the Saturation Index formula, the following results are obtained:

SI   pH + Tf + Cf + Af - TDSf
SI = 7.7 + 0.9 + 2.2 + 2.0 - 12.2
SI = + 0.6

The water is scale forming.

Saturation Index Factors

Temperature			Calcium Hardness expressed as CaCO₃		Total Carbonate Alkalinity	
°F	°C	Tf	ppm (mg/L)	Cf	ppm (mg/L)	Af
32	0.0	0.0	25	1.0	25	1.4
37	2.8	0.1	50	1.3	50	1.7
46	7.8	0.2	75	1.5	75	1.9
53	11.7	0.3	100	1.6	100	2.0
60	15.6	0.4	125	1.7	125	2.1
66	18.9	0.5	150	1.8	150	2.2
76	24.4	0.6	200	1.9	200	2.3
84	28.9	0.7	250	2.0	250	2.4
94	34.4	0.8	300	2.1	300	2.5
105	40.6	0.9	400	2.2	400	2.6
			800	2.5	800	2.9

Total Dissolved Solids Factors

Less than 1,000 ppm (mg/L)	1,000 ppm (mg/L) or greater
12.1	12.2

Illustration 6-7.

Example 6.3

You can also use the following SI Worksheet in order to calculate the SI value for your pool water. Using the factors chart in Illustration 6-7, insert the factors values for each measured variable. Note that in this example the water is not balanced with a Saturation Index value of -0.5, which means that the water is corrosive. The values given in red are possible adjustments that can be made to bring the water back into balance. These adjustments are not the only ones that can be made to bring the water back into balance.

$$SI = pH + Tf + Cf + Af - TDSf$$

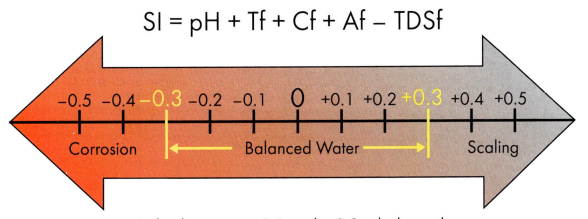

| -0.5 | -0.4 | -0.3 | -0.2 | -0.1 | 0 | +0.1 | +0.2 | +0.3 | +0.4 | +0.5 |

Corrosion ← Balanced Water → Scaling

Index between – 0.3 and + 0.3 is balanced
Index over + 0.3 is increasingly more scale forming
Index below – 0.3 is increasingly more corrosive

Illustration 6-8.

© National Swimming Pool Foundation 2017

Saturation Index Factors

Temperature			Calcium Hardness (expressed as CaCO₃)		Total Carbonate Alkalinity	
°F	°C	Tf	ppm (mg/L)	Cf	ppm (mg/L)	Af
32	0.0	0.0	25	1.0	25	1.4
37	2.8	0.1	50	1.3	50	1.7
46	7.8	0.2	75	1.5	75	1.9
53	11.7	0.3	100	1.6	100	2.0
60	15.6	0.4	125	1.7	125	2.1
66	18.9	0.5	150	1.8	150	2.2
76	24.4	0.6	200	1.9	200	2.3
84	28.9	0.7	250	2.0	250	2.4
94	34.4	0.8	300	2.1	300	2.5
105	40.6	0.9	400	2.2	400	2.6
			800	2.5	800	2.9

Total Dissolved Solids Factors

Less than 1,000 ppm (mg/L)	1,000 ppm (mg/L) or greater
12.1	12.2

	Value	Factor	New Value	Factor
pH	7.4	+7.4	7.4	+7.4
Temperature	84°F (28.9°C)	+0.7	84°F (28.9°C)	+0.7
Calcium Hardness	100	+1.6	200	+1.9
Carbonate Alkalinity	75	+1.9	80	+2.0
Sub-Total		11.6		12.0
Total Dissolved Solids	500	-12.1	500	-12.1
Saturation Index		-0.5		-0.1

Illustration 6-9. *Saturation Index worksheet.*

Ryznar Stability Index

The Ryznar Stability Index (RSI) is another saturation index that is used by some industry professionals to judge how to maintain calcium carbonate water balance and reduce metal corrosion. Like Langelier's Index, RSI estimates the degree to which calcium carbonate deposits, or scales, on surfaces or dissolves/corrodes calcium carbonate from a surface. Yet, the most common focus for use of the RSI is to minimize metal corrosion through calcium carbonate's providing a protective coating on the metal surface.

© National Swimming Pool Foundation 2017

Chapter 7:
Pool & Spa Water Problems

"Each problem that I solved became a rule which served afterwards to solve other problems."
–René Descartes

Swimming pool and spa water is part of an open system—open to the environment, air, wind, pollution, sunshine, and society's by-products, such as lawn fertilizers and weed killers. Part of the open system includes the users—more on some days, less on others. No matter how diligent the pool operator may be concerning water quality control, there will be that day when the facility's water does not meet the expected standards. This chapter will address many of these water quality issues.

Chemical Dosing

The maintenance of pool water chemistry requires that the proper chemical(s) and amounts be added to the pool or spa water, sometimes on a daily basis. This process does not have to be overly complicated and is easily turned into a routine operating procedure.

The first step in any chemical change is to determine if a change is necessary. This is accomplished by chemically testing the pool or spa water and evaluating the results against a standard. Then the operator calculates the necessary amount of chemical needed to complete the change.

The standard used for evaluation is usually state and/or local public health codes. The most common chemical range standards are shown in Appendix B-1.

When making chemical changes directly to the facility water, always follow jurisdictional regulations. Codes may require that the facility be closed for one turnover after manually adding chemicals. Adding chemicals manually is done when the pool is closed to ensure that the chemical levels have returned to allowable levels before re-opening the facility. Always follow the label instructions when adding chemicals.

Chemical Adjustments

There are three kinds of chemical adjustments that can be performed:
- Product label chemical dosage
- Product label chemical adjustment
- No product label chemical adjustment

Product Label Chemical Dosage

Some labels do not give a ppm (mg/L) adjustment amount. In this instance the label will have directions on how much to add for a given quantity of water. This could be for an initial application when a pool is opened, or to treat the pool for a water problem. Examples 7-1a and 7-1b show a product label dosing calculation.

Product Label Chemical Adjustment

It is important to always follow product label directions. Examples 7-2a and 7-2b show an adjustment calculation being made based on the product label directions. In this example the product label states that it takes 20 ounces (630 grams) of calcium hypochlorite to raise the chlorine level by 10 ppm (mg/L) in 10,000 gallons (40,000 liters) of water.

Photo 7-1. *Chemical adjustments*

© National Swimming Pool Foundation 2017

71

Product Label Chemical Dosage

You have a 96,000 gallon hotel pool. You are having recurring problems with algae blooms and decide to use an algicide. The label reads: For an initial application or when pool water is changed, use 32 fluid ounces per 25,000 gallons of water. How much do you add?

Amount of Chemical (from appendix B-2 or product label)	Actual Pool Volume	Desired Chemical Change	Total
	96,000 gallons		
	÷ 25,000 Gal. (From product label)		
32 fl.oz. (From product label)	X 3.84		= 122.9 fl.oz.

Conversion: 122.9 fl.oz. ÷ 128 fl.oz./gallon = 0.96 gallons, rounded to 1 gallon

Example 7-1a. *Product label chemical dosage*

Product Label Chemical Dosage — Metric

You have a 375,000 liter hotel pool. You are having recurring problems with algae blooms and decide to use an algicide. The label reads: For an initial application or when pool water is changed, use 1 liter per 95,000 liters of water. How much do you add?

Amount of Chemical (from appendix B-2 or product label)	Actual Pool Volume	Desired Chemical Change	Total
	375,000 liters		
	÷ 95,000 liters (From product label)		
1 liter (From product label)	X 3.95		= 3.95 liters (rounded to 4 liters)

Example 7-1b. *Product label chemical dosage — metric*

No Product Label Chemical Adjustment

Chemicals are sometimes purchased in bulk in which case there may not be a label with dosing directions. When there is not a product label, Appendix B-2 chart can be used. For some chemicals, such as calcium chloride, the concentration must be known. Examples 7-3a and b show a chemical adjustment calculation using the chemical adjustment guide in Appendix B-2.

When making chemical adjustments, follow these four steps, using the chemical adjustment worksheet:

- Determine the amount of chemical needed from the product label or the chart in Appendix B-2
- Divide the pool volume by 10,000 or the volume on the product label
- Subtract the current pool chemical reading from the level you wish to achieve; then divide that amount by the desired change on the product label or Appendix B-2
- Multiply the amounts calculated from the first three steps

NSPF and others offer smart phone apps to perform chemical dosing calculations.

© National Swimming Pool Foundation 2017

Product Label Chemical Adjustment

You have a 52,000 gallon condominium pool. There was a pool party on Friday night and the usual weekend bather load. On Sunday morning you observe the pool water to be cloudy and test a free chlorine level below 1 ppm. You decide to treat the pool with 8 ppm of additional chlorine using calcium hypochlorite. The label states that 20 ounces will raise the chlorine level by 10 ppm in 10,000 gallons. You will utilize the chemical adjustment worksheet below to determine how much cal-hypo to add.

Amount of Chemical (from appendix B-2 or product label)	Actual Pool Volume	Desired Chemical Change	Total
	52,000	8	
	÷ 10,000 Gal. (From appendix B-2 or product label)	÷ 10 ppm (From appendix B-2 or product label)	
20 oz.	X 5.2	X 0.8	= 83.2 oz

83.2 ounces ÷ 16 ounces/pound = 5.2 pounds; rounded off to 5 pounds

Example 7-2a. *Product label chemical adjustment*

Product Label Chemical Adjustment — Metric

You have a 200,000 liter condominium pool. There was a pool party on Friday night and the usual weekend bather load. On Monday morning you observe the pool water to be cloudy and test a free chlorine level below 1 mg/L. You decide to treat the pool with 8 mg/L of additional chlorine using calcium hypochlorite. The label states that 630 grams will raise the chlorine level by 10 mg/L in 40,000 liters. You will utilize the chemical adjustment worksheet below to determine how much cal-hypo to add.

Amount of Chemical (from appendix B-2 or product label)	Actual Pool Volume	Desired Chemical Change	Total
	200,000 liters	8	
	÷ 40,000 liters (From appendix B-2 or product label)	÷ 10 mg/L (From appendix B-2 or product label)	
630 grams	X 5	X 0.8	= 2,520 grams

2,520 grams ÷ 1,000 = 2.5 kilos

Example 7-2b. *Product label chemical adjustment — metric*

No Product Label Chemical Adjustment

Given: Free Available Chlorine = 1.0 ppm (mg/L)

Unknown: How much sodium hypochlorite to add to raise the chlorine level to 3.0 ppm (mg/L)

> Your chemical choice in this example is sodium hypochlorite from Appendix B-2

Dosages to Treat	10,000 Gallons			40,000 Liters		
Chemical	Desired Change			Desired Change		
Increase Chlorine	1 ppm	5 ppm	10 ppm	1 mg/L	5 mg/L	10 mg/L
Chlorine Gas	1.3 oz	6.7 oz	13 oz	40 g	200 g	390 g
Calcium Hypochlorite (67%)	2 oz	10 oz	1.3 lb	63 g	315 g	630 g
Sodium Hypochlorite (12%)	10.7 fl.oz.	1.7 qts	3.3 qts	330 mL	1.36 L	3.3 L
Lithium Hypochlorite	3.8 oz	1.2 lbs	2.4 lbs	110 g	570 g	1.1 kg

> Your actual pool volume. For example, 40,000 gallons.

> Your desired chemical change. For example, your chlorine level is 1.0 ppm (mg/L) and you want to raise it to 3.0 ppm (mg/L).
> **3.0 – 1.0 = 2.0 ppm (mg/L)**

Amount of Chemical (from appendix B-2 or product label)	Actual Pool Volume	Desired Chemical Change	Total
	40,000	**2.0**	
	÷ 10,000 Gal. (From appendix B-2 or product label)	÷ **1.0** ppm (mg/L) (From appendix B-2 or product label)	
10.7 fl. oz.	X 4	X 2	= **85.6 fl. oz.**

> Calculate the amount of chemical needed by first going down the columns and dividing the numbers.
> **40,000 ÷ 10,000 = 4   2.0 ÷ 1.0 = 2.**
>
> Finally, go across the bottom row and multiply all the numbers.
> **10.7 x 4 x 2 = 85.6 fl. oz.   — or —   85.6 ÷ 128 = 0.67 gallons**

Example 7-3a. *No product label chemical adjustment*

© National Swimming Pool Foundation 2017

No Product Label Chemical Adjustment — Metric

Given: Free Available Chlorine = 1.0 mg/L (ppm)

Unknown: How much sodium hypochlorite to add to raise the chlorine level to 3.0 mg/L (ppm)

Your chemical choice in this example is sodium hypochlorite from Appendix B-2

Dosages to Treat	10,000 Gallons			40,000 Liters		
Chemical	Desired Change			Desired Change		
Increase Chlorine	1 ppm	5 ppm	10 ppm	1 mg/L	5 mg/L	10 mg/L
Chlorine Gas	1.3 oz	6.7 oz	13 oz	40 g	200 g	390 g
Calcium Hypochlorite (67%)	2 oz	10 oz	1.3 lb	63 g	315 g	630 g
Sodium Hypochlorite (12%)	10.7 fl.oz.	1.7 qts	3.3 qts	330 mL	1.36 L	3.3 L
Lithium Hypochlorite	3.8 oz	1.2 lbs	2.4 lbs	110 g	570 g	1.1 kg

Your actual pool volume. For example, 160,000 liters.

Your desired chemical change. For example, your chlorine level is 1.0 mg/L (ppm) and you want to raise it to 3.0 mg/L (ppm).
3.0 – 1.0 = 2.0 mg/L (ppm)

Amount of Chemical (from appendix B-2 or product label)	Actual Pool Volume	Desired Chemical Change	Total
	160,000	**2.0**	
	÷ 40,000 Liters (From appendix B-2 or product label)	÷ **1.0** mg/L (ppm) (From appendix B-2 or product label)	
330 mL	X **4**	X **2**	= **2,640 mL**

Calculate the amount of chemical needed by first going down the columns and dividing the numbers.
160,000 ÷ 40,000 = 4   2.0 ÷ 1.0 = 2.

Finally, go across the bottom row and multiply all the numbers.
330 x 4 x 2 = 2,640 mL — or — 2,640 ÷ 1,000 = 2.64 Liters

Example 7-3b. *No product label chemical adjustment — metric*

1. Pool & Spa Management
2. Regulations & Guidelines
3. Essential Calculations
4. Pool Water Contamination
5. Disinfection
6. Water Balance
7. Pool & Spa Water Problems
8. Chemical Testing
9. Chemical Feed & Control
10. Water Circulation
11. Pool & Spa Filtration
12. Heating & Air Circulation
13. Spa & Therapy Operations
14. Facility Safety
15. Keeping Records
16. Maintenance Systems
17. Troubleshooting
18. Facility Renovation & Design

References

Combined Chlorine: Water and Air Quality

The Disinfection chapter summarized disinfectants and supplemental disinfectants. Since chlorine is both a disinfectant and an oxidizer, it is commonly used to solve other problems beyond disinfection.

Contaminants from users and the environment build up in recreational water. This is why requiring warm, soapy showers before people enter the water is a good idea. When free chlorine reacts with nitrogen-containing contaminants, chloramines, or combined chlorine, form. Depending on the contaminants, either inorganic chlorinamines/ammonia or organic chloramines form. The combined amount of both of these contaminants can be determined using a DPD test kit.

It is best to prevent and minimize the amount of CC in the pool or spa water since they are irritants in the water and air and slow disinfection. Regulations often limit CC to a maximum of 0.2 ppm (mg/L) in pools and 0.5 ppm (mg/L) in spas. The DPD test does not measure combined chlorine directly, as discussed in the Chemical Testing chapter. DPD measures free chlorine (FC) in step 1 and total chlorine (TC) in step 2. Total chlorine is the sum of free chlorine and combined chlorine. In other words, combined chlorine is the difference between total chlorine and free chlorine.

$$CC = TC - FC$$

When free chlorine reacts with ammonia (NH_3), an inorganic chloramine, monochloramine (NH_2Cl) is the predominant form of combined chlorine between pH 7.2 and 7.8, and the chlorine to ammonia ratio is 5:1 or less. As the amount of chlorine increases, the chlorine to ammonia ratio increases and dichloramine ($NHCl_2$) and then nitrogen trichloride (NCl_3) begin to form. Dichloramine and nitrogen trichloride are much more irritating than monochloramine to eyes and mucous membranes. Di- and trichloramine evaporate and create the chlorine-like smell in indoor facilities without proper ventilation. Therefore, breakpoint chlorination may increase the chlorine smell in indoor facilities. High doses of chlorinating agents may also increase the formation of other harmful disinfection byproducts.

Free chlorine will react with organic nitrogen-containing contaminants like urea, amino acids or proteins to produce organic chloramines (CC).

Chlorine will break down organic chloramines over days or weeks. Field test kits can not distinguish between inorganic and organic chloramines.

Removal of organic chloramines remains a big challenge with today's available technology and test methods. A detailed presentation on the chemistry on how organic chloramines, chloramides, and chlorimides are formed and destroyed is beyond the scope of this handbook.

Chloramine Prevention

Inorganic chloramines often form when free chlorine reacts with chemicals in urine and perspiration (urea) to produce organic chloramines; these chloramines degrade over the course of a week to produce inorganic chloramines. It is impossible to prevent all chloramine-producing contaminants, since perspiration and environmental contaminants will inevitably enter the water. But management practices that encourage regular bathroom breaks and pre-swim showers will reduce chloramine production and subsequently improve air and water quality.

There are several treatment methods to consider as options to reduce chloramines:
- Water replacement
- Breakpoint Chlorination (BPC)
- Ultraviolet (UV)
- Ozone
- Potassium monopersulfate (see Oxidation section later in this chapter)
- Indoor Air Handling

Research to clarify the effectiveness of these techniques continues. The latest advances are reported at the World Aquatic Health™ Conference and are available for viewing online by visiting the NSPF YouTube channel.

Water Replacement

Replacing contaminated water with fresh potable water is a reliable way to reduce inorganic and organic chloramines. In regions trying to conserve water, this method is less desirable, but still should be considered. If other methods have not reduced chloramines, then water replacement is a viable solution.

Operators must be aware that some potable water uses monochloramine (combined chlorine) as the drinking water disinfection method. Monochloramine is effective in drinking water because there is a long contact time in the distribution system; it does not act fast enough

© National Swimming Pool Foundation 2017

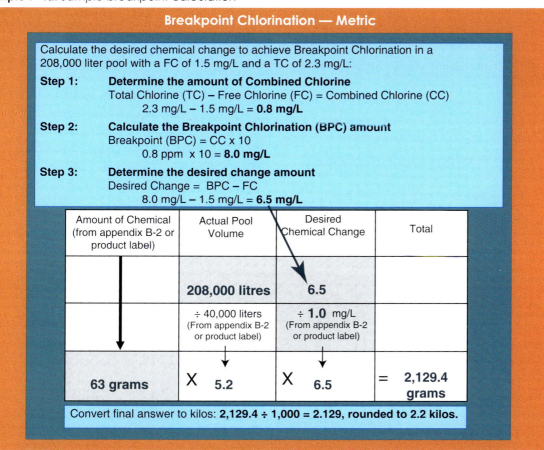

Breakpoint Chlorination

Calculate the desired chemical change to achieve Breakpoint Chlorination in a 55,000 gallon pool with a FC of 1.5 ppm and a TC of 2.3 ppm :

Step 1: **Determine the amount of Combined Chlorine**
Total Chlorine (TC) – Free Chlorine (FC) = Combined Chlorine (CC)
2.3 ppm – 1.5 ppm = **0.8 ppm**

Step 2: **Calculate the Breakpoint Chlorination (BPC) amount**
Breakpoint (BPC) = CC x 10
0.8 ppm x 10 = **8.0 ppm**

Step 3: **Determine the desired change amount**
Desired Change = BPC – FC
8.0 ppm – 1.5 ppm = **6.5 ppm**

Amount of Chemical (from appendix B-2 or product label)	Actual Pool Volume	Desired Chemical Change	Total
	55,000	**6.5**	
	÷ 10,000 Gal. (From appendix B-2 or product label)	÷ **1.0** ppm (From appendix B-2 or product label)	
2.0 oz.	X 5.5	X 6.5	= 71.5 oz

Convert final answer to pounds: **71.5 ÷ 16 = 4.468 lbs, rounded to 4.5 lbs.**

Example 7-4a. *Sample breakpoint calculation*

Breakpoint Chlorination — Metric

Calculate the desired chemical change to achieve Breakpoint Chlorination in a 208,000 liter pool with a FC of 1.5 mg/L and a TC of 2.3 mg/L:

Step 1: **Determine the amount of Combined Chlorine**
Total Chlorine (TC) – Free Chlorine (FC) = Combined Chlorine (CC)
2.3 mg/L – 1.5 mg/L = **0.8 mg/L**

Step 2: **Calculate the Breakpoint Chlorination (BPC) amount**
Breakpoint (BPC) = CC x 10
0.8 ppm x 10 = **8.0 mg/L**

Step 3: **Determine the desired change amount**
Desired Change = BPC – FC
8.0 mg/L – 1.5 mg/L = **6.5 mg/L**

Amount of Chemical (from appendix B-2 or product label)	Actual Pool Volume	Desired Chemical Change	Total
	208,000 litres	**6.5**	
	÷ 40,000 liters (From appendix B-2 or product label)	÷ **1.0** mg/L (From appendix B-2 or product label)	
63 grams	X 5.2	X 6.5	= 2,129.4 grams

Convert final answer to kilos: **2,129.4 ÷ 1,000 = 2.129, rounded to 2.2 kilos.**

Example 7-4b. *Sample breakpoint calculation — metric*

1. Pool & Spa Management
2. Regulations & Guidelines
3. Essential Calculations
4. Pool Water Contamination
5. Disinfection
6. Water Balance
7. Pool & Spa Water Problems
8. Chemical Testing
9. Chemical Feed & Control
10. Water Circulation
11. Pool & Spa Filtration
12. Heating & Air Circulation
13. Spa & Therapy Operations
14. Facility Safety
15. Keeping Records
16. Maintenance Systems
17. Troubleshooting
18. Facility Renovation & Design
References

to be effective in recreational water. When chloraminated potable water is added to the pool, this CC will show up when the water is tested. Check with your local water provider to see if the potable water is chlorinated (FC) or chloraminated (CC). If the local water supply is chloraminated, then it must be treated to remove the CC.

Breakpoint Chlorination (BPC)

Many product labels and guidelines recommend adding large quantities of free chlorine to reduce CC. The term breakpoint chlorination is used to describe the process of adding FC to treat, oxidize or remove combined chlorine. Breakpoint chlorination is an effective technique to reduce inorganic chloramines, but is not effective with organic chloramines. If an operator adds enough free chlorine to reach breakpoint chlorination and still finds measurable combined chlorine, the cause is likely due to organic chloramines present in the water. If combined chlorine is present due to organic chloramines, a technique other than breakpoint chlorination should be used to further reduce the level of chloramines.

Achieving Breakpoint Chlorination

When sufficient FC is added to pool water, the inorganic chloramines are converted to dichloramine, then to nitrogen trichloride, and then to nitrogen gas. Using calcium hypochlorite as an example:

> To achieve breakpoint, the free chlorine (FC) in the water must be raised to about ten times the amount of combined chlorine (CC).

Example 7-4: (See chart on previous page)

A 55,000 gallon pool has a FC = 1.5 ppm (mg/L), a TC = 2.3 ppm (mg/L); and a pH of 7.4. What would be the desired change to achieve breakpoint?

Since the pool already contains 1.5 ppm (mg/L) of free chlorine, the desired change is the BPC minus the current free chlorine level. Once the desired change is known, the chemical adjustment worksheet can then be used, as shown in Example 7-4.

Adding any amount of FC less than calculated may not achieve breakpoint. In addition, high chlorine levels will result in forming other disinfection by-products. Some test kits measure the monochloramine directly. If one of these tests are used, then the desired change is five times the monochloramine level.

UV Systems

Properly sized ultraviolet (UV) systems are effective at reducing inorganic chloramines. Research continues to explore if low pressure or medium pressure systems are superior at destroying inorganic chloramines, and to understand the complex chemistry between organic chloramines, UV, and chlorine.

Ozone

Properly sized ozone systems are effective at reducing chloramines in a swimming pool. Ozone breaks down both inorganic and organic chloramines. The Disinfection and Chemical Feed & Control chapters provide additional valuable information about ozone systems.

Indoor Air Handling

Inorganic chloramines like dichloramine and nitrogen trichloride are volatile and will evaporate. These chloramines are the cause of the chlorine-like smell in indoor pools. For bather comfort and safety, it is important that indoor aquatic facilities are designed and operated so that part of the air is replaced with fresh air to remove chloramines. Additional information about indoor air quality is addressed in the Heating & Air Circulation and the Facility Safety chapters.

Oxidation

The mechanical cleansing of pool or spa water is performed by the filtration system. Oxidation is the process of changing the chemical structure of contaminants so they are more readily removed from the water. In some cases, oxidation converts organic material into simple gases like nitrogen (N_2) and carbon dioxide (CO_2). In others, it adds oxygen or changes the structure of contaminant so that organic material is more readily removed by filtration. If the water looks dull or hazy, treating the water with an oxidizer often helps improve water clarity.

The process of removing contaminants from the water can be improved by a variety of oxidizer products. Some oxidizers are also disinfectants. For example, a product that releases a high dose of chlorine both oxidizes contaminants in the water and disinfects the water. Products that both oxidize and disinfect are commonly called shock or superchlorination products. The chlorine disinfectants described in the Disinfection chapter can be used to shock or superchlorinate the water. If an operator intends

© National Swimming Pool Foundation 2017

Photo 7-2. *It is important that indoor aquatic facilities are designed and operated so that part of the air is replaced with fresh air to remove chloramines so they do not redissolve into the water.*

to kill microorganisms or algae, the product must contain a disinfectant. It is important for operators to review the product labels to ensure that the product they are using contains written claims for its intended use.

Products that release an oxidizer, but not a disinfectant, are now called either shock oxidizers or oxidizing shock products according to U.S. EPA guidelines. These products often claim to reduce organic contaminants. If the operator plans a preventative treatment to only oxidize contaminants, then a disinfectant is not required. A shock oxidizer may be suitable.

Potassium Monopersulfate

Potassium monopersulfate ($KHSO_4 \cdot K_2SO_4 \cdot 2KHSO_5$) is dry, solid, granular, non-chlorine oxidizer. It is also known as monopersulfate. It is commonly used as an oxidizing shock. When used, weekly oxidizing shock doses are recommended. As an oxidizer, it reacts with contaminants and helps prevent CC from forming. The recommended dose is one pound (0.45 kg) of monopersulfate per 10,000 gallons (38,000 L) based on an active strength of 42.8%. Once the monopersulfate is dissolved, users may enter the water. Monopersulfate will reduce the water's pH. Some formulations of monopersulfate contain a less active ingredient and a more desirable neutral pH.

Monopersulfate performs oxidation of inorganic and organic contaminants. Unlike chlorine, monopersulfate oxidizes by adding oxygen to both inorganic and organic contaminants. As a result, chlorinated disinfection byproducts are not formed. The oxidation increases the contaminant's relative negative charge and promotes their removal by the filter.

Monopersulfate does not increase or decrease free chlorine levels. When performing a DPD test, monopersulfate interferes with the combined chlorine reading. A suitable test kit must be used to neutralize the interference (see the Chemical Testing chapter for more information). Monopersulfate is a NFPA Class 1 oxidizer, meaning it is an oxidizer that does not moderately increase the burning rate of combustible materials with which it comes into contact.

Colored Water

Pool and spa water should have a blue-white color, almost sparkling in appearance. Oxidized metals in the water can lead to colored, translucent water and can even stain the pool and spa wall surfaces if not treated properly. Green, red, brown, and black are some of the more common colors found in pool water when dissolved metals are present. The sources of the minerals can be
- Fill water
- Inadvertent additions of chemicals used on lawn and landscaping

1. Pool & Spa Management
2. Regulations & Guidelines
3. Essential Calculations
4. Pool Water Contamination
5. Disinfection
6. Water Balance
7. Pool & Spa Water Problems
8. Chemical Testing
9. Chemical Feed & Control
10. Water Circulation
11. Pool & Spa Filtration
12. Heating & Air Circulation
13. Spa & Therapy Operations
14. Facility Safety
15. Keeping Records
16. Maintenance Systems
17. Troubleshooting
18. Facility Renovation & Design
References

- Specialty treatment chemicals, such as algicides
- Poor water chemistry resulting in corrosion of metallic components of the pool system

Some source water contains iron and/or manganese that can give a distinctive brown or red color. Try to minimize the chance that products designed for another application, like landscaping, get into the pool. Corrosive water conditions, as discussed in the Water Balance chapter, could dissolve pool walls, hand rails, ladders, light fixtures, heater components, and pump impellers or casings.

Older pools and spas may be plumbed with iron or copper pipes, rather than with the PVC plumbing used on contemporary pools. Most heaters contain an alloy of copper in the heat exchange elements.

Stainless steel fixtures, such as ladders, handrails, and light fixtures contain iron. Again, corrosive water, usually caused by low pH, can dissolve these items. The result may be a reddish-brown water tint and perhaps a stain of the same color. When the water has a tint, it is important to determine the color before beginning a treatment program.

Green or Blue-Green Water

A turbid green pool is usually the result of an algae problem. The water should be treated with a disinfectant or an algicide. A translucent green pool most likely is caused by the presence of copper ions in the water.

Adding high levels of oxidizers like chlorine or increasing the total alkalinity can cause these metals to stain surfaces. The use of superchlorination is not often recommended due to cupric oxide formation. If the total alkalinity is increased, copper carbonate (blue-green) stains may form.

Fortunately, there are sequestering and chelating agents available that complex, or combine, with these metals and help remove them from water or prevent them from forming stains. The use of a HEDP (hydoxyethylenediphosphonic acid) or PBTC (phosphonobutanetricarboxylic acid) will complex the copper and iron and slowly break down in the presence of normal chlorine levels. As they break down, they deposit much of the metals on the filter.

The most common cause of copper in the

Photo 7-3. *Green pool water may be caused by the presence of algae or copper ions.*

water is poor water balance management (see the Water Balance chapter). Low pH makes water corrosive to copper metal, forming water-soluble copper ions. Unlike plaster or concrete, low total alkalinity and calcium hardness do not increase corrosion of copper. The source of these copper ions is the copper metal in the heater elements or the pump impeller. The copper in the water can complex with carbonate and hydroxide and form a blue-green stain on surfaces. Copper ions can also come from certain algicides.

To remove the green or blue-green tint from the pool or spa water, a sequestering or chelating agent can be added to the water to bind to the metallic ions and remove them from the surface. Label directions provide detailed guidance. The filter should be operated to assist in removal of the metal ions. After 24 hours, the water should be retested to see if the metals have been removed.

Red-Brown Water

A reddish-brown tint in the water is due to iron or manganese. Iron can exhibit brown, dark red, or a black-brown color in water. Manganese can show as a brownish-black color in water.

The source water may be the reason for the presence of the iron, or it may be due to the erosion and/or corrosion of circulation components, including the pump. Manganese may be present as a result of source water contamination or the use of certain water treatment chemicals.

To remove the red-brown tint from pool or spa water, a sequestering or chelating agent is added to the water to tie up the metallic ions and reduce the possibility that they will stain surfaces. The filter should be operated to assist in removal

© National Swimming Pool Foundation 2017

Photo 7-4. *Iron in the source water can give a reddish-brown color to the water in the pool.*

of the suspended materials. After 24 hours, the water should be retested for metals.

Chelation and Sequestration

Chelating or sequestering agents can either be liquid or granular. These products are designed to complex/combine chemically with metal ions in water. The chelating or sequestering agent forms a chemical bond to the metal. The resulting complex has different properties than the original metal. Some sequestering agents are designed to form complexes that remove or precipitate the metals from the water. Others form complexes to the metals dissolved in the water. Some of the more common sequestering or chelating agents used include HEDP (hydroxyethylene diphosphonic acid), PBTC (phosphonobutanetricarboxylic acid), oxalic acid, and less frequently EDTA (ethylenediaminetetracetic acid).

Pool water coloration, stains, and scale can be the result of copper, iron, manganese, or calcium in the source water or from contaminants in the water. Whenever pool water coloration, stains, or scale are present, it is important to use a chelating or sequestering agent and then balance the water.

Stains

The colored water conditions discussed in the previous section can quickly result in discoloration of the pool and spa wall surfaces if not promptly treated. The most common minerals that cause stains are iron, copper, and manganese. Sometimes light violet stains occur due to a complex of copper and cyanuric acid.

It is important that the source of the stain(s)

be identified and corrective steps taken to eliminate the introduction of future metal ions into the water. Failure to take these steps before undertaking a stain removal program may result in new stains forming. Stains often become more difficult to remove the longer they are present on a surface. There are many specialty products available to remove stains. Success often varies. An option that is sometimes used on pools that can be drained is to perform an acid wash after the pool is drained. Never lower water levels in regions where the hydrostatic ground water pressure can damage the pool structure.

Dark stains are often the result of plant matter like leaves, branches, acorns, etc. that fall to the bottom of the pool. The resulting stain is due to tannins. These stains can often be bleached by

Photo 7-5. *It is important that the source of stains be identified. Dark stains are often the result of plant matter that falls to the bottom of the pool.*

chlorine.

Scale

Scale is a crusty white deposit that can result in rough pool and spa wall surfaces, reduced circulation flow, and calcification of the filter media. Scale is usually dirty, giving it a grayish color. Scale on pool surfaces can cause abrasions on users. Excess calcium hardness and poor water balance result in scale formation. Usually high pH and alkalinity with high levels of calcium hardness will result in the formation of scale.

Calcium scale (calcium carbonate) is more likely to occur at locations where there is water evaporation or high temperatures. Heaters form scale because calcium carbonate is less soluble in water as the water temperature increases. The result is that a heater becomes less efficient as scale forms on the heat exchanger. If scale builds up in the plumbing, the water flow can be restricted, resulting in cloudy water. High calcium levels can be due to source water having a high calcium level; water from aquifers typically has higher calcium than surface water. The use of disinfectants like calcium hypochlorite also increases calcium and water pH, which contributes to the increased risk of scale.

To prevent scale, the alkalinity, calcium hardness, pH, and total dissolved solids (TDS) must be brought into proper balance. A portion of the pool water may need to be drained and replaced with fresh source water that is lower in hardness and TDS. Never lower water levels in regions where the hydrostatic ground water pressure can damage the pool structure. There are scale prevention products available that can be added to water to prevent formation of scale. Cleaners with a low pH/acidic are often used to remove scale from surfaces.

Cloudy Water

There are many reasons for cloudy water. The most common causes are improper filtration, insufficient water circulation or flow rate, and poor water chemistry. The early stages of algae growth also cloud the water. Cloudiness is the result of the presence of small particles that are too small to be filtered and are unable to be removed by oxidation. Environmental factors, such as wind, rain, and vegetation contribute to the existence of these particles. Users also contribute to the problem by depleting the available disinfectant and contaminating the water with dry skin flakes, bacteria, residues on the skin, and cosmetics.

The first step to correct a cloudy water situation is to check the filtration system. Clean the filter as

Photo 7-6. *Cloudy water*

necessary and re-establish the proper flow rate. There are products available that are specifically designed to clean different types of filter media.

Once the filtration system is operating properly, then proper water balance must be obtained. If the water remains cloudy when filtration, flow rate, and water chemistry are all adequate, then the likely cause for the condition is microscopic suspended particles. The next step for correcting the cloudy water condition is the use of a water clarifier.

Clarifiers

Most water clarifiers are a liquid, although products in the solid form are available. Directions often require the product to be either diluted or poured/broadcast over the surface of the water. Some products require that the pool be superchlorinated before the addition of the product; others require that chlorine be added after addition. Some solid chlorinating products contain clarifiers formulated within the product. Some clarifiers are introduced into a pool via a liquid or solid feeder.

Organic Water Clarifiers

The most common organic clarifiers are synthetic polyelectrolytes or polymeric coagulants (polyacrylonitrile or chitosan). The most frequently used clarifiers have a positive charge and are called cationic clarifiers.

The particles that cause cloudy water usually have negative electrical charges. Cationic clarifiers offer the most advantage for the widest range of situations. When combined with the small particles that have a negative charge, the positively charged clarifiers bond, or coagulate, these small particles into larger particles. The larger size helps the filter trap the material. As a result, there is less demand for the disinfectant by the contaminants and more disinfectant is available to keep the water sanitary. Water clarifiers are now available that help remove *Cryptosporidium* from water.

Inorganic Water Clarifiers (Flocculants)

The most common inorganic water clarifier is aluminum sulfate, known as alum, although new polymer-based products are also available (poly-aluminum chloride). When added to the water, alum forms a gelatinous mass that traps the microscopic suspended particles. Larger and larger particles are formed.

The circulation system should operate for a

© National Swimming Pool Foundation 2017

period of time, usually four hours, to allow proper mixing of the alum and the suspended particles. The circulation flow is then shut off for a period of 12 to 24 hours. The larger particles slowly drop to the bottom of the pool. This process is called flocculation. The flocculated particles collect on the floor of the pool and are then vacuumed to waste.

Foaming

Quaternary algicides, organic wastes, suntan lotions, body deodorants and cosmetics, and low calcium hardness can contribute to the formation of foam or suds at the surface of the water. In a spa, the aeration from the therapy jets can increase the foam. Foam is rare in pools.

If the use of a quaternary algicide is the cause, the best solution is dilution of the water. Defoamers may be used on spas and pools to reduce the visual effect of foam. Defoamers contain silicone emulsions that help break down the foam. Test kits are available that can be used to monitor the level of quaternary algicide in the water to ensure levels are not too high. Alternative algae prevention products that do not foam can also be used.

When contaminants are allowed to concentrate, foaming similar to dish soap or laundry detergent will occur. These contaminants are very undesirable. Oxidation treatments, water clarifiers, partial water replacement, or total water replacement and cleaning of a spa or wading pool may be justified.

Low calcium hardness also causes foam in pool and spa water. This foam generally occurs when the calcium hardness is 100 ppm (mg/L) or below. The calcium hardness may be increased by the addition of calcium chloride.

Photo 7-7. *The aeration from the therapy jets can increase the foaming in a spa.*

Algae

Algae are one-celled plants that are a major concern for pool/spa operators. There are several thousand species of algae that can populate a swimming pool or spa. Algae may even be present in the source water used for fill purposes. Millions of algae spores are carried by the wind every day into outdoor pools and spas. Some algae have the ability to reproduce rapidly if the conditions are favorable, turning a clear pool green in less than a day.

Algae are most commonly grouped by color into three groups: green, black, and yellow (sometimes called mustard). Green algae are by far the most common, and the most easily controlled. Black algae are usually found growing on pool walls in areas of poor circulation, such as the deep corners of the pool. Yellow algae, which are sometimes difficult to control, often require treatment with a specifically formulated algicide.

Environmental conditions, such as light and temperature, are important to support algae growth. All the nutrients algae need to grow are commonly present in swimming pool water: carbon, hydrogen, oxygen, nitrogen, and phosphorous. These nutrients come from the water itself that has hydrogen and oxygen, and from the total alkalinity (bicarbonate/carbon dioxide), which contains carbon and oxygen. Many contaminants contain nitrogen and phosphorous-like contaminants from skin fragments, dead bacteria or algae, cosmetics, some swimming pool treatment chemicals, chemical cleaners, soils, fertilizers, bird droppings, dead insects, etc. Algae can digest and store phosphorous in their bodies even if it is depleted from the water.

In most cases it is believed that algae is not harmful to users. Algae does pose a slip hazard if any is present on wet deck areas. It also clouds the water making it difficult to see a potential drowning victim. Also, algae on the pool floor can increase the risk that a person might slip into deeper water when there is a transition in the floor slope going into the deep end of the pool. The algae environment is complex, and the algae can harbor bacteria. Therefore, keeping water free of algae is more important than merely maintaining sparkling-clear water.

1. Pool & Spa Management
2. Regulations & Guidelines
3. Essential Calculations
4. Pool Water Contamination
5. Disinfection
6. Water Balance
7. Pool & Spa Water Problems
8. Chemical Testing
9. Chemical Feed & Control
10. Water Circulation
11. Pool & Spa Filtration
12. Heating & Air Circulation
13. Spa & Therapy Operations
14. Facility Safety
15. Keeping Records
16. Maintenance Systems
17. Troubleshooting
18. Facility Renovation & Design
References

Prevention of Algae

The pool operator has little or no control over the environmental factors that influence the growth of algae. Sunlight, outside temperature, and humidity are facts of nature. The nutrients can be controlled to some degree by insisting that users shower before entering the pool, especially for the removal of suntan lotions. Other nutrient factors, such as airborne debris are beyond the control of the operator. Operating factors, such as proper filtration, circulation flow, elimination of dead spots, and constant, sufficient levels of disinfection can be managed. Routine superchlorination and the use of an algicide on a maintenance basis are useful tools in the prevention of algae. Brushing the pool/spa walls on a routine basis is an important preventative measure. It is far easier to prevent algae than to remove algae.

Algicides

Disinfectants that chlorinate or brominate the water kill and prevent the growth of algae. Algae and bacteria prevention has driven more commercial facilities to install automatic chemical feeders, controllers, and probes to maintain adequate disinfectant levels at all times. Facilities without these mechanical systems are at a greater risk of algae growth, since pool water almost always contains the nutrients algae need and there are likely times when the disinfectant is absent.

Many types of algicides are sold under many different brands. Many countries require algicides to be registered with a government agency (e.g. U.S. EPA) to show active ingredients, and registration numbers. Product labels should be carefully reviewed since performance often depends on application directions. Different algicide types are described in the following sections.

Quaternary Algicides

One of the most common algicide types are quaternary ammonium algicides that are commonly called quats. The word quaternary means that there are four groups bound to a nitrogen atom (ammonium). The most common quats have chemical names like alkyldimethylbenzyl ammonium chloride (ADBAC) or dimethyldidecyl ammonium chloride (DDAC) quats.

Quats have been used for many years to kill algae. They are commonly added in small doses on a weekly schedule to maintain a quat residual, preventing algae growth in case the disinfectant ever drops to zero. The biggest disadvantage of quat algicides is that they may cause foaming if the water is agitated, but this is most prevalent where the product has been overdosed. Foaming limits their use in spas or decorative fountains. Quats do not contain metals, and there is no evidence that they contribute to surface staining.

Polymeric Algicides

Polymeric quaternary ammonium algicides are a special type of quaternary algicides that are commonly called polyquats. The chemical name of polyquats is complicated and is listed on product labels as poly{oxyethylene(dimethyliminio)-ethylene-(dimethyliminio)-ethylene-dichloride}. Polyquats have been used for many years. The chemical structure is a long molecule that does not cause foaming if the water is agitated. As a result, polyquats are often used to prevent and kill algae in recreational water that has high agitation like spas or splash pools. They do not contain metals, and there is no evidence that they contribute to surface staining.

The polymer contains a positive electrical charge that is attracted to the negative electrical charge of algae. It also attaches to dirt and debris found in pools, thus diluting its effectiveness.

Metallic Algicides

Copper is the most common metal used to kill algae. Copper metal is not soluble in water. However, copper salts like copper sulfate are soluble in water and are effective at killing most algae types. Copper algicides are sometimes sold as a solid salt or in a liquid formula. The algicide can also be dissolved in a liquid formula. Copper algicides have a deep blue to a blue-green color, so if a product is colorless or slightly yellow, it does not contain copper.

Copper algicides have excellent performance on almost all algae types. They are one of the more effective algicides against black algae, which is often difficult to kill. Despite the excellent performance, copper algicides have some disadvantages.

The biggest disadvantage is that the copper ions (Cu^{2+}) can stain pool surfaces. Higher pH can cause copper to form oxides that produce

© National Swimming Pool Foundation 2017

black stains, and hydroxides that produce pale blue stains, respectively. In addition, copper can form a bond with the high concentration of carbonate (total alkalinity; see the Water Balance chapter) and stain plaster surfaces to a blue-green color. When CyA is present at high levels, copper can form a bond of cyanurate and stain plaster surfaces to a purple color. High copper ion concentrations can give blond hair a greenish tint.

Other Algicide Types

Other algae control chemicals are available, such as ammonium sulfate, sodium bromide, and sodium tetraborate. When ammonium sulfate is used as an algicide, the chemical requires the water pH to be adjusted to about 8.0. After the algae have been killed, superchlorination is required to remove the ammonia from the water. The pH has to be checked and may need to be readjusted.

When sodium bromide is used, the bromide is oxidized by chlorine to hypobromous acid (HOBr), which is effective at killing algae. The presence of bromide cancels out cyanuric acid's ability to protect chlorine from being broken down by sunlight.

Some products recommend that a source of boron like sodium tetraborate be added to achieve 30 ppm (mg/L) of boron; this will inhibit algae growth in the water.

Phosphates and Nitrates

Phosphate levels in pool/spa waters increase over time when the source fill water contains some phosphate or when certain sequestering or chelating chemicals are used that contain phosphorous that becomes phosphate in water over time. Also, certain cleaners contain phosphates. Other sources of phosphate include fertilizers, skin, dead bacteria or algae, traces of feces carried by each user, and bird droppings. Bacteria and algae have the ability to digest phosphates and store them within their cell structure. Therefore, algae introduced into a pool from the environment can already contain phosphate or can digest and store phosphate when it is present in the water.

One common source of nitrogen, a nutrient needed by algae and bacteria, is nitrate. Nitrate sources are similar to those that contain phosphate. In addition, sweat and urine contain some nitrogen. There are several commercially available nitrate test kits on the market. Unfortunately, there is no practical method to reduce nitrates in pool/spa water other than by dilution.

Since all the nutrients that algae needs, including phosphate and nitrate, are commonly available in pool water or are stored within algae, it is very important that disinfectant residuals be maintained at all times to prevent the growth of algae.

Scum Line

It is common for deposits to form at, or slightly above, the water line to produce a scum line. Scum lines can be made of complex mixtures. The surface above the water line can get wet from waves, splashes, temporary increases in the water level as users enter, or as the water level is lowered. The thin film of water on the wall's surface can evaporate, leaving microscopic deposits of chemicals above the water line. These deposits could be from contaminants that have a low water solubility, including calcium scale, skin fragments, suntan or skin oils, debris in the water, cosmetics, detergents, and other materials. If the water is not properly balanced or is hard, scum lines may be largely due to scale.

Once the scum line starts to form, it may grow by attracting more contaminants from the water. Also, bacteria or algae may attach within the protection of the scum. There are many cleaners that help prevent a scum line from forming. It is important to select a product that has been designed for pool or spa use since some general cleaners have ingredients, such as phosphates, that are not compatible with pool water and may increase the scum line.

Photo 7-8. *Once the scum line starts to form, it may grow by attracting more contaminants from the water.*

1. Pool & Spa Management
2. Regulations & Guidelines
3. Essential Calculations
4. Pool Water Contamination
5. Disinfection
6. Water Balance
7. Pool & Spa Water Problems
8. Chemical Testing
9. Chemical Feed & Control
10. Water Circulation
11. Pool & Spa Filtration
12. Heating & Air Circulation
13. Spa & Therapy Operations
14. Facility Safety
15. Keeping Records
16. Maintenance Systems
17. Troubleshooting
18. Facility Renovation & Design
References

As with most water problems, it is best to prevent a scum line from forming. Regularly brushing the water line can help. The use of a scale inhibitor or better control of water balance properties may prevent the scum line from returning.

Biofilm

Many bacteria can protect themselves from disinfectants by forming and embedding themselves within a layer of slime called a biofilm. Bacteria in a biofilm differ from the bacteria that float freely in the water (planktonic bacteria). Biofilm bacteria may take a disinfectant level 100 times higher in concentration to achieve the same kill as required for bacteria suspended in water.

The Centers for Disease Control and Prevention estimates that 65% of human bacterial infections in aquatic environments involve biofilms. Biofilm can harbor disease-causing, or pathogenic, bacteria in filters or plumbing. Currently, industry and medical professionals and regulatory agencies are learning about biofilms and how to best control them.

Many explanations exist as to why biofilm is more resistant to treatments. For instance, the disinfectant may have difficulty penetrating the slime layer, or the bacteria on the bottom of the biofilm may be dormant. Bacteria in the biofilm secrete a plastic-like substance called extra-cellular polysacchrarides (EPS), which forms the protective slime layer around the cells and binds them together. Biofilms are a dynamic, organized, cooperative community of bacteria. They communicate through chemical signals that allow them to attach and detach in an organized pattern to help the biofilm survive.

Enzymes

Living cells in plants and animals make proteins from long strings of different amino acids. Cells bend and twist proteins into a specific three-dimensional arrangement. When in that arrangement, proteins are called enzymes because they cause chemical reactions (catalysts) required by the body for life to exist. For example, the food we eat is broken down in part by enzymes. Pool and spa enzyme products are made from living cells that are broken apart and claim to contain enzymes that react with and degrade contaminants in water.

Unfortunately, over time, enzymes lose their three-dimensional structure and no longer act as enzymes when they are outside of a living cell; thus they can no longer react with the contaminants in water. This inactivation occurs faster when the enzyme is exposed to chemicals like water, algicides, and oxidizers. Research sponsored by NSPF® demonstrates that some fat-destroying enzymes are present in commercial formulas. Once an enzyme is inactivated, it becomes a protein contaminant in the water itself. There has not been adequate study at this time to quantify the degree to which the nitrogen atoms in proteins or enzymes contribute to combined chlorine residuals.

© National Swimming Pool Foundation 2017

Chapter 8:
Chemical Testing

"The meeting of two personalities is like the contact of two chemical substances: if there is any reaction, both are transformed."

–Carl Jung

Swimming pool and spa environments are dynamic systems in which conditions constantly change. When disinfection and water balance chemicals are added, chemical reactions and by-products are the result. Evaporation and water loss due to patron use requires water replacement. User waste, environmental debris, and rainfall in outdoor pools affect the pool's chemistry. The system is never the same, and yet the certified operator or service professional must minimize the potential for hazards at all times. Pool and spa water testing is an essential tool in this task. The more accurate the water analysis is, the better prepared the operator is to address user hazards, automated controller performance, and pool maintenance.

The certified operator or service professional must determine what tests should be performed, the frequency of testing, and the method of testing. In many cases the local laws and codes establish minimum standards for testing. The aquatic facility will often have an automatic control system that constantly monitors water chemistry and makes adjustments as required. Even so, it may be necessary to perform manual water testing to ensure that the calibration of the automatic equipment is correct.

Testing validates water quality and guides changes that must be made to the water to protect users and the facility. For all tests described in this chapter, it is important to understand the label directions. Slight variations on how the test is performed can give inaccurate results. Guidance like "take the reading with the sun to your back" or "hold the reagent bottle vertically" have been developed to yield accurate readings. In addition, manufacturers provide guidance on maintaining equipment and reagents. Always follow health codes and laws concerning proper disposal of sample water containing testing reagents, the mixture used to perform the water analysis.

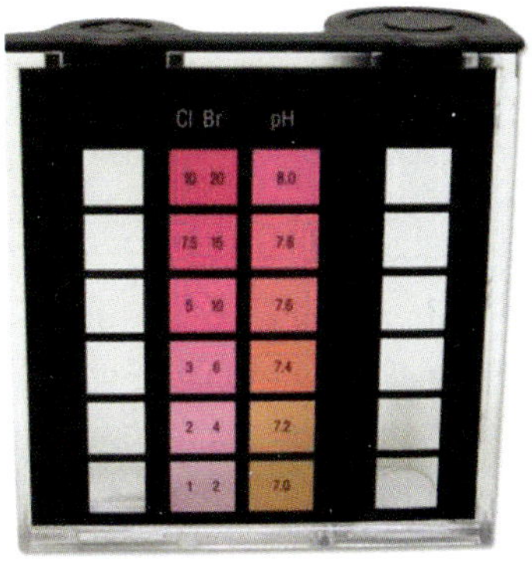

Test Methods

There are four basic methods used to test pool/spa water. They are
- Colorimetric—this also includes photometric testing (examples: disinfection and pH)
- Titrimetric (examples: disinfection, total alkalinity and calcium hardness)
- Turbidimetric (example: cyanuric acid)
- Electronic (examples: total dissolved solids and pH)

Colorimetric

Colorimetric testing relies on color matching. An indicator reagent is added to the water sample in a comparator test block and a chemical reaction takes place. A chemical product is produced that varies in color intensity depending on the concentration of the chemical being tested. The sample color is then compared to

Photo 8-1. *The most common form of testing uses a colorimetric test block comparator with printed standards.*

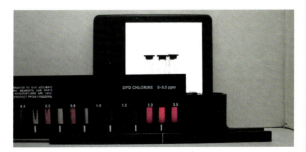

Photo 8-2. *The colorimetric slide comparator uses liquid color standards.*

© National Swimming Pool Foundation 2017

a set of standard liquid or printed references. The accuracy of the test results can vary by individual and may depend on lighting conditions. Some pool operators may be unable to properly differentiate between certain color variations, especially different shades of the color red.

Colorimeter (Photometer)

Color matching is still the basis, but a colorimeter, or photometer, uses instrumentation. The photometer uses a beam of fixed wavelength light that is passed through the sample and the emerging light is analyzed electronically. The light absorbed by the sample water, which is affected by its color, is calculated and displayed as a direct reading on the instrument. Since lighting conditions and human bias are no longer a factor, photometer testing is more accurate than comparator testing. Multiple parameter photometers are capable of accurate readings for all pool and spa water analyses. Many times the certified operator will rely on photometer readings in order to calibrate automated controllers.

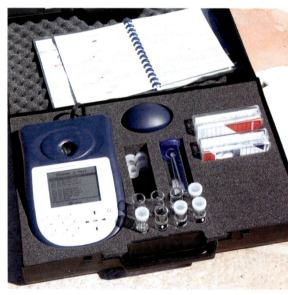

Photo 8-3. *The photometer uses a beam of fixed wavelength light that is passed through the sample and the emerging light is analyzed electronically.*

Dip-and-Read Test Strips

Chemically treated reagent pads are affixed to plastic strips. The strips are dipped into the pool water and removed. After the appropriate time (usually 15–30 seconds), a color develops, which is then compared to the standard printed on the packaging container. This method is not approved for commercial aquatic facilities in all regions, but it provides a quick way of

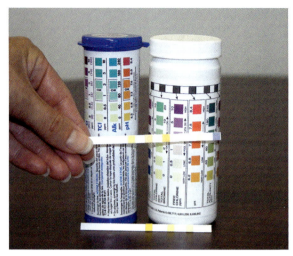

Photo 8-4. *Dip-and-read test strips have a comparison standard printed on the packaging.*

determining if the water quality parameters are within the minimum and maximum range and if more involved testing is necessary. Test strips are commonly used by consumers to verify water conditions.

Dip-and-read test strips are commercially available for chlorine, bromine, pH, total alkalinity, calcium hardness, cyanuric acid, polymeric biguanides, nitrites, nitrates, salt, total dissolved solids, potassium monopersulfate, iron, copper, and borate. The certified operator should check with their local health department to determine whether test strips are approved for commercial pools and spas since they may not provide the accuracy necessary for making chemical adjustments.

Titrimetric

Titration is a test method that determines the unknown concentration of a chemical by using a standard concentration of a known reagent. It is more or less a chemical balance test. The standard reagent solution is called the titrant. There must be a way of determining when the balance or end point is reached to know that the test is complete. The end point occurs when all of the unknown concentration of chemical has reacted with the standard titrant. A third chemical, usually an indicator, is used that changes color when the end point is reached. Individuals who have problems distinguishing color variations with a comparator test block will be able to see the color variations as the end point is reached. Titration is more accurate for pool/spa water testing than comparator test blocks.

© National Swimming Pool Foundation 2017

Turbidimetric

Turbidity is a measure of the amount of solid particles that are suspended in water and that cause light rays shining through the water to scatter and appear cloudy. In pool/spa water testing, a standard reagent is added to a known sample of water. The reagent reacts with the unknown concentration of the sample, causing the sample to turn cloudy in proportion to the concentration. The cloudiness, or turbidity, is then measured by use of a calibrated cell.

Photo 8-5. *Calibrated cell for turbidimetric testing*

At the base of the cell is a black dot; the cell is filled with the cloudy sample until the dot can no longer be seen. The test results are then known by reading the calibrated markings on the cell at the level of the sample water. Other tests use a dipper rod to lower the black dot into the sample until it is obscured. There are some testing procedures that may use a photometer to measure the results in nephelometric turbidity units (NTU) with greater accuracy.

Nephelometric Testing

Turbidity is based on the amount of light that is reflected off particles in the water. Turbidity can be tested electronically by the use of a nephelometer. The results are given as nephelometric turbidity units (NTU). Nephelometric testing is not performed as a normal routine at most pools; the accepted practice

Photo 8-6. *Handheld NTU electronic test meter*

is that the main drain must be clearly visible from the pool deck. Water must have a turbidity level that does not exceed 0.5 nephelometer turbidity units, as determined by the NSF standard.

Water Clarity (Secchi) Disk

Some health departments use a water clarity disk to determine the turbidity of the water. Clarity is considered acceptable when the disk can be seen in the deepest part of the pool. The operators should check with their local codes to determine the acceptable parameters of the disk. The size and color is usually specified by the codes. Some may require an all black disk, others may require an alternating black and red quadrant disk. Some codes require a two inch disk, while others may require a six inch disk.

Illustration 8-1. *Water clarity disk used to determine water turbidity*

Electronic Testing

Portable, handheld electronic test meters are available for pool-side use. There are a wide range of features available from simple to complex. All electronic meters require frequent calibration and probe cleaning, sometimes on a daily basis. Test devices are available for pH, total dissolved solids, oxidation-reduction potential, nitrates, and others.

Test Procedures

Pool water chemistry is a science, and accurate test results are necessary if the certified operator is going to maintain the facility in a clean, healthful condition. Errors in testing may lead to unsafe pool water conditions and damage the facility operating system components. Some errors may include the use of chemical reagents that are not full strength, inaccurate addition of reagents, inaccurate water sample volume, poor light conditions, and inaccurate color interpretation. It is important that the test kit instructions are followed to minimize errors.

Test Kit Care

Most test kit reagents may be affected by improper storage conditions. Test kits must be protected from heat, light and exposure to chemical fumes and air-borne debris. The

Photo 8-7. *Always store test kits according to the manufacturer's instructions.*

following guidelines should be considered when liquid reagents are used:

- Replace and tighten all caps after use; some reagents may be affected by oxygen or other external contamination
- Store the test kit out of direct sunlight, maintaining the storage temperatures between 36°F and 85°F (2°C and 29°C). Never store the test kit with chemicals.
- Allow frozen reagents to thaw at room temperature before using. Make sure the dropper tip is not cracked.
- Use reagents prior to the expiration date. Colored reagents usually have a shorter shelf life than colorless reagents. Care should be taken as to the size of reagent bottle used. The longer time a reagent is in use, the greater the chance for a problem to develop.
- Reagents in brown bottles are usually oxidizing and reducing agents. They normally have a shorter useful life and are particularly sensitive to poor storage conditions.
- Discard and replace reagents if there is any change in color or the appearance of suspended material in the reagent
- Never replace reagents using bottles from other test kits or other manufacturers. As an example, one manufacturer makes several different concentrations of phenol red for pH testing. Each reagent is formulated for a specific volume of water and view depth of the test sample container; reagents cannot be mixed and matched.
- Make sure that all test kit vials, caps, cells, and blocks are rinsed out completely with fresh tap or sample water after using. Colored solutions may stain the side walls of cells. Sample residue left in cells may interfere or contaminate the next test.

Tablet or powder reagents are also affected by the above mentioned precautions. Most tablet and powder reagents are hermetically sealed to eliminate or minimize degradation by temperature and exposure to airborne chemicals. The extended shelf life is typically four years for these sealed reagents. Contact the manufacturer for specific care and shelf life information.

Collecting the Sample

The pool or spa water sample should be taken from a location that is representative of the water as a whole. It may be appropriate for some facilities to take samples from more than one location.

The sample should be taken from a depth of at least 18 inches (45 cm) below the water surface and from a location well away from any return inlets. Never use glass or metallic objects as sample collectors, but the sample can be transferred into a glass testing tube away from the pool deck. Insert a clean plastic bottle, bottom-side up, to the required depth. Turn the bottle top-side up to release the air and collect the water. Remove the bottle making sure there is no air at the top and cap the bottle.

Take the sample to a location removed from the pool or spa area for testing. In this manner, facility users will not be a distraction by asking if the water is safe. By testing the water away from the facility, the operator will not be tempted to throw the test water back into the pool or spa.

Performing the Test

The following are steps to follow when performing the water test:

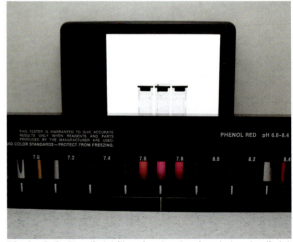

Photo 8-8. *Daylight illuminator to simulate daylight conditions for indoor facilities*

© National Swimming Pool Foundation 2017

- **Volume:** The sample of water must be the correct volume as indicated in the instructions if the test results are to be accurate. Water has surface tension that causes it to cling to surfaces. When placed in a test cell, this property causes the water to curve downward at the surface center, a characteristic called the meniscus. All cells should be filled with water to a level such that the bottom of the meniscus is even with the fill-to line on the cell wall. The fill-to line should be at eye level when filling the cell.
- **Light:** When using a color block comparator, always hold the comparator at eye level to the to the horizon opposite the sun to properly match the sample color to the standard. Do not hold the block towards the only available clear patch of sky or towards the sun. Never perform color comparator tests with fluorescent light as the source. If necessary, purchase a daylight illuminator to simulate daylight conditions for indoor facilities.
- **Drop Size:** When adding reagent drops to the sample, hold the dropper bottle straight up and down. This will insure the correct drop size and give accurate test results. Holding a dropper bottle on an angle while adding reagent may distort the drop size and thus give inaccurate results. Static electricity sometimes builds up around the tip of the dropper, making the drops difficult to push out or reduce in size. To correct this problem, wipe around the dropper tip with a clean damp cotton cloth or paper towel.
- **Mixing:** Proper end points can only be detected if the reagents and the sample water are properly mixed. When titrating, the sample must be swirled after each drop of titrant is added. The end point must be

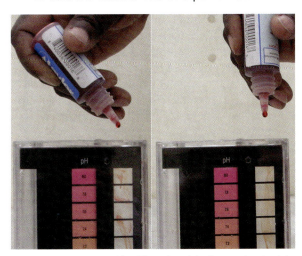

Photo 8-9. *Reagent bottles should always be held in a vertical position to ensure the correct drop size.*

Photo 8-10. *The comparator test block should be held up at eye level to the horizon opposite the sun for the best comparison to the printed standard.*

permanent and not fade back toward the previous color. Add titrant until no further color change is observed, and then do not count the last drop.

Testing Frequency

Health codes and laws often dictate how frequently pool and spa water must be tested. The operator must meet or exceed the minimum requirements for testing based on conditions of use and environment. Excessive or heavy user loads may require testing every hour.

Disinfectant and pH

These two tests have a direct bearing on the safety of the patrons and facility. They are the most frequently performed tests because disinfectant levels and pH are the factors that change most rapidly. User load, sunlight, and rainfall can quickly reduce disinfectant levels and change pH levels.

Most health codes require disinfection and pH testing several times per day whenever the pool or spa is open for use. Less frequent testing is sometimes allowed if an automated system is installed that constantly monitors water properties.

The facility's water should always be tested before opening to ensure that conditions are acceptable for patrons. The facility's water should also be tested at the highest user and environmental load conditions to assure that the disinfection system is keeping up with the user load. Finally, if water balance adjustments are to be made, the facility should be tested at closing, before and after the balance chemicals are added.

© National Swimming Pool Foundation 2017

Total Alkalinity

Chlorine efficiency is affected by pH (see Disinfection chapter). The change in pH is governed by total alkalinity. Maintaining proper total alkalinity is, therefore, important for proper disinfection control. It is also important for maintaining water balance as discussed in the Water Balance chapter.

Low levels of total alkalinity may result in pH bounce. High levels of total alkalinity will allow the pH to rise, make it difficult to lower, and could cause cloudy water.

The environment has a bigger impact on outdoor pools and spas. Conditions such as heavy rains can result in a rapid reduction of total alkalinity. The use of low pH disinfectants, such as chlorine gas, trichlor, and bromine tablets or potassium monopersulfate, will cause the total alkalinity to drop.

Source water may be high in total alkalinity, or the use of carbon dioxide gas as a pH control may cause total alkalinity to rise. The common industry standard is to check total alkalinity on a weekly basis or after every heavy rain storm. The use of low pH disinfectants may require more frequent testing. Local codes and regulations may have requirements concerning total alkalinity testing.

Calcium Hardness

Source water, evaporation, and the addition of pool chemicals cause the calcium concentration to increase. Heavy rainfall, system leakage in the shell or piping, and source water low in calcium hardness result in a decrease of calcium concentration.

Because of the importance of calcium hardness to water balance, determining the correct frequency for testing is important. Low calcium hardness in the source water may require testing as frequently as every two weeks. High calcium source water may allow the testing to be as infrequent as every month or two.

Cyanuric Acid (CyA)

Cyanuric acid is increased by manual addition or by the use of stabilized chlorine. CyA is decreased by dilution. If a form of stabilized chlorine is used, CyA should be tested weekly.

Other Testing

Testing for nitrates, phosphates, metals, and TDS should be performed on an as-needed basis. Testing monthly will, in most cases, be sufficient to spot any developing trends, allowing the pool operator time to respond accordingly. Testing for salt concentration, hydrogen peroxide, and potassium monopersulfate should be performed according to existing conditions or the manufacturer's recommendations.

Disinfectant Testing

Tests for residual disinfectant and disinfectant by-products like free chlorine and combined chlorine or others, such as bromine or biguanide, are the most important water chemistry tests the certified operator can perform. Only by constantly monitoring, testing, evaluating results, and taking corrective steps when necessary can the pool/spa operator be assured that the water is sanitary and the patrons are protected from disease-causing germs/pathogens.

There are many choices as to the method for testing disinfectant:

- Some use **Orthotolidine (OTO)**, which only measures total available chlorine. This is unacceptable for public pool/spa use since free chlorine is the active disinfectant and is what the codes and laws require operators to test. Others test for free chlorine using syringaldazine by the **FACT** (free available chlorine test) method.
- **DPD (N,N-diethyl-p-phenylenediamine)** has the capability of measuring both free and total chlorine and is available as a colorimetric and titration test. Most states and local codes require the use of a DPD method for chlorine and bromine testing.
- **Oxidation-Reduction-Potential (ORP)** is the most common method to approximate the disinfectant level in automatic chemical feed systems. ORP is a method of chemical analysis that measures the electrical potential of chlorine or bromine, or any other oxidizer in the water. Most health codes and all chemical product labels require a manual test based on DPD to be used to measure the amount of disinfectant, even when ORP is employed.

© National Swimming Pool Foundation 2017

DPD Testing

DPD is used to measure chlorine, bromine, iodine, ozone, and chlorine dioxide in pool/spa water. Here the discussion will be limited to chlorine and bromine determination.

There are three DPD test methods available: colorimetric, photometric, and titrimetric. The colorimetric test using a color comparator test block is by far the most common of the methods available. The titration test, called Ferrous Ammonium Sulfate-DPD (FAS-DPD), does not have the visual uncertainty that is sometimes associated with colorimetric test block comparator. Colorimetric photometer equipment is available to measure the amount of color due to DPD and remove variability due to the human eye and lighting conditions.

Photo 8-11. *DPD has the capability of measuring both free and total chlorine.*

DPD Colorimetric Test Block

Test kit manufacturers formulate the DPD reagents in different ways. Liquid, tablet, and powder reagent tests offer a reagent DPD #1 as the first step in chlorine testing. Others offer separate liquid reagents DPD #1 and DPD #2 as the first step in chlorine testing. Both of these test protocols give free chlorine as the result. Most test kit manufacturers refer to the second step reagent in the chlorine test as DPD #3. When added to the water sample already indicating free chlorine, DPD #3 will react and give total chlorine as the result. Remember:

- Step 1 in the DPD chlorine test adds DPD #1 (or DPD #1 and DPD #2, depending on the manufacturer) to the sample water to obtain the free chlorine reading
- Step 2 in the DPD chlorine test adds DPD #3 to the sample results of Step 1 to obtain the total chlorine reading

The amount of combined chlorine may now be calculated from the results of Step 1 and Step 2 The results can be shown in the relationship:

$$\underset{\substack{\text{Combined} \\ \text{Chlorine} \\ \textbf{Result}}}{\text{CC}} = \underset{\substack{\text{Total} \\ \text{Chlorine} \\ \textbf{Step 2}}}{\text{TC}} - \underset{\substack{\text{Free} \\ \text{Chlorine} \\ \textbf{Step 1}}}{\text{FC}}$$

The sample water in Step 1 will turn a noticeable pink color if there is chlorine or bromine present. The color intensity is proportional to the chlorine or bromine concentration. If there is any combined chlorine in the sample water, the sample will turn a more intense color when Step 2 is performed. The same procedures may be followed using DPD test kit reagents based on powder or tablets rather than liquid reagents.

Test kits vary, but most test blocks measure concentrations up to 5.0 ppm (mg/L) chlorine. Above 5.0 ppm (mg/L) concentration, a dilution of the sample water is usually recommended, unless FAS-DPD or photometer methods are used. Dilution is discussed later in this chapter.

Total bromine may be determined using standard chlorine test procedures. To learn the total bromine level in a sample known to contain bromine, multiply the observed free chlorine level by 2.25. Many test kit manufacturers will provide a calibration for bromine on the test block comparator.

Bromamines react with DPD #1 and DPD #2 in a manner similar to both hypobromous and hypochlorous acids. This means combined bromine cannot be distinguished from free available bromine. Consequently, you only test for the total bromine residual.

False DPD Readings

Bleaching of the DPD reagents is a major limitation of this test method. At free chlorine concentrations of 10 to 15 ppm (mg/L) and normal pH levels, the chlorine content of the sample may cause the coloration to be less intense or even colorless. As a result, the facility operator could incorrectly judge the test result for chlorine to be zero ppm (mg/L) and mistakenly add

Photo 8-12. *False DPD reading; if a temporary pink color appears, the sample water has a high chlorine content.*

more chlorine. Errors of this type could result in chlorine concentrations above 100 ppm (mg/L).

If the certified operator notes a zero chlorine result, the following procedure is recommended:

- Add an additional drop (or tablet) of DPD to the sample
- If a temporary pink color appears, the sample water has a high chlorine content, and dilution is necessary to achieve accurate results
- If no color develops, then the chlorine level is zero

A false DPD reading may develop with a high chlorine concentration or a high pH in the water sample. The chlorine activity is much lower at a high pH, and the DPD will not bleach out.

Instead, the coloration intensity will appear to be 5.0 to 10.0 ppm (mg/L) when in fact it is much higher. This situation could come about when a pool operator adds a high pH disinfectant, like sodium hypochlorite, directly to the pool and neglects to correct the pH. If and when the pH is normalized, the chlorine becomes active and the subsequent test could bleach out as previously described.

Another false free chlorine reading can be obtained when the combined chlorine is very high. Combined chlorine reacts slowly with DPD, so slowly that normally it does not interfere with the free chlorine reading. If the combined chlorine concentration is high, some DPD can be oxidized to give a red color. This reaction is faster when the temperature is high. Pay close attention to the test.

If no color develops when the DPD is added to the solution, but over time color slowly develops, this is a sign that there is a high combined chlorine level. Although this is rare, it more typically occurs during spring opening or if the water is filled with potable water from a municipal system that uses combined chlorine as the disinfectant.

FAS-DPD Titration Testing

DPD titration testing does not use a color comparator. Titration (as explained earlier in this chapter) uses a balancing reagent known as a titrant, and a visual end point is easily observed.

Manufacturers state that FAS-DPD is more accurate at both high and low concentrations as compared to colorimetric block comparator. The FAS-DPD titration method allows users to measure both free and combined chlorine as low

as 0.2 ppm (mg/L) and as high as 20 ppm (mg/L). To obtain the free chlorine reading, a buffered DPD indicator powder is added to the water sample. The reaction with chlorine produces the pink color characteristic of the standard DPD test. Ferrous ammonium sulfate (FAS) titrating reagent is then added, counting the drops, until the pink color permanently disappears, signaling the end point. The number of drops is then converted to the concentration ppm (mg/L) of free chlorine or bromine according to the manufacturer's instructions. The distinct change from pink to no color eliminates the need for color matching. This is beneficial when testing samples with high level of disinfectant where color comparisons become more difficult.

The second part of the FAS-DPD test determines the amount of combined chlorine present. This also involves turning the sample from a pink to a colorless endpoint. Note: If the water sample being tested contains trace amounts of a potassium monopersulfate-type shocking agent, this will oxidize the DPD #3 reagent in the FAS-DPD test. This interference must be removed prior to testing otherwise a false high combined chlorine reading with result. Check with the test kit for the removal of this interference.

Photo 8-13. *Titration DPD can easily determine chlorine concentrations as low as 0.2 ppm (mg/L) or as high as 20 ppm (mg/L).*

Photometric Disinfectant Testing

The photometer uses proportional color to determine specific disinfection levels using a beam of fixed wavelength light. The light is passed through the colored sample and the emerging light is analyzed electronically. The light absorbency factor of the sample water, which is affected by its color, is calculated and the results are given on a digital display.

Photometry is very accurate and has its own

© National Swimming Pool Foundation 2017

light source, making it independent of daylight or artificial daylight. The results of the test are automatically displayed on the digital display. In some instances concentrations as low as 0.01 ppm (mg/L) can be detected and displayed. Photometer testing is also preferred for pool operators who have problems discerning slight difference in colors.

Photo 8-14. *Photometric testing is ideal for use by pool operators who have problems discerning slight color differences.*

Disinfectant Sensors

There are many types of probes that can measure and provide output signals for control monitoring. The most commonly used is Oxidation Reduction Potential (ORP). ORP, sometimes called redox, is a measure of the oxidizing capacity present in water expressed in millivolts (mV). Oxidizers, such as chlorine, bromine, potassium monopersulfate, and ozone accept electrons. Reducers like sodium bisulfite and sodium thiosulfate lose electrons. An increase in oxidation will result in a decrease in reduction and vice versa. When water is being superchlorinated or de-chlorinated, ORP readings may be erratic as the water and chemicals mix.

Since most disinfectants are oxidizers, they provide a positive ORP reading that increases as the oxidizer concentration increases. ORP is an indirect method to approximate disinfectant level and does not measure disinfectant directly. ORP and disinfectant concentration do not have a linear relationship. In other words, at low chlorine concentrations, the ORP increases quickly with a small change in chlorine concentration. At high chlorine concentrations, ORP increases slightly with a large change in chlorine concentration. To ensure accuracy, probe readings need to be periodically calibrated to a known standard.

Despite the tremendous utility ORP probes provide, health codes still require periodic chlorine measurements to be taken. This is a good idea since many chemicals used in water impact the ORP reading (potassium monopersulfate, cyanuric acid, dirt, etc.). All chemical disinfectant labels guide users to periodically measure disinfectant levels with a chemical (DPD) test.

ORP probes are most commonly used as part of an automated chemical feed system. The ORP probe reading signals a controller to turn on or off chemical feeders. Hand-held ORP probes are available but are not commonly used. See the Chemical Feed & Control chapter for more information about controllers and feeders.

Monthly cleaning of probes is commonly advised. More frequent cleaning may be needed in heavy use environments and when cyanuric acid is present. Swimming pools that use cyanuric acid as a stabilizer pose a unique challenge for pools automated with ORP controllers. It is well established that ORP readings decline as cyanuric acid levels increase. A reduction in chlorine's oxidation potential occurs as more chlorine connects to the cyanuric acid in the water.

The second effect on ORP readings happens when a microscopic layer of residue, called fouling, forms on probes. Fouling can result from cyanuric acid (Aquatics International, June 2002) and/or other contaminants in the water. Fouling reduces the probe accuracy and slows the response to changes in disinfectant levels.

It is difficult for an operator to determine how

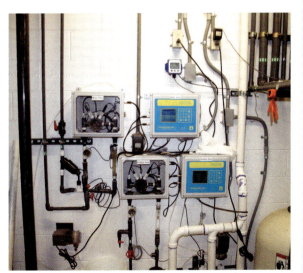

Photo 8-15. *The ORP probe reading signals a controller to turn on or off chemical feeders.*

© National Swimming Pool Foundation 2017

much the ORP is lowered due to cyanuric acid's lowering the oxidization potential of the chlorine and how much is due to probe fouling. The only way for an operator to gauge the amount due to fouling is to clean the probe and to observe the change in ORP readings.

Another probe used to detect disinfectant is the amperometric probe. While ORP probes have been more commonly used in the past, amperometric probes are a newer technology, proving more effective at detecting changes in the chlorine level. See the Chemical Feed & Control chapter for more information on chemical sensors.

Water Balance Testing

The factors that contribute to water balance are pH, total alkalinity, calcium hardness, temperature, and total dissolved solids. These factors are discussed in detail in the Water Balance chapter.

pH Testing

pH is a measurement of the acidity of water and is measured on a logarithmic scale. The term parts-per-million has no relationship to the measurement of pH. A pH sample may not be diluted to obtain proper measurement results.

The pH of pool and spa water is usually measured by adding **phenol red** (phenol-sulfonphthalein) indicator to a pool water sample. The phenol red indicator is yellow at a pH of 6.8, orange at 7.6, and red at 8.4. The color developed is caused by the pH of the water. The color is then compared to a standard on the colorimetric block comparator.

Pools and spas are normally operated at a slightly alkaline pH, with an ideal pH range of 7.4 to 7.6. There are other pH indicators that provide results in this range (bromthymol blue, 6.0–7.6; and cresol red, 7.2–8.8), but they are not commonly used.

The pH test is performed by placing the proper volume of water in the sample tube in the block comparator. The phenol red reagent is then added and the sample is capped and properly mixed. The resulting color is then matched to the color standard on the block.

Electronic meters are also used to measure pH. Two types of meters are used: the first is a photometer, typically the same that is used to measure disinfectant. Some photometers will measure the pH of a water sample within plus or minus 0.05 of their range.

The second is a pH meter. pH meters have become more portable and less expensive than in the past. They have a longer shelf life than reagents and are not subject to the interferences and pH range limitations of indicators. Thus, they have become a good alternative to the pH indicator field kit. However, a pH meter is an electronic instrument and it must be properly calibrated and maintained.

pH meters need to be calibrated daily by measuring the pH of a standard buffered solution to ensure accurate measurements. Some meters can be calibrated by two to three different solutions to give accurate readings over several pH units. However, pool and spa water pH is between 6.5 and 8.5, so a single calibration to a pH 7.0 buffer is adequate.

The most vulnerable part of the meter is the electrode. It must be stored wet in either pH buffer or electrolyte solution. However, tap water will suffice if these solutions are not available. Do not store an electrode in deionized or distilled water, since this will destroy the electrode. It is important to protect the electrode from physical damage due to impact. Electrodes are normally designed to protect the electrode surface with a plastic shield. pH electrodes are commonly installed in automated chemical feeder systems with controllers.

pH Adjustment Testing

Many test kit manufacturers offer a convenient method of determining the proper amount of chemicals to add to correct for an improper pH condition. This involves two additional reagents known as Base Demand Reagent (BDR) and Acid Demand Reagent (ADR).

Should the initial pH test have a higher pH than desired, the ADR reagent is added by drops until the sample coloration matches the desired pH on the comparator standard. On

Photo 8-16. *Acid demand and base demand reagents are useful in making the proper pH adjustments.*

© National Swimming Pool Foundation 2017

the other hand, should the initial pH test have a lower pH than desired, the BDR reagent is added by drops until the sample coloration matches the desired pH on the comparator standard. By counting the drops and using the manufacturer's reference charts, the proper amount of pH corrective chemical can be easily determined.

False pH Readings

Phenol red will only provide correct results when the pH is in the range of 6.8 to 8.4. If the sample water has a pH lower than 6.8, the color saturation will appear as if it were a pH 6.8. If the sample water has a pH higher than 8.4, the color saturation will appear as if it were a pH 8.4. In either case, the pH must be corrected. The ADR and BDR reagents will prove useful. However, the large correction required should alert the operator that there is a definite problem with the water balance that must be identified and corrected to prevent this problem from happening again.

High halogen levels from chlorine or bromine will react with the phenol red indicator for the pH test to create either chlorophenol red or bromophenol blue. Both of these reactions result in a dark purple color whenever the sample pH is above 6.6. This purple color is often confused with a pH of 8.4, and pool operators mistakenly add acid to correct what they believe to be a high pH.

To overcome the presence of high halogen levels, the sample cell should be rinsed out and refilled with the sample water. A chlorine-neutralizing reagent, which is normally used in the total alkalinity test, is then added to neutralize the chlorine or bromine. The phenol red reagent is then added to obtain the pH reading. Adding too much of the chlorine-neutralizing reagent will influence the pH test.

Chlorine-neutralizing reagents can impact the pH. This is one of the reasons that different test kits give slightly different pH readings. When neutralizing the pH with sodium thiosulfate, the pH reading may go higher. Test kit manufacturers provide instructions concerning the number of drops of sodium thiosulfate necessary for high-chlorine correction. Some test kit manufacturers use blends of chemicals to minimize the impact on the pH reading when the chlorine has to be neutralized.

Photometers utilizing phenol red in tablet form typically prevent false readings due to high halogen levels by incorporating chlorine-neutralizing agents in the dry tablet. The halogen level can be as high as 25 ppm (mg/L) without any adverse effect on pH readings.

Total Alkalinity Testing

Total alkalinity is the measure of the ability of water to resist changes in pH. It is a determination of all the alkaline components in the sample that act as a buffer against pH changes. The test method used in normal pool/spa total alkalinity testing is titration.

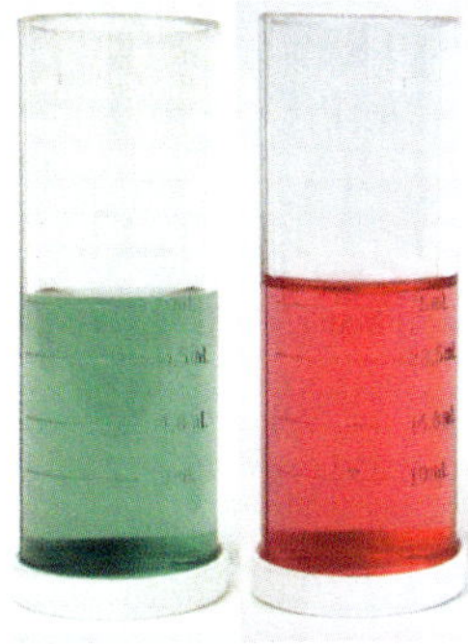

Photo 8-17. *The normal beginning (green) and end (red) point for the titration of total alkalinity.*

The amount of total alkalinity is determined by the use of an acid to titrate or neutralize the total alkalinity. The proper volume of sample water is treated with sodium thiosulfate to remove the halogen. A colored indicator reagent, usually a mixed reagent of bromcresol green/methyl red, is then added. If there is any total alkalinity present, the sample will turn green. The sample is then titrated drop-wise with an acid, usually sulfuric acid, until a reddish-pink color develops. The number of drops is then multiplied by a calibration factor, usually 10, to determine the level of total alkalinity.

Photometers used for total alkalinity may utilize a different reagent and indicator in a single tablet or powder form. These are typically buffered to eliminate any halogen interference, thus preventing any false total alkalinity readings.

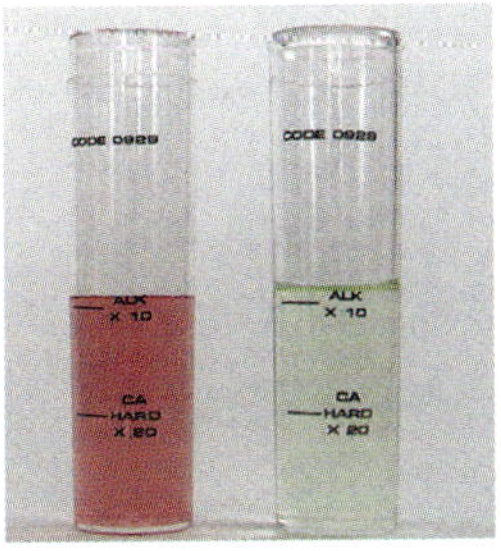

Photo 8-18. *The normal end point (red) and false end point (yellow) for the titration of total alkalinity.*

False Total Alkalinity Readings

High levels of chlorine or the presence of biquanides can result in an end point different from the expected reddish-pink color. The result is usually a yellow color.

The presence of high levels of chlorine will oxidize one of the two

© National Swimming Pool Foundation 2017

total alkalinity color indicator reagents in the sample. If this occurs, follow the manufacturer's instructions to destroy the excess chlorine in the sample. This usually involves repeating the test with additional drops of sodium thiosulfate added before adding the colored indicator reagent.

Cyanuric Acid and Total Alkalinity

The total alkalinity (TA) test measures all buffering capability in the water by determining how much of known acid must be added to react with the alkalinity in the water. The total alkalinity test measures many ions in the water, such as carbonate, bicarbonate, hydroxide, cyanurate, sulfate, and nitrate. The Water Balance chapter provides guidance on how to subtract out the contribution cyanuric acid makes to alkalinity.

Calcium Hardness Testing

Calcium is a metal, and the calcium ion (Ca^{2+}) is determined in water by titration. The most commonly used titrant is ethylenediamine-tetraacetic acid (EDTA). See the Water Balance chapter for chelation or sequestering agents, and EDTA is one of these items. Therefore, the titration test for calcium is one of tying-up the calcium until the end point is reached.

The usual first step in the calcium hardness test is to raise the pH using a base reagent, commonly sodium hydroxide. If the pH is raised high enough, any magnesium present in the water will be eliminated as an interfering factor. Also, at a high pH, the color saturation is more distinct and thus more easily seen.

The second step is to add a color indicator to the sample. The usual color change is from a light red to a sky blue as the titrant is added.

The third step is to add the EDTA drop by drop until the end point is observed. Good lighting is important to observe these results with accuracy. The number of drops is then multiplied by a calibration factor, usually 10, to determine the level of calcium hardness.

Many photometers utilize a different chemistry and do not include EDTA. The tablet reagent is specific to calcium and do not require an end point determination. Depending on the manufacturer they may not be subject to interferences from magnesium hardness or other trace metals in the water.

Photo 8-19. *False calcium hardness endpoint*

False Calcium Hardness Readings

The presence of small concentrations of iron or copper in the sample water may result in an end point that is difficult to interpret. The false end point may appear in one of two ways: either the initial color after adding the indicator never changes or the end point color turns purple. A normal color change takes place at the beginning of the titration, but the transition falls apart. The test kit manufacturers specify corrections to the procedure that can correct for this condition. In some cases, while titrating, small purple clumps will appear to float in the sample. This occurrence will not affect the end point color but is rather an indication of the presence of magnesium hydroxide (MgOH) in the sample.

Temperature Testing

Measuring the temperature is usually accomplished by a thermometer placed in the circulation line after any heating mechanism and before the water is returned to the pool. There are thermometers made for placement in the pool/spa water or as part of the deck plate for a skimmer mechanism. It is not suggested that these items be used for public pool/spa operations. A handheld thermometer is a good tool for an operator to have especially if caring for a spa where a temperature over 104°F (40°C) can pose a safety risk. To prevent the possibility of contamination, thermometers that contain mercury must not be used.

Total Dissolved Solids Testing

Total Dissolved Solids (TDS) is a measurement of all products dissolved in the water including chemicals, user waste, cosmetics, pollution, and wind-borne debris. The usual method of testing is to use a conductivity meter. There are also titration test methods and test strips for the measurement of TDS.

The conductivity meter is calibrated with a solution of known conductivity that is available from the meter manufacturer. The sample is

© National Swimming Pool Foundation 2017

Photo 8-20. *The usual method of testing TDS is to use a conductivity meter.*

then tested by passing an electrical current through the water. The results are given either as microhms or ppm (mg/L). Handheld devices are available from various manufacturers.

Sample Dilution Method

Water samples that read at the upper limit of a test kit's color comparator may have a chemical level above the kit's measuring ability. In this instance, the sample dilution method is recommended.

In the sample dilution method you need to fill the sample with 1/2 sample water and 1/2 distilled water. The test is then performed according to the test kit directions. The result is then doubled. Other dilutions can be used, such as 1/3 sample water and 2/3 distilled water, in which case the result would be tripled.

Dilution works for quantitative tests, or tests that determine the total quantity of substance in the water sample. It requires the addition of water that is free of the chemical being tested. For example, pH cannot be measured using the dilution method because the added water will have its own pH, and the resulting water sample will be different. Qualitative tests are those describing quality, such as the presence or absence of algae and turbidity, as opposed to quantitative test and give a resulting measurement that is counted. Qualitative measures are not made by the dilution method.

Other Testing Concerns

Many other tests can be valuable tools for the pool operator. Some, like that for cyanuric acid, may be required by local codes and regulations.

Others, like those that test for metals or phosphates, will assist in keeping the facility's water in the best condition possible. The operator should review his or her testing requirements and contact the test kit manufacturers for in-depth assistance in selecting the appropriate test apparatus.

Cyanuric Acid (CyA) Testing

Cyanuric acid (s-triazinetrione) is sometimes called stabilizer. When CyA is added to pool water, the chlorine depletion by sunlight is inhibited.

The effect of CyA increases as more is added to the water. Many health departments limit CyA to 100 ppm (mg/L), although some allow less and others allow more. Testing and control of CyA is important to comply with local codes.

The most common CyA test is a turbidimetric test. It uses a reagent called melamine to precipitate the CyA. The resulting sample is then added to a calibrated cell as discussed earlier in this chapter. The ppm (mg/L) determination is based on the observance of a black dot in the test cell. This test is influenced by lighting conditions and by personal abilities. If the result of the CyA test using this method is 100 ppm (mg/L) or above, the sample should be diluted and retested to ensure accuracy.

CyA testing may also be performed electronically and by the use of dip-and-read test strips. A more recent test utilizes a photometer. A one step addition of a tablet reagent is used to display results as low as 2.0 ppm (mg/L) and as high as 200 ppm (mg/L). At 30 ppm (mg/L) the accuracy may be within 1.0 ppm (mg/L).

Testing for Metals

Iron or copper in low concentrations in pool or spa water can result in unsightly stains and colored water conditions. It is always wise to test the source water on a routine basis for these metals.

Both iron and copper are tested with colorimetric test kits and photometers or by the use of dip-and-read test strips. The results of these tests may be used to determine the need for a sequestration or chelation metal control program.

Photo 8-21. *Phosphates and nitrates are derived from the breakdown of natural vegetation.*

Testing for Phosphates and Nitrates

Phosphates are used in fertilizer, detergent formulations, and other cleaning materials. Phosphates and nitrates are present in source water and waste water. They are derived from the breakdown of natural vegetation, the use of fertilizers, and the oxidation of nitrogen compounds.

Phosphates and nitrates provide a nutrient base for algae in swimming pools and spas if a disinfectant is absent. Testing for phosphates can be done colorimetrically, photometrically, or by dip-and-read test strips. Nitrates are tested colorimetrically (using zinc reduction), photometrically, or by dip-and-read test strips.

Testing for Salt Concentrations

The rising popularity of chlorine generation systems and their need to maintain proper salt levels makes testing for salt concentration increasingly important. Sodium chloride tests are available using titration or a dip-and-read test strip. Some chlorine generators have an automatic tester built into the unit.

The titration test accuracy is between 20 ppm (mg/L) and 880 ppm (mg/L) per titrant drop, with the most common being 200 ppm (mg/L) per drop. Photometers can also be used to test for salt concentrations with a common accuracy of less than 200 ppm (mg/L).

Testing for Hydrogen Peroxide

Unlike chlorine, hydrogen peroxide (H_2O_2) is not degraded by sunlight. If the pool/spa disinfection system uses hydrogen peroxide (with PHMB), then tests must be performed on a routine basis to assure proper oxidizer levels. Testing for hydrogen peroxide is most commonly performed using a titration test or photometer, although dip-and-read test strips are available. The titration test can be performed with results being given as a percentage or in ppm (mg/L). The available photometric test range can be from 0–100 ppm (mg/L).

Testing for Polyhexamethylene Biquanide (PHMB)

PHMB marketers provide PHMB-specific test kits. Color comparator blocks or photometric means of testing PHMB are available. PHMB testing in residential applications is usually performed on a weekly basis. Where PHMB disinfection is allowed for public pools, more frequent testing may be required. The usual operating level for PHMB is maintained between 30 and 50 ppm (mg/L).

Testing for Non-Halogen Oxidizers

Swimming pools and spas may use ozone (O_3) or potassium monopersulfate ($KHSO_4 \cdot K2SO_4 \cdot 2KHSO_5$) as supplemental oxidizers. The same DPD methods used for testing chlorine are used for testing ozone. The presence of chlorine in the sample water will make the ozone concentration determination very difficult. The proper method of introducing ozone to swimming pool or spa water insures that no ozone gets to the pool or spa. Therefore, any ozone levels found in pools or spas should be very minimal and not necessary to test.

Some test kit manufacturers offer a deox reagent as part of a titration FAS-DPD chlorine test. This reagent allows the determination of potassium monopersulfate in ppm. The test is not designed to determine potassium monopersulfate directly, but rather to eliminate it as an interfering factor in the determination of total chlorine. Photometer test kits also have this reagent. Determination of the potassium monopersulfate concentration can also be determined.

© National Swimming Pool Foundation 2017

Chapter 9:
Chemical Feed & Control

"If everything seems under control, you're just not going fast enough."

–Mario Andretti

Adding chemicals to pool water can be as simple as dumping a bag of material into the water or as complex as having a computer controlled system that automatically analyzes the water and makes adjustments accordingly.

Any system, simple or complex, requires the manual handling of chemicals at some point in time. Certain rules must be followed when manually adding chemicals to pool water. Carefully read and follow the instructions on chemical labels and use the recommended personal protective equipment. To ensure the safety of the staff, the users of the facility, and the population in the surrounding areas, chemicals should never be mixed, even if you think they are the same chemical or compatible. Proper handling of chemicals is discussed in greater detail in the Facility Safety chapter.

Hand feeding is considered acceptable for residential pools. Manual chemical dosing of a commercial pool is only allowed when the pool or spa is closed to the users. A sufficient time should be allowed for the chemicals to dissolve and disperse before the commercial facility can be re-opened.

Pool and spa chemicals usually have characteristics that can be harmful to operating equipment. For this reason, chemicals should be introduced into the system downstream from all equipment, with the possible exception of the flow meter. Cyanuric acid, water clarifiers or flocculants, and diatomaceous earth are further exceptions to the rule, and can be added upstream. There is, however, a cyanuric acid feed pump available for downstream injection.

It is important to ensure that the chemical feeder is the correct size for the body of water it will treat. Feeders that are too large can over-feed chemicals. Feeders that are too small can cause the water to be unsanitary or have undesirable pH levels if the feeder cannot keep up with the needs of the system. Feeder size is often dictated by public health codes. Many codes dictate a disinfectant feeder that delivers chlorine and is capable of providing a specific volume of chemical into a given volume of water. Most states require feeders to be tested to meet the NSF/ANSI 50 Standard. While other organizations and agencies can perform the testing, such as Underwriters Laboratories (UL), only those tested by NSF® International (NSF) will have the NSF logo on the feeder's face plate and operation manual. Part of the testing includes verifying the amount of chemical that the feeder releases. The operators should check with their local codes for the requirements in their area. In addition, the NSF listing demonstrates that the feeder's materials of construction have been tested and do not degrade in the presence of the chemical they contain.

Photo 9-1. *The operator should check the face plate on the feeder to verify that it has been tested and certified by a recognized organization.*

Manually Adding Chemicals

Before any chemical is added to pool or spa water, the label instructions must be read and understood. Some chemicals are diluted in a container before being added to the pool. Others are evenly broadcast over the water's

© National Swimming Pool Foundation 2017

surface. Pool operators should always follow the instructions on the packaging label for all products.

Some chemicals have instructions on their label that limit the amount of product that may be added per 10,000 gallons at one time. Dosage amounts outside the U.S. are usually per 40,000 liters. If the amount of chemical that is necessary to add exceeds this maximum amount, then the chemical must be added in multiple doses, allowing sufficient time between additions.

The operator should be aware of and comply with federal and state regulations that pertain to safe use, handling, and storage of pool chemicals. When handling chemicals, the operator should always take the necessary protective measures as detailed in Safety Data Sheets (SDS) for each specific chemical. Eye protection and gloves may be required, at a minimum.

All users must be excluded from the pool and deck area while chemicals are being added. The pool or spa should be closed until the chemicals are properly dispersed or for the length of time dictated by the jurisdictional code. Some additional basic rules are

- NEVER ADD WATER TO CHEMICALS. ALWAYS ADD CHEMICALS TO WATER. As a way to remember this think of AAA, Always Add Acid. Pour chemicals into water slowly.
- Never mix chemicals. Do not add different chemicals to the same bucket. Do not add different chemicals to the pool or spa water over one another without giving the previous chemical time to disperse.
- Never siphon chemicals by mouth
- Never flush excess chemicals into any sewer line, especially those that may lead to a septic system
- Always use a clean scoop or dipper. Never use the same scoop for different chemicals. Tag or label scoops as to the chemical with which they are to be used. Using the same scoop for different chemicals may cause a fire.
- Always keep chemicals in their original containers
- Always replace chemical container covers in a proper manner
- Always clean up spills immediately. Use clean, dry utensils according to the instructions on the SDS for the chemical being used.
- Empty chemical containers or packaging

should be discarded in a manner consistent with the label's instructions and local codes
- Always interlock the chemical feeder to the circulation pump to prevent chemical feeding without water circulation

Photo 9-2. *Always keep chemicals in their original containers.*

Addition by Dilution

When label directions call for the chemical to be diluted in water before adding to the pool, directions typically contain guidance, such as

- Use a 5 gallon or 20 liter bucket, filled ½ to ¾ with pool or spa water
- Pour the necessary amount of chemical into the bucket of water. The amount of water should always be much larger than the amount of chemical.
- Stir the bucket contents with a piece of plastic pipe or other noncombustible material. Never use your hand. Some chemicals give off a large amount of heat when mixed with water.
- Walk around the deep two-thirds of the pool and pour the mixture evenly
- The above steps may need to be repeated several times for larger pools
- Once the chemical addition has been completed, rinse the bucket and store any unused chemicals according to the label's instructions

Addition by Broadcast Method

Some chemicals have instructions that require the material to be broadcast directly from the packaging. Directions typically include guidance, such as

- Chemicals should not be broadcast if there is a wind because the wind can carry and deposit the chemicals around the pool where exposure can take place, possibly in the face or eyes
- Close the facility and make sure everyone is out of the pool

© National Swimming Pool Foundation 2017

- Open the container or package as instructed
- Slowly pour the chemical broadly over the water's surface. Keep the packaging near the water's surface and away from your face and body. To spread the chemicals throughout the water, kneel down and pour some of the chemical into the pool water close to a return fitting.
- Repeat several times if necessary, adding equal amounts of chemical around the deep portion of the pool. Always be mindful of the wind direction.
- Use appropriate personal protective equipment

Mechanical Feeders

Pool and spa chemicals can be a gas, a liquid, or a solid. There are mechanical chemical feed designs for each of these types. Mechanical feeders require some type of energy to work. The energy source could be electrical, which operates a motor driven pump, piston or diaphragm. The source of energy could be from the flow of circulation water through a housing, such as a chlorinator or bromine feeder.

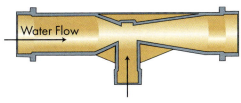

Vacuum Chemical Feed

Illustration 9-1. *A venturi creates a vacuum as the water flows through it. This vacuum may be used to "pull" chemicals into the water circulation.*

The flow of circulation could be due to the hydraulic principle of the venturi effect, the reduction in fluid pressure that results when a fluid flows through a constricted section of a pipe. The venturi effect provides the energy to create suction and draw the chemical into the water. Or the energy source could be from a gas that is under pressure and condensed into its liquid state.

There are different ways to adjust the amount of chemical added through a mechanical feeder. Mechanical feeders may use electrical timers and work semi-automatically. They can also be wired to a controller that opens and closes valves, which makes the feed system function totally automatic. Mechanical erosion feeders usually have a means to adjust the flow of the water, and thus manually control the amount of chemical.

Liquid Solution Feeders

Liquid solution feeders deliver a liquid chemical or a liquid solution slurry containing solid chemical particles. Liquid chemicals should be fed into the circulation downstream from the filters and heating systems. Unless a venturi is used, the liquid solution pump must have a high enough effluent pressure to ensure that the liquid will be pumped into the circulation line. This type of mechanism is a **positive displacement pump**.

Positive displacement pumps are commonly used for the injection of sodium hypochlorite, and liquid chemicals for pH adjustment. In some cases, labels instruct operators to dissolve sodium bisulfate, which has a low pH, into an excess of water, and then to feed the slurry to lower the pH. It is important to follow label directions.

Use caution and the appropriate personal protective equipment when adding products to water. Never add water to a chemical. Chemicals should always be added to a large amount of water. Acids should not be put through metal pipes or allowed to contact metals, including some pump impellers, since the acid can corrode the metal. If a slurry of soda ash, or sodium bicarbonate, is used to raise pH, then label directions should be followed and appropriate personal protective equipment should be used. A separate electrically operated mixer is needed to keep the soda ash slurry well distributed in the reservoir tank.

There are two common designs for positive displacement pumps. The peristaltic pump uses rollers that squeeze a feed tube, moving the fluid through the tube. The piston or diaphragm pump operates with check valves.

The output of the positive displacement pump

Mixing Chemicals
Always follow the instructions of the chemical manufacturer when mixing chemicals with water. Always add the chemical to the water. Read and understand the Safety Data Sheets provided by the manufacturer and kept at the job site.

© National Swimming Pool Foundation 2017

Photo 9-3. *Gas chlorine systems often use a solution of soda ash dissolved into water for pH control. Positive displacement feeders introduce the solution into the circulation system.*

should be introduced into the circulation flow by means of a special connection, sometimes called a corporation cock. This is a connector that is easily removed for periodic cleaning.

Peristaltic Pumps

In peristaltic pumps, a motor-driven roller assembly squeezes a flexible tube. As the rollers rotate, a constant volume of fluid is discharged under pressure for each cycle of the rollers. On the input side of peristaltic pumps, a suction is created to pull more fluid into the system. On the output side of peristaltic pumps, the pressure is usually about 25 psi (172 kPa). Some models can go as high as 100 psi (689 kPa).

Peristaltic pumps require that the feed lines be maintained free of sediment clogging on the input side and at the injection point. The flexible tube is the main source of failure. It may prove useful to have replacement hoses in inventory to minimize downtime.

Care should be taken as to the proper placement of the peristaltic pumps relative to the chemicals being fed. Follow these guidelines:

- The pumps should not be mounted directly above the chemicals. Over time, fumes from the chemicals could harm the equipment.
- The pumps should not be mounted above other operating equipment. A flexible tube failure could release chemicals that might cause equipment damage.
- The pumps should never be mounted above chemicals of a different type. A flexible tube failure could release chemicals that are incompatible resulting in the release of dangerous gasses.

Perform regular maintenance on peristaltic pumps. Clogged lines can result in higher than normal back pressure resulting in line failure.

Expect the flexible feed lines to operate about 400 hours between replacements. Clogged lines will shorten this life expectancy. Whenever lines are cleaned, extreme care must be taken to ensure that any sodium hypochlorite and acid do not contact each other because dangerous chlorine gas will be released.

Diaphragm and Piston Pumps

These two pumps use check valves and cams. The diaphragm pump uses a flexible membrane that displaces fluid as it moves in and out. The piston pump is activated by a cam. Both the diaphragm and piston pumps operate with the use of check valves.

The diaphragm pump has a casing that encloses the diaphragm. The in-and-out motion of the diaphragm is controlled by a rotating cam or solenoid. The outward motion of the diaphragm produces a vacuum inside the feeder housing. This in turn causes the suction-side check valve to open and draw chemical fluid into the chamber. As the chamber becomes full, the pressure is equalized and the suction check valve closes. The fluid is trapped in the chamber.

The inward motion of the diaphragm causes the fluid to be pressurized. The fluid is forced up through the out-port check valve and into the

Photo 9-4. *Feed pumps often have lines that can break or rupture. Care should be taken as to how these pumps are mounted above incompatible chemicals.*

> **Caution**
> Never attempt to clear a clogged line by switching chemicals. Switching the muriatic acid and sodium hypochlorite lines can result in these chemicals mixing and releasing toxic chlorine gas.

© National Swimming Pool Foundation 2017

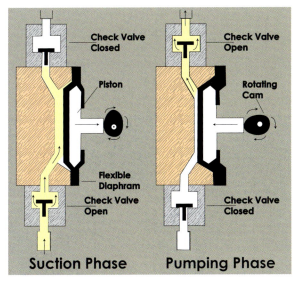

Illustration 9-2. *Diaphragm pumps use check valves for liquid control. These check valves should be cleaned according to the manufacturer's recommendations.*

injection feed line. This completes one cycle. The feed rate of the chemical is determined by the cycle rate of the cam or solenoid.

The check valves in a diaphragm pump are spring loaded. There are usually four, one-way check valves for each pump: one at the strainer side of the tubing in the chemical vat, one at the entrance side of the feeder, one at the exit side of the feeder, and one at the point of injection. If any of these valves stop operating properly, then the disinfection system could fail to maintain proper sanitation levels. It is important to flush the diaphragm pump as often as once a week to avoid failures.

A piston pump works in much the same way as a diaphragm pump, except that the out-port pressure is created by the movement of the piston. The same recommendations for flushing the feed lines apply.

Liquid Vacuum Induction Feeders

Liquid bleach vacuum induction feed systems and erosion feeders are both listed by NSF Standard 50 as "flow through chemical feeders." The difference between the two feed systems is that one feeds sodium hypochlorite/liquid bleach and the other feeds an average of 1% eroded slurry from calcium hypochlorite. Liquid bleach vacuum induction employs venturi-type injection. The venturi produces a vacuum, which first draws chemical from a liquid storage tank through the feeder. The chemical is then injected into a dedicated bypass line and added into the circulation line downstream.

Feed rates are controlled by a simple metering valve, which controls a flow meter. The feeder is operated by an automated chemical controller, which signals a solenoid valve to turn the feeder off and on. Variable high capacity adjustable feed rates allow an operator to regulate flow by enabling set point control under any demand.

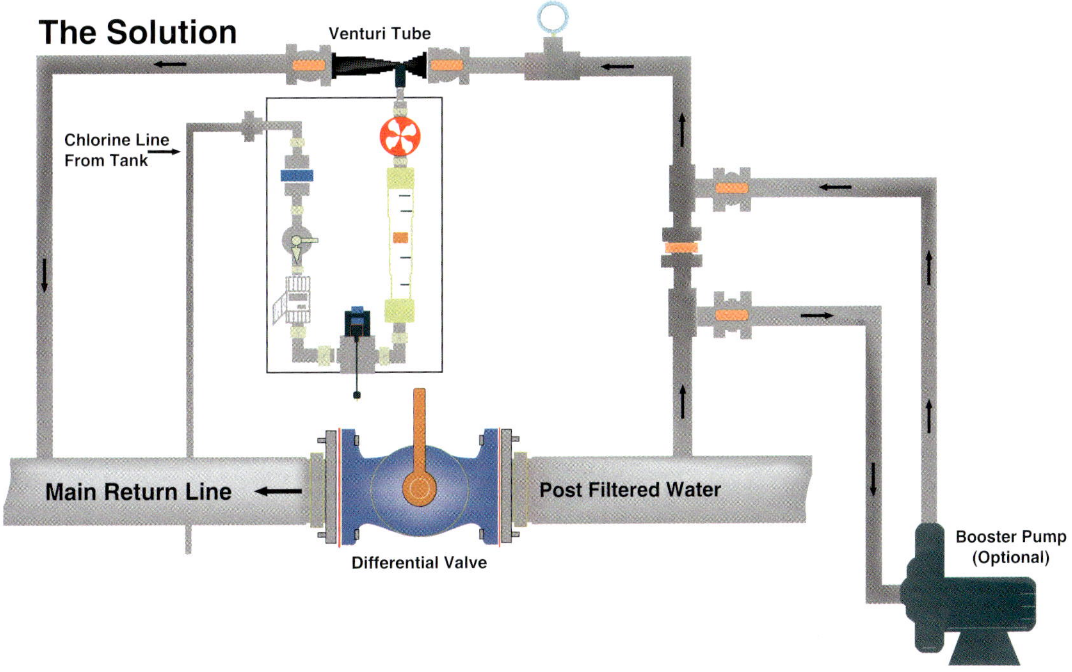

Illustration 9-3. *Typical installation of a liquid vacuum induction feeder.*

1. Pool & Spa Management
2. Regulations & Guidelines
3. Essential Calculations
4. Pool Water Contamination
5. Disinfection
6. Water Balance
7. Pool & Spa Water Problems
8. Chemical Testing
9. Chemical Feed & Control
10. Water Circulation
11. Pool & Spa Filtration
12. Heating & Air Circulation
13. Spa & Therapy Operations
14. Facility Safety
15. Keeping Records
16. Maintenance Systems
17. Troubleshooting
18. Facility Renovation & Design
References

© National Swimming Pool Foundation 2017

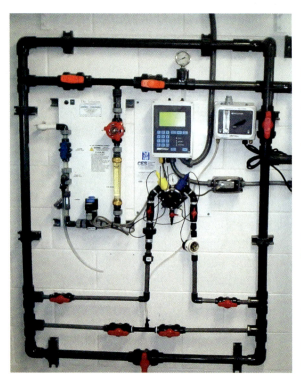

Photo 9-5. *Chemicals can be evenly distributed throughout the pool system through liquid solution feeders.*

Dry Chemical Feeders

Dry chemicals can be granular or tablets in various sizes and shapes. These chemicals can be fed in one of two ways: one method is through erosion feeders, which use a stream of water to contact the dry chemical, causing the chemical to erode and dissolve. Another method is mechanical dry feeders, which use a mechanical gate or a rotating screw to move granules into a water stream where the granules are dissolved; then the chemical is fed into the pool or spa. The operation of a dry chemical feeder relies on the pressure and/or suction created by the circulation pump or the differential pressure between the suction and pressure side of the pump.

Erosion Feeders

NSF calls erosion feeders flow through chemical feeders. There is a gradual wearing-away or erosion of the solid tablet in the feeder. As the tablet erodes, the chemicals dissolve. The effectiveness of this type of system is dependent on four basic factors:

- The solubility of the chemical product
- The flow rate of the water through the erosion device
- The total surface area of the exposed chemical pellets

- The temperature of the water flowing through the erosion feeder

Installation and Operation (I&O) manuals state the pool or spa size that the feeder is designed to treat. In addition, the I&O manual includes information about how to plumb the feeder into the circulation system. There are also directions covering how to connect the feeder to an electronic controller or timer. Failure to comply with operational I&O directions can make the operation more difficult or place people in danger.

It is important that the pool operator understand the safety information provided by the manufacturer to minimize any risk. Improperly operated feeders could rupture or explode.

Erosion feeders work by relatively simple principles. The chemical is placed into the body of the feeder and the feeder housing is secured usually by a cap and gasket. The chemical remains stationary while water flows over or is sprayed on the chemical. This causes the chemicals to erode and dissolve. The water flow must be carefully controlled to maintain the proper amount of disinfectant output. Most commercial erosion systems have one or more flow regulating valves. Codes may require the use of a flow meter for erosion systems.

Photo 9-6. *Erosion feeders use a stream of water to contact the dry chemical, causing the chemical to erode and dissolve.*

© National Swimming Pool Foundation 2017

Solid chlorine-releasing tablets and bromine-releasing tablets are commonly used in erosion feeders. Hence the names chlorinator and bromine feeder have evolved. Chlorinators and bromine feeders both work on the principles of pressure and pressure differential, through in-line and venturi systems, respectively. Vacuum systems also exist, using the suction side of the pump. Pump warranties may be voided, however, if high chemical concentrations are fed through the pump.

> ### Caution
> Never add chemicals to an erosion feeder other than those specified by the feeder manufacturer. An explosion or fire could result.

Pressure Erosion Feeders

Pressure erosion feeders are installed downstream from the filter and heater in the circulation line and are under full line pressure. If the pump and filter are installed below the water surface level, it is important that isolation valves are installed on each side of the feeder and that these valves are closed before opening the unit.

Any feeder that is designed to operate under pressure includes a bleed valve. The bleed valve is designed to relieve pressure from the feeder before it is opened. No feeder should be opened unless it has been determined that there is no pressure within the feeder. Circulation systems have enough internal pressure to blow a lid off and project it through the air at speeds that could damage or destroy equipment and injure or kill a person.

Pressure Differential Erosion Feeders

Pressure differential erosion feeders are installed downstream from the pump. Water under pressure from the pump flows through the feeder and returns to the circulation line at a point farther downstream that is at a lower line pressure. This difference in pressure is what causes the water to flow through the erosion feeder. To create the pressure differential, one of the following methods are used:

- A booster pump to introduce the chemically treated water from the feeder to a circulation line that is under pressure
- A venturi loop that can create a vacuum, which draws chemical from the feeder to the venturi
- A throttling valve loop with a valve restriction on one leg of the loop

Photo 9-7. *Booster pumps are often used to introduce chemicals into the circulation line.*

In all cases, filtered water should be used as the source water for the erosion feeder. Some feeder installations take the water from the pump discharge line before it is filtered. The erosion feeder outlet line is connected to the circulation return line after the heater. This method uses the pressure drop across the filter and heater to develop positive flow through the feeder.

Spray Erosion Feeders

Spray Erosion Feeders are sometimes used with calcium hypochlorite systems. The calcium hypochlorite tablets are sprayed with water rather than being immersed in the water. With this type of system, a venturi loop or a booster pump is often used. It is important that regular preventative maintenance be performed to control calcium scale in the system, which can cause lines to plug and the feeder to fail. Although these feeders are designed to reduce any scale formation, scale can form because calcium hypochlorite has a high pH and high calcium content. Therefore, it is important that the plumbing lines and fittings that transport water from the feeder have large diameters and are regularly cleaned as directed by the manufacturer.

> ### Caution
> Never open a pressure erosion feeder unless the pump has been turned off and the internal pressure has been released. Check the manufacturer's instruction manual.

Pressure to Vacuum Feeders

It is best to feed chemicals later in the circulation system after the pump, filter, chemical-sensing probes, and heater, to reduce the risk that the chemicals damage the circulation system parts. It is important for the pool operator to recognize that some feed systems are installed in a pressure-to-vacuum arrangement. In this case, water from a portion of the circulation that is under pressure is tapped and directed through a flow meter and then into the chemical feeder. Then the water containing chemicals exits the feeder and returns to a location upstream to the pump, which is under vacuum.

Some manufacturers and facilities recommend this type of system. One of the reasons this type of plumbing arrangement is selected is cost. A pressure-to-vacuum system is relatively inexpensive since a booster pump or a venturi system is not needed. The flow through the feeder is controlled with a valve and flow is driven by the pressure differential.

There are certain drawbacks when operating a pressure-to-vacuum system. Many of the fed chemicals may cause deterioration to the pump impeller and heater and possibly to the pump housing. If the system uses probes to measure chemical levels, the system design must ensure that the probe measurements are not false readings as a result of the newly chemically treated water passing by the probes.

Mechanical Dry Feeders

Chemicals can be metered into a chemical feed tank by a screw mechanism or a mechanical gate or shutter mechanism. The output of the feed tank is drawn into the circulation line by venturi action, or by using a booster pump. The tank must be sized to allow time for the chemical to be dissolved or eroded.

Gas Feed Systems

There are three gasses commonly used in aquatic facility operations. First, chlorine gas is used for disinfection. Second, carbon dioxide is used for lowering the pH, usually with sodium hypochlorite as the disinfectant. Both gasses are contained in pressure vessels in a liquefied state. Third, ozone is generated on-site and is used as an oxidizer and supplemental disinfectant.

The pressure cylinders are attached to a

Photo 9-8. *Most gas feed systems rely on the venturi principle to mix the gas into the circulation water flow so that the gas is properly dissolved.*

feed device by means of a yoke mechanism. There is an adjustable control device to properly meter the desired amount of gas. Finally, there is an injection device to place the gas into the circulation line.

Gas feed systems rely on either a venturi principle or a contact chamber to dissolve the gas into the circulation water. The desired chemical reaction, being disinfection, pH control, or oxidation, can occur after dissolution takes place. Some gas feed systems rely on booster pumps that utilize side-stream injection.

Chlorine Gas Feeders

Chlorine gas has a green color and is heavier than air causing it to collect in low areas. It has a distinctive odor and is easily detected at concentrations as low as 0.2 to 0.4 parts per million (or mg/L). Acute, or short-term, exposure to high levels (>30 ppm or mg/L) of chlorine results in chest pain, vomiting, toxic pneumonitis, pulmonary edema, and death. At lower levels (<3 ppm or mg/L), chlorine is a potent irritant to the eyes, lungs, and upper respiratory tract. Several studies have reported the following effects:

- 0.014 to 0.054 ppm (mg/L): tickling of the nose
- 0.04 to 0.097 ppm (mg/L): tickling of the throat
- 0.06 to 0.3 ppm (mg/L): itching of the nose and cough, stinging, or dryness of the nose and throat
- 0.35 to 0.72 ppm (mg/L): burning of the conjunctiva and pain after 15 minutes
- above 1.0 ppm (mg/L): discomfort ranging from ocular and respiratory irritation

© National Swimming Pool Foundation 2017

Photo 9-9. *Mounted on the chlorine tank is a regulating chlorinator. A new lead gasket is always used anytime the chlorinator is removed from the cylinder.*

to coughing, shortness of breath, and headaches

(E.J. Calabrese and E.M. Kenyon. <u>Air Toxics and Risk Assessment</u>, Lewis Publishers, Chelsea, MI. 1991) For the above reasons, all gas chlorine feed systems and control equipment should be located at or above ground level. The gas chlorine feed systems should be installed in an equipment room with a forced-air ventilation system capable of a complete air exchange in one minute or less.

The chlorine storage area must be posted properly with signs in accordance with local codes and state and federal laws and regulations. Access to storage areas by unauthorized personnel should be restricted.

Although chlorine gas is an effective disinfectant, relatively few pools use chlorine gas due to the regulatory restrictions driven by the hazard of a potential release. Chlorine gas is more commonly used on larger pools and in

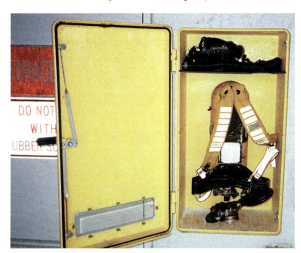

Photo 9-10. *A self contained breathing apparatus should be located just outside the chlorine room.*

some regions by licensed service companies. The greatest hazard occurs if a large cylinder ruptures or develops a leak. Evacuation plans for the facility and local community are needed.

Any operator who uses gaseous chlorine should consult with the state or local health department on proper training requirements concerning the use of this product. Additional information about chlorine can be obtained from the Chlorine Institute.

Chlorine Gas Cylinders

All gas chlorine is shipped and stored in pressure vessels as a liquefied gas under pressure resulting in the presence of both liquid and gas phases in the containers. Cylinders used at pools and spas should always feed chlorine as a gas. Most chlorine gas cylinders are portable and are filled off-site by the chlorine gas supplier. The most common sizes are 100 lbs (45 kg) and 150 lbs (68 kg). Cylinder valves are equipped with a pressure relief device consisting of a fusible metal plug in the valve body, located below the valve seat. Some larger facilities may have gas storage tanks that have a one ton capacity requiring on-site replenishment.

Cylinders should always be stored upright. To prevent accidental damage to the cylinders, both full and empty cylinders must be individually chained or strapped to a wall or other fixed device. When not in use, all cylinder valves and outlets should be protected by caps as provided by the supplier. The storage of cylinders should have a system for use. The cylinders should be tagged with the arrival date, and the oldest inventory cylinder should be placed online when cylinders are changed. This is called the first-in, first-out principle.

Carbon Dioxide Gas Feeders

Swimming pools and spas using sodium hypochlorite or calcium hypochlorite as the primary disinfectant often use muriatic acid to lower the pH. Over the past 10 years, the use of carbon dioxide gas has become a popular choice as an alternative method for pH control.

Carbon dioxide when dissolved in water produces carbonic acid, which at normal pool pH will react with base chemicals in the water to produce bicarbonate and carbonate. When carbon dioxide is inserted into the circulation line, the resulting carbonic acid will reduce the pH of

Photo 9-11. *Carbon dioxide may be used instead of acids to lower the pH of pool/spa water.*

pool or spa water. When CO_2 is used, it has a tendency to increase the total alkalinity.

Carbon dioxide may be delivered to the swimming facility in high-pressure tanks (50 lbs/23 kg or 150 lbs/68 kg). For larger facilities, up to 750 lbs/340 kg permanently installed tank systems are available.

The release of the carbon dioxide must be controlled and therefore a release regulator is required. A rapid release of carbon dioxide can result in a freeze-up of the injector system.

The carbon dioxide regulator is usually connected to the automated feeder control system and is discussed later in this chapter. Injection is usually accomplished by means of a venturi or a booster pump. Injection into the circulation line should occur downstream from all other circulation system components, including disinfectant injection.

Caution
Carbon dioxide is heavier than air and is colorless and odorless. Any storage of carbon dioxide should be in a forced ventilation room. Storage tanks should be chained or strapped in a manner similar to a chlorine gas tank to prevent accidental damage to the cylinder. If carbon dioxide is released in great amounts, oxygen could be displaced, resulting in suffocation and possibly death.

Ozone Generators

Ozone is an unstable bluish gas. The oxygen molecule (O_2) can be split and chemically bound to another oxygen molecule creating ozone (O_3).

Ozone is not stable and cannot be stored and transported; it must be produced on-site. The chemistry of ozone as it applies to swimming pool and spa operations is discussed in the Disinfection chapter. This chapter focuses on the mechanics of ozone production and how it is introduced into the pool or spa water.

Even at low levels, ozone is not safe for humans. There are maximum exposure limits for people. The OSHA level is 0.1 ppm for an eight-hour exposure. When ozone equipment is operated at a pool or spa facility, the placement of the generation equipment should be carefully considered. Fresh air circulation is a must, particularly in indoor environments. Never install ozone generation equipment below ground level. State and local health regulations may require the installation of an ozone detection system and alarm.

There are two methods of ozone production: **corona discharge** and **ultraviolet light**. Regardless of the method of manufacture, for ozone to work properly, it must be introduced into the circulation water in an effective manner. This is best accomplished by the means of a venturi injection system. The ozone injection placement should be downstream from all operating equipment and before the injection point of the disinfectant.

The amount of ozone that will dissolve in water depends on three factors: 1) the concentration of ozone in the air coming out of the ozonator, 2) the size of the bubble, since smaller bubbles have a greater surface area to contact the water, and 3) the temperature of the water; at higher temperatures, less ozone gas dissolves in the water.

In some installations, the ozone is introduced into a circulation side stream. This method utilizes a separate booster pump. The side stream water is taken from the main circulation line, after the filter and before the heater. The ozone is applied to the side stream flow and the ozonated water is returned to the main circulation flow after the heater and before the disinfectant injection.

All ozone should be depleted or used up before the circulation water returns to the pool. Ozone is heavier than air and could possibly collect and concentrate at the water's surface. This could result in discomfort to the eyes and respiratory systems of pool or spa users. For this

© National Swimming Pool Foundation 2017

reason, the method of ozone-to-water contact is very important.

In addition to the venturi injection, some systems may also employ a contact column. This device allows for thorough mixing and increased contact time to ensure that no gaseous ozone is allowed to reach the pool or spa area.

Corona Discharge Ozonators

A corona discharge generator is sometimes referred to as a CD ozone generator. Corona discharge systems produce a much higher concentration and quantity of ozone compared to the ultraviolet (UV) ozone generators. CD generation systems may be more expensive to purchase and install than UV generation systems; however, the cost per gram of ozone produced is less with the CD generation system.

In the CD ozone generator, air is exposed to multiple high-voltage electrical discharges. Air contains 20% oxygen (O_2) and 80% nitrogen (N_2). A ring of energy is created, the corona, and hence the name. As the air flows through the corona, some of the oxygen molecules are split apart, or disassociated, and then reassembled with the oxygen that remains to form ozone.

Before being exposed to the CD, the moisture in the air is removed. If the moisture

Photo 9-12. *A corona discharge ozone generator may have a contact column to increase the mixing time to achieve the greatest amount of ozone in solution.*

is not removed, nitric acid can form inside the generator, resulting in a decrease in ozone production or corrosion to equipment. For this reason, most CD ozone generators use a desiccant air dryer to remove the moisture.

> ### Advice
> Since an ozone residual is not maintained in pool or spa water, it is used to supplement disinfectants like chlorine or bromine. Humans should not be exposed to ozone in pool/spa water.

The corona discharge generators must have an electrical interlock with the main circulation pump. When the pool or spa circulation system is not active, the production of ozone must cease. Often a second fail-safe device is used, such as a pressure switch on the circulation line.

Ultraviolet Ozonators

Ultraviolet (UV) ozone generators produce a lower output of ozone and a lesser concentration than CD generators. Air is passed over UV lamps. The energy from these lamps splits the oxygen molecules in the air. The resulting oxygen atoms, seeking stability, attach to other oxygen molecules, forming ozone.

The ultraviolet lamps emit light at 185 nanometers (nm). Ultraviolet lamps have been used for many years to generate ozone. The air used is ambient air, the natural state of air in the outdoor environment, under normal pressure. With UV systems, less ozone dissolves into the water, since the ozone concentration in the air when subjected to energy is lower in UV systems than in CD systems. Due to the lower output and concentration of ozone, UV ozone generation systems are less common in larger commercial pools and spas.

Ultraviolet Radiation (UV)

Ultraviolet (UV) systems utilize ultraviolet lamps to generate UV radiation to disinfect the water. It is typically added after the filter. Water in the pool or spa is flowing continuously through the UV system where it is exposed to the UV radiation. The UV light will not only inactivate the bacteria and viruses, but it will also oxidize chloramines.

After the pool or spa water has passed

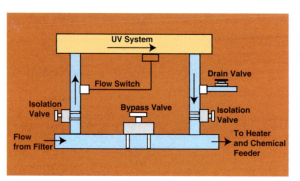

Illustration 9-4. *Diagram showing the typical installation of a UV disinfection system*

through the filter it is diverted to flow through the UV system via an inlet and outlet line. A flow switch is typically installed with the UV system that would shut the system down if the water flow is interrupted. Since all the pool or spa water is diverted through the UV system, treatment occurs in all the water on every pass.

There are different lamp output levels available, low pressure and medium pressure UV lamps. Low pressure lamps have a lower power density, which results in a larger number of lamps being needed for high flow rates. Medium pressure UV lamps have a lower effective output of UV light but have a higher power density, thus requiring fewer lamps. UV lamps have a long lifetime lasting anywhere from 4,000 to 9,000 hours.

Factors that should be considered when installing a UV system include the type of pool, volume of water, and turnover rate.

> **Warning**
> Radiation from UV lamps is harmful to eyes and skin. Equipment using these lamps must screen them completely from direct view

Photo 9-13. *A UV system is installed so that the water flow can be bypassed so that it passes by the UV lamps.*

Chlorine Generators

On-site chlorine generation is growing in popularity in North America. Most new residential pools have generators installed when the pool is built. These systems are popular in other parts of the world too. The majority of pools in Australia have them. By creating free chlorine in the water, chemical storage, transportation, installation of chemical feeders, and handling is reduced. It is important that a qualified technician or contractor install the chlorine generator. The operation manual should be carefully reviewed. A spectrum of chlorine generators are available. Additional information about these systems is provided in the Disinfection chapter.

In-Line Generators

In-line generators introduce chlorine directly into the circulation line of the pool or spa. First, salt is added to the water. Usually 3,000 to 3,500 ppm (mg/L) of salt is added to the pool or spa water. Some systems may use salt levels as high as 8,000 ppm (mg/L). To achieve 3,000 ppm (mg/L) of salt, at least 250 lb (115 kg) of salt is added for every 10,000 gallons (38,000 liters) of water. The salt itself is not the disinfectant. The circulation system forces water through an in-line unit also called a cell installed in the circulation system. The cell contains layers of plates that are electrically charged by the generator's power supply. The plates in the cell convert salt to free chlorine by a chemical process called electrolysis. The chemical reaction that takes place is shown in the Disinfection chapter.

The free chlorine that is produced has only a minor effect on water chemistry. The pH tends to increase slightly over time.

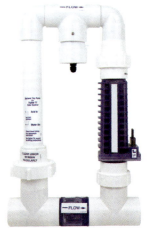

Photo 9-14. *In-line chlorine generators may have self-cleaning cells and be compatible with ORP control systems.*

© National Swimming Pool Foundation 2017

Photo 9-15. *On-site chlorine generation reduces hazards of chemical storage and transportation.*

Traces of hydrogen gas are produced, but they are vented to the atmosphere. These systems have an interlock so that the chlorinator is shut down if the pump is off and the small level of hydrogen gas does not build up to create an explosion hazard. Additionally, to prevent scale build-up on the plates, the generator's control unit periodically reverses the charge on the plates. Care must be taken to ensure that the hydrogen gas does not interfere with the probe readings.

In-line chlorine generation is almost self-sustaining. The chlorine generated by the system reverts back to salt and water and is thus available to be oxidized again to chlorine. Salt addition is necessary to replace losses due to filter backwash, rain water dilution, user drag-out, and splash out.

Chlorine generators can be automated. Newer generators also measure the amount of salt in the water and provide an electrical adjustment to compensate for a steady chlorine generation level. Some generators can sense if the salt level in the water is outside the desired range and signal the operator with a warning light.

Brine-Tank Generators

The brine method of on-site chlorine generation is a miniature chlorine plant converting salt into free chlorine. Brine-tank generators are less common than in-line generators. In the brine generation method, sodium chloride (NaCl) is dissolved into water at high concentrations creating brine. The brine is passed through an electrolytic cell and free chlorine is produced with concentrations of 4,000 to 8,000 ppm (mg/L). Some electrolytic cells have a membrane separating the anode and cathode; some do not.

This system is not in the circulation system of the pool or spa. The free chlorine solution is collected in a storage tank with a low-level switch to activate and a high-level switch to send the system to standby when the tank is full. The solution is sometimes called a sodium hypochlorite solution, or one manufacturer calls it a mixed oxidant solution. Use of a storage tank ensures enough disinfectant is available and can be delivered to fulfill demand when needed. These systems can use chemical sensors and controllers to measure the water chemistry, activate a pump to feed disinfectant, and turn off the feed pump.

Feeder Automation

Two pool and spa water chemical variables change rapidly: pH and the level of disinfectant. Proper water balance can help ensure that pH is buffered from any rapid changes due to various factors, such as the amount of the disinfectant added, the pH of the disinfectant used, user load, and environmental factors like rain. The level of disinfectant in pool water can also change rapidly due to user loading and environmental factors such as sunlight.

Without some form of automatic sensing and chemical feeding, the pool operator must adjust feed rates manually. For some pools this is an easy task, requiring minor adjustments on an infrequent basis. For other pools, maintaining proper pH and disinfectant levels may require adjustments on a daily basis, or even more often. A pool that requires constant feed adjustment for pH and disinfectant control is an ideal environment for an automated feeder control system. Generally, the smaller the body of water (spas and wading pools), the higher the user

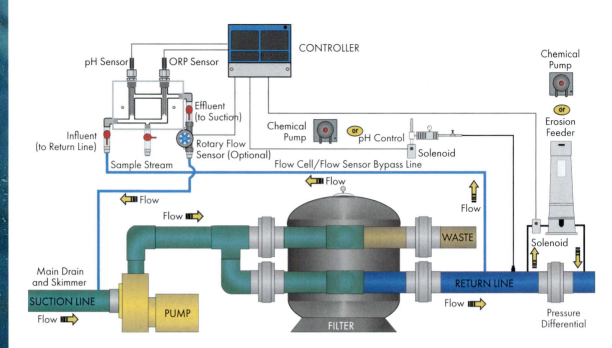

Illustration 9-5. *Courtesy of Chemical Automation Technologies, Inc.*

load; or the more intense the sunlight, the harder it is to maintain the chemical levels.

Control Systems

Electronic controllers fitted with chemical-sensing probes are becoming more prevalent in the pool and spa marketplace. Public health departments, facility managers, and residential pool owners are driving this growth in an attempt to better ensure that sanitary conditions are being continuously maintained. Being assured that disinfectant levels are maintained at all times reduces the risk of disease outbreaks and the hardship that could result.

Several states require some form of automatic chemical control for pH and disinfectant levels for spas. In addition, there is strong justification that high risk environments like wading pools should also use control systems to ensure that sanitary conditions are maintained.

Chemical probes and controllers help prevent feeding too little or too much disinfectant. In addition, they can help respond quickly to changes in the water by feeding chemicals when they are needed. Many of the items discussed in the earlier sections of this chapter may be controlled by an automated system. Turning a chemical feed pump on or off and opening or closing a circulation valve can be accomplished by an automated, chemical feed control system.

Chemical Sensors

The first step in automated control is to measure the chemical factor or parameter to be controlled. This is accomplished with a sensor called a probe. These probes send signals to the controllers that operate feeders, which introduce more disinfecting and pH-controlling chemicals into the water. Only the probes designed to work with a specific controller should be used. There

Photo 9-16. *Simple ORP control systems consist of two probes (to measure pH and disinfectant), a control processor, and feed pumps to introduce chemicals.*

© National Swimming Pool Foundation 2017

are many types of probes that can measure and provide output signals for control monitoring:

- pH probes
- Oxidation-Reduction Potential (ORP) probes
- Amperometric probes

pH Probe

Most pH probes consist of a body, an electrode, and a cable. If the probe is more than 20 feet (6 meters) from the controller, a preamplifier is needed to ensure the proper signal is sent to the controller.

Temperature can affect pH probe readings in two ways. The pool water pH and the probe electrode output will both change with temperature. These two effects, either together or separately, can lead to errors in measurement, control, and calibration.

An acidic substance is able to donate an H^+ ion. A basic, or alkaline, substance is capable of accepting an H^+ ion. The pH probe has an element with a thin membrane that allows H^+ ions to pass through. The probe electrode is filled with a neutral solution, or an equal number of H^+ and OH^- ions. When the probe is immersed in an acidic environment, H^+ ions pass through the membrane and develop a positive potential on the sensing electrode. This potential difference between the electrode and the reference is measured by a pH meter and displayed on the controller as a pH reading.

If the probe is in an alkaline environment, there exists within the probe a higher concentration of H^+ ions than outside the probe. This causes H^+ ions within the probe to pass through the membrane, leaving an excess of OH^- ions within the probe. A negative potential is thus sensed by the pH meter. Once again, the pH reading is displayed on the controller.

ORP Probe

The concept of ORP is discussed in the Chemical Testing chapter. An ORP, sometimes referred to as redox, probe indicates the oxidizing/reducing capability of pool water by measuring the electron activity. A reducing agent is a substance capable of donating an electron. An oxidizing agent is capable of accepting an electron. There can be no oxidation without simultaneous reduction.

The ORP probe measures electron activity. This requires that the probe must be both chemically inert and an electron conductor.

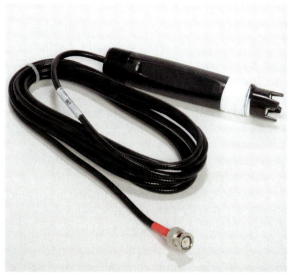

Photo 9-17. *An ORP probe indicates the oxidizing/reducing capability of pool water by measuring the electron activity.*

Platinum is the most frequently used material for ORP electrodes, except in applications containing very strong reducing solutions. In these applications, gold is the material chosen.

ORP probes only measure the ratio of oxidized to reduced forms of all chemicals in pool water. Calibration with a known standard is important for the ORP reading to be meaningful.

ORP Probe Cleaning

The most common probe used to estimate disinfectant levels is the ORP probe. Unfortunately, these probes foul or get dirty, causing the ORP reading to change even though the true ORP of the water does not. Manufacturers recognize that probes get dirty and include instructions in their manuals on how to clean them.

Signs that the probes are dirty include a slow response to disinfectant level changes in the water and low or inaccurate readings. Probes get dirty when materials accumulate on their surfaces in a thin film, which is often invisible to the human eye. The time it takes for ORP probes to foul varies from pool to pool, depending on what is present in the water and on the probe itself. Components in water that contribute to probe contamination include minerals, organics, perspiration, suntan lotions, body oils, urine, and cyanuric acid. Probe fouling can occur within days or weeks if cyanuric acid is present in the water.

Automated control system manufacturers include detailed instructions in their maintenance manuals on proper probe cleaning procedures. It is helpful to post these procedures near the probes for easy reference. Generally, these instructions are

- Turn off the power to the controller
- Remove the probes from the flow chamber
- Gently scrub with a clean soft brush, such as a toothbrush; use any mild detergent, such as hand soap, or toothpaste
- Reinstall the probes and turn on the power to the controller

In certain cases, ORP probe fouling is so rapid that an automatic ORP cleaner is more desirable than manually cleaning them. Manufacturers make automatic ORP cleaners designed to resolve the probe-fouling problem and permit long-term use of a probe.

Amperometric Probe

Amperometric probes detect disinfectant residual level changes by measuring the amount of current flow between the electrodes in the probe. They have a faster and more linear response to changes in the chlorine level in the water than ORP probes. There is a membrane that protects the sensing surface of an amperometric probe, so frequent probe fouling is greatly reduced.

Amperometric probes and controllers are used to a greater extent in Europe as a control for drinking water and swimming pool water. Their use in the North American market is growing, however, and these probes are also finding use in some automated residential spa applications.

Probe Location

Accurate chemical control cannot be accomplished unless the probes provide accurate readings. A key factor in obtaining accurate readings is the source of the water to be measured. Detailed considerations for source water to the probe chamber are

- The probe chamber source water should be downstream from the filter. Unfiltered water will plug some flow cells and may cause the probes to become dirty, providing inaccurate measurements.
- Water from the flow cells that contain the probes should not be plumbed to the suction side of the pump since the vacuum may damage the probe
- The probe chamber source water should be upstream from the pool/spa heater. Changes in water temperature can affect the accuracy of measurement.
- The probe chamber source water should be

upstream from the chemical injection point into the circulation line
- If possible, the probe chamber should not be installed in direct sunlight

Chemical Controllers

A chemical controller uses a microprocessor as its basis for operation. These devices can be simple, with only the ability to adjust pH and disinfectant levels, or complex, with the ability to incorporate remote communication, data logging, and water control factors other than pH and disinfectant level. These devices can control more than one pool or spa.

The simplest, most basic system does not display the actual pH and ORP readings. It has small indicator lights that inform the pool/spa operator whether or not the probe-measured values are within the operator-set limits.

As more functions are added, the control system becomes more complex. Digital readouts and alarms can be incorporated. Data storage, which is unaffected by power loss, can record disinfectant and pH values, circulation line pressures, backwash times, and chemical feed times.

Whether a system is a simple basic design or a complex multi-function device, there is one important common requirement: all feed systems, manual or automatic, must shut down if circulation to the pool or spa ceases. In addition, if the controller malfunctions, the fail-safe mode stops all feeder activation.

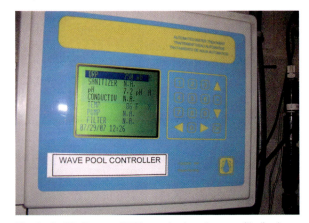

Photo 9-18. *Some ORP control systems will display pH and ORP levels and have warning alarms.*

Proportional Feed

Basic systems use a simple on/off control signal to the chemical feed pumps. This can result in greater changes to the pool/spa water chemistry

© National Swimming Pool Foundation 2017

than is desired. In this situation, the water chemistry may fluctuate from highs to lows and back again, or yo-yoing.

A proportional controller measures how far off the probe reading is from the desired set point. The chemical feeders are activated for a short period of time when the reading is close to the set point. When the reading is far away from the set point, the chemical feed will be activated for a longer period of time. This process continues until the set point is reached and maintained. This feature minimizes the highs and lows.

Remote Alarms

Most controller manufacturers offer a wide variety of alarm options, some of which are

- Chemical supply vat empty
- Chemical being fed for extended time
- pH too high and not correcting with chemical feed
- pH too low and not correcting with chemical feed
- Disinfectant too high
- Disinfectant too low
- Low circulation flow to the probes
- Low circulation flow to the pool

These alarms can be installed to activate lights, buzzers, or even horns.

Many systems can be connected to the internet to store data and send alarms to remote

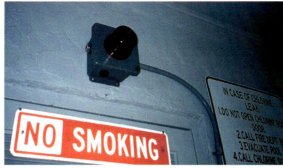

Photo 9-19. *Automated systems may incorporate a variety of alarms.*

locations. Systems can send alarms via various technologies/methods: calling a pager or cell phone, texting a smart phone, sending an e-mail or a fax, or a combination of these methods. The result is that operators can be notified about issues when they are at the pool or on the other side of the world. This helps to solve small problems before they become big problems to minimize the downtime of the pool or spa. Some systems interface with websites so the pool can be monitored and controlled remotely. Despite these advances, it remains vital to have an educated pool operator on site to diagnose and fix problems. It is ineffective to send an alarm and not have a person there who can fix the problem. These new technological systems do not replace the need to have people thinking and acting.

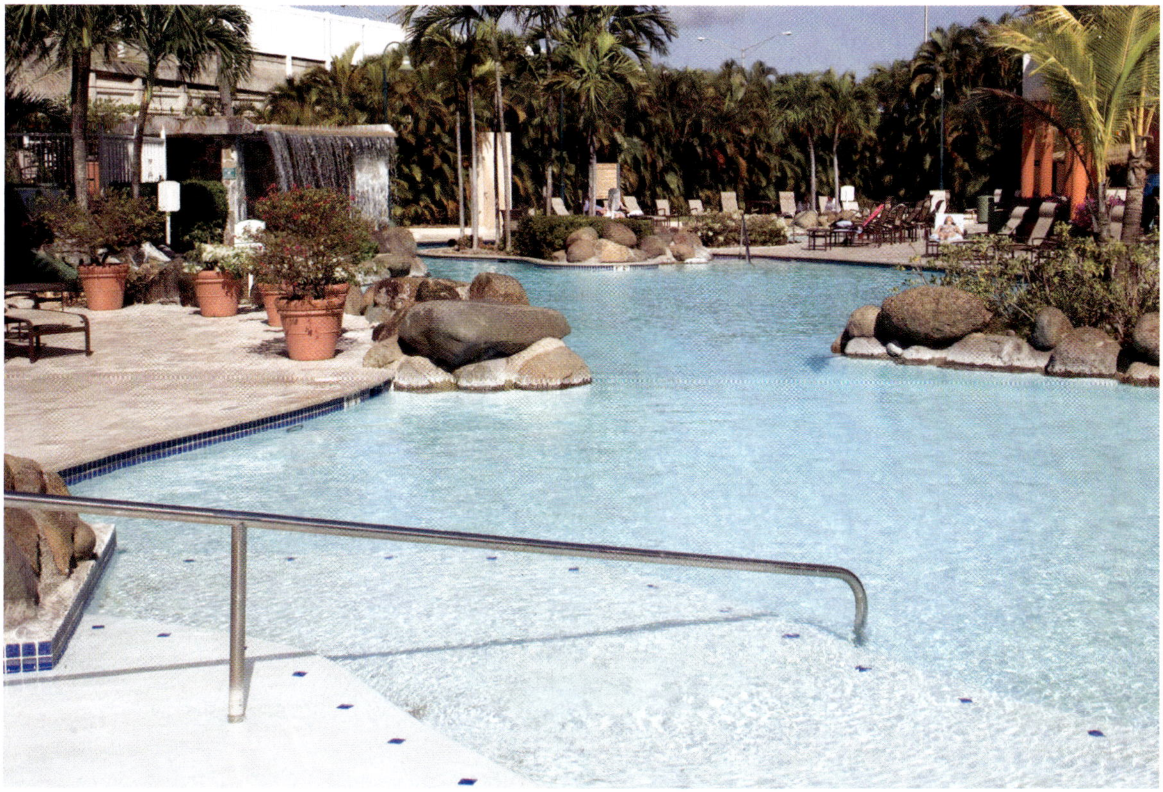
Photo 9-20. *Automatic controllers are recommended for shallow pools with high sun exposure.*

© National Swimming Pool Foundation 2017

1. Pool & Spa Management
2. Regulations & Guidelines
3. Essential Calculations
4. Pool Water Contamination
5. Disinfection
6. Water Balance
7. Pool & Spa Water Problems
8. Chemical Testing
9. Chemical Feed & Control
10. Water Circulation
11. Pool & Spa Filtration
12. Heating & Air Circulation
13. Spa & Therapy Operations
14. Facility Safety
15. Keeping Records
16. Maintenance Systems
17. Troubleshooting
18. Facility Renovation & Design
References

Notes

118

© National Swimming Pool Foundation 2017

Chapter 10:
Water Circulation

"Like swift water, an active mind never stagnates."

–Author Unknown

Swimming pool and spa water must always be maintained at proper disinfectant levels and kept free of harmful microorganisms, chemical consuming organics, and turbidity. For this to be accomplished, it is best to continuously circulate and filter the water. Circulation is the movement of water in the pool. Water circulation is influenced by many factors and is governed by the physical laws of hydraulics. Circulation is influenced by

- Inlet placement and design
- Circulation pumps
- Pool shape and contour
- Piping and fittings

Other system components, such as heaters, heat pumps, solar heating systems, and surface and main drain location, will also influence circulation to a lesser degree.

A proper circulation design will provide effective removal of surface water, which has the highest concentration of pollutants. There must be a constant and uniform dilution of treated and filtered water returning into the pool. There is no perfect pool circulation system. The calculations that describe the circulation of pool water are theoretical, and real-world pools will always fall short of meeting the mathematical model.

Circulation Systems

The main feature of a circulation system is the pump. The pump provides the motion of the water through the piping. Other necessary water quality functions, such as filtration, chemical treatment, and temperature control are meaningless unless the water is moving.

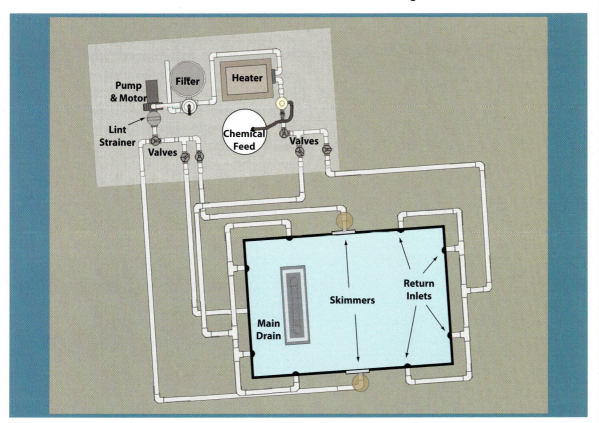

Illustration 10-1. *Direct suction circulation systems include the pump, filter, piping, valves, inlets, outlets, meters and gauges.*

© National Swimming Pool Foundation 2017

Circulation systems can be one of two designs: direct suction or overflow. Direct suction means the pump is drawing water directly from the return outlets or skimmer. In an overflow system, as people enter the pool, water is displaced. The displaced water is collected and held either in the gutter, skimmer system, or in a collection tank. The collection tank—sometimes called a surge tank or balance tank—collects and holds displaced water in a reservoir, which is open to the atmosphere, before the water goes to the pump. The water held in the gutter is pumped through the strainer, and water that is held in the skimmer is connected directly to the pump.

Once water is collected, it is moved to the pump by gravity toward the vacuum created by the pump. The pump provides the necessary force to move the water through the piping, pressure system components, and back into the pool through the return inlets.

It is common practice for public circulation systems to operate 24 hours per day. Residential circulation systems typically run fewer hours per day. Local codes may allow for the system to be idle for periods of time, or operate at a reduced flow using variable speed motors, discussed later in this chapter.

Labeling all circulation components helps operators understand the operation of the system. Color-coding also helps identify the lines and avoid any potential plumbing error. All equipment in the circulation system must be easily accessible for maintenance and replacement purposes.

Turnover Rate

Turnover rate is the time it takes for the circulation system to move the number of gallons equal to the volume of water in the pool through the filtration equipment. Water is processed through the filter, chemically treated, and then returned to the pool. In the pool, the filtered water is diluted with the unfiltered water. Continuous removal of pollutants occurs by the process of partial dilution. This course of action must be repeated enough times to achieve acceptable water quality standards.

The mathematical model standard for one turnover is the filtration of 63% of the water molecules, leaving 37% of the water unfiltered. A second turnover reduces the unfiltered level to 14%. After a third turnover, the unfiltered water is 5%. It is only after four turnovers that the amount of unfiltered water is reduced to 2%, which many codes require on a daily basis. For this reason, the turnover rate requirement or code standard for most commercial swimming pool operations is six hours.

These calculations are based on the theory of partial dilution, and the calculations assume that there is no further addition of pollutants. In the real world of pool operations, a pool is receiving continuous pollutant loading, even during the hours when the pool is closed. For this reason, pools are often designed to circulate water at least 25% above the code requirement. Larger pumps should not be added to existing systems since the higher flow may exceed the maximum flow velocity for the anti-entrapment drain covers, filters and piping.

Turnover rate requirements vary for different

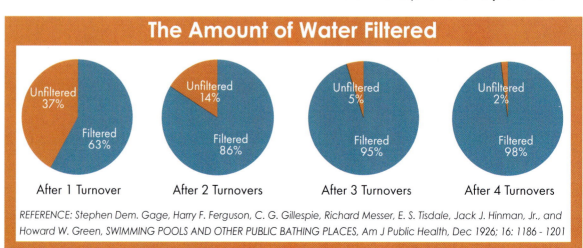

The Amount of Water Filtered

After 1 Turnover — Unfiltered 37% / Filtered 63%

After 2 Turnovers — Unfiltered 14% / Filtered 86%

After 3 Turnovers — Unfiltered 5% / Filtered 95%

After 4 Turnovers — Unfiltered 2% / Filtered 98%

REFERENCE: Stephen Dem. Gage, Harry F. Ferguson, C. G. Gillespie, Richard Messer, E. S. Tisdale, Jack J. Hinman, Jr., and Howard W. Green, SWIMMING POOLS AND OTHER PUBLIC BATHING PLACES, Am J Public Health, Dec 1926; 16: 1186 - 1201

Illustration 10-2

© National Swimming Pool Foundation 2017

types of water use. This has to do with pollution load based on the type of activity and the volume of water in the facility. The code requirement of turnover rate determines the necessary minimum flow rate for any pool operation. The following turnover rates are considered standard in most jurisdictions:

- Swimming pools—six hours
- Spas—30 minutes
- Wading pools—one to two hours
- Waterparks/specialty pools—one to four hours
- Hospital/health club pools—as low as three hours

The turnover rate is calculated in hours using the following formula:

$$\text{Turnover Rate (hr)} = \text{Pool Volume} \div \text{Flow Rate} \div 60 \text{ min/hour}$$

Example 10-1:

You have a 200,000 gallon pool with a flow rate of 750 gpm. What is the turnover rate?

$$\text{TOR} = 200,000 \div 750 \div 60$$
$$\text{TOR} = 4.44 \text{ hours}$$

Example 10-1: Metric

You have a 756,000 liter pool with a flow rate of 3,000 lpm. What is the turnover rate?

$$\text{TOR} = 756,000 \div 3,000 \div 60$$
$$\text{TOR} = 4.2 \text{ hours}$$

Flow Rate

If the pool volume is in gallons, the flow rate must be in gallons/min. If the volume is in liters, then the flow rate must be in liters/min. Flow rate is measured with a flow meter installed on the return flow line downstream from all equipment and just before the water is returned to the pool. There must be sufficient flow rate to achieve the required turnover rate. The relationship between flow rate and turnover rate is

$$\text{Flow Rate} = \text{Pool Volume} \div \text{Turnover Rate} \div 60 \text{ min/hour}$$

The flow rate necessary to meet all operational requirements is called the design flow rate and should always be a higher requirement than the minimum code standard. The actual flow rate should always be maintained near or above the calculated minimum code flow rate. Obstructions to water flow result in a decrease in flow rate.

Simply cleaning the filter and removing debris from the skimmer or from hair and lint baskets will usually return the flow to the proper level.

Suction Side Elements and Entrapment

In a circulation system, water must be pumped from one location to another. The process of pumping water creates a risk to people, who can be entrapped in the vacuum flow created by the pump. Once entrapped, a person is at risk of injury or drowning in a pool or spa. There are five different types of entrapment:

1. Hair entrapment
2. Limb entrapment
3. Body entrapment
4. Evisceration/disembowelment
5. Mechanical entrapment

Entrapment types are discussed in greater detail in the Facility Safety chapter.

A system can be designed and operated to reduce or eliminate the possibility that direct suction can entrap and injure a person. The first line of defense involves ensuring that a drain cover is in place over any suction outlet to prevent entrapment or evisceration. Cover removal should require the use of a tool. Manufacturers often sell screws that are different colors to make them more obvious when the pool or spa is being inspected.

According to the Virginia Graeme Baker Pool & Spa Safety Act (VGB Act), anti-entrapment drain covers must be used. In the U.S., effective December 20, 2008, all drain covers for public pools and spas are required to comply. Compliant covers display specifications indicating maximum flow rate, model number, lifespan, whether the cover is suited for floor or wall use, and a statement indicating that a third party has tested

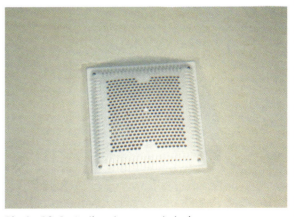

Photo 10-1. *Anti-entrapment drain cover*

and certified that the cover complies with the ANSI/APSP-16 standard. The ANSI/APSP-16 standard is the successor standard to the ASME/ANSI A112.19.8-2007 standard. These covers should be installed so that the maximum flow rating is not exceeded. The anti-entrapment covers are designed to keep body parts from blocking the cover. In addition, they prevent hair from entangling around the cover.

Entrapment can be further minimized by other design criteria. Dual main drains, which are covered with an anti-entrapment cover, further reduce the risk of entrapment when plumbed and spaced at a sufficient distance apart to ensure that an individual cannot block both drains.

Removing direct suction is the most effective way to reduce entrapment risk. Unfortunately, many laws require main drains and direct suction outlets in pools and spas. Some systems remove direct suction outlets from the pool or spa by using a gutter system or a surge tank (gravity systems). In these systems, water leaves the pool by atmospheric pressure and flows to a collection pit or balance tank. The water in the collection or balance tank is then drawn up by the pump's suction. The pump creates pressure, forcing water through the piping, the other system components, and back to the pool.

Properly engineered and maintained atmospheric vents can be incorporated in circulation systems to reduce the risk of evisceration and body and limb entrapment (Aquatic Safety Compendium™ - Chapter 7). There is no evidence that vent lines prevent hair entrapment. Alternatively, manufactured Safety Vacuum Release Systems (SVRS) are included in the circulation system to help prevent entrapment. SVRS devices should comply with the ASME/ANSI A112.199.17 "Safety Vacuum Release Systems for Swimming Pool Suction Fittings and Drains" and successor standard ANSI/APSP 16-2011. SVRS may provide additional protection against body and possibly limb entrapment. There is no evidence that SVRS prevents hair entrapment or evisceration.

Main Drains

Main drains are usually located at the deepest part of the pool. A controlled amount of water is drawn through the main drain to the circulation system.

Main drains are sized during the pool design phase by the engineer or architect. There should be no changes made to the size, design, location, or operation of the main drain in later years, unless approved by the local health agency and supported by an engineering evaluation. Dangerous conditions could result, with the possibility of serious trauma or even death to a user.

Photo 10-2. *There is usually one valve to control the flow from the main drain and one valve to control the surface flow.*

© National Swimming Pool Foundation 2017

The openings in the main drain covers are part of the original design and are controlled by standards. The main drain should be visually observed on a daily basis as part of the vacuuming process and any cracked or broken element is cause for pool closure until the cover is replaced. Fingers or hair could become entrapped in the defect.

There should be a method of controlling the amount of water exiting the pool from the main drain. It is important to maximize the flow from the surface, which has the greatest concentration of pollutants and floating debris.

It is also important to minimize the flow through the main drain for entrapment considerations. The flow velocity through a main drain must not exceed the maximum flow for the main drain cover. In the case of dual drains that are connected, the flow velocity should not exceed half of the maximum flow rate for each cover. Following this procedure ensures that, should one cover be blocked, the maximum flow for the other cover will not be exceeded. Jurisdictional codes may have requirements about the water flow velocity through a main drain. At a minimum, the pool operator should always follow code.

Surface Water Removal

The surface of a pool is where the highest concentration of contamination exists. Windborne debris, algae spores, user bodily discharge, and user oils all collect at the surface. The pool's disinfectant level is usually lowest at the surface. It is at the surface that the user may swallow water. In addition, the user's nose, ears, and eyes have the greatest exposure to water at the surface.

Water flow patterns are almost completely determined by the surface and return inlet placement and control. These patterns eliminate the presence of dead spots or areas of poor circulation. Dead spots can support algae growth and collect dirt and debris.

Health departments often require that the surface water be the highest percentage of the circulation. Some codes may require that under certain circumstances, all of the circulation water must be removed from the surface. The commonly accepted practice is that 75% of the water be removed from the surface. Some codes allow a 50/50 ratio, and others have no

requirement at all. Codes may also require that the skimmer system or main drains be able to handle 100% of the flow.

Water may be removed from the surface throughout the entire perimeter of the pool or through selected point removal locations. Perimeter removal is through gutters, while point removal is through a box-like device called a skimmer.

Gutters

Gutters are trough-like designs that work on the principle of surface tension removal during periods of pool non-use. The water level must be carefully controlled to no more than ¼ inch (6 mm) above the lip of the gutter. In this manner, a surface tension draw of the top layer of the pool water is maintained. Surface debris and contamination are removed from the pool and filtered or oxidized.

During periods of use, user action creates a wave motion or a rolling effect. The surface water is trapped in the gutter and removed for processing.

There are several types of gutter designs. Older pools have what is called a scum gutter. This is a rather narrow gutter that can be recessed or partially open. The volume capacity of a scum gutter is very low and it may be difficult to achieve a 50% circulation draw through these older devices.

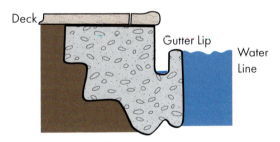

Scum Gutter

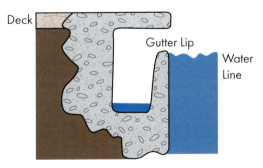

Surge Gutter

Illustration 10-3. *Two styles of gutter design*

Photo 10-3. *A rim-flow gutter system with grating. Since users come in direct contact with the grating in a rim-flow system, the grating should have tamper proof fasteners holding it in place.*

Surge gutters have a much larger capacity and are usually recessed. Both surge and scum gutters require frequent maintenance to prevent the build-up of oils and debris that can contribute to the growth of algae.

Scum and surge gutters must be monitored by the pool lifeguard staff. Young or inexperienced users can use these gutters as a hand-hold device. They are able to wall walk down the pool to depths that are over their heads. When they release their grip, these users can then panic when they realize their predicament, and a drowning can occur.

Surge gutters are highly effective at removing large quantities of water for filtration and chemical processing. They can be designed for wave suppression in competition pools, and provide for easy maintenance access by having removable top plates. Surge gutters can store huge quantities of water and provide surge control for large numbers of users.

Rim flow gutters are 1 foot wide and generally have a 2 inch slope from the water-edge tile to the back where the outlet drains are located. There is little or no storage capacity in these gutters for user load surge. It is easy to flood this type of gutter, which results in loss of skimming action under heavy user loading.

Rim flow gutters are perimeter gutters that are more typically found on recreational pools. An integral part of the rim-flow system is the grating.

The grating acts as a skimmer, preventing large debris from entering the filter system. Since users come in direct contact with the grating in a rim-flow system, the grating should have tamper proof fasteners holding it in place.

Surface Skimmers

Skimmers are box-like openings in the pool wall, located at the surface. Pool codes and regulations commonly require one skimmer for each 400 to 500 square feet (37 to 46 square meters) of water surface area or fraction thereof. Skimmers are located to maintain effective skimming over the entire surface area of the pool.

Some codes limit the size of the pool that can use skimmers. Limits may also be placed on the number of square feet or square meters of water surface area that a skimmer can service. The minimum water flow through a skimmer may be defined by code—for example, 30 gallons or 114 liters per minute—as well as manufacturer's specifications.

The operation of a skimmer is engineered into the pool operation at the design stage. No later changes should be made without specific health department approval and a professional engineering review.

The construction of skimmers today utilizes PVC or other plastic materials. The skimmer is installed so that the pool wall opening is midway up the skimmer face.

Mounted at the entrance to the skimmer body or housing is a floating weir. This weir will always adjust to the level of the water, providing the skimming or sheeting action. The operation of the circulation pump draws water from the pool. The water flows through the pool wall opening and over the weir. The weir acts as a barrier for water and debris, not allowing a backwards motion into the pool.

Inside the skimmer housing is a basket for the collection of larger debris. The skimmer basket must be cleaned on a routine basis to maintain proper water flow. Most skimmers have a design feature to adjust flow through the skimmer. This allows for the adjustment of individual skimmers to work as part of a system, providing surface water removal from all areas of a pool.

Some skimmer designs may have an equalizer line attached to the skimmer body. A springloaded check valve will be a part of this design. Some skimmers will also come with a

© National Swimming Pool Foundation 2017

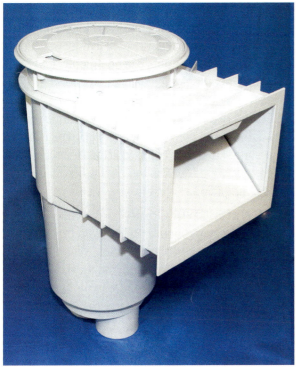

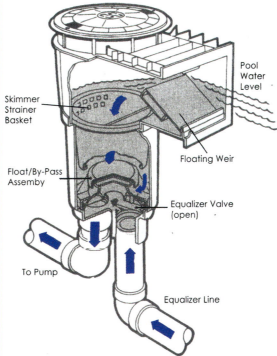

Skimmer Strainer Basket

Pool Water Level

Floating Weir

Float/By-Pass Assemby

Equalizer Valve (open)

To Pump

Equalizer Line

Illustration 10-4. *Surface skimmers are usually used for spas and smaller pools.*

float valve. The normal flow of the water through the skimmer keeps the equalizer valve closed. Should there be an interruption of the water flow through the skimmer, the float valve closes and the springloaded equalizer valve opens, causing water to flow out of the pool through the skimmer equalizer line. If the water level falls below the skimmer wall outlet, the equalizer line becomes active. This ensures that the pump will have adequate water flow and not lose prime.

Care must be taken to never allow direct suction to occur with an equalizer line. These lines are usually located about one foot below the water surface. If the water level drops below the skimmer opening, the pool should be closed.

Photo 10-4. *Vacuum outlet cover*

Vacuum Fittings

One of the basic considerations for any pool operation is that of maintaining a clean pool floor surface. This requires frequent vacuuming of the pool bottom. To assist in this effort, most codes require that every pool and spa have some method to draw water from the pool, either portable or plumbed directly.

The vacuum may be provided by the main circulation pump, a secondary dedicated vacuum-only pump, or even a robotic vacuum device. Pools that have skimmers may provide the vacuum through the skimmer itself. When using the skimmer to vacuum, it may be necessary to change the restriction or even close off other skimmers to achieve the necessary water flow. The normal valve settings should be marked so that each skimmer may be returned to its proper setting once vacuuming is completed.

Some wall vacuum outlets are plumbed directly to the suction or influent side of the pump. This can result in severe trauma or death if the vacuum line is operational while the pool is open for use. The pool operator should insure that the vacuum outlet is always covered and the vacuum line is inoperable when the pool is open for use. Vacuum outlet covers should be spring-loaded and in place at all times. This item should be inspected daily for damage and operability.

The distance between wall vacuum outlets is

© National Swimming Pool Foundation 2017

usually no more than 50 feet (7.62 meters). This will allow for the use of a shorter vacuum hose, which makes vacuuming more efficient. Some codes specify the distance in their requirements.

Collection or Balance Tanks

In certain regions, collection or balance tanks are commonly installed with a pool. In these systems, the water is collected in a tank called a collection tank or, in a more complex system, a balancing tank. One function of these devices is to isolate the pool from direct suction to the pump. They are open to the atmosphere and must be sized to provide an adequate reservoir for the pump suction.

A collection tank could be used for other purposes, such as maintaining water levels in rim flow gutter systems and in vacuum filtering. It is not normally recommended that chemicals be added to the collection tank, especially if there is a vacuum filter. The pH and possible corrosivity of chemicals could cause harm to circulation system components downstream. Chemicals added to the vacuum filter collection tank may result in an increased need for filter maintenance and a shorter life span of the filter elements.

The balancing tank or surge tank is more complex than the simple collection tank. These systems actually hold water in reserve that has been displaced by users. This allows for skimming to be maintained at all times, whether the pool is in use or not. The commonly accepted user displacement is 20 gallons (76 liters) of water per adult using the pool. If a pool had a user load of 200 persons, this would require a storage capacity of 4,000 gallons (15,142 liters). The surge capability of this device allows for the release of water back to the pool as users exit, thus maintaining skimming.

Pool Water Level Control

Often there is an equalizing line from the pool to the collection or balancing tank. When the circulation pump is turned off, the level of the pool water and the level of the water in the tank will be equal due to atmospheric pressure. The equalizer line, with the use of an elbow and a vertical pipe section, can be used for pool water level control. The water level in the equalizer vertical section will always be equal to that in the pool, whether the pump is operating or not.

Pool water level control devices can be either simple float valves that actuate a mechanical auto-fill valve or complex probes that provide signals to microprocessors. In either case, the operator must remember that the pool water level should be controlled to ¼ inch (6 mm) maximum above the gutter lip to maintain proper skimming.

Vacuum Filters

This filter will be discussed in more detail in the Pool & Spa Filtration chapter. The placement of

Illustration 10-5. *Balance tank with float valve and atmospheric vent*

Photo 10-5. *Vacuum style filters are installed in a tank of water open to atmosphere, prior to the pump.*

© National Swimming Pool Foundation 2017

the filter prior to the pump requires an impeller that has more suction capability. A large amount of the work that an impeller must perform is now on the influent side of the pump. As the filter becomes loaded with oils and debris, the water flow to the pump is decreased. This can result in pump and motor failure if proper water flow is not maintained for a period of time.

Vacuum filters are easily damaged by excessive vacuum forces. Over time, the filter elements may be damaged allowing water to flow into the pump unfiltered. In turn, this lowers the water quality in the pool and increases the demand for chemicals. Vacuum filter elements should be manually examined on a regular basis to ensure that no water can pass unfiltered.

Vacuum Gauges

The influent or incoming flow of water to a pump should never be restricted under normal operating conditions. Restrictions do occur, however, as hair and lint baskets, skimmer baskets, or vacuum filters become clogged with debris. This causes the pump to work harder to maintain prime. A vacuum gauge located just prior to the pump allows the pool operator to measure just how hard the pump is working on the suction side.

The vacuum gauge may be mounted on the drain port of the hair and lint basket assembly, if there is one, or on the piping just prior to the pump inlet port. Vacuum is negative pressure, and a vacuum gauge measures this as inches of mercury (in. Hg) or kilopascals (kPa).

The pool operator should know what the base, or clean, normal vacuum gauge reading is for

the system. As debris builds up, there will be an increase in vacuum. Over time, by observing the system, watching the flow meter for a decrease in water flow, and listening to the pump for sounds of cavitation, the maximum vacuum reading for normal operation of the system can be determined.

Both the base and upper limits of the vacuum should be posted in the pump room for reference. The vacuum gauge reading is very important in determining when to clean a vacuum filter or the hair and lint basket.

Circulation Pumps

The pump is the main part of the circulation system. It is the component that causes the water to move. Swimming pools use only one type of pump for circulation purposes: a centrifugal pump. A centrifugal pump has an impeller that rotates on an axis creating a centrifugal force and displacement of the water.

There are two types of centrifugal pumps used. The most common is the self-priming pump. This type of pump can re-prime itself using only the water in the pump housing. The self-priming pump will not lose prime even with large amounts of air in the system. Pool pumps that are located above the pool water level must be of this type.

A flooded suction pump will lose prime when air is in the system. A flooded suction pump generally runs at lower revolutions per minute, and, therefore, has a longer life expectancy. Flooded suction pumps are used in systems where the pump is located below the pool water level.

Every pump has the same basic components:
- The volute or pump housing
- The shaft, which is an extension of the pump motor
- Mechanical shaft seals
- A motor adaptor and seal plate
- The impeller

The volute is sometimes called the diffuser. It gives the self-priming pump the ability to handle air and re-prime itself. The shaft is an extension of the pump motor and provides the mechanical motion to the impeller. (See Illustration 10-6.)

Older pumps may still use lubricated fiber rings to seal the shaft. Most pumps today use a mechanical shaft seal that operates without

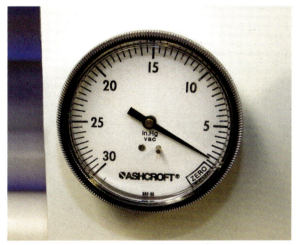

Photo 10-6. *Vacuum gauges measure in inches of mercury or kilopascals.*

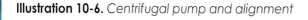

Illustration 10-6. *Centrifugal pump and alignment*

Shaft

Motor Adaptor and
Seal Plate

Mechanical Seal

Impeller

Volute

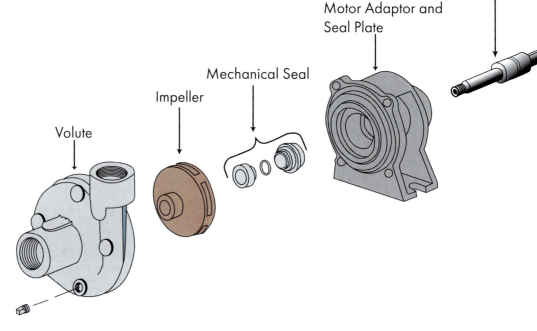

external lubrication and does not require adjustment.

Some pumps have their own shaft that must be coupled to the motor shaft. These are called frame-mounted pumps. The close-coupled pump uses the motor shaft and relies on the bearing support of the motor.

Impeller

The impeller causes the water to flow. As it rotates, the center or eye of the impeller draws water in from the suction or influent piping from the pool. The water is then thrown out as with a flinging motion by the centrifugal movement

of the impeller. The volute, or housing, collects the water, and as the velocity of flow increases, pressure is created. The water exits the pump through the effluent or out-going piping. It is at this point that the necessary force is developed to push water through the circulation system and back to the pool.

Centrifugal pumps are not positive displacement pumps. For each revolution of the impeller, a different amount of water will be discharged depending on conditions. The most important factors are exit pressure, air in the system, and a restricted influent line. A blocked suction line and air in the system can cause cavitation and damage the pump.

Cavitation

Cavitation occurs when the impeller is starved for water and cannot maintain the discharge requirements. The sound of the pump changes when it is cavitating. In severe cases the pump and motor may vibrate. The operator must check the obvious reasons for cavitation:

- Debris in the skimmer basket
- Debris in the hair and lint basket
- A dirty vacuum filter
- A partially closed or restricted suction line
- A throttling valve on the effluent line not properly restricted
- A leak in the plumbing on the vacuum side of the circulation system

Cavitation is a symptom of a problem and the

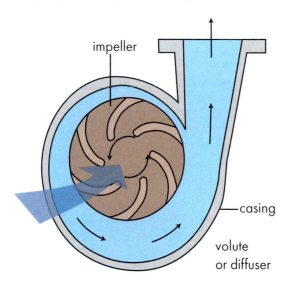

impeller

casing

volute
or diffuser

Illustration 10-7. *Centrifugal pump*

© National Swimming Pool Foundation 2017

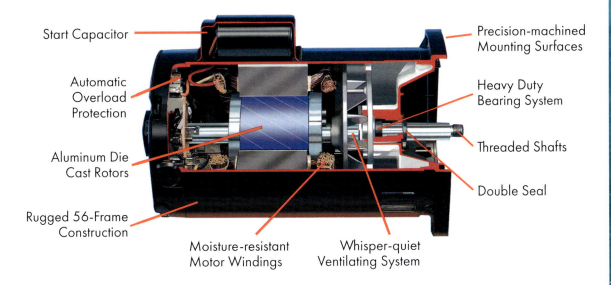

Start Capacitor

Automatic Overload Protection

Aluminum Die Cast Rotors

Rugged 56-Frame Construction

Moisture-resistant Motor Windings

Whisper-quiet Ventilating System

Precision-machined Mounting Surfaces

Heavy Duty Bearing System

Threaded Shafts

Double Seal

Illustration 10-8. *Pool pump motor. The pool operator should look to outside professional, licensed help when servicing or repairing motors.*

operator must take immediate corrective action. If allowed to continue, cavitation may result in serious damage to the pump, motor, or both.

Output Pressure Gauge

A pressure gauge should be mounted on the discharge piping immediately after the pump. This gauge measures the output performance of the pump and is important to the understanding of the overall operation of the circulation system. The output pressure is the driving force for circulation and is measured in pounds per square inch (psi). In Europe and other countries, this pressure is measured in bar or kilo pascals (kPa).

If the pressure reading is too low, the necessary flow and turnover rates will not be achieved. The pump vacuum and pressure gauges can be used to evaluate the circulation system performance or total dynamic head.

Total Dynamic Head

Total dynamic head (TDH) is a measure of the total resistance to flow in the system. All components,piping, pipe fittings, filters, heaters, outlets, inlets,and the water level of the return fittings into the pool have a resistance to flow. This is calculated by the design engineer and is required to properly size the pump and motor.

The TDH can be measured for any operating system by using the pump vacuum and pressure gauges. The vacuum gauge reading is multiplied by the factor 1.133 to determine the suction side head. The pressure gauge is multiplied by 2.31 to determine the pressure side head. The two heads are added together to find the actual operating TDH of the system.

The TDH should be measured and recorded on a regular basis using a clean filter. Variations over time may indicate that the impeller is wearing or the filter media needs to be replaced.

Motors

Pump motors used in pool and spa operations have many variations in design and installation. Smaller pump motors (three horsepower or less) are usually compact, open designs. They have an extended shaft that allows the pump adapter to be mounted directly to the housing. Larger motors follow the design standards of the National Electrical Manufacturer's Association (NEMA). Quite often these motors are of the frame-mounted design requiring a coupling to the pump.

Motors used on pools or spas are normally 115/230 volt, single phase, or 230/460 volt 3-phase AC. Motors at 5 horsepower and above are usually 200 volt AC or 230/460 volt AC. The 230/460 volt AC is obsolete, and the operator should be aware of this for replacement purposes.

The operator should look to outside professional licensed help when servicing or repairing motors. Most motors are capable of handling two voltages, and the motor terminals must be connected properly to the available voltage supply.

The motor name plate provides the necessary replacement information, and this data should be part of the operator's files. With the availability of digital cameras today, it is easy to take a picture of the motor name plate for file purposes. This should be done while the motor is relatively new and the name plate is easily readable.

Motor Energy Efficiency

Some states have enacted new regulations requiring more energy efficient motors. For example, the California Energy Commission Title 20. This regulation requires the use of variable speed motors, which are significantly more energy efficient. Pool pump motors with a capacity of 1 hp or more must have the capability of operating at two or more speeds with a low speed having a rotation rate that is no more than one-half of the motor's maximum rotation rate.

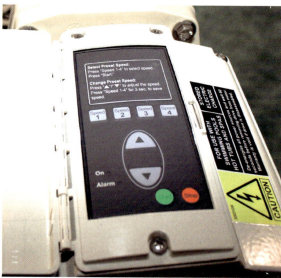

Photo 10-7. *Installing variable speed motors can significantly reduce energy costs.*

Pool pump motor controls must have the capability of operating variable speed pool pumps with at least two speeds. The default circulation speed shall be the lowest speed, with a high speed override capability being for a temporary period not to exceed one normal cycle. Having

the motors run at the slower speed overnight when the pool is not being used is a significant energy savings.

While these energy efficient regulations are primarily for residential applications, new laws may apply to commercial facilities. The pool operator should check with their jurisdictional codes.

Valves

Valves control or regulate the flow of the water in pool and spa circulation. There are several common types of valves. They are

- Gate valves
- Ball valves
- Butterfly or wafer valves
- Multi-port valves
- Globe valves
- Check valves

Valves can be operated manually, which is more common, or automatically in sophisticated, electronically controlled systems. All valves create a resistance to flow and thus must be part of the engineering of the system. Valves can be located on the suction side and/or the pressure side of the pump.

> ### Warning
> Always open all air bleed valves and turn off the pump before changing valve positions or removing any clamps or fittings. Failure to follow proper procedures could result in violent separation of the equipment causing possible serious injury or death.

Gate Valves

Gate valves are either totally open or totally closed. A gate valve should never be in a partial position. To close a gate valve, the handle is turned clockwise, to screw down the gate. Follow the old axiom righty tighty, lefty loosey.

Ball Valves

Ball valves have a housing that encloses the ball. The valve handle is usually shaped like a pointer. When the handle is in-line with the piping, the valve is open. Usually the valve is closed when the valve is at a right angle to the

© National Swimming Pool Foundation 2017

Photo 10-8. *Ball valves come in different configurations. Three-way and two-way valves are shown.*

piping. This is not always the case; some valves have the opposite orientation. The valve handle is connected to a ball with a circular bore through it. Ball valves are regulating valves because they can be totally closed, totally open, or any position in between.

Butterfly Valves

A butterfly or wafer valve is commonly used in larger, more complex, multi-filter systems. The valve positioning is the same as the ball valve. When the handle is in-line with the piping, the valve is open. The valve is closed when the valve is at a right angle to the piping. The butterfly or wafer is attached to the handle and rotates on axis as the valve handle is turned.

Multi-port Valves

There are two types of multi-port valves: slide and rotary. Multi-port valves are usually found on smaller pool operations or residential pools. It is important that the pump motor is always turned off and the air bleed valves opened up before changing a multi-port valve position.

The purpose of a multi-port valve is to reduce the number of valves necessary to operate a system. The piping from the pump, filter, and waste lines can all be attached to just one component valve.

Rotary Valves

The function of the circulation system may be easily changed with a rotary valve. Some rotary valves have simple filter and backwash positions. Others are more complicated with bypass, rinse, circulate, and off positions. The operator must always follow the manufacturer's instructions carefully when using this type of valve. It is usually suggested that a rinse cycle be used between backwash and filter operations to reduce the possibility of dirt particles becoming trapped in the mechanism.

Rotary valves are not designed for universal operations but are media dependent. A different valve may be necessary for a sand filter as opposed to a D.E. filter.

Photo 10-10. *Some rotary valves have bypass, rinse, circulate, and on-off positions.*

Photo 10-9. *Butterfly valves with electric actuator*

Push-Pull Valves

The push-pull or slide valve is usually a large cylindrical body with incoming and outgoing ports. The cylinder contains a movable shaft that has wafers to direct the flow of the water. There is no standard for the normal operating position and the manufacturer's operating instruction manual must be consulted for safe procedures. The pump must always be turned off before changing this valve position.

Check Valves

These valves are usually cylindrical in shape. Inside they contain a spring-loaded device that requires a certain pressure to depress the spring and allows liquid to flow in one direction through the valve. The valve is designed to seal and prevent flow in the opposite direction. Valves contain an arrow on the outer body to show the direction of flow. Water that contains particles can prevent the valve from sealing and may allow liquid to pass in the wrong direction.

Piping

If the pump is the heart of the circulation system, then the suction-side piping components are the veins and the pressure-side components are the arteries. Every foot (or meter) of pipe and every fitting, elbow, connection, and tee contribute to total dyanamic head and subsequent resistance to flow or friction loss. The diameter of the pipe and the material used to manufacture the pipe also factor into the total dynamic head losses.

The efficiency of water flow is also affected by the velocity of the water. The velocity of water as it flows through a pipe is determined by two elements:

- The size of the pipe in which the water is flowing
- The head pressure developed by the pump

The faster the water moves the more friction it creates. For a given pipe diameter, if the flow rate is doubled, the friction loss will increase by approximately four times. As a result, installation of large diameter pipe and as few elbows and fittings as is reasonable is ideal for energy conservation. Once the piping is installed, however, the operator has limited ability to alter pipe size.

PVC piping and fittings shall be non-toxic

Potable water	Dark Blue
Filter water	Aqua
Skimmer or gutter lines	Olive Green
Main drain line	Black
Alum	Orange
Chlorine	Yellow
Soda ash	White
Ozone	Light Green
Acid	Pink
Backwash waste	Dark Brown
Sewer	Dark Grey
Deck drains	Light Brown
Compressed air	Dark Green
Gas chlorine	Red

Illustration 10-9. *Sample color-coding for pool and spa piping*

and able to withstand the design operating pressure. The pool circulation piping shall be at least schedule 40 PVC weight and comply with ANSI/NSF Standard 14 "Plastics Piping System Components and Related Materials."

Piping that is exposed to damage by freezing shall have a uniform slope in one direction and be valved to facilitate drainage. As an alternative, the piping should be designed to allow for water removal to prevent damage from freezing. Plastic pipe subject to a period of prolonged sunlight exposure should be coated to protect it from ultraviolet light degradation.

Pump room re-piping must be accomplished by a trained, licensed pool professional. All new piping should conform to the original specifications. Any changes must have prior approval from the appropriate authority.

To assist the pool operator in performing the daily maintenance requirements, all circulation components should be labeled, tagged, or even color-coded. To assist in operations, a valve identification and performance chart should be

Water Circulation

© National Swimming Pool Foundation 2017

developed and posted in the pump area. Many states and local agencies have specific color-coding requirements. The color coding helps the operator identify the flow of water through the pipes, such as filtered water, backwash water, heated water, etc. A sample color coding system is shown in Illustration 10-9. Pool operators should abide by any color-coding system regulations that may apply where they work.

Pressure Side Elements

All equipment located after the pump operates under pressure and must be designed and operated with this in mind. The pool operator must be aware at all times of the dangers associated with pressurized systems. A normal by-product of a centrifugal pump is the creation of air in the system. This air will collect at the highest point in the system, usually the filter, and is compressible. Any change in the hydraulic flow, such as changing a valve position, can result in a water-hammer effect, causing the system components to separate in a violent manner. Before adjusting any pressurized component, shut the pump off and bleed the air from the system.

Pressure Filters

This filter will be discussed in more detail in the Pool & Spa Filtration chapter. The placement of the filter after the pump requires an impeller that has more pressure capability. A large amount of the work that an impeller must perform is now on the effluent side of the pump. As the filter traps oils and debris, the water flow from the pump, or the flow rate, decreases, the influent pressure before the filter increases, and the effluent pressure after the filter decreases.

Pressure filter media is easily affected by excessive pressure forces. Over time, the filter media may be damaged or by-passed and water can flow to the pool unfiltered. This, in turn, lowers the water quality in the pool and increases the demand for chemicals. Pressure filter media should be manually examined on a regular basis to ensure that no water can pass unfiltered.

Separation Tanks

Separation tanks are utilized to collect spent D.E. rather than dumping the used material into

Photo 10-11. *Separation Tanks have internal bags to collect the spent D.E. powder.*

the environment or local sewer systems. Many regulations dictate the use of a separation tank. As the vacuum or pressure D.E. filter is cleansed, the spent media is forced under pressure to the separation tank. A dedicated backwash pump, a vacuum pump, or the main circulation pump could be used for this purpose.

An important consideration is that the separation tank is a pressure vessel and all of the warnings and guidelines associated with pressure operations must be followed. Separation tanks need to have a manual means to release air or a lid that allows pressure to be released slowly and safely. Not all regulations allow for the slow release design and require air release valves.

The interior of the separation tank contains a collection bag that separates the spent D.E. from the effluent filter water. The water is then discharged from the system into the sewer inlet. The contents of the collection bag are then transferred to a refuse bag and discarded into the solid waste disposal.

Heaters

Pools have been heated for more than 70 years. The heat source can be electric, natural gas, propane, solar, air or geothermal heat pumps, or even oil-fired. In all cases, there is a hydraulic or friction loss as the water moves through the device.

Before being heated, the pool or spa water must be properly filtered. The water then enters the heater through the inlet fitting. In some cases, there is a metallic heat sink made of copper or

Photo 10-12. *Natural gas pool heater*

Photo 10-13. *Flow meters are generally mounted on the return piping after all other system components but before any chemical feed injection.*

stainless steel attached to the inlet and outlet fittings. The purpose of the heat sink is to radiate the high temperature of the water and cool it enough to allow the remainder of the circulation piping to be PVC.

In most cases, heater manufacturers require a check valve between the filter and the heater as well as between the heater and the chemical feeders. In this manner, hot water cannot back-flow into the filter and distort the elements when the pump is turned off. Likewise, chemicals cannot back-flow into the heater, which could corrode or create scale on the heater elements.

In some installations, the heater piping is equipped with a bypass line and valve. This allows for a controlled amount of circulation through the heater to control heat rise. It also allows for a minimal amount of water flow through the heater in the warm season. Always follow the installation and operating instructions provided by the heater manufacturer.

Flow Meters

All public pools and spas should be equipped with a flow measuring device that indicates the rate of flow through the circulation system. The flow meter usually reads in gallons per minute as well as liters per minute.

The flow meter should be properly sized for the design flow rate and must be capable of measuring from ½ to at least 1½ times the design flow rate. The clearances upstream and downstream from the flow meter must comply with manufacturer's installation specifications.

The flow meter is generally mounted on the return piping after all other system components but before any chemical feed injection. Once more, follow the manufacturer's instructions.

When water changes flow direction, a certain amount of turbulence is created. Because of this, there is a requirement of ten times the pipe diameter of equivalent straight pipe before the flow meter and four or five times the pipe diameter of equivalent straight pipe after the flow meter.

Most gauges can be remotely located for easy observation. The flow meter is no exception. Some manufacturers offer rotary flow meters that feature a digital read-out at a pump room location of your choice. If your flow meter is in a difficult-to-read location, a digital flow meter may be a wise investment.

Electronic Control Systems

A wide variety of automated system controls are available. Pool filters can be backwashed, pool water chemistry can be monitored, and chemicals can be fed automatically to maintain disinfection and pH without manual operation. Pool water level, water temperature, lighting, and air blowers have all been incorporated into automatic monitoring and control systems. A full discussion of ORP is provided in the Chemical Feed & Control chapter.

Chemical Feeders

Chemicals can be introduced into the circulation system in a number of ways. Positive displacement pumps inject the chemicals into the return flow after all other equipment. Erosion feeders can be installed either in-line or off-line to the circulation flow.

The performance of erosion feeders is dependent on two circulation factors: first, the water temperature; and second, the flow rate of water through the device. Many manufacturers specify the need for a flow control valve and a flow meter on the chemical feed line. Several health departments have the same requirement.

© National Swimming Pool Foundation 2017

Photo 10-14. *Chemical-venturi feed piping and ball valve arrangement*

For a heated pool, the recommended location for the chemical erosion feeder is after the heater. If this is not possible, the erosion feeder can be installed after the heater.

Another alternative is to install the erosion device with the output port leading to the suction port of a venturi. The flow of the water through the venturi pulls the water through the erosion feeder. The amount of water pulled through the venturi is controlled with a ball valve.

Return Inlets

Once water is filtered and chemically treated and its temperature is adjusted, it is returned to the pool. The method and placement of the return inlets are critical to the overall development of flow patterns within the pool. Flow patterns provide equal distribution of chemicals and warm water throughout the entire body of water and help eliminate dead or stagnate areas.

Return inlets are sometimes called discharge outlets or inlet fittings. The inlet fittings can be installed in the pool wall, in the pool floor, or a combination of both. The locations, numbers, and types of inlet fittings are part of the design

Photo 10-15. *Adjustable eyeball wall return inlet (left) and bottom floor return (right)*

engineering phase of the pool facility. It is important that any inlets be replaced with items that comply with the original specification.

Wall inlet fittings are usually shaped like an eyeball and are adjustable as to flow direction. Bottom floor returns are designed with rotating face plates or internal valves for the control of return flow output.

Floor inlets should be designed and installed so that they do not extend above the pool floor. All inlets should be designed and installed without sharp edges or extensions hazardous to pool users. Wall inlets should be installed a minimum of 12 inches (30 cm) below the normal operating water level. This would not apply to returns in areas, such as entry ways or benches.

The number of return inlets is often dictated in codes and regulations based on the pool surface area. Often, a minimum of one return inlet per 300 square feet (28 square meters) of pool surface area is required. Some codes base the requirement for inlet spacing on the width of the pool. The general requirement is that the distance between inlets does not exceed 20 feet (6 meters).

Hot water therapy pools and spas use an aerated, jetted return design in addition to standard returns. These inlets are designed with a venturi tube or have a fitting that allows forced air from a blower to be utilized. The return lines of spa-type therapy or jet systems are independent of the circulation-filtration and heating systems. The water flow through an aerated jetted return is not considered as part of the requirements.

Verifying Circulation

Rare circumstances occur requiring operators to check or verify circulation. Signs of poor circulation can include conditions such as repetitive algae growth or lack of disinfectant residual in a particular location. To troubleshoot, operators may consult with the pool designer, verify water flow to all return inlets, or adjust inlet flow. If necessary, an operator may perform a dye test to observe circulation.

Dye Testing

One option to confirm the effectiveness of water distribution throughout the pool is to perform a dye test. Before the test is performed, the material that is to be used should be checked for compatibility with the system components. The

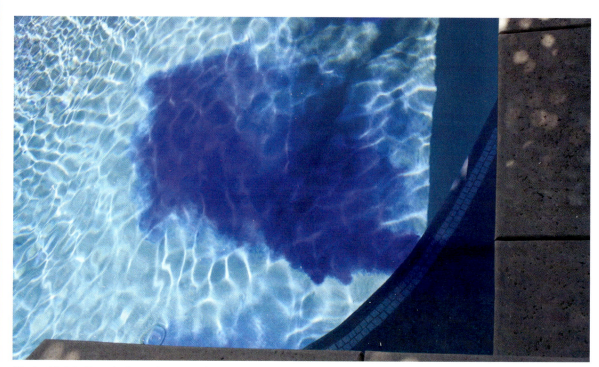

Photo 10-16. *The design characteristics of some pools may require a dye test to insure proper water distribution patterns in every area of the pool.*

dye should not stain the pool wall, inlet or outlet fittings tiles, or grout.

Before the test, the pool water level should be set and controlled to no more than ¼ inch (6 mm) above the lip of the gutter. The proper ratio of surface draw to main drain removal should be established. Direction of the return inlets should be adjusted and the outlet flow set to normal.

Most dyes are incompatible with chlorine, requiring the use of a chlorine neutralizer, such as sodium thiosulfate or sodium sulfite. The two dyes typically used are crystal violet and sodium fluorescein. Ozone and carbon filtration systems should be bypassed and the flow rate adjusted to the level of operation as if these systems were in use.

With the circulation pump turned off, the dye is added into the circulation line as close as possible to the normal disinfectant injection point. Often a positive displacement pump is used for this purpose. The circulation pump is then turned on to achieve normal flow.

Staff members should be positioned around various areas of the pool deck to record the time of emergence of the dye from each return inlet. The overall pool is observed to determine the time necessary to reach a uniform coloration. A video tape of the entire pool shot from an elevated position will provide a helpful tool to analyze the test at a later time.

Once the pool has reached a uniform color, the disinfectant and ozone system operations may be resumed. The dye will be oxidized and the color removal can serve as a second test to confirm the results of the original test. For evaluative purposes, uniform color distribution should occur in 50% of the time of a normal turnover or less.

© National Swimming Pool Foundation 2017

Crystal Violet Water Distribution Test Procedure

Initial Conditions

1. Pool filled with water
2. Filter in operation and pool water filtered
3. pH of pool water 7.8
4. No chlorine in water. Test value of chlorine = 0.0 ppm (mg/L).
5. All required personnel (photographer, timer, data taker, filter operator, video operator, and other observers) are briefed and ready to conduct test
6. All inlets are positioned and functional. All outflows are set to required proportional flow and are functional.
7. Filter is operating at rated flow
8. Crystal violet solution is prepared (20 grams per 50,000 gallons (189,271 liters) of pool water). Crystal violet is mixed in two gallons or 8 liters of water in a five-gallon or 20 liter bucket.

Test Procedure

1. Place D.E. filter in pre-coat mode, sand filter in circulation mode, or remove cartridges from the filter housing
2. Dump one gallon or 4 liters of crystal violet dye solution in to the surge tank
3. After solution is thoroughly mixed, alert all personnel to start of test
4. When all ready response is given, commence zero time of test by placing filter in normal mode
5. Note exact elapsed time when dye is first observed in pool
6. Observe and take digital images or video of dye pattern, and note and record all significant movement and times
7. After 4 minutes, dump one-half gallon or 2 liters of dye solution into surge tank. After 4 more minutes, dump the remaining one-half gallon or 2 liters of dye solution into surge tank.
8. When pool water is completely and uniformly dyed, record end of test
9. To remove dye, introduce sodium hypochlorite to the surge tank. (Use six quarts/5.7 liters per 50,000 gallons/189,271 liters of pool water). More sodium hypochlorite may be necessary. Add as much as four additional quarts (3.78 liters) if necessary.

Figure 10-1.

Notes

© National Swimming Pool Foundation 2017

Chapter 11:
Pool & Spa Filtration

"You don't get anything clean without getting something else dirty."

–Cecil Baxter

Filtration and circulation are the means that provide clean, clear water. Filtration is important because it removes contaminants that can promote the growth of bacteria or algae. Filters also remove particles that can make the water cloudy. Clear water is needed to easily observe people in the water to avoid collisions or to identify a person in distress. Clear water allows operators to see and ensure that main drains are properly secured to prevent injury or death due to entrapment.

A properly designed and operated pool filtration and circulation system will dilute and flush all areas of the pool equally and will mechanically remove insoluble solid matter from the water. The filtration and circulation systems also provide for equal distribution of cleansed water to all areas of the pool.

The equipment involved in this process includes pumps and filters; and gravity, vacuum, and pressure piping. Although chemical treatment usually takes place during the filtration cycle, the system for adding chemicals is generally considered to be separate from the filtration and circulation process.

Pool water is physically cleansed by passing through a filter. The material doing the filtering is called the media and is comprised of either sand, fibrous cartridge, or diatomaceous earth (D.E.). Filtration is a process where particles are captured in the media's pores or on the media's surface.

Filter Media

The physical properties of each media type determine the size of the trapped particles (see Illustration 11-1). Consider these factors when selecting a media for use: space, maintenance time, and budget.

Sand filtration is the oldest type of pool water filtration dating back to the very first pools. Granular media for sand filters is generally a fine, high-grade silica sand, or high-rate sand; or rapid-rate sand, a combination of coarser sand and gravel. Rapid-rate sand filters, not commonly used except in older installations, use sand closer to 0.56 millimeter size in combination with support beds of gravel. High-rate sand filters use much smaller and higher quality sand, generally without the gravel support. Sand media usually has a long life and is replaced about every five to 15 years.

Cartridge filtration is the newest form of filtration. The filter media is either spun-bonded polyester or treated paper in a cylindrical pleated arrangement. Cartridge filtration is said to be in the 10–25 micron range for the size of particles it will filter. Cartridge filters offer a compact design with a large filter area and a relatively small foot-print. A cartridge filter usually will require about half the filter room area as a comparable sand or diatomaceous earth filter. Cartridge filters are found on smaller pools and are utilized extensively for spa filtration. Cartridge filter elements are considered replaceable. The normal life of a commercial cartridge element is about six months. Several cartridge filter cleaning products

Photo 11-1. *A modern high rate sand filter system*

are commercially available to clean cartridges and may extend their useful life.

Diatomaceous earth (D.E.) removes the smallest particle size of any pool/spa filtration device. Tiny fossilized skeletons of small sea plankton, or diatoms, are used to trap undissolved material. D.E. filtration is said to be in the 2 to 6 micron range. The D.E. is held against a grid device or septum by the movement of water. The grid is covered with a cloth-like material and the D.E. forms a cake or coating on the cloth. Water passes through the D.E. with the suspended material trapped in the channels of the skeletal material. D.E. is considered to be a disposable filter media.

Water Clarity

Good water clarity is the result of proper filtration, circulation, and chemical treatment. It is important to ensure that people can see users in distress and the presence of all drain covers. Clarity is a qualitative, subjective term and will vary according to the observer. Turbidity is a quantitative measurement of the amount of suspended matter in the water. Clarity and turbidity have a reverse relationship: the more turbidity, the less clarity.

Water is cleansed mechanically by the passage of water through the filter media to remove suspended particles. This movement is accomplished by the circulation system described in the Water Circulation chapter. Failure to remove the suspended matter can result in unhealthy and unsafe water and increase the consumption of pool chemicals.

Two types of equipment used to measure turbidity, or clarity, are a nephelometer and a turbidimeter. NSF® International (NSF) recommends that pool water turbidity should not exceed 0.5 Nephelometer Turbidity Units (NTUs) or 0.2 Jackson Turbidity Units (JTUs). However, for short times during peak user load, turbidity should not exceed 1.0 NTU, and the pool filtration system should be capable of returning this water to 0.5 NTUs within 8 hours following peak use. A pool at 0.6 NTUs is visibly turbid or cloudy and levels approaching or exceeding 1.0 are generally unacceptable to both users and the pool operator. Most jurisdictional codes include a reference to the NSF standards for water clarity. Several states do not allow turbidity to exceed 0.5 NTUs.

In the absence of a nephelometer or turbidimeter, common methods of noting water clarity described in many state regulations include:

- Being able to see the pool drain clearly from the pool deck
- Being able to see a two-inch disk with black and red quadrants through 15 feet (4.6 meters) of water

It is important to always make sure that the pool's main drain cover is properly attached and not damaged before opening the pool. A visual inspection of the attached main drain cover requires acceptably clear water.

What Do Filters Remove?

The size of suspended particle removal is generally measured in the unit of a micron. The pictorial below uses a grain of table salt as the reference at 100 microns. The other designations are relative to the salt diameter. A micron is one millionth of a meter.
There are approximately 25 microns in 1/1000 of an inch.

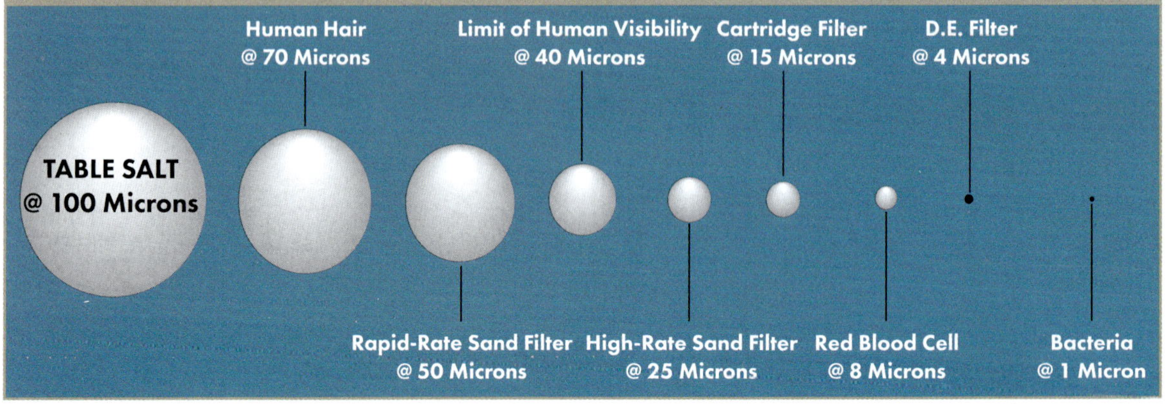

TABLE SALT @ 100 Microns

Human Hair @ 70 Microns
Limit of Human Visibility @ 40 Microns
Cartridge Filter @ 15 Microns
D.E. Filter @ 4 Microns

Rapid-Rate Sand Filter @ 50 Microns
High-Rate Sand Filter @ 25 Microns
Red Blood Cell @ 8 Microns
Bacteria @ 1 Micron

Illustration 11-1

© National Swimming Pool Foundation 2017

Filter Media Rate (FMR)

An important consideration in pool water management is the rate of flow of water through a filter. This factor is called the Filter Media Rate (FMR). Sometimes FMR is called the filter flow rate or the filter factor. When the pool is designed, the flow rate (FR) is determined by the need to obtain adequate dilution based on how the particular pool will be used. Once the design flow rate has been determined, the FMR is used to calculate the necessary minimum filter area.

The FMR for a particular filter type is determined as part of the filter manufacturer's compliance with the NSF International Standard 50, "Equipment for Swimming Pools, Spas, Hot Tubs, and Other Recreational Water Facilities." The NSF public pool standards for FMR are shown in the following chart:

Filter Type	Filter Media Rate
High-Rate Sand	5 – 20 gpm/ft^2 204 – 813 lpm/m^2
Cartridge	0.375 gpm/ft^2 15 lpm/m^2
Diatomaceous Earth	2.0 gpm/ft^2 81 lpm/m^2
Diatomaceous Earth with Slurry	2.5 gpm/ft^2 102 lpm/m^2
Rapid-Rate Sand	3 gpm/ft^2 122 lpm/m^2

Table 11-1. *Filter types and corresponding filtering rates*

Outside the United States, sand filters are most common. Big or heavily used commercial pools will normally use LOW filtration rates. Schools, hotels, other commercial pools, and heavily used private pools will usually have a MEDIUM filtration rate. HIGH rate filtration is usually only suitable for private home pools. The Filtration Rate is measured in cubic meters of water per square meter of filter surface area per hour (m^3/m^2/hr) The use of flocculants is common in medium rate sand filters. NOTE: many sand filters have a maximum Filtration Rate of 45 m^3/m^2/hr.

Filtration Rates for Sand Filters (Metric Rates)
Low Rate Filtration – Less than 10 m^3/m^2/hr
Medium Rate Filtration – 11 m^3/m^2/hr to 30 m^3/m^2/hr
High Rate Filtration – 31 m^3/m^2/hr to 50 m^3/m^2/hr

Table 11-2. *Metric sand filter filtration rate standards*

Filter Area

The pump's maximum flow rate must be used to calculate the minimum filter area. The filter area is the surface area of filter media through which the water flows. The filter area is printed on the filter's data label. In addition, the manufacturers provide specifications to match their filters to the pool size and the desired turnover rate. By matching the correct filter area to the amount of water that must pass through the filter to achieve the proper turnover rate, the quality of the water can be maintained. Exceeding the FMR for any type of filter may have undesirable consequences, including:

- **Sand Filters:** dirt material is driven further into the sand bed, making cleaning more difficult during the backwash cycle. Channeling can bypass the filtration process, resulting in unfiltered water returning to the pool.
- **Cartridge Filters:** dirt, minerals, and oils can be driven into and through the filter element and back into the pool. Cartridge filters are much more affected by high water velocity than sand or D.E. filters. Particles can become embedded so deeply in the cartridge that they are not released during cleaning.
- **D.E. Filters:** D.E., minerals, and oils will be forced into the grid cloth and cause the D.E. to stick to the cloth. Some of the D.E. will not be released during the backwash or cleaning cycle. This causes an increase in force, either vacuum or pressure, on the grid element and shortens grid life.

The maximum flow rate through any filter should never exceed the filter's capacity. Filter area has a relationship between the necessary minimum filter size to properly manage the design flow rate or engineered flow rate as discussed in the Water Circulation chapter.

© National Swimming Pool Foundation 2017

There are three factors in this relationship. They are

Filter Area, called FA
Flow Rate, called FR
Filter Media Rate, called FMR

The relationship between theses factors is

Filter Area = Flow Rate ÷ Filter Media Rate

Using the abbreviations, the relationship is

FA = FR ÷ FMR

This formula can also be expressed in two other ways:

FMR = FR ÷ FA
FR = FA x FMR

The actual flow rate can be observed by watching the flow meter. Observation of the flow meter is important to insure that the FMR is never exceeded. With a vacuum filter there is a valve, often called a throttling valve, just after the pump. This valve can be used to control the flow rate. The throttling valve may need to be adjusted throughout the filter cycle. The flow rate minimum must be known and maintained so that the turnover rate required by code is achieved.

Metric Filter Sizing

The flow rate of a metric filter is measured in cubic meters per hour, m^3/hr. The surface area of the filter is in m^2. Since flow is in liters per minute (lpm), the liters per minute need to be converted into m^3. The formula for calculating the filter size is

lpm x 60 = liter per hour
Liters ÷ 1,000 = m^3
FR (m^3) ÷ FMR ($m^3/m^2/hr$) = FA (m^2)

Example 11-1:

The maximum output flow from the pool's pump is 350 gallons per minute. The D.E. filter system uses square 2 feet x 2 feet grids. How many grids are required? Vacuum D.E. grids filter from both sides. One grid is 2 ft. x 2 ft. = 4 square feet on one side. This becomes 8 square feet for both sides for one grid. The FMR is 2.0 gpm/ft^2 for a vacuum D.E. filter without a slurry.

FA = FR ÷ FMR
FA = 350 gpm ÷ 2.0 gpm/ft2
FA = 175 ft2
Number of grids = 175 ft2 ÷ 8 ft2/grid
Number of grids = 22 (rounded up)

Example 11-1: Metric

The Filtration Rate is measured in cubic meters of water per square meter of filter surface area per hour, $m^3/m^2/hr$. The pool has a medium rate sand filter capable of 11 $m^3/m^2/hr$. The circulation rate (flow rate) is 95 m^3/hr. How many m^2 of sand filter will be needed?

FA = FR ÷ FMR
FA = 95 m^3/h ÷ 11 $m^3/m^2/h$
FA = 8.64m^2

Example 11-2:

The pool has four, 4 foot diameter high-rate sand filters. What is the filter area of the system? For sand filtration, only the top of the sand is considered when discussing filter area.

Area = R x R x 3.14
Diameter = 4; Diameter ÷ 2 = Radius
Radius = 2
Area = 2 x 2 x 3.14 =
12.56 ft^2 for one filter
Total filter area = 12.56 ft^2 x 4
= 50.24 ft^2 (for four filters)

Example 11-2: Metric

The pool has four 1.5m diameter low-rate sand filters. What is the filter area of the system?

Area = R x R x 3.14
Diameter = 1.5; Diameter ÷ 2 = Radius
Radius = 0.75 m
Area = 0.75 x 0.75 x 3.14
Area = 1.77 m^2 for one filter
Total filter area = 1.77 m^2 x 4 = 7.08 m^2

Using a 15 gpm/ft^2 FMR, what is the maximum flow rate this system can support?

FR = FA x FMR
FR = 50.24 ft^2 x 15 gpm/ft^2
= 753.6 gpm

Metric

Using a FMR of 10$m^3/m^2/h$ for the filter size of 7.08 m^2, what is the maximum circulation rate (flow rate) this system can support?

FR = FA x FMR
FR = 7.08 m^2/h x 10 $m^3/m^2/h$
FR = 70.8 $m^3/m^2/h$

© National Swimming Pool Foundation 2017

Filtration

Filters are classified by the media type and the mode the filter uses. The three most common media types are sand, cartridge, and diatomaceous earth (D.E.). The two modes refer to whether the filter is exposed to either the pressure-side or the vacuum-side of a pump. Pressure and vacuum filters can be sand, cartridge, or D.E.

When selecting a filter, remember that not all water loss is bad. Proper water management often involves a planned dilution of the pool to control the buildup of undesirable materials. The local weather conditions, water availability, and regulations regarding waste discharge are all important considerations.

A pressure filter is downstream from the pump in the water flow and is in a closed tank. The water is forced through the tank by the output head pressure of the pump. As the particles in the water are trapped by the media, there is an increase in pressure going to the filter (influent pressure) and a decrease in flow.

A vacuum filter is before the pump in the water flow and is usually in an open-to-atmosphere tank. The water is pulled through the media by the suction of the pump. As the media collects the pollutants, there is an increase in vacuum on the pump suction side and a decrease in flow.

Photo 11-2. *Valves should be properly tagged and a valve identification chart should be close at hand for reference by the pool operator.*

Sand Filtration

As stated earlier, sand filtration is the oldest type of filtration. Sand is considered a permanent media, lasting between five and 15 years before replacement. When new sand is looked at under a microscope, the particles have sharp edges.

Old sand will be smooth in shape, indicating that it is time for replacement. The ancient Greek and Roman baths used water that was passed through a bed of sand, collected and then returned to the baths through a variety of gravity-based mechanisms.

All sand filters today work on a similar principle of moving water from the top of the filter to the bottom. Water with suspended pollutants passes through the grains of sand and the dirt is entrapped in the small crevices and openings between sand particles. As debris attaches itself to the sharp edges of the sand grains, the gaps between sand grains become smaller. This allows suspended pollutants, such as dirt, body waste material, and lotions to further embed, creating a fibrous maze.

As the filter cycle continues, progressively smaller particles are removed. The smallest possible material is filtered just prior to the backwash, or cleaning cycle.

There are two types of sand filters. The earlier sand filtration category utilizes sand and gravel, and is called a rapid-rate sand filter. A more fitting term for this older type of filter would be a sand and gravel filter. The more modern sand filter is the high-rate sand filter, which filters water at a much faster rate. These filters were developed in the 1950s and use #20 mesh crystal silica.

High-Rate Sand Filtration

The most common high-rate sand filters are pressure filters, although there are vacuum high-rate sand filters. Recreation pools, competition pools, and major resort pools may use high-rate sand filters.

The pressure filter tank is cylindrical, with diameters that most commonly range from 2 to 4 feet (0.61 to 1.22 meters). Larger facilities, such as parks, schools, and competition pools have pressure high-rate sand filters with diameters as large as 10 feet (3.05 meters). The pressure filter, regardless of the diameter, can be assembled as part of a modular system utilizing multiple tanks.

The sand used in a high-rate sand filter has particle sizes generally between 0.018 in. (0.35 mm) to 0.022 in. (0.56 mm). This size sand is sometimes called #20 standard silica sand. It will pass through a mesh screen with 20 wires per inch (20 mesh) and collect on a screen with 30 wires per inch (30 mesh). Failure to use the correct sand can result in poor pool water quality, sand particles

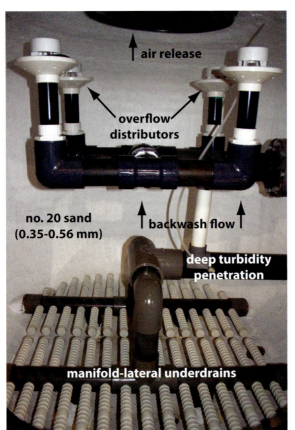

air release

overflow distributors

no. 20 sand (0.35-0.56 mm)

backwash flow

deep turbidity penetration

manifold-lateral underdrains

Illustration 11-2. *Cross section of a high-rate sand filter*

passing into the pool, or filter failure. Particle size entrapment for sand filtration is in the 25 to 100 micron range. Other media, such as crushed garnet or zeolite can be used, but #20 sand is the most common.

The filter tank or housing can be made of stainless steel, plastic, fiberglass, or a combination of materials. There are single piece tanks with only a removable lid to access the internal parts. The larger vertical tanks are usually welded steel and have access covers in the top for maintenance purposes.

The water that enters the top of the filter housing goes through a fixture that spreads the water over the top of the sand bed. This fixture is typically called a baffle or a distributor. Underneath the baffle is an open space between the baffle and the sand bed. This open space is called a freeboard.

Freeboard is critical because it allows the sand bed to expand during the backwash cycle. The amount of freeboard is an engineering factor built into each filter manufacturer's engineering specification. Generally, it is one-half the depth of the sand bed. Manufacturers often do not dictate the freeboard, but rather specify the amount of

sand that should be added for the specific filter model. This amount of sand will leave the proper freeboard.

When replacing sand, always make sure to maintain the proper amount of freeboard. Failing to do so will result in extended flush times during the backwash cycle and may even redistribute the sand over time.

Underneath the sand at the bottom of the filter is the underdrain or laterals assembly. The laterals are slotted to allow water to pass, but are too small for the sand to pass.

Valves are used to direct the water flow in the proper direction. Smaller filters make use of multi-port, rotary, or ball valves, while larger filters utilize butterfly and gate valves.

The design flow rate for high-rate sand filters is 5 to 20 gpm/ft^2, with 15 gpm/ft^2 being the most typically used. The design backwash and design filter rates are approximately the same for most high-rate filters. High-rate sand filters primarily filter in the top several inches of sand. The depth to which particles penetrate will be proportional to the flow rate.

Automated filter operation is possible. Filters can be controlled by a small microprocessor. Solenoid valves can be activated to control the water flow for each filter unit or the entire system. The microprocessor monitors the incoming or influent flow, the outgoing or effluent flow, and the flow rate, utilizing a remote digital flow meter. When the system performance falls below preset levels, the backwash sequence is activated.

Warning
Pressure filters operate under high pressure. Always open all air bleed valves and turn off the pump before changing valve positions or removing any clamps or fittings. Failure to follow proper procedures could result in violent separation of the equipment causing possible serious injury or death.

Backwashing Sand Filters

Backwashing is required when the water entering the filter (influent) and the water exiting the filter (effluent) reaches a 10 to 20 psi (69-138 kPa) pressure difference. This difference is noted by observation of the pressure gauges, installed on each side of the filter flow per code in many

© National Swimming Pool Foundation 2017

areas. If there is only one pressure gauge, the filter should be backwashed when the pressure increases 8 to 10 psi (55-69 kPa) over the starting pressure.

Always follow the written directions of the filter manufacturer. Generally the backwash rate is equivalent to the flow rate, but to achieve the necessary agitation of the sand, 15 gpm/ft^2 is considered necessary. In some modular systems, the backwash water is already filtered, but in most systems, unfiltered pool water is used.

During backwash, the water flow is reversed. The flow is from the bottom laterals to the top. As the sand is lifted, it expands, becomes agitated, filling the freeboard area. The agitation removes the trapped particles and material, which is flushed out the distributors to waste. In manual systems, the backwash waste water is observed through a sight glass until the effluent water becomes clear.

Photo 11-4. *Backwash waste water is observed through a sight glass until the effluent becomes clear.*

Photo 11-3. *During backwash the water flow is reversed using the valve system.*

After the backwash cycle is complete, the cleansed sand begins the process of filtration again. The dirt particle size removed is usually above 50 microns during this initial phase of the cycle. With each turnover, the voids between the sand become progressively smaller, and the dirt particle size removed from the flow also becomes smaller. It is at the latter stages of the filter cycle that the smallest of particle size is removed. For high-rate sand filters, this is about 25 microns but can be smaller.

Backwashing a high-rate sand filter on a time schedule will result in the inability to remove the smaller particles because the sand voids never become properly constricted. Poor water clarity can result over a period of time. When filter

aids or flocculants, such as aluminum sulfate (alum), potassium aluminum sulfate, or poly-aluminum chloride are used, they can fill gaps between sand particles. The short-term results are improved filtration and higher filter pressures. The long-term result is that gaps between sand particles can become filled with the filter aid, causing the bed of sand to stick together to form a large mass with poor filtration properties.

When replacing sand, always follow the manufacturer's instructions. For new sand, most of the small sand particles, referred to as fines, are removed while the supplier is processing and washing the sand. These fines are further removed during a series of backwash cycles at new filter start-up or after the replacement of the sand bed. It is important that the fines are removed so that oils do not adhere to them, causing the premature development of mud-balls.

Rapid-Rate Sand Filtration

Rapid-rate sand filters are a series of large tanks with diameters of eight feet (2.44 meters) or more. This type of filter was commonly found on large municipal and competitive pools during the first half of the 1900s. A few of these filter types remain in operation today in regions around the world.

The term rapid-rate came about as a descriptive or comparative term. The original gravity or slow-rate filters had a FMR of ½ to 1 gpm/ft^2. As engineering designs improved, the FMR improved to 1.5 to 5 gpm/ft^2, with 3 gpm/ft^2 considered the standard; thus the term rapid-rate.

The rapid-rate media consists of a series of

1. Pool & Spa Management
2. Regulations & Guidelines
3. Essential Calculations
4. Pool Water Contamination
5. Disinfection
6. Water Balance
7. Pool & Spa Water Problems
8. Chemical Testing
9. Chemical Feed & Control
10. Water Circulation
11. Pool & Spa Filtration
12. Heating & Air Circulation
13. Spa & Therapy Operations
14. Facility Safety
15. Keeping Records
16. Maintenance Systems
17. Troubleshooting
18. Facility Renovation & Design

References

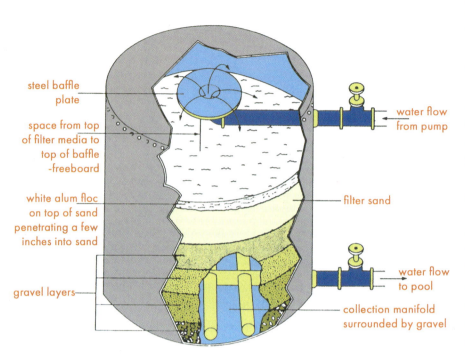

steel baffle plate

space from top of filter media to top of baffle -freeboard

white alum floc on top of sand penetrating a few inches into sand

gravel layers

water flow from pump

filter sand

water flow to pool

collection manifold surrounded by gravel

Illustration 11-3. *Cross section of a rapid rate sand filter*

Horizontal Modular High-Rate Sand Filtration

These systems consist of a single tank, multiple tanks, and even multiple modules of tanks. Incoming water flow is directed toward the top of the tank to prevent channeling of the sand. The engineering is such that during backwashing, each sand particle is moved to the top of the fluidized bed every 30 seconds. This provides for an aggressive scrubbing action for the release of suspended solids.

Many of these systems are backwashed automatically with the use of a microprocessor. Maintenance of the auto-features and remote flow meter on these specialized systems is important.

Multi-Cell High-Rate Sand

A multi-cell filter consists of one or more vertical tanks containing two or more cells each. This concept allows for more filtering with less floor space.

The piping can be quite complex, and careful consideration must be given to the manufacturer's instructions at all times. Backwashing is relatively easy with one filter. In larger commercial facilities where there may be many sand filters, backwashing can be a more time-consuming process since each filter cell is backwashed separately. Automatic backwash control technology can be installed that automates multi-cell filter backwash control.

Vacuum High-Rate Sand

These systems are in a large open steel tank, which is placed with the top at ground level. The vacuum high-rate equipment package is placed in an adjacent pit and the result is an energy-

multiple sand layers and gravel. The finest sand is on the top and is supported by courser sand. The gravel is also graded and provides support to the sand, with the courser gravel on the bottom.

The courser material is also the densest and after backwash settles more quickly. In this manner the layering is maintained. The backwash rate is 12 to 15 gpm/ft^2 and is achieved by cleaning one filter at a time independent of the remaining tanks, using all of the system's water flow.

As with high-rate filters, there is a baffle or distributor, freeboard, and bottom laterals. A layer of flocculant like aluminum sulfate is usually added to the top of the sand to assist in the formation of a soil layer in the first few inches of the sand.

Other Sand Filters

Technological improvements have resulted in several other filter choices, such as horizontal modular high-rate sand, multi-cell high-rate sand, and alternative media such as zeolite. A newer design concept called vacuum high-rate has developed based on older style gravity sand filters.

© National Swimming Pool Foundation 2017

efficient system. These systems can be as much as 8 feet (2.44 meters) deep, making servicing the equipment more difficult for the pool operator. Consideration should be given to the placement of the vacuum and pressure gauges and flow meter for ease of observation.

There is sufficient space in the tank above the sand to allow backwashing and provide surge capability for level control. The pool water flows by gravity from the main drain and surface gutters.

Zeolite

Zeolite is a granular volcanic material that is extremely porous and is capable of removing particles down to five microns in size. Manufacturers claim that activated zeolite has the capability to absorb ammonia from the pool water. Removal of this contaminant is desirable since chlorine reacts with ammonia to form chloramines that are irritating to users' eyes and have a pungent odor that impacts the indoor air quality.

The active ingredient of the zeolite is clinoptilolite, a mineral with an exceptionally high surface area. It has an extended three-dimensional cage-like structure with large internal pore spaces. This material has the ability to chemically capture pollutants by a mechanism called cation exchange. Before using this product, check with the product supplier and filter manufacturer for instructions.

Cartridge Filtration

Cartridge filtration is used in swimming pools, and, to a greater extent, to treat spa water. There are two basic concepts to cartridge filtration. The oldest is the depth penetration filter, which was designed for a FMR between 3 and 8 gpm/ft² (122 - 325 lpm/m²). The cartridge filter of today is a surface type with FMR between 0.375 and 1.0 gpm/ft² (15 - 41 lpm/m²). Cartridge filters are considered replaceable media.

The depth penetration filters are called fabric cartridges. The

Photo 11-5.
Cartridge filters elements are not backwashed, but cleaned.

surface filters are constructed of synthetic fabric in a pleated arrangement around a cylindrical or oval core.

In most cases, cartridge filtration is operated in the pressure mode. There are some commercial instances where cartridge filters have been installed in the vacuum mode, similar to a vacuum D.E. system.

The most obvious reason for choosing cartridge filtration is its compact size. The normal installation will require about half the floor space of an equivalent sand or D.E. system. Cartridge filters do not require backwashing to clean the cartridge so water is conserved. This is a cost saving advantage. The disadvantage of using a cartridge filter is lack of dilution or replacement of dirty water with fresh potable water.

Water containing suspended material passes through the filter element, depositing the debris on the surface. As the cycle continues, more dirt is deposited, causing the passageways to become more constricted. Smaller and smaller particles are trapped as the process continues. The cycle continues until the influent pressure increases to 10 psi (70 kPa) above the cycle starting pressure. Excessive water velocity has a greater negative effect on cartridge filtration than any other type. Debris can be driven through the filter and back into the return water flow and can damage the cartridge element.

Cleaning Cartridge Filters

Cartridge filters are not backwashed but are removed from the filter, hosed off, and cleaned. Shut off the pump and follow the manufacturer's instructions. If high water velocities or mineral build-up has occurred, then further steps are necessary:

- The element should be soaked in a commercial filter-cleaning product. It is important to review label directions since often two filter cleaners are needed. One removes oils and greases and another may remove scale deposits. The order in which the cleaners are used may affect how the cleaners perform. Often grease cleaners must be used before acid cleaners. Failure to do so may result in the acid causing the oil materials to set into the cartridge media.
- After a thorough rinsing, any minerals can be removed with a light acid wash
- The filter element(s) should be replaced back into the filter tank and the housing

secured. The O-ring should be visually inspected for wear before closing the housing. O-ring lubricant should be applied as necessary, or once per month. Failure to maintain the O-ring can result in water loss or air entering the filter.

Many operators eliminate downtime by keeping a spare cartridge filter element on site so that when one needs to be cleaned, it can be replaced with a clean cartridge. In some instances it is a code requirement to have an extra cartridge.

Diatomaceous Earth

Diatomaceous earth, known as D.E., is a type of disposable filter media. At each filter cycle, the D.E. media is discarded and replaced with new. The replacement process is called pre-coating.

D.E. is a white powder material made up of the skeleton-like fossils of diatoms. It has sponge-like qualities and can absorb huge quantities of water. The porous D.E. particles are layered on top of one another to form a very fine screen. The D.E. powder is held on the filter elements, which are called the septum. The septum is covered with a fine weave cloth material made of synthetic fabric. The D.E. powder forms the cake on the septum between 1/16 to 1/8 inch (1.6 to 3.2 mm) thick.

It is the flow of the water that holds the D.E. in place. Insufficient water flow can cause the D.E. to fall off the grid. The openings of the D.E. cake are extremely small, allowing the passage of the water but trapping even the smallest of suspended solids.

D.E. filtration can be either in the pressure or vacuum mode. In the pressure mode, the D.E. filtration operation is much like a sand filter. The filter is backwashed when the incoming (influent) pressure increases 8 to 10 psi (55-69 kPa) above the starting pressure and the flow is reduced.

Handling D.E. Powder

The pool operator should use great care in the storage and handling of D.E. powder. A copy of the Safety Data Sheet for the D.E. powder in use should be obtained from the supplier. The operator should become familiar with all aspects of this information.

First, like most powders, D.E. is extremely sharp at the microscopic level. The D.E. should never be stored near the operating equipment or other chemicals. D.E. becomes airborne easily and could be attracted to the windings of a circulation pump motor, causing premature failure. D.E. powder could also contaminate chemicals and test kit reagents that are not properly stored.

Second, D.E. is extremely hazardous when the pool operator fails to utilize breathing protection. This is a statement taken from the label of one D.E. supplier:

> "Breathing crystalline silica dust in excess of the permissible exposure limit, over a prolonged period of time, can cause silicosis, a progressive, sometimes fatal lung disease. Crystalline silica has been classified as a known carcinogenic for humans."

Vacuum D.E. Filtration

In a vacuum D.E. system, the pool water flows by gravity from the main drain and surface to an atmospheric filter tank. It is important to maintain a proper FMR with a vacuum D.E. system. If the FMR is below 1 gpm/ft^2 (41 lpm/m^2), the D.E. may not properly coat the grids. If the FMR is above 2 gpm/ft^2 (81.5 lpm/m^2), the D.E. powder and filter debris may be forced into the fabric weave, causing a blocking effect. To control the flow rate throughout the filter cycle, the circulation pump flow may have to be throttled, or restricted.

Any vacuum filter system must be operated with the use of a vacuum gauge which measures in. Hg or kPa. A clean set of filter grids, freshly coated with D.E. powder, should read no

Photo 11-6. *A vacuum D.E. filter system*

© National Swimming Pool Foundation 2017

Photo 11-7. *A vacuum D.E. filter slurry feed system*

more than 8 inches of mercury (expressed as 8 in. Hg or 27 kPa). When the starting vacuum increases by 10 in. Hg (34 kPa), the filter cycle is complete, and the D.E. powder must be replaced. Observation of the flow meter is also part of this determination.

Pre-coating a Vacuum D.E. Filter

The replacement of the used D.E. powder with fresh powder is called pre-coating. To start a new filter cycle, the filter tank must be drained and the soiled D.E. properly collected and discarded. The filter tank is isolated from the pool by valves, and then the tank water is drained, usually with an auxiliary pump. As the water is pumped out, the grids become exposed. The pool operator uses a hose to dislodge any used powder remaining on the exposed grids.

The filter tank water and used D.E. should be pumped into a separation tank, which collects the used D.E. The material should then be disposed of in a manner compliant with local codes. Never use sewers or open bodies of water for D.E. disposal.

The filter tank is then filled with pool water by opening the control valves. After filling the filter tank, the auxiliary pump is re-valved so as to circulate only the filter tank water. New D.E. powder should be mixed into a bucket of water to make a slurry. The slurry should be added evenly around the surface of the filter tank. The water in the tank is observed for consistent color indicating an even distribution of powder. Then the main circulation pump is started, and the auxiliary pump is turned off. The precoating process is now complete.

The amount of new D.E. powder used is critical to proper filter operation. Too little powder will not adequately coat the fabric weave, allowing oils and debris to clog the openings. This will result in reduced flow and, eventually, grid damage. Too much powder will result in the D.E. cake from one grid coming in contact with the D.E. cake from an adjacent grid. This is sometimes referred to as bridging.

Follow the directions as provided by the filter manufacturer concerning the proper amount of D.E. to use. The normal amounts range from 1 to 1.5 pounds (0.5 - 0.7 kilos) for every 10 square feet (1 square meter) of filter area. The commonly accepted value is 1.25 lbs/10 ft^2 (0.6 kilos/m^2).

Pressure D.E. Filtration

Most pressure D.E. systems have vertical filter tanks with a top and a bottom. The two halves are held together by locking devices, such as compression clamps, bolts, or locking screw closure rings. There is generally a seal between the two halves consisting of an O-ring or gasket.

The water inlet and outlet lines are usually located on the bottom half of the filter tank. This facilitates the removal of the top half for servicing and repair. There is an air relief valve (manual, automatic, or both) on the top of the filter to allow internal pressure release before servicing. Always shut off the pump and release the air pressure before attempting to service any type of pressure filter.

Internally, the filter has a grid assembly that can be of different sizes and shapes. The grids are made of plastic and covered with a synthetic cloth. The cloth is the support base for the D.E. cake. The grids are held together by a collection manifold and support bracket with connecting rods.

Water enters the filter tank through a series of valves or a multi-port valve. The water is then directed to the bottom of the tank without contacting the grids. This action collects the D.E. from the bottom of the tank and deposits it on the grids. Suspended dirt is then trapped on the D.E. powder as the cleansed water passes through. Water leaves the filter through the output port and is returned to the pool.

Backwashing a Pressure D.E. Filter

During a filter cycle, the collection of suspended dirt in the passageways of the D.E. cake causes an increase in pressure and a decrease in flow. When the pressure for a single gauge operation

© National Swimming Pool Foundation 2017

reaches 10 psi (70 kPa or 1 bar) higher than the cycle starting pressure, the filter must be cleaned.

Backwashing is accomplished with the use of valves or a multi-port valve. The flow of the water is reversed, with the water action causing the D.E. cake to break off. The dirty water is then directed to the separation tank and then to waste. Always follow the instructions of the filter manufacturer.

Many states require that pressure systems have a sight glass installed in the waste effluent line exiting the filter tank. Watch the sight glass until the backwash water runs clear. The pump should be turned off and restarted, repeating the backwash cycle three times. This process removes contaminated cake which adheres to the filter grids.

To increase the length of time between backwashes, a slurry feed system can be installed. A slurry solution of D.E. is continuously fed into the filter tank to create new surfaces of D.E. on the filter grids. In this situation, the operator needs to make sure that the filter operating pressure continues to work within the manufacturers specifications. If it doesn't, the filter should be cleaned.

Manual Grid Cleaning

Commercial D.E. filter grids, both vacuum and pressure, need to be manually cleaned on a regular basis, generally every three months of filter operation. The procedure is as follows:
- The grids should be removed from the filter as per the manufacturer's instructions
- The grids should be sprayed down with water and the grid cloth inspected for any tears or other damage
- The elements should be soaked in a commercial filter cleaner to remove any buildup of oily compounds and rinse
- If necessary, the grids should be soaked in an acidic filter cleaner to remove any calcification or other mineral buildup, then rinsed
- Lastly, the filter mechanism should be reassembled

Alternative Material for D.E. Type Filters

There are several alternative materials available as a substitute for D.E. The most popular is based on wood pulp fiber. These materials are attractive in that they are biodegradable and can be flushed to waste without the need for separation tanks. As always, check with your filter manufacturer's manual before using a substitute product.

The wood fiber material is also useful in coating a cartridge filter, especially for spa operations. Use about 1 ounce per 25 ft^2 (28.3 grams per 2.32 m^2) to make oil removal very easy. Remember, all materials used for filtration must have NSF and the manufacturer's approval.

Regenerative Filters

Regenerative filters utilize D.E. or a synthetic substitute. The regeneration process is a mechanical means of dislodging the D.E. and dirt to allow better, more efficient use of the D.E. Manufacturers claim that the differences between these types of filters and sand filters fall into several categories including design, installation, operation and performance.

The difference between regenerative filters and conventional high-rate sand filters is that sand filters use the entire sand bed for filtration, while a regenerative filter has water flowing through multiple outlet tubes covered in fabric, coated with filter media. This greatly increases the filter's surface area, which means that

Photo 11-8. *Regenerative filters require a much smaller footprint for installation compared to sand filters.*

150

© National Swimming Pool Foundation 2017

Pool & Spa Filtration

Photo 11-9. *Turnover rates and flow rates must be carefully considered based on the design size of the pool.*

regenerative filters require a much smaller footprint for installation compared to sand filters.

Bumping is what is referred to as the regeneration process. This process agitates the media and trapped dirt particles off the leaves that it is attached to. Regeneration redistributes the media thus extending the life of the media.

Another advantage that comes from the regeneration process is that less water is sent to waste, which conserves water. Some manufacturers claim that regenerative filters can save as much as 90-95% of waste water associated with sand filter backwashing. Eventually the dirt will build up in these filters and the media will have to be replaced.

Filtration Summary

The design size of the pool is determined by the expected pool usage requirements, including what programs or features will be offered in the pool: lap swimming, diving, water polo, wading, swim lessons, water features, etc. The more

people in a pool and the more strenuous the activity means more gallons of water, or a faster turnover rate, are needed to maintain acceptable water quality and proper sanitation.

Turnover rate is a function of code requirements and expected user loading. More demanding conditions require more filtration and faster turnover rates. For example, spas and wading pools have a faster turnover rate than a large swimming pool.

The flow rate in a system is determined by the turnover rate, how quickly the volume of the pool must be passed through the circulation system. In other words, it is the flow rate that provides the actual turnover rate.

Filter area is determined by the circulation pump output or flow rate, which at a minimum must meet the turnover rate code requirements. Filter area is a function of the Filter Media Rate (FMR) or the capacity of the filter to process water.

Notes

152

© National Swimming Pool Foundation 2017

1. Pool & Spa Management
2. Regulations & Guidelines
3. Essential Calculations
4. Pool Water Contamination
5. Disinfection
6. Water Balance
7. Pool & Spa Water Problems
8. Chemical Testing
9. Chemical Feed & Control
10. Water Circulation
11. Pool & Spa Filtration
12. Heating & Air Circulation
13. Spa & Therapy Operations
14. Facility Safety
15. Keeping Records
16. Maintenance Systems
17. Troubleshooting
18. Facility Renovation & Design
References

Chapter 12:
Heating & Air Circulation

"It doesn't make a difference what temperature a room is, it's always room temperature."

–Steven Wright

Nothing makes the use of a swimming pool or spa more enjoyable than to have the correct water temperature for individual comfort and for the aquatic activity being performed. In addition, if the facility is indoors, the temperature and humidity of the environment surrounding the pool or spa must be maintained for the comfort of the facility staff, visitors, and users. The decision on how warm to keep the pool is up to the individual facility. The American Red Cross recommends a temperature of 78°F (25.6°C) for competitive swimming. However, this may be too cold for young children and the elderly who may require 80°F (26.7°C) or higher.

The recommended pool water temperatures for various activities are

- Recreational swimming: 82°F (27.8°C)
- Infant/preschool (ages 4 and under) swimming and therapy: 90–93°F (32.2–33.9°C)
- Children instructional classes: 84–89°F (28.9–31.7°C)
- Competitive swimming and diving, including training and fitness swimming: 77–82°F (25–28°C)
- Spas: ≤104°F (40°C)

The energy content of pool or spa water is determined by the temperature of the water. The water's energy content is somewhat like the monetary value of a bank checking account: constant deposits and withdrawals cause the bank balance to rise and fall. In a pool or spa, there are constant heat gains and heat losses causing the temperature to rise or fall. Pool or spa water becomes colder when energy is withdrawn. The water becomes warmer when energy is added at a rate faster than it is withdrawn. To maintain a constant temperature, energy must be added at the same rate that it is withdrawn.

Energy Losses

The mechanisms of surface loss are evaporation, convection, and thermal radiation. Conduction does not occur at the surface and has little effect on the total heat loss. In addition to the thermal mechanisms, another heat loss occurs as a result of user load. As the number of users increase, the volume of water lost due to splash-out and drag-out increases, requiring replacement with source water. The source water is usually at a lower temperature than the pool or spa water, which lowers the pool or spa water temperature.

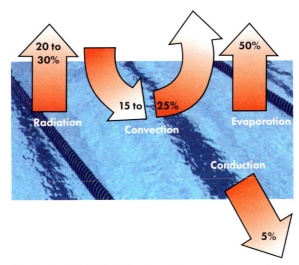

Illustration 12-1. *Relative heat losses from pools*

Evaporative Losses

Water at the surface is constantly changing into water vapor. This evaporation requires energy, known as the heat of vaporization. The heat required to turn liquid water into water vapor is removed from the body of water that remains, lowering its heat content and thus its temperature.

Evaporation is increased by high wind speeds, high air temperature, low relative humidity, and high water temperature. As evaporation takes place, the pool operator must replace the water, which further lowers the pool or spa water

© National Swimming Pool Foundation 2017

Photo 12-1. *Evaporation is increased by high water temperature relative to the air temperature.*

temperature. Evaporation causes about 50% of all energy losses.

The energy loss for one gallon of water evaporation is 8,730 British Thermal Units (BTUs). For example, if a 55,000 gallon pool lost one inch of water due to evaporation, the loss would be 781 gallons. The total BTUs lost would be 781 times 8,730 or 6,818,130 BTUs. 55,000 gallons is 458,150 pounds of water, which is also the number of BTUs necessary for a 1°F temperature change. Dividing 6,818,130 by 458,150 represents a BTU loss that is equivalent to a temperature decrease of 15°F, for 1 inch of water loss due to evaporation.

In hot outdoor environments, pool water tends to get too hot. Often waterfalls or other features are designed to help cool the water. The cooling occurs by evaporation and convection.

Metric

It takes 4.18 kilojoules to heat 1 liter of water by 1 degree Celsius. If you have a pool that is 200,000 liters in volume, you would need 836,000 kilojoules to raise the temperature by 1 degree Celsius. If you want to raise the temperature 5 degrees higher than the unheated water, how many kilojoules would be needed to reach the desired temperature?

5°C x 200,000 liters x 4.18 kilojoules = 4,180,000 kilojoules required to raise the temperature 5°C.

Convection Losses

Convection losses are closely related to the evaporative losses for a pool or spa. Convection, like evaporation, occurs when heat from the water's surface is transferred to the cooler surrounding air. The movement of air across the water's surface cools the water in a manner similar to blowing across a hot cup of coffee or tea before drinking. Convection losses can account for 15% to 25% of total heat losses.

There are other commonly observed forms of convection loss. People experience convection loss when they leave the water and feel chilled as air blows against their skin. The wind chill factor is based on the increased cooling due to wind blowing against people and increasing the convection of heat.

Thermal Radiation Losses

A warm pool will radiate heat to a cooler sky. This thermal radiation is similar to the heat felt across the room from a fireplace. These losses increase when there is no cloud cover, when the relative humidity is high, and when the pool temperature is relatively high. The losses due to thermal radiation account for about 20% to 30% of the heat lost from a pool or spa.

Conduction Losses

Conduction is the movement of heat through an in-ground pool's structural components. It is the only heat loss that does not occur at the surface. The amount of heat lost after the pool's components reach an equilibrium temperature is small, accounting for about 5% of all heat losses. Pools built in a high water table environment will experience a much higher rate of conductive heat loss.

Controlling Energy Losses

Sheltering the surface of a pool from the wind will reduce the energy losses associated with evaporation and convection. Heating costs will increase for an open body of water as compared to one that is sheltered from the wind. Movable planters or wind blocks can shelter a pool in cooler months. Allowing wind to blow across the pool during hot weather can help cool the water, which might otherwise be too warm for some pool activities.

© National Swimming Pool Foundation 2017

Indoor pools must control the amount of relative humidity for the comfort of the users and visitors and also for the protection of the building and equipment. The indoor air temperature should be kept 2°F to 5°F (1°C to 2.5°C) above the temperature of the pool water. The relative humidity should be maintained between 40% and 60%, which will help to reduce the amount of evaporation.

Evaporation occurs in both indoor and outdoor pools. One method to reduce the amount of evaporative losses is to cover the pool or spa water surface during non-use periods.

Pool and Spa Covers

The use of a pool cover reduces the heat loss due to evaporation, thermal radiation, and convection, which account for about 95% of losses. Depending on the length of the swimming season, pool covers can reduce heating costs by 50% to 70%. In addition, pool covers reduce the amount of dirt and debris in the water, which in turn lowers the demand for chemical consumption.

Photo 12-2. *Pool covers reduce heat losses due to radiation, evaporation, and convection.*

There are three basic types of pool covers:
- Translucent air cell (bubble)
- Insulating foam wrapped in vinyl
- Specialty vinyl with sewn, weighted edges

Most pool covers are removed during daylight hours, and any heat gain potential is therefore not realized. However, on those days when a bubble cover is used, it can absorb about 80% of the heat energy striking the surface and transfer it to the water.

Pool covers can be manually placed or can be semiautomatic or fully automatic in their operation. Fully automatic systems only require operator activation. A motor reel system pulls the

Photo 12-3. *Fully automatic pool cover with a motor reel system that pulls the cover into place*

cover into place without any operator assistance. The semiautomatic system requires the operator to guide the cover into place.

Some pool and spa cover designs are considered to be a barrier to access. These are called safety covers and must meet the requirements of ASTM standard F1346-91 (2003). Covers that do not meet this standard must never be in place while the pool or spa is open for use.

Some covers are designed for winter use to keep dirt and other debris from entering the pool during the closed winter season. With any cover, chemical treatment of the water must be carefully controlled so as not to damage the cover and void the manufacturer's warranty. Read the manufacturer's instructions carefully. No pool cover should be in use or in place when the pool or spa is being used.

Heat Gains

Swimming pools and spas gain heat in three ways. The first is natural sunlight, absorbed directly by the water. About 90% of the sunlight that reaches the surface of a pool is absorbed. Time of year, shade availability, pool location, and layout affect the amount of sunlight that can be absorbed. Secondly, an indirect energy source is sunlight that has been absorbed by the pool deck and transferred by conduction to the water through the pool wall structure. The third source of heat gain is by fossil fuel, electric, heat pump, heat exchangers or solar heating systems.

Gas Heaters

The fuel in a typical gas heater system is natural gas or propane. Natural gas is lighter than air. If the heater burner tray is flooded with gas but not ignited, the natural gas will escape. Natural gas has an additive, giving it an odor that can be detected.

Propane gas is heavier than air and also has an additive to give it an odor. If for some reason the propane fails to ignite, it will remain on the bottom of the heater. Should the concentrated propane ignite suddenly, a violent explosion will occur. The force of this energy release will blow out through the open front panel of the heater, possibly causing serious injury or death to anyone standing close to the heater. The pool and spa operator should always follow the manufacturer's troubleshooting instructions for ignition problems.

There are two methods of ignition for a gas fired heater: millivolt and electric pilot. Millivolt ignited heaters have a pilot light that is constantly burning. The heat of the pilot is converted to a small amount of electricity by a thermocouple. With the proper switches, the thermocouple creates a control circuit. Electricity passes through the circuit when it is closed, opening the main gas valve. The gas floods into the burner and is ignited by the pilot light. State or local codes may ban millivolt ignition. The temperature in the burner chamber can approach 1,100°F (593°C).

Electronic ignition heaters produce an electronic spark when they are turned on. This spark ignites the pilot, which then ignites the gas in the burner in the same way as in the millivolt ignited heater. The control circuit is usually 25 volts AC.

Photo 12-4. *All pool/spa heaters should be positioned so their controls are not accessible to unauthorized users.*

Electric Heaters

Electric immersion element heaters are often used for spas. They have a high cost of operation and a slow heat rise or recovery time. An electric coil is immersed in water that flows through the unit.

Heat Exchangers

Many large aquatic facilities heat their pool by installing heat exchangers. In large recreation centers there already exists heating for water in the bathrooms and showers. A by-pass line is taken from this hot water system, which comes into contact with a by-pass line from the swimming pool return line. Heat is exchanged between the two lines.

Photo 12-5. *Heat exchangers utilize the existing hot water supply of a building to heat the swimming pool water.*

The heat exchanger usually has an outer shell which contains multiple small diameter tubes. Hot water from the building's hot water system, and possibly the building's heating system, circulates to the heat exchanger and the small tubes are heated by the hot water. The pool water, which surrounds the small tubes, is heated by the heat exchanged through the small tubes.

There should be a pool water thermostat that controls the pool temperature. When the pool water needs to be heated, a small circulation pump turns on to draw water from the building heating system through the heat exchanger.

© National Swimming Pool Foundation 2017

Heat Pumps

Heat may be extracted from the air or water and transferred to the water by the use of a heat exchanger. This system is called a heat pump.

This system does exactly what its name implies: it moves heat from one location to another. Heat pumps involve a change of phase using a refrigerant vapor compression cycle to move heat from the source to the pool or spa water. The only costs are for electricity to operate the compressor and the pumps.

A phase change heat pump uses a liquid with a low boiling point. This was typically freon, comprised of chlorofluorocarbons (CFC); but now is generally hydrofluorocarbons (HFC), which are not destructive to the earth's ozone layer. The liquid requires energy to evaporate, and it obtains that energy from a heat exchange with the surrounding air. When the vapor condenses, it releases the energy as heat.

First the liquid's pressure and temperature are lowered by an expansion valve, forcing the liquid to evaporate and extract heat from its surroundings. The vapor is then pumped to the compression side, the compressor, where it is compressed into a high pressure, high temperature state. As this vapor travels through the pool water heat exchanger, it gives up its heat and condenses back to a liquid and the cycle begins again.

On the output side of the pump where the heat is transferred, the heat that was extracted from the air, plus the amount of heat that corresponds to the electrical power used to run the system, is available for use.

Air Heat Pumps

For an air-source heat pump, the amount of heat that can be pumped depends on the air temperature and humidity of the air. The colder the air, the less heat can be extracted and pumped.

A newer technology involves the use of scroll compressors. Conventional heat pump compressors use a piston and two check valves to compress refrigerant to make heat. The scroll compressor has two scrolls that rotate around

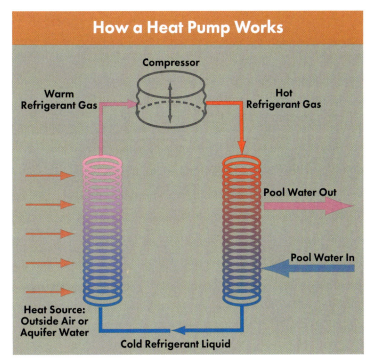

How a Heat Pump Works

Compressor

Warm Refrigerant Gas

Hot Refrigerant Gas

Pool Water Out

Pool Water In

Heat Source: Outside Air or Aquifer Water

Cold Refrigerant Liquid

Illustration 12-2. *Heat pump diagram*

each other to continuously compress refrigerant with no valves. Scroll compressors are more expensive but offer the following advantages:

- Higher heat output at lower air temperatures
- Fewer operating parts and related maintenance problems
- Lower operating noise

Geothermal Heat Pumps

These heat pump systems use aquifer or surface water as the source of heat energy. Instead of an air-to-water system, it is a water-to-water system. These are commonly referred to as geosource heat pumps. The only outside energy requirement is electricity to operate the compressor and the pumps for the source water. Water is pumped through a heat exchanger in the heat pump. Heat is extracted and the water is then returned to the ground, either through discharge on a drain field or through a closed earth loop system.

If aquifer water is used, the source water is between 55°F and 75°F (12.8°C and 23.9°C), depending on location. A closed loop system pumps the source water to the heat exchange system. The water is then returned to the source by use of a pump. Geothermal Heat Pumps are typically more efficient than air source units due to ground water being more stable in temperature than air.

Coefficient of Performance (COP)

When comparing the performance of heat pumps, it is best to avoid the word "efficiency," as it has many different meanings. The term coefficient of performance (COP) is used to describe the ratio of heat output to electrical power consumption. The higher the COP, the more efficient the heat pump is. A typical heat pump has a COP that can range from three to eight, compared to an electric heater, which has a COP of one.

Solar Heating

The surface of pool water can be expanded by the use of solar panels. The solar panels absorb heat energy from the sun, which is then transferred to the water. The amount of energy absorbed is related to the size of the solar panels and their orientation to the sun. Usually, the panels face the equator, southwest in the northern hemisphere, or northwest in the southern hemisphere, and have an area equal to 50% or 120% of the pool surface area.

Photo 12-6. *Solar panels absorb heat energy from the sun, which is then transferred to the water.*

Solar energy should be added to the water prior to any other type of heating system. The heat gain from the solar heating system can then be augmented if necessary by a supplemental system. The solar system has sensors that detect the amount of heat on the panels. These sensors control motorized valves that allow the water to enter the panels if sufficient heat energy is available for transfer. Otherwise the water bypasses the panels and is heated strictly by the auxiliary system.

Thermostats and time clocks are used for the control of solar panels. With a well designed and operated system, it is possible to add too much heat to the water. Solar panels may also be operated at night during warm weather months to cool the pool water by radiation.

The process of continuously passing water through solar panels and then to the pool is called the open loop system. There is no additional medium for the transfer process other than unglazed collectors. A different system uses glazed collectors containing transfer fluids and a heat exchanger. The internal fluid is heated by the sun and is transported to the heat exchanger, which then heats the pool water flowing through the system. This process is called the closed loop system.

Gas Heater Sizing

The main concern in properly sizing the heating system is to understand what the desired water temperature is and the amount of time it will take to achieve that temperature under normal conditions. A heater that is too small will have a long heat rise time. A heater that is too large will increase the initial installation cost.

The process of selecting the type and size of heater will differ as to whether the heater is for a pool or a spa operation. The main consideration for a pool is the amount of heat loss through the surface. For a spa, the main consideration is the amount of time to reach operating temperature. Another concern is whether the heat will be used to maintain a certain temperature or will be used intermittently. For maintenance heating, surface area is important. For intermittent heating, water volume is important.

Other decision factors include wind, altitude, and how the pool is shaded. For every 1,000 feet (300 meters) above sea level, the heater output requirements increase by 4%.

For fossil fuel heating, the availability of fuel is important. In some regions, natural gas may not be available. Propane or fuel oil need to be examined for pricing and availability.

When sizing a heater, multiply the number of gallons by 8.33 pounds per gallon, and by the

Photo 12-7. *Properly sized heaters will ensure that the desired water temperature will be reached in a timely manner.*

© National Swimming Pool Foundation 2017

temperature rise. The answer is the number of BTUs required to heat the pool or spa initially but is not a good representation of the maintenance heating needs.

Example 12-1

Here's an example using a 6 degree temperature rise in a 40,000 gallon pool. You want to raise the temperature of your 40,000 gallon pool from 74°F to 80°F. How many BTUs will this require?

$$BTUs = Gallons \times 8.33 \times °F \text{ temp. rise}$$
$$BTUs = 40,000 \text{ gallons} \times 8.33 \times 6$$
$$BTUs = 1,999,200$$

Example 12-1: Metric

It takes 4.18 kilojoules to heat 1 liter of water by 1 degree Celsius. Therefore, if you have 1,500,000 liters and you want to go from 23°C to 27°C, how many kilojoules would you need?

$$Kilojoules = Liters \times 4.18 \times °C \text{ temp rise}$$
$$Kilojoules = 1,500,000 \times 4.18 \times 4$$
$$Kilojoules = 25,080,000$$

Example 12-2

Here's an example using a 40 degree temperature rise in a 1,400 gallon spa.

$$BTUs = Gallons \times 8.33 \times °F \text{ temp. rise}$$
$$BTUs = 1,400 \text{ gallons} \times 8.33 \times 40$$
$$BTUs = 466,480$$

This number can either be divided by the desired heat-up time to give you the required heater output, or it can be divided by the heater capacity to give you the heat-up time a given model will provide.

The amount of heat required to maintain a pool at a specified temperature is usually much less than the initial heat up requirements. Determining site conditions, such as air/water temperature difference, wind conditions and shade levels will be necessary to calculate maintenance heating requirements.

In worst case situations unblanketed pools can lose as much as 50% of total pool temperature rise. Blanketed pools reduce these losses to the 15% to 25% range.

Example 12-3

Using a 10 degree temperature rise in a 40,000 gallon pool. You want to raise the 40,000 gallon pool from 72 degrees to 82 degrees and maintain it at that 82 degree temperature. Your pool uses a bubble blanket for heat retention.

$$BTUs = Gallons \times 8.33 \times \text{degrees of temperature rise} \times 0.20 \text{ (20\% of daily loss factor)}$$
$$BTUs = 40,000 \times 8.33 \times 10 \times 0.20$$
$$BTUs = 666,400$$

Cost of Operation

Once you know how many BTUs per hour the heater provides, you can calculate the number of therms provided. Divide the BTUs used per hour by 100,000 to calculate the therms per hour consumed. Multiply this number by the hours operated per day to get the daily consumption of therms. The cost per therm is shown on most gas bills.

Metric Cost of Operation Example

You have a 5,300 liter spa and wish to raise the temperature by 4.5 degrees Celsius. How many kilojoules are needed?

$$5300 \times 4.18 \times 4.5 = 99,693 \text{ kilojoules}$$

There are 3,600 kilojoules per kilowatt hour. Daily kilowatts required to raise the temperature are

$$99,693 \div 3600 = 27.7 \text{ daily kilowatts}$$

If your heater output is 5 kilowatts, then your heater will need to run for

$$27.7 \div 5 = 5.54 \text{ hours}$$

Multiply the 27.7 kilowatts by the cost per kilowatt to know the final cost.

Heater Installation

The American National Standards Institute offers guidelines on heater installation in ANSI Standard 2223.1. This standard sets clearance requirements based on the external temperatures of heaters, which may vary from manufacturer to manufacturer.

All heaters must be installed at least five feet from the inside wall of a spa unless the heater is separated from the spa by a fence, wall or other permanent barrier.

The heater must be installed on a level, non-combustible base, such as brick or concrete. If concrete blocks are used as a base, they must be aligned so the cells are all pointing in the same direction; the end should be left open. When such hollow masonry is used, the pad must be at least four inches high and covered with at least a 24-gauge piece of sheet metal.

If the heater is placed in an area exposed to

© National Swimming Pool Foundation 2017

high winds, the unit either must be installed at least three feet from the nearest wall or a wind block must be constructed to help minimize the wind effect.

The heater should be installed downstream of the pump and filter and upstream of any automatic chlorinating, brominating, or ozone disinfecting equipment.

If the circulation system is run with a timer, the heater should be equipped with a separate low-voltage switch that deactivates the heater before the pump is turned off. This useful circuit is known as the heater's fireman switch. On a millivolt heater, the length of wire between the heater and the timer should not exceed 30 feet. Resistance on longer runs will reduce the millivolts to a level that will not support reliable operation of the gas valve.

Air Circulation

Indoor pools and spas require that the relative humidity levels be maintained between 40% and 60%. This level provides for the comfort of the users and guests, assists in the control of energy consumption, and provides for proper building protection. The American Society of Heating, Refrigerating and Air-Conditioning Engineers (ASHRAE) has established standards for ventilation rates for indoor environments, including swimming pools, for acceptable indoor

air quality. The ANSI/ASHRAE Standard 62.1-2016, "Ventilation for Acceptable Indoor Air Quality," requires 0.48 cfm (cubic feet per minute) of outdoor air per square foot on pool and deck area (2.4 liters per second per square meter).

Indoor air circulation designs must consider the following items:

- Humidity control
- Ventilation requirements for air quality, such as outdoor air and exhaust air
- Air distribution
- Air duct design
- Evaporation rates
- Pool water chemistry

The purpose of air standards is to specify minimum ventilation rates and indoor air quality that will be acceptable to human occupants. ASHRAE defines acceptable indoor air quality as

"air in which there are no known contaminants at harmful concentrations as determined by cognizant authorities and with which a substantial majority (80% or more) of the people exposed do not express dissatisfaction."

Fluctuations in relative humidity outside the 40% to 60% range can increase levels of bacteria, viruses, fungi and other factors that reduce air quality. For users, 50% to 60% relative humidity is most comfortable. High relative humidity levels are destructive to building components. Mold and mildew can attack wall,

Photo 12-8. *Humidity control is an important design consideration for large indoor pool facilities.*

© National Swimming Pool Foundation 2017

Photo 12-9. *Ventilation system design and operation is important to achieve good air quality at indoor aquatic facilities. Low level air returns help to carry away gasses evaporating from the water.*

floor, and ceiling coverings. Condensation can degrade many building materials. In the worst case, the roof could collapse due to corrosion from water condensing on the structure.

Total heat loads, or gains and losses, for the air environment in a spa enclosure include outdoor air, lighting, walls, roof, and glass, with internal heat gains coming from people and evaporation.

Water, air temperature, and relative humidity conditions must be carefully controlled and regulated. Air temperatures in public and institutional pools should be maintained 2°F to 4°F (1°C–2.0°C) above the water temperatures. The maximum comfort level for air temperature is 86°F (30°C). These temperatures are important to minimize the pool water evaporation as well as to avoid chilling users as they leave the water.

Recommendations are as follows:

- Relative humidity should be maintained at the recommended levels because of the evaporated cooling effect on a person emerging from the pool and because of the increased rate of evaporation from the pool, which increases pool heating requirements
- Humidity that is higher than recommended encourages corrosion and condensation problems as well as occupant discomfort.

Air velocities should not exceed 0.4 feet/sec. (0.13 m/sec) at a point 8 feet (2.4 m) above the walking deck of the pool.

- Ventilation is important, especially if chlorine is used to treat the pool water. Ventilation is also used to prevent temperature stratification in areas with high ceilings. Since exhaust air will have chloramines from the chlorine treatment and also have high moisture content, care must be exercised to vent this air to the outside environment and not into dressing rooms, bathrooms, or showers.
- Low level return vents can be used to extract air from the surface of the water
- Pool areas should have a slight negative pressure and automatic door closers to prevent the contaminated air, laden with moisture and chloramines, from migrating into adjacent areas of the building
- Six to eight air changes per hour should occur, except where mechanical cooling is used. With mechanical cooling, the recommended rate is four to six air changes per hour for therapeutic pools.

Since natatoriums, or indoor pools, can create a major energy burden, energy conservation should be considered in any facility housing a natatorium. This includes evaluating the primary heating and cooling systems, fan motors, backup water heaters (in the case of geothermal energy use), pumps, and heat recovery ventilation.

Natatoriums with fixed outdoor air ventilation rates without dehumidification generally have seasonally fluctuating space temperatures and humidity levels. Since these systems usually cannot maintain constant humidity conditions, they may encourage mold and mildew growth and poor indoor air quality. In addition, varying activity levels will also cause the humidity level to fluctuate, and thus change the demand on ventilation air. The presence of aquatic play features with turbulent water will also increase humidity.

Heat Recovery Ventilation

In colder climates, a vast amount of energy is required to heat air exchanged from the outside. To avoid wasting the heat from the extracted air, it may be necessary to install an air heat exchanger unit which transfers the heat into the incoming air. These heat recovery systems can provide significant energy savings.

Heat recovery ventilation is a ventilation system that employs a counter-flow heat exchanger between the inbound and outbound air flow. It provides fresh air and improved indoor air quality, while also saving energy by reducing the heating, or cooling, requirements.

Heat recovery ventilators (HRVs), as the name implies, recover the heat energy in the exhaust air, and transfer it to fresh air as it enters the building.

There are a number of heat exchanger methods used in air-to-air HRV devices. The most common method used for indoor swimming pools is a counter current heat exchanger, which is up to 99% efficient.

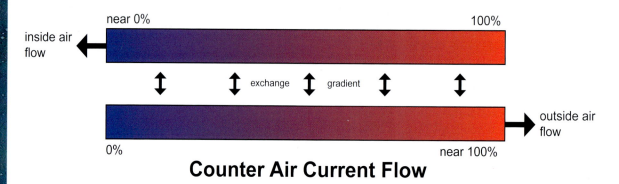

Counter Air Current Flow

Illustration 12-3. *Diagram demonstrating the heat exchange that occurs between outside and inside air in a heat recovery ventilation system*

© National Swimming Pool Foundation 2017

Chapter 13:
Spa & Therapy Operations

"I can't think of any sorrow in the world that a hot bath wouldn't help, just a little bit."

–Susan Glasee

Spas, hot tubs, and therapy pools provide for relaxation, rehabilitation, and may provide for respiratory and cardiac exercise. The use of hot water for purposes of tranquility and social interaction has existed for over 2,000 years in locations as diverse as ancient Rome, Japan and India, and continues with the use of hot springs in North America. The hot water environment brings about a level of relaxation, both mental and physical, that is hard to achieve by any other means.

The healing benefits of warm water became well known in Europe as early as the 15th century. Today, therapeutic benefits are one of the driving forces in the rapid growth of spas and hot tubs. Often, people who use a warm water facility have severe physical afflictions, such as arthritis, and may be taking prescription medication.

The use of medications combined with warm water immersion could result in serious physical consequences for bathers. This is just one of many special concerns of operating a warm or hot water facility. Warm water and high user loads can also produce unhealthy and unsafe conditions.

A spa or hot tub is a structure containing water with a depth not to exceed 48 inches (1.22 meters). The structure can be made of many different materials, such as concrete, fiberglass, thermoplastic, or stainless steel. The wall finish can be acrylic, marcite, exposed aggregate, tile, wood, or marble. The water circulates through two types of returns: circulation and therapy jets. There is a high water velocity from the circulation return jets and a separate control capability for air injection into the therapy returns.

Some confusion exists as to the proper terminology for these warm water facilities. There are many names, such as spa pools, swim spas, and therapy pools, to name just a few. The word Jacuzzi has been also used, but the name Jacuzzi® is a trade name for a particular manufacturer and should not be used as a generic description of a spa.

The term spa originally was used for natural

> **Warning**
> A casual attitude regarding maintenance and safety standards for spas, hot tubs, and hot water therapy pools can quickly produce an unhealthy and unsafe environment.

Photo 13-1. *Spas provide for relaxation and socialization. The water should always be free of foam and have no color tint, except beautiful blue.*

© National Swimming Pool Foundation 2017

hot and cold immersion baths. The term hot tub has traditionally been thought of as a wood structure. In today's language, hot tub has evolved to describe a portable spa.

Innovative swim spa is terminology used to describe a combination of a spa and a short-length pool. Swim spas propel water, creating a current for bathers to swim against.

In an effort to standardize definitions, the pool and spa industry has recently begun to review spa and hot tub terminology. Regardless of the name, the common thread in all of these facilities is higher temperatures and rapid water movement. Throughout this chapter we will refer to hot tubs, spas, or swim spas as spas.

In addition to spas, hot tubs, and therapy pools, another type of therapy vessel is a float tank, also known as a floatation tank, float room/pod/chamber, isolation tank, or sensory deprivation tank. Used for meditation and relaxation, a float tank contains a saturated solution of magnesium sulfate (Epsom salt) having a specific gravity of 1.23 to 1.3, provides a light and sound free environment, and is maintained at a temperature of approximately 93.5°F (34.1°C). With the rising interest in commercial float tanks has come demand for information on their proper regulation and operation. See Appendix C-4 for more information on safe and effective operation of float tanks.

Hot Water Health Benefits

The question driving many to use spas is, "How can immersion in hot water benefit my health?" As people experience life, they often feel pain and sore muscles and joints. Healing happens faster as blood flow to the injured location increases. Bodies make adjustments when they are immersed in water. These changes are similar to those that occur during exercise. The changes include increased circulation, more efficient breathing, and improvement in mood.

There are several ways in which hot-water immersion improves healing:

- Immersion increases circulation. When muscles are warmed and the body is immersed, the blood supply to the area muscles increases.
- When the body is immersed, water exerts pressure on the body. This increased pressure tends to reduce swelling.

- The buoyancy of the water provides unique benefits that are significant. Immersion in water reduces the amount of weight people bear on their joints due to gravity.
- Water plays a useful role for people who suffer from arthritis, knee, hip, or other joint problems. Immersion in warm water tends to increase joint mobility, reduce joint stiffness, and increase flexibility and range of motion.

> **Warning**
> Do not allow the use of a spa for therapeutic purposes without a doctor's permission. A licensed hydrotherapy technician should supervise any and all therapy sessions. Individuals who are on medications should not use any hot water facility without doctor's permission, and then only under the supervision of a licensed hydrotherapist. Never allow hot water use to exceed 15 minutes. Any immersion in hot water at 104°F/40°C for longer than 15 minutes could result in hyperthermia. Hyperthermia is the over heating of the body's internal temperature.

It is well known that when a person's body is immersed in water, the water's pressure affects almost every part of the body. When immersed, the body must adjust to the pressure from the surrounding warm water. The result is greater cardiac output and lower resting pulse. Also, the water pressure and hot temperature help the body to release chemicals/hormones that help perople relax and improve mood. For more information about health benefits see Hot Water and Healthy Living available for no charge at www.nspf.org.

Often, therapy facilities will use alternate hot and cold water immersion. Individuals on heart medications must be cautioned against using a hot water immersion and then taking a dip in a cold pool. This type of therapy must only be performed with professional supervision. The water temperature in spas is normally maintained between 98–104°F (36.7–40°C). Therapy pools and some spas designed for physical exercise, however, are maintained at lower temperatures.

© National Swimming Pool Foundation 2017

Safe Use Guidelines

Many codes have regulations covering the safe use of hot water facilities. The Consumer Product Safety Commission (CPSC) recommends the following safety precautions when using a spa. Although developed for residential use, many of these precautions apply to commercial applications:

- Always use a locked safety cover when the spa is not in use, and keep young children away from spas unless there is constant adult supervision
- Make sure the spa has dual drains and anti-entrapment drain covers, and complies with the Virginia Graeme Baker Pool & Spa Safety Act
- Regularly have a professional check the spa and make sure it is in good, safe, working condition, and that drain covers are in place and not cracked or missing. Check the drain covers throughout the year.
- Know where the cut-off switch for the pump is so it can be turned off in an emergency
- Be aware that consuming alcohol while using a spa could lead to drowning. Commercial facilities often require signs warning against the use of alcohol or medication when using a spa.
- Keep the temperature of the water in the spa at 104°F/40°C or lower

Photo 13-2. *The common practice is to limit the use of the spa to 15 minutes.*

In addition, the following items must also be part of the compliance:

- Always maintain a disinfectant residual because bacteria grow faster in hot spa water
- Monitor and control water pH more closely because the air and hot water cause pH to rise, thus lowering the ability of the disinfectant to kill bacteria

Signage

Rules governing the use of a spa should be posted at the entrance to the facility. The objective of the signs is to help users reduce any risk of injury. Always follow the requirements of jurisdictional codes and regulations. In the event the state and/or local code does not provide specific guidance, guidelines from the Centers for Disease Control & Prevention (CDC) can help an operator or facility management determine suitable signage. The CDC recommends that the following items should be listed on signs:

- Caution: pregnant women, elderly persons, and persons suffering from heart disease, diabetes, or high or low blood pressure should not enter the spa without prior medical consultation and permission from their doctor
- Do not use the spa while under the influence of alcohol, tranquilizers, or other drugs that cause drowsiness or that raise or lower blood pressure
- Do not use at water temperatures greater than 104°F (40°C)
- Do not use alone
- Unsupervised use by children is prohibited.
- Enter and exit slowly
- Observe reasonable time limits (that is,10–15 minutes); then leave the water and cool down before returning for another brief stay

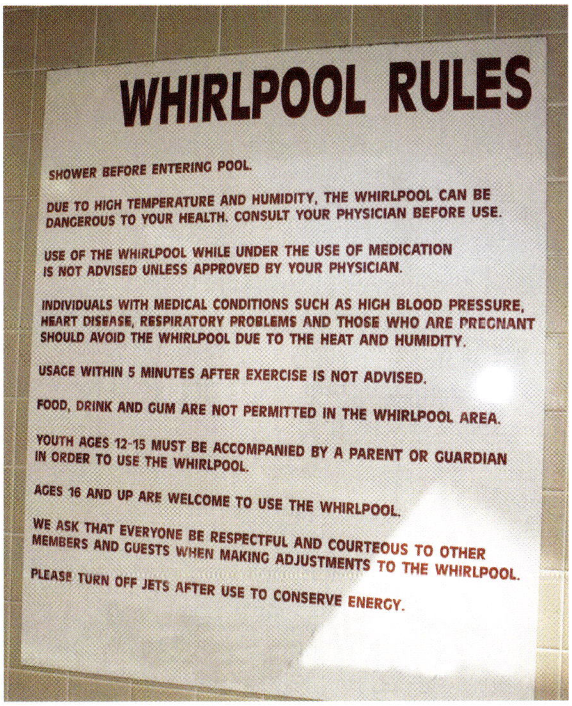

WHIRLPOOL RULES

SHOWER BEFORE ENTERING POOL.

DUE TO HIGH TEMPERATURE AND HUMIDITY, THE WHIRLPOOL CAN BE DANGEROUS TO YOUR HEALTH. CONSULT YOUR PHYSICIAN BEFORE USE.

USE OF THE WHIRLPOOL WHILE UNDER THE USE OF MEDICATION IS NOT ADVISED UNLESS APPROVED BY YOUR PHYSICIAN.

INDIVIDUALS WITH MEDICAL CONDITIONS SUCH AS HIGH BLOOD PRESSURE, HEART DISEASE, RESPIRATORY PROBLEMS AND THOSE WHO ARE PREGNANT SHOULD AVOID THE WHIRLPOOL DUE TO THE HEAT AND HUMIDITY.

USAGE WITHIN 5 MINUTES AFTER EXERCISE IS NOT ADVISED.

FOOD, DRINK AND GUM ARE NOT PERMITTED IN THE WHIRLPOOL AREA.

YOUTH AGES 12-15 MUST BE ACCOMPANIED BY A PARENT OR GUARDIAN IN ORDER TO USE THE WHIRLPOOL.

AGES 16 AND UP ARE WELCOME TO USE THE WHIRLPOOL.

WE ASK THAT EVERYONE BE RESPECTFUL AND COURTEOUS TO OTHER MEMBERS AND GUESTS WHEN MAKING ADJUSTMENTS TO THE WHIRLPOOL.

PLEASE TURN OFF JETS AFTER USE TO CONSERVE ENERGY.

Photo 13-3. *Spa rules, emergency telephones, and emergency off switches may be required by local codes. The Centers for Disease Control & Prevention has similar recommendations.*

- Long exposure may result in nausea, dizziness, or fainting
- Keep all breakable objects out of the area

In addition to the above sign suggestions, any applicable signage used for pool use rules should also be used for spas; included would be the maximum user load.

The CDC goes on to recommend that a sign be posted in the immediate vicinity of the spa stating the location of the nearest telephone and indicating that emergency telephone numbers are posted at that location. Those emergency telephone numbers should include the name and phone number of the nearest available police, fire and/or rescue unit, physician, ambulance service, and hospital. A sign should also be posted requiring each user to shower prior to entering the spa.

Photo 13-4. *An emergency script next to the emergency telephone may help in calming the caller by providing necessary guidance.*

Timers and Emergency Switches

Commercial spas are typically equipped with a 15-minute timer controlling the hydrotherapy jets and blower operation. The switch to turn on the jets is typically located at a distance such that the spa user is required to get out of the water for reactivation. This action allows the body to cool and helps prevent users from losing consciousness and drowning.

An emergency shut-off switch should be located close to the spa to stop all circulation and activate an audible alarm. Local codes may require that the emergency shut-off switch be visible from the spa.

Photo 13-5. *Should entrapment occur, a means of quickly shutting off the circulation system may assist in the rescue efforts.*

Showers

Nude showering with soap removes bacteria from the skin and buttocks and washes away sweat, oils, suntan lotion, and dirt that can quickly use up the disinfectant in a spa. Soil and sweat can also transmit bacteria to the water. It is recommended that all individuals take showers before entering the spa. To encourage use, the showers should be provided with hot water. The location of the shower should be close to the spa. Codes and regulations may dictate what this distance should be.

Hyperthermia

Hyperthermia occurs when the internal body temperature reaches a level several degrees above the normal body temperature of 98.6°F (37°C). Symptoms include dizziness, fainting, drowsiness, lethargy, and an increase in the internal body temperature. The effects of hyperthermia include:

- Lack of awareness that the user is losing their ability to physically leave the spa
- Failure to recognize how hot the water is
- Failure to recognize need to leave the spa
- Physical inability to leave the spa
- Damage to fetus of pregnant women
- Unconsciousness, resulting in a danger of drowning

In 1987, the CPSC helped develop requirements for temperature controls to make sure that spa water temperatures never exceed 104°F/40°C. The smaller the child, or adult, the greater the likelihood that their core body temperature will increase when exposed to hot water. Women who may be pregnant, women who are pregnant, and young children should only use a spa after consulting with a physician. Some state or local codes may limit spa temperature to 102°F/38.9°C. The pool operator should always follow local code requirements.

Main Drain

The CPSC has reported several incidences and deaths after users' hair was sucked into and tangled behind the pool or spa suction fitting, causing the victims' heads to be held under water. These incidences of hair entrapment are most common in spas because of the shallow water depth. In other cases, the CPSC reported that suction from drain outlets was strong enough

© National Swimming Pool Foundation 2017

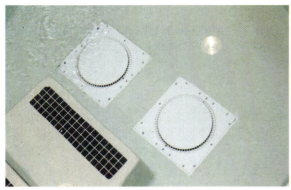

Photo 13-6. *Main drain covers should be selected so as to reduce or prevent the chance for hair entanglement or entrapment.*

to cause entrapment of a body or a limb causing injury or drowning.

The Aquatic Safety Compendium™ published by the National Swimming Pool Foundation®, contains a chapter entitled, "Suction Entrapment and Hair Entanglement/Entrapment." This is included to provide additional information about the prevention of entrapment. The report concludes, "suction entrapment is entirely preventable...[with] proper covers or grates, split drains, specified suction, side flow rates and maintenance." The report reinforces data from the CPSC showing that most incidences of entrapment have occurred in spas.

Hair entanglement and body entrapment are the most common forms of entrapment occurring in spas. The Facility Safety and Water Circulation chapters provide additional information and guidance on how to avoid these and other forms of entrapment.

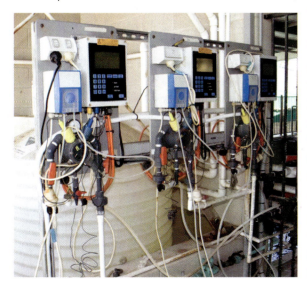

Photo 13-7. *An ORP system for chemical control is often required by codes for spas, which helps to maintain proper disinfectant levels.*

Hot Water Diseases

A small volume of hot water with air bubbling through it is a good environment for bacterial growth. The temperature of the water in spas causes the level of active chlorine or bromine in the water to dissipate more quickly than in cooler swimming pools. As the disinfectant level becomes lower, there is an increased risk for a bacterial growth. This situation is made worse by high user density. Every person that enters a spa or pool carries bacteria into the water. Compared to a swimming pool, there are far fewer gallons per user in a spa; therefore, the concentration of bacteria is higher in the spa than in the pool. It is common to have only 200 gallons (757 liters) per person in a spa as compared to 1,800 gallons (6,814 liters) per person in a pool. Six people in a 1,200 gallon (4,543 liters) spa are equivalent to 275 people in a 55,000 gallon (208,198 liters) pool. Since spas are shallower than most pools, the amount of chlorine or bromine destroyed by sunlight is greater in outdoor spas. These different factors make it more difficult to maintain disinfectant levels.

This chapter reviews many elements that demonstrate the unique operation of a spa. There are increasing numbers of health departments and regulations requiring automatic controllers. As discussed in the Chemical Feed & Control chapter, controllers can help ensure that disinfectant levels are monitored and maintained at all times. Spas are more challenging to maintain than pools. Therefore, control systems are considered a good tool to help maintain sanitary water and prevent excessive addition of chemicals.

Medications and Drugs

Spa users who are taking medications, such as tranquilizers, antihistamines, vasoconstrictors, vasodilators, anticoagulants, and diuretics must have their physician's permission to use the facility. Any person using recreational drugs, including alcohol, should not use the facility while under the influence.

Legionnaires' Disease

In the Pool Water Contamination chapter, Legionnaires' disease was described as caused by *Legionella pneumophilia* bacteria. The risk of contracting Legionnaires' disease is much greater in and around a spa than a pool. Although these bacteria are quickly killed by chlorine or bromine, the risk is greater in spas because the spa environment is favorable for bacteria growth. These commonly found bacteria infect the lungs through tiny water droplets, or aerosol, given off by the bubble action from a spa. The aerosol droplets are small enough that they float in the air and are inhaled by people in or near the spa. The droplets deposit bacteria in the lung, which begin to grow and cause pneumonia.

Although people immersed in spa water are at a greater risk, these bacteria can and have infected people who were near a spa and inhaled the contaminated aerosol from the spa water that had not been sufficiently treated with a disinfectant (MMWR 1994, 43:521).

Dermatitis

Dermatitis is an infection that causes the skin to become itchy and develop a bumpy red rash. The skin may also become tender and develop pus-filled blisters surrounding the hair follicles. The rash may be worse under a person's swimsuit because the swimsuit keeps contaminated water in contact with the skin longer. Because of its association with spas, the rash is sometimes called hot tub itch or hot tub folliculitis. Most rashes clear up in a few days, but if a rash persists, a health care provider should be consulted.

Dermatitis is caused by contact with water contaminated with a type of bacteria called *Pseudomonas aeruginosa* (see Pool Water Contamination chapter). The bacteria cannot be seen with the naked eye, which is why it is important to test the water in the spa frequently. The rash usually appears within a few days after contact with the contaminated water. Studies on persistent dermatitis (J. Clinical Micro 1988, 1650–1654) helped establish the need for higher disinfectant levels in spas versus pools.

This same bacteria causes outer ear aches in users. Since the head and ears are not usually immersed in spa water as frequently, ear aches are rarely caused by spas.

Hot Water Systems

Spas and other hot water amenities include the same system components as found in swimming pools, such as filter pumps, motors, valves, surface water removal, inlets and outlets, heating system, circulation piping, and a disinfection system. In addition, hot water systems may also have

- Hydrotherapy pumps
- Hydrotherapy jets
- Air blowers
- Timers
- Emergency shut-off switches

Hot Water Circulation

The most common standard turnover rate required in codes for spas is no more than 30 minutes. For therapy pools, the turnover rate requirement is typically four hours, and some hospital/health club pools could be as low as three hours. The operator should consult local codes and regulations to obtain the turnover requirements. Turnover requirements must be met by the facility's main circulation system, not including hydrotherapy jet circulation.

Spa circulation systems are usually required to operate 24-hours a day. Maintaining constant circulation allows the water to be filtered, oxidized, and disinfected, ensuring that the water quality recovers after heavy use periods. It may be helpful to reduce after-hours use by controlling the heating and jet circulation systems with a timer.

Filters

The Pool & Spa Filtration chapter covers in detail how filters operate. Spa filters operate in the same manner as pool filters. Spa filters can be high rate sand, cartridge, or diatomaceous earth.

High rate sand filters are used less in spas due to the high concentration of body oils and the potential for scale formation. These two items can result in the sand grains becoming encased in a clay-like medium, providing little filtration and a blockage of flow. When this occurs, the sand must be replaced. To help sand filtration operations, the sand should be regularly degreased with a commercial cleaner. Degreasing frequency depends on spa user loading over time.

In environments that receive very heavy user loads, such as cruise ships or resorts, the CDC and the U.S. Public Health Service have provided guidance relative to filters (National Center for Environmental Health, Vessel Sanitation Program Operations Manual, 2000). A spare replacement cartridge should be on hand. Every week, or

© National Swimming Pool Foundation 2017

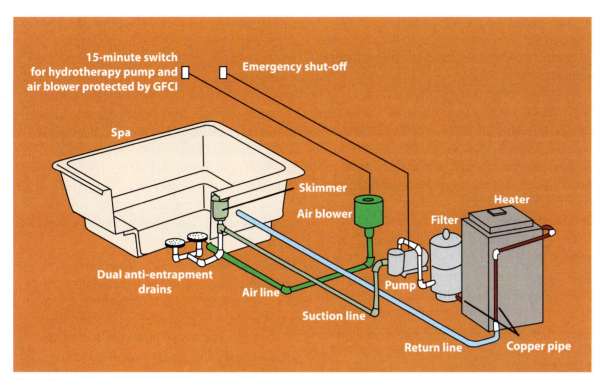

Illustration 13-1. *A hot water system includes many system components as found in pools, as well as hydrotherapy pumps and jets, air blowers, timers and emergency shut off switches.*

more often, cartridge filters should be opened and inspected for cracks, tears, or holes. Similarly, every month, sand and D.E. filters should be opened and inspected for cracks, mounds or holes; in addition, a core sample of the sand should be taken and inspected for excessive organic matter. The CDC also recommends that the sand be replaced at least every six months in cruise ship spas, unless the inspection suggests replacement sooner.

Air Blowers

An air blower is simply an air pump with a motor. The air blower must be sized to meet the hydraulic requirements of the piping and air jets. The design must not allow for water to come into contact with the blower motor, and a check valve or Hartford loop, a piping loop that has its highest point above all circulation components, is used to prevent this from happening.

Hot Water Chemistry

Studies published by the CDC have verified that spas are less likely to have proper disinfectant level compared to pools. Several factors contribute:

- Spas have higher user to water ratios
- Water aeration affects the pH and air contamination

- Water temperature accelerates the amount of user waste released into the water
- Higher water temperatures accelerate the loss of disinfectant chemicals
- Higher temperatures promote bacteria growth

Disinfectants

Government authorities commonly require higher levels of disinfectant in spas. This is confirmed by guidance from the CDC, chemical manufacturers, most public health departments, and voluntary standards. Chemical reactions in hot water occur at a faster rate.

The suggested ideal free chlorine level is 3.0 to 5.0 ppm (mg/L), with a maximum combined chlorine level of 0.5 ppm (mg/L). For bromine, the suggested ideal total bromine level is 4.0 to 6.0 ppm (mg/L). Where allowed by local codes, the PHMB (biguanide) level should be maintained ideally between 30 and 50 ppm (mg/L). A greater percentage of spas use bromine to disinfect the water. This is due to bromine's superior disinfectant performance at a higher pH. As discussed in the Disinfection chapter, spas typically have higher levels of contaminants, which increase the formation of bromamines in bromine-treated spas or chloramines in chlorine treated spas. The bromamines that form are less irritating to eyes and mucous membranes than chloramines. In addition, bromamines are more effective at killing bacteria than chloramines. Bromines may contribute to rashes called bromine itch described in the Pool Water Contamination chapter.

With the problems of elevated water temperature, aeration, and high user load, in spas the disinfectant levels and pH can quickly change. The spa operator should consider checking the disinfectant level and pH every hour. The trend is to use an automated chemical control system to feed pH and disinfection chemicals for spa operations.

More intense chemical treatments are often needed in spas. For example, there may be a need for increased oxidation on a regular basis to prevent the build-up of unwanted contamination. The development of a biofilm in the circulation piping may warrant the use of high concentrations of disinfectants. See the Disinfection chapter for a more complete discussion.

Water Balance Concerns for Hot Water

The Langelier Saturation Index (SI) applies to hot water facilities just as it does for pools. This topic is discussed fully in the Water Balance chapter. Although ideal ranges for the different water parameters are given below, as with pools, it is most important that the SI be maintained at all times. Closer care is needed to make sure the disinfectant remains effective by keeping an ideal pH level. Water balance will help protect against corrosive water dissolving metal and destroying heating elements. In addition, water balance will help protect against scaling conditions that can coat surfaces or heater elements, causing energy costs to increase. Since water balance changes more quickly in spas, chemical controllers are more useful in helping the operator maintain proper pH and water balance.

pH
The aeration typically found in spas and therapy pools, causes carbon dioxide to evaporate from the water. The loss of carbon dioxide will increase the pH and decrease the alkalinity. Much as a can of soda loses its fizz and is no longer acidic to the stomach, the pH of a hot water facility has a tendency to rise. BCDMH, often called bromine, which is commonly used to treat spa water, is acidic and tends to lower the water's pH. If alkalinity is low due to the loss of

carbon dioxide, the pH can drop quickly. The pH of the water has a tendency to go up and down as a result of these counteracting effects.

The usual requirement for pH adjustment is in the downward direction. If manual adjustments are made, muriatic acid may be too aggressive for the small volume of water in spas. A milder approach would be to use dry acid (sodium bisulfate) or carbon dioxide injection (see Chemical Feed & Control chapter).

The ideal pH is the same as with swimming pools: 7.4 to 7.6. The pH should not go below 7.2 or above 7.8.

Total Alkalinity
The role of alkalinity in a spa is the same as in a swimming pool; it acts as a buffer against a shift in pH. The total alkalinity in a hot water facility should be tested on a daily basis. The ideal alkalinity should be maintained just as with a swimming pool as described in the Water Balance chapter. Alkalinity is consumed faster in spas than in pools because carbon dioxide gas is driven from hot water that has air pumped through it. When operating a spa, operators should pay closer attention when the alkalinity gets lower. Once it is too low, the pH can quickly change, causing the disinfectant to become less effective, scale to form, or corrosion of surfaces or heating elements. If the disinfectant used lowers the pH, then it is best to have a higher total alkalinity.

Calcium Hardness
As the temperature of water increases, the solubility of calcium decreases. In spas this is a critical concern. The tendency for calcium to precipitate out of solution could result in a reduced flow rate as piping becomes constricted. Since every spa has a heater, the temperature within the heater and at the surfaces of the heating elements is higher. As a result, scale tends to form within the heater, lowering its efficiency. It is a common practice to use a scale inhibitor in spa water to help protect the heater and keep it working efficiently.

Photo 13-8.
Failure to maintain proper water balance conditions may result in scale and a reduction in water flow.

© National Swimming Pool Foundation 2017

The ideal calcium level for a hot water facility is 150 to 250 ppm (mg/L). Regulations may govern the calcium hardness level.

Temperature

The higher water temperature and aeration found in spas results in the water evaporating at a faster rate than in swimming pools. The vapor does not remove the minerals or total dissolved solids in the water. As the evaporated water is replaced, more minerals and solids are added to the water.

Therapy pools may have temperatures as low as 92°F (33.3°C). Spas and hot tubs usually operate between 98–104°F (36.7–40°C) depending on the requirements and wishes of the users. Often users will try to increase the temperature above the setting offered by the spa operator. This is very dangerous. All temperature controls for commercial hot water facilities must be locked or otherwise made inaccessible to users.

Total Dissolved Solids

As hot water ages, the concentration of minerals, unoxidized organics, and unfilterable material increases. The amount of total dissolved solids (TDS) in the water must be tested on a routine basis. As the TDS increases, the disinfectant may become less able to control bacteria and oxidize contaminants. This usually results in unattractive and cloudy water. TDS can also promote galvanic corrosion. The heater elements are more easily attacked by the spa water chemistry and unsightly staining may occur.

It is commonly recommended that the TDS not exceed 1,500 ppm (mg/L) above the start-up level (see Water Replacement section later in this chapter).

Photo 13-9. *High total dissolved solids, lack of proper water balance, and perhaps improper bonding of metallic components, may result in galvanic corrosion and staining.*

Cyanuric Acid (CyA)

Although many spas use bromine as a disinfectant, others use chlorine. In some cases, chlorinated isocyanurates are used, which release chlorine and cyanuric acid into the water. Although spa water requires more disinfectant, the chance that cyanuric acid levels can build higher than in pools is reduced because spa water is replaced with fresh water more frequently. It is important that the operator be familiar with local codes, since some health departments limit cyanuric acid use in spas and others limit its use indoors. The product label directions do not restrict the use of isocyanurates in these applications.

Other Hot Water Concerns

There are three additional items that must be given consideration when operating a hot water facility. They are
- The small volume of water and the potential for severe overdosing on chemicals
- Foaming
- Full replacement of the body of water

Chemical Overdosing

Based on the small volume, dosing a little more chemical can have a big impact on the chemical concentrations in the spa. Most chemical parameters are maintained in a range. Falling outside the ideal ranges can have negative consequences.

The Chemical Testing chapter summarizes interferences in many tests. For example, if disinfectant levels are too high, the pH test reagent can give false readings. Also, the free chlorine or total bromine test reagents can be bleached out, making it look like there is no chlorine when there is actually too much.

Overdosing any chemical can have negative effects. For example, dosing too much disinfectant can have negative consequences. High chlorine levels are no more effective at inactivating most pathogens, and more potentially toxic disinfection byproducts may form as a result of high chlorine. Bleaching of swim suits and hair becomes more likely at high disinfectant levels. Even adding too much of a water balance chemical can make the water corrosive or scale or make the disinfectant less effective.

Photo 13-10. *Foam on the spa water can form as a result of contaminants and poor oxidation. Foam can be a health concern.*

Foaming

Poor filter maintenance and poor oxidation may result in high levels of organic wastes in the water. Quaternary algicides are often used in outdoor spas. Aeration of spa water that contains either high levels of contaminants or certain algicides by the hydrotherapy inlets causes foaming. There are silicone-based products called defoamers that can help break up and dissipate the foam. However, defoamers only mask the real problem.

It is important to determine the cause of foaming and correct the underlying reason. The presence of an algicide is not a public health concern and the use of a defoamer is a reasonable solution. However, if the foam is due to the buildup of contaminants in the water because of poor oxidation and improper filter maintenance, there is a health concern. A buildup of contaminants in the water can promote the growth of bacteria in the water. If contaminants from heavy use or lack of disinfectant are the cause of the foam, the spa should be drained, cleaned, and refilled. In heavy use environments like on cruise ships, the CDC/U.S. Public Health Service recommends that water be replaced every day.

Water Replacement

Although spas are more difficult to maintain in many ways than pools, water replacement is much more easily accomplished due to their small size. The first step is to drain the water. Next, the spa can be cleaned, disinfected, and refilled relatively easily and inexpensively. Although disinfectants, water clarifiers, oxidizers, and the other chemicals used to treat spa and pool water are effective, they do not remove or oxidize all of the contaminants that go into water. Therefore, water replacement is a good periodic preventative practice.

As the levels of TDS and nuisance chloramines rise, the water becomes ever more difficult to maintain properly. The level of contaminants increases, and they can inhibit the disinfectant or act as nutrients for bacteria or algae. This can result in sustained levels of bacteria and other hazards to users' health.

The water in a spa or therapy pool should be replaced based on user loading. This replacement interval can be calculated as follows:

**Replacement Interval (days) =
Spa Gals ÷ 3 ÷ Users pers day
or in metric, Replacement Interval =
Spa Liters ÷ (3 x 3.78) ÷ Users per day**

© National Swimming Pool Foundation 2017

Photo 13-11. *Spa water replacement is a good periodic preventative practice.*

An alternative method would be to use the TDS test results as a guideline. The general guideline is to replace the water if the TDS increases by 1,500 ppm (mg/L) above the start-up water TDS.

When operating a spa or therapy pool, observe it closely. Several other factors suggest when to replace the water: foam, odor, or cloudy water. Depending on experience and the above factors, some facilities schedule water replacement after a defined number of days.

> **Caution**
> To prevent damage to the structure, in places with a high ground water table, always make sure the facility is protected by a hydrostatic relief device before draining the water.

Notes

© National Swimming Pool Foundation 2017

Chapter 14:
Facility Safety

"It is one of the worst errors to suppose that there is any path for safety except for that of duty."

–William Nevins

ater is a foreign environment for human beings, and immersion into this environment is potentially dangerous for them. Swimming and other water-based activities, such as diving, sliding, or water games, require entering this environment with a proper understanding of water safety.

Many of the chemicals used to maintain a pool and spa facility are classified as toxic and dangerous. Chemical accidents result from chemical contact with the skin or the eyes; or from inhaling or swallowing the chemical.

Some facilities may have lifeguards who have the responsibility of preventing and responding to emergencies. Other facilities are available for use with no lifeguard oversight. Either way, owners of aquatic facilities have a responsibility to provide a safe recreational environment. Water and chemical related accidents around the pool or spa environment are often the result of failing to abide by known safety practices and standards. It is the duty of facility management and the pool operator to be knowledgeable of the safety practices and standards as they apply to their facilities. The prime responsibility of every aquatic facility staff member is the prevention of accidents. This chapter provides general safety guidelines for aquatic facilities. Please consult the specific laws, rules, and regulations that may apply in your particular area.

Photo 14-1. *After-hours use of a facility with no staff on site is a very high-risk behavior.*

Training

This handbook provides a summary of various safety topics relevant to aquatic facility operators or management. Additional training is often required and helpful for compliance with laws. NSPF® provides additional training and educational programs online at www.nspf.org, as well as at the World Aquatic Health™ Conference (WAHC™). Courses available include Aquatic Risk Management, Emergency Response Planning, Aquatic Facility Audits, Aquatic Play Feature, HAZMAT, Bloodborne Pathogens, and many others.

Access

A first step in the prevention of an accident is prevention of people being in places when they should not be. After-hours use of a facility with no staff on site is a high-risk behavior. Failure to properly secure chemical storage areas can lead to unintentional and disastrous results. Every facility needs to be evaluated for the possibility of unauthorized access, and proper methods and practices should be developed and implemented to prevent this possibility.

At facilities that are required to provide lifeguards during operating hours, it is important to deny unauthorized access to all pool and spa facilities when the facility is closed. It is also important to do so for those facilities that do not provide lifeguards, in order to prevent access by unsupervised children.

Barriers

Barriers can only act as deterrents and should never be considered a guarantee of protection. There is no substitute for direct supervision by a lifeguard, parent, or other responsible individual.

Aquatics facilities are not generally open 24-hours-a-day, seven-days-a-week. During the closed times, an effective barrier is necessary

Photo 14-2. *Signs encourage a change in behavior. Barriers are a deterrent. There is no substitute for supervision.*

to prevent individuals from gaining access. A commercial pool or spa should have a barrier that completely encloses the area, such as a building, wall, fence, or any combination of these items. The barrier should inhibit trespassing or casual foot traffic through the area when the facility is not opened for use.

The industry has worked closely with government agencies to develop barrier guidelines. The Consumer Product Safety Commission (CPSC) has issued publication number 362, "Safety Barrier Guidelines For Home Pools." The terms home and residential are used interchangeably. In some cases, local governments have adopted these guidelines into barrier code requirements for commercial pools, in order to restrict access and lessen unauthorized entry into the aquatic area.

The following are the CPSC recommendations:
- The top of the barrier should be at least 48 inches (1,219 mm) above grade, measured on the side of the barrier that faces away from the swimming pool. The maximum vertical clearance between grade and the bottom of the barrier should be 4 inches (102 mm). When the grade is a soft surface, such as grass or ground/natural surface, the bottom of the fence should be no more than 2 inches (51 mm) above grade. All measurements should be taken on the barrier side farthest from the pool.
- Openings in the barrier should not allow passage of a 4-inch (10 cm) diameter sphere or disk. This is the approximate size of a child's head.

- Solid barriers, which do not have openings, such as a masonry or stone wall, should not contain indentations or protrusions except for normal construction tolerances and tooled masonry joints
- Where the barrier is composed of horizontal and vertical members and the distance between the tops of the horizontal members is less than 45 inches (1,143 mm), the horizontal members should be located on the swimming pool side of the fence. Spacing between vertical members should not exceed 1¾ inches (44 mm) in width. Where there are decorative cutouts, spacing within the cutouts should not exceed 1¾ inches (44 mm) in width.

Photo 14-3. *Openings in the barrier should not allow passage of a 4-inch (10 cm) diameter sphere or disk.*

© National Swimming Pool Foundation 2017

- Where the barrier is composed of horizontal and vertical members and the distance between the tops of the horizontal members is 45 inches (1,143 mm) or more, spacing between vertical members should not exceed 4 inches (102 mm). Where there are decorative cutouts, spacing within the cutouts should not exceed 1¾ inches (44 mm) in width.
- Maximum mesh size for chain link fences should not exceed 1¼ inch (32 mm) square [1¾ inches (44 mm)]. A larger mesh size may be used if slats fastened at the top or bottom of the fence are used to reduce mesh openings to no more than 1¾ inches (44 mm).
- Where the barrier is composed of diagonal members, such as a lattice fence, the maximum opening formed by the diagonal members should be no more than 1¾ inches (44 mm).
- Access gates to the pool should be equipped to accommodate a locking device. Pedestrian access gates should open outward, away from the pool, and should be self-closing and have a self-latching device. Gates other than pedestrian access gates should have a self-latching device. Where the release mechanism of the self-latching device is located less than 54 inches (1,372 mm) from the bottom of the gate.
  - (a) the release mechanism should be located on the pool side of the gate at least 3 inches (76 mm) below the top of the gate
  - (b) the gate and barrier should have no opening greater than ½ inch (13 mm) within 18 inches (457 mm) of the release mechanism
- Barriers should not have any openings, external footholds or handholds, indentations or protrusions, or horizontal members that would make it easy to climb
- Barriers should be installed in such a manner as to prevent other objects, building walls, or permanent structures from being used to climb into the pool area

Fences, gates, or any other type of barrier should never be considered a substitute for direct supervision. Unsupervised pools are a hazard and pose potential legal action against the facility.

Photo 14-4. *Safety covers provide an extra layer of protection, especially when there is no supervision.*

Safety Covers

Another deterrent to unauthorized entry into the pool or spa is a safety cover. Safety covers must meet strict performance standards as set by the American Society for Testing & Materials in ASTM Standard F1346-91(reapproved 2003), "Performance Specification for Safety Covers and Labeling Requirements for All Covers for Swimming Pools, Spas and Hot Tubs."

Safety covers are installed in guides, a track, a rail, or are otherwise secured into the deck. These covers provide a continuous union with the deck, allowing no passage. In the case of a pool with a width or diameter greater than 8 feet (2.4 m) from the periphery, the cover should be able to hold a weight of 485 pounds (220.0 kg). If the pool width or diameter is less than 8 feet (2.4 m) the cover should hold a weight of 275 pounds (125 kg).

There should be a means of removing standing water, such as with a pump. All standing water should drain substantially from the cover within 30 minutes after cessation of normal rainfall.

Photo 14-5. *Access must be denied when pool covers are in place, even if they meet ASTM standard F1346-91 for safety covers.*

Pools should not be used if a cover is in place. There is a serious risk of drowning if a user is ever allowed to enter the water with a pool cover either totally or partially in place. Warning labels in compliance with the ASTM standard should be attached to the cover.

Alarms

Alarms can be installed to protect against unauthorized entry onto the deck area as well as into the water itself. On the deck, the use of laser beams or infrared sensors can be coupled with radio frequency receivers to activate the remote alarm system. In the pool, pressure wave sensors or sonar devices can be permanently installed and can detect entry into the water.

For larger more sophisticated aquatic facilities, an underwater digital video system is available to assist lifeguards in early distress detection. The system, through sophisticated monitoring of swimmers' trajectories, can alert lifeguards in the event of a dangerous situation and help them initiate a rescue more quickly.

The CPSC has published an article, "An Evaluation of Swimming Pool Alarms," dated May 2000. The conclusion was

> "Test results showed that the subsurface pool alarms generally performed better. They were more consistent in alarming and less likely to false alarm than the surface alarms. When a test object, intended to simulate the weight of a small child, was pushed into the pool, the subsurface sensors detected it most reliably. The subsurface alarms can also be used in conjunction with solar covers, whereas the surface alarms cannot."

A pool alarm can only be considered an additional layer of protection against drowning in swimming pools. It is recommended that pool alarms be made active immediately upon closure of the facility. Pool alarms should never take the place of an effective barrier or supervision.

Safety in the Water

Swimming pools and spas provide the means for individuals and family groups to escape from the heat, to exercise, to compete in games or events, or to simply relax. Along with the joys of water use, consideration should be given to the responsibility for safety. Safety in the water is the responsibility of everyone: individuals, parents, group leaders, friends, lifeguards, facility owners/managers, and pool operators.

Drowning

The World Health Organization (WHO) defines fatal and non-fatal drowning as "the process of experiencing respiratory impairment from submersion/immersion in liquid." The WHO also states that drowning outcomes should be classified as either death, morbidity, or no morbidity. Morbidity is a disease state or symptom. An example of morbidity could be an individual who becomes ill with pneumonia or suffers from brain damage following a drowning incident. Additionally, in order to simplify how drowning is defined, the WHO states that the terms wet, dry, active, passive, silent, and secondary drowning are no longer used. However, some of these terms may still be used by other organizations.

A drowning may result in neurological damage. Successful recovery depends on prompt rescue and resuscitation. Children younger than five years are at greatest risk of drowning. In teenagers and adults, drowning is common in those who are intoxicated or those who have taken sedatives or drugs. People who intentionally hyperventilate and hold their breath under water for extended periods may pass out and be unable to surface, thus increasing the risk of drowning.

For children, a lack of adult supervision is the single most important contributory cause of drowning. Children with minimal swimming skills can get into trouble if they attempt activity beyond their capabilities or if they are injured due to unsafe behavior in the water.

Photo 14-6. *Teaching children and adults to swim is an important first step in the prevention of drowning.*

© National Swimming Pool Foundation 2017

According to the CDC (www.cdc.gov), drowning is the second leading cause of unintentional death for children between one and 14 years of age; motor vehicle accidents are the leading cause. From 2005-2014, there were 3,536 unintentional drowning deaths annually in the United States, averaging ten deaths per day. About 20% of the unintentional drowning deaths were to children between the ages of 1–14.

In swimming pools, hot tubs, and spas there are a number of contributing factors to drowning. The strong suction at outlets of a pool or spa can entrap body parts or hair and hold the victim's head under water, causing drowning. The clarity of the water in pools can also be a factor. In turbid water the lifeguard may not be able to identify someone in need of help. Crowded swimming pools present a similar problem.

Drowning Prevention

Teaching children and adults to swim is an important first step in the prevention of drowning. Education about the risks of swimming in certain situations is essential to reduce the risk of drowning. It would be helpful if all aquatic facilities promoted learn-to-swim programs for all ages and especially for children. Some other preventive measures include:

- Making sure an adult is constantly watching children swimming or playing around the water, including staying within arm's reach of inexperienced swimmers while they are in the water
- Controlling access around pools and spas, especially those without lifeguards, with four-sided isolation fences using self-closing and self-latching gates in the fence with latches out of the reach of children
- Checking the water depth before entering

Photo 14-7. *Children with minimal swimming skills can get into trouble if they attempt activity beyond their capabilities. Noodles and armbands cannot replace personal flotation devices (life jackets).*

- Not using air-filled or foam toys, such as water wings, noodles, or inner-tubes in place of life jackets, or personal flotation devices. These are toys and are not designed to keep swimmers safe and can provide a false sense of security.
- Not swimming alone or in unsupervised places. Instructing children and adults to always swim with a friend.
- Instructing individuals never to attempt to swim in situations beyond their skill level
- Reducing the risk of drowning through the presence of trained lifeguards
- Warning individuals to refrain from alcohol or drug consumption before and during swimming
- Ensuring that suction outlets (main drains) in pools and spas are certified as compliant with the Virginia Graeme Baker Pool & Spa Safety Act (VGB Act), have not exceeded their installed service life, are secured in place, and are not damaged or discolored. The VGB Act is discussed later in this chapter.
- Having staff members trained in CPR (cardiopulmonary resuscitation) and the use of Automated External Defibrillators (AEDs)
- Only allowing swimming when the bottom of the pool, or its main drain, is clearly visible

Drowning Signals

If a person is unable to breathe for more than four minutes, it is possible that irreversible brain damage or death can occur. The longer a person is without oxygen, the more severe the outcome. Death has been known to result from submersion of less than one minute.

Active drowning victims remain at the surface for less than one minute. They may be able to struggle for as little as 20 seconds. A passive drowning victim does not struggle at all.

Time is critical in life-threatening situations. In the first minute, breathing stops, and the heart ceases to beat shortly thereafter. Brain damage is quite possible when the brain is deprived of oxygen for four to six minutes. Brain damage is likely after oxygen deprivation of six to 10 minutes. With no oxygen for ten minutes, brain damage is certain. Before help can be provided to a distressed swimmer, the rescuer must be aware of certain signs of distress. It is important to note that most drowning victims cannot or do not call for help.

Distressed swimmers are aware that they are in trouble. They are conscious but in many cases are unable to call for help. Usually they are in a diagonal position, at or just below the surface of the water. There may be some motion as they attempt to swim, without any effective results. If they are not helped, they may lose the ability to float, thus becoming a drowning victim.

Active drowning victims will usually have their head back with the face looking up. Their bodies are usually vertical or slightly diagonal to the water. Their eyes, if open, have a surprised disoriented look. Often the mouth is in a round "O" open position. It is rare that an individual in this condition can call for help. They are usually gasping for air or not breathing at all.

An active drowning victim may progress to a **passive drowning victim**. These individuals are unconscious. Their bodies can be either limp or rigid. They can be floating face down on the bottom or near the surface of the water. There is no motion except for possible convulsive jerks as a result of lack of oxygen to the brain.

Making Swimming Safer

When a person visits an aquatic facility for the first time, they are at the greatest risk for injury. First-time visitors should be made aware of all safety rules before being allowed to enter the water. Never allow anyone to swim alone. Children should be supervised at all times. Children should never be left in the care of an individual, such as an older sibling, unless the caretaker is a capable and responsible person as it relates to the pool/spa environment.

All rules must be enforced. Local regulations often dictate specific minimum rules that must be posted. These rules are only a minimum requirement and usually address items, such as user loads, times of operation, shower requirements, and diving. Any aquatic facility can post additional rules as long as they are not discriminatory in nature. Remember, Your Pool, Your Rule. Rules can cover a wide range of concerns, prohibiting:

- Consumption of food, drugs, and alcoholic beverages
- Glass containers in the facility
- Diving or jumping from the deck into the diving board pool area
- Diving outside designated areas
- Throwing objects, such as balls or other personal items

Photo 14-8. *Your Pool, Your Rule. Signs should address specific risks regarding pool use.*

- Horseplay, such as running, shoving, dunking
- Improper behavior, intoxication, and profanity
- Use of electrical appliances, such as radios or hair dryers
- Swimming if you have/had diarrhea
- Diaper age children without swim pants
- Entering the pool without showering or washing hands when leaving the bathroom
- Urinating in the pool
- Changing diapers outside designated rest room areas
- Swimming outside designated areas
- Swimming alone
- Remaining in the pool and deck area during electrical storms
- Swimming without a lifeguard or other suitable supervision

The list of possible rules is almost endless. The facility and its program use, as well as the make-up of the community of pool users, can guide in the selection of those specific rules that may apply. Under Resources, the NSPF® website links to other organizations which are good sources of safety information.

Rules should be written in easy-to-understand phrases. If the community of users is diverse, multi-language signs may be helpful. One rule that should be posted and enforced is that hold-your-breath games or long underwater swims are not allowed. Children and teenagers as well as young adults seem to enjoy this type of activity, which can quickly lead to a water emergency and death.

POOL RULES

- All children under 6 years and any non-swimmers **MUST** be within parent's reach at all times.
- 1 person at a time on the slide.
- Children must be this tall (36") to use cargo net.
- Slide must be ridden feet first lying on back or sitting, facing forward.
- Keep arms and hands in the slide at all times.
- Do not hang on or swing from ropes.
- Do not run, dive, stand, kneel, rotate or stop on slide.
- Clear the landing zone immediately upon entering pool from slide.

CAUTION: For safety reasons, pregnant women and persons with heart conditions or back trouble should not ride this slide.
For complete pool rules, please see the sign on the far end of the natatorium."

MUST BE 36" FOR CARGO NET

© National Swimming Pool Foundation 2017

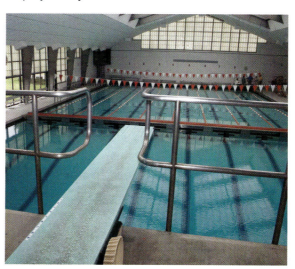

DO NOT HOLD BREATH UNDER WATER

DO NOT PLAY "HOLDING BREATH" GAMES

Photo 14-9. *Games involving holding breath underwater may lead to serious injury or death.*

Non-Swimmers

Individuals who do not possess a minimum proficiency for swimming can be at great risk, particularly if they are unsupervised. This is true for all age groups.

Non-swimmers should be advised to remain in water that is not above their shoulders in depth. Water deeper than this is an area in which non-proficient swimmers should only be when they are being instructed and under direct supervision. A floating lifeline, also called a safety line, should be used to indicate the transition between shallow and deep water. Local codes may specify the exact location; however, according to some industry guidelines, the line should be placed between 1 foot (305 mm) and 2 feet (610 mm) toward the shallow end from the transition. It is advised by industry groups that a wide tile line be placed on the pool walls and across the floor of the pool at the transition, usually at the water depth of 5 feet (1,524 mm). Some codes require that the floating safety line should be in place at all times, except when the pool is under the supervision and observation of a lifeguard, or during supervised activities with a swimming coach in attendance.

Non-swimmers should be supervised carefully and observations made as to their well-being. Becoming chilled or overly tired can lead to dangerous results for a less than confident swimmer. Weak swimmers often use wall-walking to travel from shallow water to deeper water. They often can be observed bouncing from shallow to deeper water. Non-swimmers and weak swimmers should be allowed and encouraged to use life-jackets when in water over their shoulders. However, this should never take the place of direct supervision.

Making Diving Safer

Serious head, neck, or back injury may occur when diving head-first into a pool. Permanent paralysis or even death can occur when the diver's head comes into contact with other individuals, objects, or portions of the pool structure, such as the walls, pool deck edge, or flooring. When the head contacts an object, even at slow speeds, the chin rotates into the chest. The upper and lower body parts continue to move due to inertia, and the neck and spinal cord are subjected to severe strain that could break the neck, sever the spinal cord, or both.

Swimmers should always enter a pool feet-first initially, to become familiar with the physical characteristics of the pool. No head-first diving should be allowed in any pool unless the pool meets all standards that pertain to diving, such as provided by the diving board manufacturers, pool industry groups, the United States Diving Association, or FINA; or by recommendations as provided by the American Red Cross or the YMCA; as well as any applicable local codes and regulations.

Non-diving areas should be clearly marked with NO DIVING signs that meet the requirements of ANSI Z535. In addition, the international No Diving symbol should be placed in the deck at intervals consistent with local code. This symbol may be located in any area where diving is not appropriate, regardless of depth. The ANSI/APSP-1-2003 standard states that all pool areas of five feet (1,524 mm) or less depth should display the symbol.

Photo 14-10. *If a pool facility allows diving, all other water-related activities should be stopped in the diving area.*

If a pool facility allows diving, all other water-related activities should be stopped in the diving area. Lap swimming, recreational water play, or any other activity should not be allowed in the dive zone while diving is taking place.

No diving equipment should be installed on any pool unless the equipment is installed and used according to the manufacturer's instructions and specifications. All diving equipment should have slip-resisting tread surfaces. In addition, a manufacturer's label is affixed providing information as to the necessary water depths, widths and maximum user weights.

The pool operator should maintain the treads and labels as part of the overall maintenance program. Diving equipment should be kept in good repair. Daily inspection should verify that the equipment is firmly in place. Loose fittings should be tightened and any sharp edges should be repaired.

Starting blocks should be made available for use during practices and competition and only under supervision by a coach. The blocks should be removed or covered at other times so that casual swimmers are not tempted to use them.

Rules related to diving and the use of diving equipment should be developed and displayed in the dive area or near the equipment. The following suggestions are typical of such signs:

- Use the equipment only under the direct supervision of a coach or lifeguard
- Dive or jump only in a straight line from the end of the equipment
- Swim to the closest pool exit or wall immediately after completion of the dive
- Look before diving to make sure the area is clear
- Only one person is allowed on the equipment at a time
- No multiple bounces are allowed
- The ladder is the only means allowed for climbing aboard equipment

The casual non-trained diver can pose a risk to themselves and others. People often overestimate their skills and attempt to perform feats for which they have not been properly trained.

Headfirst Entry Dives

Most accidents involving headfirst entry dives occur in shallow water, less than 5 feet in depth. A shallow water dive requires expert skill and most individuals risk serious injury by attempting such a dive. Literature on safe diving techniques

Photo 14-11. *The casual, non-trained diver can pose a risk to themselves and others.*

is available from the American Red Cross and the YMCA. Signs are available that provide safe diving messages.

Running and diving into a pool should not be allowed, and this should be included in pool rules. Diving across narrow areas of the pool should not be allowed.

Jumping into shallow water can be dangerous. Injuries such as a broken leg can occur if the bottom of the pool is hit with sufficient force. Jumping into submerged obstacles, surface objects, or other swimmers can cause serious injury. If jumping is allowed, rules should be posted, and the need to jump directly forward from the edge of the pool should be included.

Slides

Many of the potential dangers discussed in the previous section concerning the use of diving equipment also apply to the use of slide equipment. Headfirst sliding and headfirst diving follow the same laws of physics. Falls from slides as a result of standing on the slide, diving or jumping from the slide, and horseplay on the slide can result in serious injury or paralysis.

If a pool slide is available, there should be proper deck clearance around the slide, proper vertical clearance above the deck and pool edge, and an appropriate area and depth of water. Local codes may provide necessary requirements. Follow the slide manufacturer's instructions and specifications concerning installation and use.

According to the American Red Cross, there is

© National Swimming Pool Foundation 2017

Photo 14-12. *Riders should only go down a slide feet first.*

only one safe way to go down a slide, and that is feet first. Facility rules should address the proper use of the slide equipment, and these rules must be enforced. Typical rules may include the following:

- Only one person is allowed on the slide at a time
- Enter, ride, and exit the slide feet first
- Move away from the bottom of the slide quickly
- Do not wear glasses on the slide
- Standing, stopping, and sliding down headfirst are not allowed
- Keep hands inside the slide

Slide rules should also address the problem of horseplay. A facility that has a slide that exits into water over five feet in depth should prohibit use by non-swimmers. Facilities often limit access to children based on height. More information about slides and other aquatic play features can be found in the NSPF® Aquatic Play Feature™ online course and handbook.

Wading Pools

Wading pools are shallow. As a result, they can have hazardous suction outlets located near children. The International Swimming Pool and Spa Code (ISPSC) prohibits the use of suction outlets in new wading pools, but to prevent entrapment in any wading pool environment, close adherence to the VGB Act must be enforced. This chapter and www.nspf.org have more detailed information about the VGB Act and entrapment prevention.

Wading pools have similar features as spas and, as a result, are often more difficult to maintain compared to pools. For example, both are shallow and have high user loads, warmer temperatures, and high sunlight exposure. As a result, some of the operational guidance for spas or therapy pools also applies to wading pools.

Wading pools should have their own filtration and circulation system. Additionally, it is recommended that an automatic control system be used to maintain a consistent disinfectant level. In some cases an automatic control system may be required by jurisdictional codes and supplemental disinfection may also be required. Pool operators should check for the requirement in their area.

Typically it is small children that use the wading pool. It is important that adequate supervision, which may include the parents or guardians, is provided. Wading pools are more likely to have fecal contaminants due to the presence of diaper-age children. Research presented at the 2008 World Aquatic Health™

Photo 14-13. *Adult supervision is recommended at wading pools.*

© National Swimming Pool Foundation 2017

Conference demonstrates that swim diapers do not readily prevent fecal contamination.

Other innovative water play features create fun but present unique risks. The Aquatic Play Feature™ online course and handbook has more information about play features, management, operations, and safety.

Entrapment

The Consumer Product Safety Commission (CPSC) has documented that from 2011–2015, there were 23 reported incidents associated with suction entrapment, including one death and 19 injuries. As with all reporting of this type, it is likely that more incidences occurred than were reported in the CPSC study. Upon review of these cases, it was determined that there were five different ways that caused a user to be entrapped:

- Hair entrapment is the most common and most difficult to identify. It occurs when the suction outlet (drain cover) has a certified flow rating too low for the pumping system. Exceeding the flow limit causes long hair to tangle on and in the fitting. This hazard is increased when the suction pipe is too shallow for the specific drain cover, causing hair to twist and tangle after passing through large opening grates common in public pools.
- Limb entrapment occurs when the cover is missing or broken, allowing curious children to reach into the pipe and get their hand and arm stuck. Other reported limb entrapments include fingers stuck in pre-VGB covers with ½" circular holes, and feet/ankles lodged in covers that have broken.
- Body entrapment occurs when a large part of the body is able to seal the suction outlet. This happens when covers break, become loose, and/or are missing. It also happens with flat drain covers that are not VGB Act compliant.
- Evisceration/disembowelment occurs when an individual's buttocks form a seal over an open suction outlet when the cover is missing, causing the rectum to burst and viscera to be withdrawn from the body
- Mechanical entrapment occurs when something attached to the user, such as a necklace, bellybutton piercing, bathing suit string, etc., tangles in the large openings of a cover or grating

NSPF® is committed to working with government and industry groups to protect the

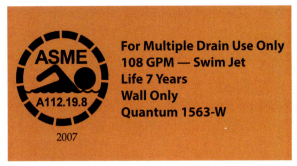

Illustration 14-1. *Example of markings that must be visible on a drain cover.*

public by minimizing any chance of entrapment. Pool operators should perform careful inspections prior to facilities being opened to ensure that the facility minimizes risk of entrapment.

Prevention is the most important way to avoid entrapment. The pool operator plays an important role to ensure that protective suction outlet covers are properly installed and operating to minimize entrapment. The ANSI/APSP/ICC-7-2013 standard for "Suction Entrapment Avoidance in Swimming Pools, Wading Pools, Spas, Hot Tubs, and Catch Basins" should be followed.

If someone does become entrapped, it is important that the emergency cut-off switch be activated. Once the pumps are off, try to roll the entrapped victim off, rather than pulling them up. You may need to wedge something between the victim and the suction outlet to break the seal.

Virginia Graeme Baker Pool and Spa Safety (VGB Act)

The VGB Act is a federal law that was designed to improve swimming pool and spa safety. After a decade since its adoption, it has had a 100% success rate, with no reported entrapments in any pool or spa that meets all requirements. Enacted into law in December 2007, the "Virginia Graeme Baker Pool and Spa Safety Act" is often shortened to the P&SS Act or the VGB Act. The law is focused on drowning prevention, and addresses suction entrapment hazards, fencing, and pool alarms.

The VGB Act directly regulates suction outlet fitting assemblies, not just drain covers. It also regulates public pool suction systems, allowing for either no drains at all, a single drain that qualifies as unblockable according to the CPSC's 2011 definition, or two or more drains that are properly separated. Public pools that do not meet one of these requirements are required to

© National Swimming Pool Foundation 2017

be equipped with a secondary device or system designed to prevent suction entrapment. The most common of these systems is a public pool gravity system that has a second body of water, such as a surge tank or collector tank, between a single blockable drain and the circulation pump or pumps. Other options include Safety Vacuum Release Systems, suction pipe vents, or drain disablement devices or systems. In all cases, these systems are intended to prevent a high-vacuum condition capable of holding a swimmer against a blockable drain cover.

The VGB Act required that drains be installed in all public pools and spas by December 2008, and that going forward the drains be replaced before the end of their service life, which begins the month and year they are installed, with or without water being present. The standard requires all suction outlets to have a life in years designation; a pool or spa is no longer VGB Act compliant if the outlets expire while installed. The act requires all suction outlet drain covers manufactured, distributed, or entering commerce (installed) in the United States to conform to ASME/ANSI A112.19.8 (2007) or successor standard ANSI/APSP-16, the suction outlet fitting assembly test and certification standard.

The requirements of the law include:

- Each swimming pool or spa cover shall conform to the entrapment protection standards recognized by one of the following marks: ANSI/APSP-16, ASME/ANSI A112.19.8, and/or VGB-2008 performance standards. All covers in commerce must comply.
- All suction piping systems must have compliant configurations to help prevent or mitigate high-vacuum entrapment
- Any pool or spa with a single main drain other than a single unblockable drain must also be equipped with one of the following devices or systems:
  - Safety Vacuum Release System
  - Suction-Limiting Vent System
  - Gravity Drainage System
  - Automatic Pump Shut-Off System
  - Drain Disablement
  - Other systems approved by the Consumer Product Safety Commission (CPSC)
- Covers must include permanent labeling with the maximum flow rate, which is often different for floor versus wall installations; the installed service life in years; the certifying agency mark; and the version of

the standard to which it was tested, ASME/ANSI A112.19.8, VGB 2008, or ANSI/APSP-16

- Public pool and spa facilities with Field Fabricated Outlets that have been certified by a Registered Design Professional must retain a copy of the certification report at the property, to document full compliance with the drain cover standard. These field-built outlets are not required to be permanently marked like purchased manufactured mass-produced drain covers.

To further minimize the five forms of entrapment:

- No pool or spa should be operated at any time if any of the covers of the vacuum outlets are missing or damaged
- Some local codes still require dual-drains in order to minimize the potential for direct suction that can entrap a person. These drains must be at least three feet (0.91 meter) apart, measured center-to-center, or be on two separate planes.
- Drain covers should be selected so the suction system is capable of handling 100% of the circulation system flow. Suction system flow ratings are calculated as follows:
  - Single unblockable drain system: the VGB Act cover/grate must be rated for 100% of the flow
  - Multiple unblockable drain systems: the sum of VGB Act cover/grate flow ratings must equal at least 100% of the flow
  - Dual blockable drain systems: each VGB Act cover/grate must be rated for 100% of the flow
  - Three or more blockable drain systems: subtract the flow rating of one VGB cover/grate from the sum of all other covers and the result must be rated for 100% of the flow
  - In the event a pump is replaced, the manufacturer can assist in selecting a pump that draws flow to not exceed the cover's maximum rating in the case that 100% of the circulation system flow passes through the cover(s)

Suction entrapment hazards can further be minimized by certain other design criteria. Overflow skimmer/gutter systems that do not incorporate main drains eliminate all suction outlet hazards.

Existing pools and spas that were constructed

before the VGB Act often include a single, blockable drain cover that must be supplemented with one or more VGB Act systems or devices designed to prevent suction entrapment. These systems are NOT designed or tested to address all five forms of entrapment; they can only limit the amount of suction present under drain covers, or they limit the amount of time a swimmer is exposed to the full vacuum of a pump. It is very important to understand that none are tested to prevent hair, limb, mechanical, or evisceration hazards.

Safety Vacuum Release Systems (SVRS) are a type of device that are tested to respond to a full vacuum, stopping and releasing a vacuum within 4.5 seconds after a drain is fully blocked. These systems must be tested and certified to be in conformance with ANSI/PSPS/ICC-7-2013 "Manufactured Safety Vacuum Release Systems (SVRS) for Residential and Commercial Swimming Pool, Spa, Hot Tub, and Wading Pool Suction Systems" or ASTM F2387 "Standard Provisional Specification for Manufactured for Swimming Pools, Spas, and Hot Tubs." These standards establish requirements for manufactured SVRS devices: the dimensions and tolerances, materials, installation instructions, testing requirements, and markings and identification. An SVRS can be installed as an independent system or can be incorporated as part of the pool pump.

Suction-Limiting Vent Systems are circulation systems that incorporate a tamper-resistant atmospheric vent that is hydraulically located between the suction outlet and the circulation pump, allowing air to enter the circulation system and release the vacuum within the system when the suction outlet is blocked and the circulation pump is operating. These systems must be carefully engineered to work effectively. If the vent connection point is too shallow or too close to the pump, it can allow air into the system during normal operation; conversely, a connection point that is too deep will not release the vacuum as intended.

Gravity Drainage Systems are powered circulation systems which utilize a collector tank located between the pump and the suction outlet. The tank is filled by the gravitationally induced flow of water from the suction outlet, and is vented to the atmosphere by a tamper-resistant opening.

Automatic Pump Shut-Off Systems are systems designed to sense blockage of the suction fitting and then turn off the power to the pump, and subsequently release the vacuum in the circulation system when a blockage is detected. It is extremely important that no check valves are installed anywhere in the system that would prevent the suction pipe from equalizing with atmospheric pressure through the return side of the pump.

Other Systems—Any other system determined by the Consumer Product Safety Commission to be equally effective as, or better than, the systems described above at preventing or eliminating the risk of injury or death associated with pool drainage systems.

> More detailed information about the Virginia Graeme Baker Pool and Spa Safety Act (VGB Act) can be found in Appendix C-1. The Virginia Graeme Baker Pool & Spa Safety Act online course is available for no charge at www.nspf.org.

Unblockable Drain

The use of unblockable large-size grate drain covers can also help to reduce the risk of body entrapment. Unblockable drains can be flat and flush mount with the pool or spa interior surface, where blockable drains cannot be flat and flush mount. Another significant difference is how the suction system flow rating is calculated; the rating is simply the sum of all unblockable drains connected together without valves. These drains are not subject to the three feet (0.91 meter) separation requirement of blockable drains.

The CPSC voted to change the definition of unblockable drains in September 2011. Before the change, unblockable was defined by the size of the cover. Unblockable is now defined by the size of the opening in the pool or spa. A drain is unblockable if the suction outlet, including the sump, has a perforated (open) area that cannot be shadowed by the area of the 18"x23" Body Blocking Element of ANSI/APSP–16 2011, and the rated flow through any portion of the remaining open area cannot create a suction force in excess of the removal force values in Table 1 of that Standard. This 2011 policy change impacted many public pools that were previously retrofitted with unblockable covers over blockable

© National Swimming Pool Foundation 2017

sumps to be VGB Act compliant. By now these facilities should have been updated again with one or more of the additional VGB Act systems or devices designed to prevent suction entrapment, or modified to include an unblockable drain and sump, or a multiple drain system.

Safety Around the Water

Not all pool-related accidents happen in the water. The area around the pool and spa should contain important safety and rescue equipment and warning signs to prevent injury and to help treat anyone who is injured. There is the possibility of slip-and-fall accidents as a result of poor deck maintenance or because of personal items left on the deck. Some slip-and-fall accident victims can end up in the water, resulting in serious injury or death. In the event there is an accident or injury, proper safety and rescue equipment needs to be accessible around the pool or spa. In addition, operators must consider how to handle electrical storms, store and handle chemicals, maintain indoor air quality, and use electricity safely.

Other accident victims could be staff, employees, or the surrounding community. Intense fires, toxic smoke, chemical burns, or debris in the eyes are just few of the potential hazards associated with an aquatic environment. The pool operator should evaluate his or her facility and help implement the necessary safety programs to ensure the continued well-being of users and employees.

Safety and Rescue Equipment

Local code requirements vary as to the type of safety and rescue equipment required for swimming pools and spas. A pool operator should meet the code requirements at minimum.

The safety and rescue equipment should be easily accessible around the pool. The following items may be addressed in local codes (there may be additional requirements for public pools that have diving boards and/or slides):

- A light, strong, non-telescopic reaching pole not less than 12 feet long (3.66 meters). Many times 16 feet is required (4.88 meters), including a securely attached body hook or shepherd's crook type of pole having blunted ends. These poles are constructed of fiberglass or some other electrically non-conducting material.

Photo 14-14. *Most codes require a facility to have a backboard to respond to spinal injuries.*

- A United States Coast Guard-approved ring buoy with an outside diameter of 15 to 24 inches (381 to 610 mm) to which has been firmly attached a throwing rope with a diameter of ¼ inch to ⅜ inch (6.35 to 9.5 mm) that is at least as long as two-thirds of the maximum width of the pool
- A rope and floating lifeline separating the shallow area from the deep area at the transition point (five feet or 1.5 meters)
- At least one rescue tube for each lifeguard on duty. A polypropylene line or webbed towline and shoulder strap are attached to the tube at one end. There may be a clip device on the end of the tube opposite the towline so that the tube can be fastened around a victim or rescuer.
- One or more backboards with a minimum of three tie-down straps and a head immobilizer for back and neck injuries
- A first aid kit meeting an appropriate standard (OSHA). First aid kits shall be housed in a durable weather-resistant container and kept filled and ready for use. Disease transmission barriers and cleansing kits that meet OSHA standards must be included.

As stated in the Pool & Spa Management chapter, swimming pool and spa facilities exist in all sizes and vary greatly as to the activity or programs provided. The safety and rescue equipment possibilities are as varied as the types

1. Pool & Spa Management
2. Regulations & Guidelines
3. Essential Calculations
4. Pool Water Contamination
5. Disinfection
6. Water Balance
7. Pool & Spa Water Problems
8. Chemical Testing
9. Chemical Feed & Control
10. Water Circulation
11. Pool & Spa Filtration
12. Heating & Air Circulation
13. Spa & Therapy Operations
14. Facility Safety
15. Keeping Records
16. Maintenance Systems
17. Troubleshooting
18. Facility Renovation & Design
References

of pool and spa facilities. Further considerations are used for clearing

- Automated External Defibrillators (AEDs) are easy to use by trained people and provide correction for sudden cardiac arrest (SCA)
- Mechanical and manual suctioning devices are used for clearing a victim's airway
- Resuscitators are easy to use and provide superior pulmonary ventilation than what can be obtained from mouth-to-mouth resuscitation. Also, resuscitation can be performed with supplemental oxygen.
- Survival blankets can be used for hypothermia or shock victims

Emergency Telephones

Time is critical when professional help is needed. Some pool and spa facilities at home-owner associations or condominiums and apartments are open much later than the administrative offices. There may be no telephone close by unless an emergency phone is installed. Certain local or state regulations require an emergency telephone within a certain distance of the pool or spa (usually 200 feet or 61 meters). Often it is required that the sign

Photo 14-15. *There may be no phone in the pool unless an emergency phone is installed.*

next to the telephone give the dialing directions, the exact location of the pool, the phone number, and other directions to help give guidance to the emergency medical service (EMS) personnel.

Signs

Signs around aquatic facilities are a means of providing information. The type and number of signs, their location, and the message to be communicated should be chosen with great care. Signs provide facility guests and employees with important messages regarding the proper use of the pool or spa, any hazards that may be present, and ways to avoid personal injury.

A well-written sign will warn people about any threat to their well-being that physical conditions or chemicals may present. Signs

may act as a means to encourage a change in behavior and induce people to act in a safer manner. Most visitors to an aquatic facility are unaware of the hazards to which they may be exposed. Warnings should be provided to reduce the risk of accidents. Warnings can only encourage people to do the right thing; they cannot fix physical problems.

Photo 14-16. *Warning signs such as Caution should be posted in areas around the pool that have a potential for slip-and-fall.*

Signs should warn users of physical hazards, such as shallow water, diving areas, and slippery areas. Signs should warn of chemical hazards related to the storage of chlorine, acid, and cleaning materials. There may be times when warnings are given for environmental conditions involving lighting, glare from surfaces, algae, or cloudy water. Finally, signs warn of behavioral hazards, such as horseplay, running, shoving, jumping, hours of use, and shallow-water diving.

Local code requirements often dictate sign requirements. An example of minimum code signage could be

- A sign stating No Diving or Diving Prohibited should be posted

Photo 14-17. *Signs should warn of chemical hazards related to storage.*

© National Swimming Pool Foundation 2017

DIVING BOARD RULES

1. ONLY ONE PERSON ON BOARD AT A TIME
2. NO RUNNING ON BOARD
3. CARTWHEELS OR OTHER RELATED FORMS OF WATER ENTRY ARE NOT ALLOWED
4. DIVING AREA MUST BE CLEAR OF SWIMMERS WHILE THE BOARD IS OPEN
5. NO HORSEPLAY
6. ONLY ONE BOUNCE ON BOARD
7. DIVER MUST SWIM TO LADDER OR UNDER BUOY ROPE BEFORE NEXT DIVER MAY GO

Photo 14-18. *Some state or local jurisdictions require a separate rules sign be posted for diving.*

- A sign shall be conspicuously posted in the pool area stating:
  - The maximum number of users who may use the swimming pool at one time
  - The hours that the swimming pool is open and that pool use is prohibited at any other time
- A sign, or signs, stating the following shall be posted conspicuously at the swimming pool or enclosure and in the dressing rooms and offices of all swimming pools where applicable:
  - Pollution of swimming pool is prohibited
  - Urinating, discharge of fecal matter, expectorating or blowing the nose in any swimming pool is prohibited
  - Swim diapers must be worn by users who are incontinent, lack toilet training, or are otherwise lacking voluntary control of excretory functions
- For pools with deck slides:
  - Sliding shall not occur in water less than four feet deep
  - Sliding shall be performed only in a feet-forward position
- For pools with starting blocks:
  - Use of starting blocks is prohibited except during competitive swimming or swimmer-training activities
- For facilities with spas:
  - Spa Warning Sign should be conspicuously posted in the immediate vicinity of the spa, a minimum of 3 square feet (1 meter) in size. The Spa & Therapy

Operations chapter lists what should be included on the Spa Warning Sign.

Some jurisdictions require a separate rule sign be posted by diving boards. It is important that the pool operator review the warning signs posted around the pool or spa and help the facility post signs that are appropriate for the activity and risk involved.

Depth Markings

Depth markings inform people in and around the facility of the water depth in any given area. Many codes require depth marking signs to help prevent drowning and diving injuries. Codes may require the size and location of the depth markings. For example, markings may need to be placed on the pool wall and the deck and be a clearly visible.

Photo 14-19. *Many codes require depth marking signs. It may be advisable to have the markings in both feet and meters.*

Decks

Deck areas of swimming pools and spas have three areas of concern: deck obstructions, the condition of the decking material, and entrance and exit areas.

The deck should be kept free of equipment and personal belongings. Lounge chairs, umbrella tables, and other deck furniture should be well back from the pool or spa edge. It is common to find state or local regulations that require a 4 foot clearance around the pool's edge. Food or drink on the pool deck is often regulated as well. Glass objects must never be allowed on the pool deck.

The deck should be checked on a daily basis for standing water or slippery areas. Any damage to the deck material, such as loose or broken material, should be noted and repaired as soon as possible. Warning signs such as Wet Floor should be posted in areas of potential slip-and-fall. There should be a strict rule against running and horseplay on the deck.

Photo 14-20. *There should be adequate clearance around the pool to avoid tripping near the water's edge.*

Entrances to pool decks should be in areas where the hazards are the lowest level. This usually is at the shallow end of the pool.

All ladders, ramps, hand-holds, and hand-rails should be checked on a daily basis to insure they are properly secured and in good repair.

Electrical Storms

The swimming pool industry has not reached a consensus of agreement concerning the timing as to clearing a facility of patrons during an electrical storm, particularly as it affects indoor pools.

Local code requirements may provide specific guidelines on this matter. Power may be interrupted, causing lights to go out, which can cause a dangerous environment in indoor pools or outdoor pools in the evening, due to lack of light. The American Red Cross advises that a safe practice is to clear all patrons from the water at the first sound of thunder. The suggested procedures are

- When a thunderstorm threatens, clear the pool. This also applies to the surrounding deck area. If possible, get all patrons inside and away from the water.
- Keep everyone away from windows inside. People can be injured by flying debris or glass if the window breaks.
- Do not let anyone take a shower during a thunder storm. Water and metal can conduct the electricity of lighting.
- Do not use the corded telephone except for emergencies

- Keep away from water and grounded objects, such as metal fences, tanks, rails, and pipes

In many instances the facilities follow the requirements of the National Fire Protection Association (NFPA) 780 "Standard for the Installation of Lightning Protection Systems." This standard provides information regarding a complete lightning protection system and its installation. It is important that lightning protection equipment be inspected and tested on a regular basis. Make sure that the manufacturer's instructions are being followed.

It is recommended that a facility conduct a lightning risk assessment. The risk assessment should include items, such as building environment, type of construction, structure occupancy, structure contents, and lightning strike consequences. Lightning risk for a structure is the product of the lightning strike frequency and the consequence of the strike to the structure.

Individual patron conduct at a facility is very important, especially patron response to lightning warnings. Lightning warning systems are available to provide early warning of lightning activity. Strict adherence to facility rules during a lightning storm is important. The NFPA recognizes that certain locations are extremely hazardous during thunderstorms and should be avoided. These locations include both indoor and outdoor swimming pools.

The National Lightning Safety Institute recommends a cautionary approach when it comes to indoor swimming pools. They recommend the following steps be taken during a thunderstorm:

- Recognize the threat. Use detection methods, such as the TV Weather Channel; a weather radio; seeing lightning and/or hearing associated thunder; or subscription services such as www.www.intellicast.com
- Identify in advance SAFE and NOT SAFE places:
  - SAFE = dry areas inside large permanent buildings
  - NOT SAFE = near electrical conductors, electrical equipment, metal objects (lifeguard stands, ladders, diving board stanchions), and water, including showers
- Take action to suspend activities. When lightning is within 6–8 miles, evacuate

© National Swimming Pool Foundation 2017

people to safe areas. Guards should secure the entrance to the pool deck.

- Determine when activities should be resumed. Wait 30 minutes after the last observed lightning or thunder, since lightning may visit from the back end of the passing thunderstorm.

Chemical Safety and Storage

Pool chemicals may become a hazard when contaminated by a small quantity of water or when they are improperly mixed or contaminated. Fires, toxic vapor releases, and personnel injuries can occur if pool chemicals are not stored in a proper manner.

Pool chemicals, especially those that are oxidizers, may be highly reactive and capable of generating intense fire, high temperatures, and toxic gases if improperly handled or stored. Reactivity may be triggered by water wetting the chemical or by the inadvertent mixing of a pool chemical with an incompatible material. An oxidizer can begin to degrade if stored improperly. As degradation occurs, these chemicals become less stable. These chemicals are packaged in breathable containers to avoid pressure buildup while in storage. As pool chemicals decompose, the result may include chlorine gas, which may cause the corrosion of the product packaging, piping, electronics, and other metal equipment in poorly ventilated areas.

Pool chemicals that release disinfectants, like chlorine or bromine, into the water have the potential to release toxic vapors if they ignite or are contaminated. Chemicals that release chlorine or bromine are among the group of chemicals that are classified as oxidizers. Three things are required to initiate and sustain a fire: heat, oxygen, and fuel. Oxidizers pose a unique hazard because they can release oxygen and heat if contaminated or heated.

All that is then required is fuel, which is present as packaging. These pool oxidizer chemicals include calcium hypochlorite, sodium dichloro-s-triazinetrione, 1-bromo-3-chloro-5, 5-dimethyhhydantoin, trichloro-s-triazinetrione, and potassium monopersulfate. It is extremely important to have proper ventilation in any chemical storage area. The NFPA provides guidance on oxidizer storage with NFPA-400 Hazardous Materials Code. The code applies to the storage, use, and handling of the following

Photo 14-21. *Incompatible pool chemicals are often stored in an improper manner, with liquid above or beside solids.*

hazardous materials in all occupancies and facilities:

- Corrosive solids and liquids
- Flammable solids
- Organic peroxide formulations
- Oxidizers—liquid or solid
- Pyrophoric solids and liquids
- Toxic and highly toxic solids and liquids
- Unstable (reactive) solids and liquids
- Water-reactive solids and liquids

Moisture

Under normal circumstances, pool chemicals are intended to be added to large quantities of water. If a limited amount of water is added to certain chemicals, an unwanted reaction may occur. The result may be an increase in temperature and the release of toxic gas. Even a small amount of water or perspiration splashed onto certain chemicals may in some cases trigger a strong reaction.

Although the pool chemicals are usually packaged in plastic bags or drums, accidents have occurred when water leaked into damaged or open containers. According to the EPA, possible sources of water entry have been traced to

- Rain water from a roof leak or from an open or broken window
- A wet floor where stored chemicals were not elevated off the floor
- Leakage from fire suppression sprinkler system
- Hose-down water generated during area cleanup

Photo 14-22. *Chemicals must be stored so that the container and packaging are not damaged by contact with water, even if they are packaged in drums.*

Another source of water that may come in contact with pool chemical packages is high humidity in summer weather. However, the effects of humidity are more likely to be slow-acting, with the rate of temperature buildup and chlorine gas release being minimal.

Chlorine gas is corrosive to metals, such as steel and copper. Instances have been reported where exposed water piping has become corroded, causing leaks, and also where metal storage shelves have corroded and collapsed, causing chemical spillage.

Improper Mixing

The most common pool chemicals are incompatible with each other. Intentional or accidental mixing of incompatible chemicals is likely to lead to a chemical reaction that may generate temperatures high enough to ignite nearby combustible materials. Mixing can also lead to the release of highly toxic and corrosive chlorine gas. Reactions have also been traced to the mixing of old, partially decomposed, and new chemicals of the same type. The mixing of pool chemicals with completely unrelated materials, such as material swept from the floor, oily rags, and other miscellaneous materials, have been known to cause strong reactions, with the potential for a resulting fire.

Improper chemical mixing incidents have been reported when

- Tools and equipment used to handle one chemical were used with a different chemical before being cleaned

- Spilled substances (e.g., from damaged containers or from sloppy handling) and other miscellaneous substances on floors were swept up together and mixed
- Containers that were not properly cleaned and held small residues of product were contaminated from dirty water, liquids, or solid contaminants in the refuse

Liquid chemicals, such as sodium hypochlorite, if spilled, can leak into other containers or seep into cracks in the floor. A spill containment device is often required. Liquids, because of their properties, can create hazards not associated with solid or granular products and must be carefully handled.

Control of Chemical Hazards

The pool operator is responsible for knowing and understanding the hazards associated with pool chemicals and ensuring that the chemicals are safely stored and handled. In addition to operator training, hazardous material training is required. Hazardous substances are capable of being safely handled day after day through a management system that ensures that good, written procedures are prepared, posted, and followed by trained employees. Also, the facility needs to be properly designed and maintained. Finally, the facility owner/operator should plan for emergencies and work with local agency responders to lessen the impact of any incidents that may occur.

Product labels and Safety Data Sheets (SDS) include information about how to store chemicals. EPA recommendations for addressing the major hazards associated with pool chemicals are discussed here.

Photo 14-23. *Use SDSs for guidance concerning the appropriate personal protective equipment.*

The EPA recommends to **keep pool chemicals dry**. The aquatic facility should design and maintain designated areas for pool chemical storage so that water does not come in contact with containers or packaging. Any evidence of

© National Swimming Pool Foundation 2017

potential water entry from the following possible sources should receive prompt corrective attention:

- Roof, windows, and doors
- Wall and floor joints
- Water pipes or hoses and sprinkler systems
- Drains

The pool operator should look for ways to prevent water contact with stored pool chemicals by

- Closing containers properly
- Covering opened or damaged packaging
- Storing chemicals away from doors and windows
- Ensuring that there are no roof leaks, open or broken windows, or leaks from water pipes, hoses, or the sprinkler system
- Ensuring that floors are sloped to floor drains to keep water drained away from chemicals
- Storing chemicals on shelves or pallets to keep containers from direct contact with the floor
- Using waterproof covers on packaging
- Exercising particular caution to prevent water contact with stored chemicals any time water is used for cleanup of floor areas near stored packages
- Ensuring that water will not back up from faulty or clogged floor drains

The EPA recommends to **avoid mixing chemicals**. The pool operator should conduct a review of chemical storage arrangements and chemical handling tasks to identify situations where chemicals could be intentionally or accidentally mixed:

- Separate incompatible substances; avoid storing containers of liquids above containers of other incompatible substances
- Do not mix old chemicals with fresh chemicals, even if they are the same type
- Use separate, designated tools for each chemical. Handle only one chemical at a time and make sure that tools used with one substance are not used with another unless all residues are removed.
- Use separate, designated containers for cleanup of spilled materials to avoid inadvertent mixing of spilled substances. Consult the manufacturer or a hazardous waste disposal facility for more detailed information on proper waste disposal.
- Make chemical storage area housekeeping a priority. Don't allow rags, trash, debris, or other materials to clutter hazardous material storage area. Keep combustible and flammable substance storage areas tidy.

For storage and handling of large quantities, see the EPA Safety Alert, "Safe Storage and Handling of Swimming Pool Chemicals" (2001).

The EPA further advises on fire prevention through the following safe practices. The pool operator should prevent a chemical reaction ignition by avoiding wetting or mixing chemicals as described above. Avoid having combustible or flammable materials near the chemicals, particularly gasoline, oil, paint solvents, oily rags, etc. Do not allow ignition sources, such as gasoline, diesel, or gas-powered equipment, such as lawn mowers, motors, or welding machines, in the storage area. Also, do not allow smoking in the chemical storage area. Review bulk storage, including packaging and chemical storage locations, relative to potential for accidental contact with water, including sprinkler systems, rainwater, etc.

The EPA advises on **emergency response planning** and **fire fighting**. The pool operator should work with local first responders, such as fire departments, and emergency medical teams, as well as their Local Emergency Planning Committee (LEPC). Once started, fires involving pool chemicals are difficult to extinguish. The first responsibility is to safely evacuate people from the area and call the fire department. Self-contained breathing apparatus should be used by all firefighters. The EPA recommendations are

- Do not use dry chemical or halon-type fire extinguishers where chlorine gas may be involved. These agents can result in explosive reactions with chlorine.
- Large quantities of water should be applied to the burning combustibles to remove heat and for fire intensity control.
- When extinguishing a fire, only large volumes of water should be applied and then only by persons trained in chemical fire response. Caution must also be exercised to protect against environmental and wildlife damage due to contaminated water runoff.
- Once started, the reaction of wetted or mixed chlorinated pool chemicals may continue generating heat, unless the material is cooled below its reaction temperature or until all chlorine is used

Protective Measures

Pool chemicals can cause injury if they directly contact a person's skin, eyes, or respiratory or digestive system. The chemicals may immediately react when wetted by perspiration, tears, mucus, and saliva in the nose, throat, and

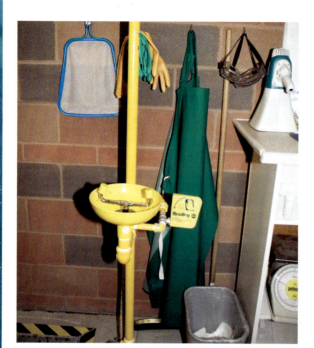

Photo 14-24. *There should be ready access to eye and body wash stations for the removal of chemicals, as well as personal protective equipment.*

respiratory and digestive systems. Such reactions may result from direct chemical contact with the skin or if chemical dust in the air contacts eyes, is inhaled, or settles on food that is consumed.

Consult the chemical manufacturer's safety instructions as well as the SDS for guidance on the appropriate personal protective equipment (PPE) necessary to protect your employees. Share SDS with local emergency medical responders and LEPC. The following protective measures address conditions that may arise during normal operations or during the performance of routine tasks. If, however, additional information is needed for fire, spill, or release intervention, contact the LEPC.

The following are some protective measure guidelines:

- See that personal protective equipment is kept clean, in proper operating condition, and available for use when needed
- Use basic PPE including, as a minimum, chemical goggles and liquid impervious gloves and boots for any chemical handling activities. For frequent or extended chemical handling activities, add a face shield and liquid impervious apron or coveralls to the basic PPE.
- As a minimum, use a National Institute for Occupational Health & Safety (NIOSH) approved air-purifying respirator when

airborne chemical dust or mist may be present. 29 CFR 1910.134 "Respiratory Protection" covers the OSHA requirements for respiratory protection.

- Develop work practices to minimize dust generation and accidental contact with pool chemicals
- Provide a means of ready access to water (e.g., safety showers, eye wash stations, etc.) for removal of chemicals that may accidentally contact employees
- Post the numbers for the local emergency responders and medical practitioners that are familiar with the appropriate treatment for the chemical present
- Consider appropriate first aid and coordinate with local first responders and medical professionals for treatment of accidental exposure until professional medical treatment can be provided
- Keep safety equipment in a separate location from the pool equipment or stored chemicals

Additional training on Chemical Safety, Fire Safety, PPE, and Flammable Liquid Safety is available at www.nspf.org.

Indoor Air Quality

Air circulation in the indoor pool/spa environment is at risk of containing airborne contaminants. This condition may lead to an increase in respiratory problems and complaints among facility users, and even more so among the employees. Poor air circulation also leads to the potential for deterioration of equipment and building components, such as structural steel, ceiling or roof material, and air handling equipment.

Air pollutants travel from high air pressure to lower air pressure areas. The indoor pool/spa area should have a positive air pressure compared to the outdoor ambient pressure. The pool/spa area should have a negative pressure compared to surrounding areas, such as locker rooms and chemical storage sites. In this way, air pollutants will not build up in the storage area or the pool/spa area. Some of the key provisions from the ANSI/ASHRAE Standard 62.1-2016 for indoor facility (natatorium) air ventilation include:

- Compliance with ANSI/ASHRAE Standard 62.1-2016, "Ventilation for Acceptable Indoor Air Quality"
- Compliance with ASHRAE Standard 55-

© National Swimming Pool Foundation 2017

2013 "Thermal Environmental Conditions for Human Occupancy" should be observed

- 0.48 cfm (2.4 liters per second) of outside air for each square foot of natatorium area
- Between six to eight complete air exchanges per hour
- Maintain CO_2 levels below 0.1% or 1,000 ppm (mg/L)
- Percentage of fresh air introduced: suggested minimum 40%, maximum 100% depending on usage patterns, natatorium design, and the type of equipment installed
- The air temperature in the pool area should be maintained at 2°F to 4°F (1°C to 2.0°C) above pool water temperature

See the Heating & Air Circulation chapter for more information. Additional online training on Indoor Air Quality is available at www.nspf.org.

Electrical Safety

Electrically operated equipment and power supplies installed at aquatic facilities can create shock hazards to facility employees and users. Electrical equipment should only be installed, repaired, or replaced by qualified licensed personnel. Defective electrical devices are those with ground faults or shorts. In the pool or spa environment, the water in the facility and the moisture on the surfaces, equipment, and skin provides a path of low electrical resistance. Current can easily flow from the defective device through a person's body to ground. One of the most dangerous hazards to the pool and spa user is the underwater light fixture.

An individual may receive a shock when touching an energized piece of metal equipment while also touching an metallic object that is at a different electrical potential. An example of this would be holding onto a pool exit ladder with one hand and having the foot come into contact with the metallic ring of a defective underwater light.

It is also possible for a defective underwater light to generate and sustain a charge in the surrounding water. If a user touches a grounded object, the user can be shocked.

Electrical Shocks

When an individual is subjected to an electrical shock, vital organs can be damaged and there could be a loss of muscular function. This loss of function can result in a person not being able to let go of the item causing the shock. The degree of severity is determined by the level of current entering the body. Other factors include the path taken by the current through the body, the size of the person, and the health of the individual.

Small currents of less than one milliampere are usually felt as a slight tingle by a healthy person. People with coronary conditions may be injured by this small current. Currents of about 16 milliamperes are the maximum that a male can endure and still let go using body muscles. The "let go" current for females is generally accepted to be 10 milliamperes. Let go current usually has no effect on the body tissue.

Death can occur in healthy individuals when the current flow reaches 18 milliamperes. At this level, the chest muscles could contract, causing breathing to stop. If the current is allowed to continue at this level, unconsciousness and death may result.

Sources of Shocks

The CPSC has reports of 14 deaths related to electrocutions in swimming pools from 2003–2014. Hot tubs and spas may present the same electrical hazards as swimming pools. The following present risk of electrocution in or around the pool:

- Underwater lighting
- Electrical pool equipment—pumps, filters, vacuum, etc.
- Extension and power cords
- Electrical outlets or switches
- Radios, stereos, TVs and other electrical products
- Overhead power lines

The installation of electrical equipment and wiring in or adjacent to swimming pools and spas is governed by the requirements of the National Electric Code (NEC 70), Article 680. There may be further local requirements applied to electrical equipment and accessories used around aquatic

Photo 14-25. *One of the most dangerous hazards to the pool and spa user is the underwater light fixture.*

Photo 14-26. *Violations of the National Electric Code, NEC 70, such as this make-shift electrical service, can lead to fires and serious injury.*

environments. There are five general elements of consideration for aquatic facilities: grounding, bonding, safe distances, ground fault circuit interrupters (GFCIs), and warnings, labels and procedures. For more information, see NSPF® Electrical Safety Work Practices & Standards (NFPA 70E) online course.

Grounding provides a low-resistance path from the equipment to ground for fault currents. A ground is a connection between an electrical device and the earth, which is at zero voltage. NEC Article 680 requires the following equipment to be grounded:

- Electrical equipment located within five feet (1.5 m) of pool or spa walls
- Electrical equipment associated with pool water circulation
- Junction boxes
- Transformer enclosures
- Circuit boards associated with the pool's electrical supply
- Ground Fault Circuit Interrupters (GFCIs)
- Wet and dry niche underwater lighting
- Panel boards that are not part of the service equipment and that supply any electrical equipment associated with the pool water

Bonding is the act of tying or fastening electrical devices to the same ground potential. Bonding all required pool elements connects the devices by means of a low-resistance path to ground using a solid copper wire. In essence, everything within touch is connected to ground potential. NEC Article 680 requires the following pool/spa items to be bonded:

- All metal parts of the pool structure,

including the reinforcing metal in the shell and the deck

- All metal fittings within or attached to the pool structure, such as ladders and handrails
- Metal parts of equipment associated with the pool water circulating system, such as pump motors
- Underwater lighting
- Metal parts of equipment associated with pool covers, including electrical motors
- All fixed metal parts, cables, and raceways that are not separated from the pool by a permanent barrier. If these items are within 5 feet of the pool wall horizontally, they must be bonded.
- In some cases, electric pool heaters should be bonded

Safe distances for electrical receptacles, lighting fixtures, and similar equipment must be maintained from the pool or spa and any other area that is likely to become wet. NEC Article 680 requires that receptacles be located no closer than 10 feet (3 meters) from the pool wall.

Ground Fault Circuit Interrupters (GFCIs) measure the difference between the input and output current through a circuit. When a person is being shocked, there is a rapid discharge of electricity, which results in a large difference between the input and output current. When the difference is about 5 milliamperes, the GFCI opens the circuit and the duration of the shock is limited.

A shock can occur when a fault or electrical leak occurs. If the current flowing out of the neutral conductor of a device is less than the current flowing into the device, then a current leak has occurred. GFCIs respond to these situations. Older pools, spas, and hot tubs may not have adequate GFCI protection. In particular, pools older than 30 years may not have GFCI protection on underwater lighting circuits. Because the NEC provision for spas only became effective in 1981, even somewhat newer spas or hot tubs may not be protected. NEC Article 680 requires that GFCIs be installed when

- Underwater lighting fixtures are operating at more than 15 volts
- 15- and 20-ampere receptacles are installed outdoors having grade (ground-level) access to the receptacles
- Lighting fixtures and lighting outlets are installed in the area extending between 5

© National Swimming Pool Foundation 2017

feet and 10 feet (1.5 and 3 meters) from the pool walls

- Motor and controller electrical circuits are used in electrically operated pool covers
- 125-volt receptacles are located within 20 feet (6 meters) of the pool wall

Warnings, labels, and procedures should be developed for every facility regarding electrical safety. Electrical radios, sound systems, and hair dryers should not be used close to the pool or spa. Extension cords should not be allowed close to the pool or spa or in any other wet area. The electrical system should be shut off prior to servicing any electrical equipment. Written instructions should be developed covering the use of electrically operated equipment, including circulation system components, pool vacuums, and pool covers.

Preventing Electrocutions

Insulation is a primary protection against electric shock, but it can get worn or cracked. Regular inspections can detect hazards. For example, look for frayed cords on power tools. In addition, the CPSC offers the following recommendations:

- Plug grounded (3-wire) tools only into grounded outlets
- Don't pick up power tools by their power cords
- Read and obey all signs and posted warnings. Don't let these important sources of information become an unnoticed part of the landscape.

- Don't use electrical appliances in the rain
- Leave tasks involving electricity to electricians and other specialists. A little knowledge can definitely be a dangerous thing when it comes to wiring, troubleshooting, and repairing electrical devices and circuits.
- Use a wood or fiberglass ladder if you are working with or around electricity

Lock Out/Tag Out

The Lock Out/Tag Out (LOTO) standard, Occupational Safety & Health Administration (OSHA) Regulation 29 CFR 1910.147, "The Control of Hazardous Energy," applies to all employees servicing and maintaining machines and equipment in which the unexpected energizing or start up of the machines or equipment or release of stored energy could cause injury to the employee. Often people performing this work are required to be licensed.

Training is to be provided to ensure that the purpose and function of the energy control program (LOTO) are understood by employees and that the knowledge and skills necessary for the safe application, usage, and removal of energy controls are acquired by employees.

LOTO is the physical restraint or limit of all hazardous energy sources that supply power to a piece of equipment, machinery, or system. LOTO also includes applying a **warning tag** on the physical limiting device. This documents

Photo 14-27. LOTO is the physical restraint or limit of all hazardous energy sources that supply power to a piece of equipment, machinery, or system.

the authorized LOTO personnel and the date. LOTO operations must be done on all equipment, machinery, or system **shut downs** before **authorized personnel** can perform repairs or service.

Most equipment and machinery have an energy isolation device. These devices are usually put into the off position to shut down the hazardous energy source. Physical limits, such as lock out devices, can be put onto the energy isolation device and secured with padlocks. Examples of lock out devices include: ball valve and gate valve lock outs, circuit breaker lock outs, plug and wall switch lock outs, and pneumatic lock outs. The total shutdown and restraint of all hazardous energy sources, including the safe release of stored hazardous energy, such as capacitors and water pressure in a pool circulating line, must be accomplished.

Additional online training on Electrical Safety is available at www.nspf.org.

Sun Exposure

Exposure to the sun's ultraviolet (UV) rays is the most important environmental factor in the development of skin cancer and a primary factor in the development of lip cancer. Protection from sun exposure is important not only for patrons using the aquatic facility but also for the staff.

Individuals need to protect themselves from excessive exposure to the sun's UV rays, which can cause skin damage during any season or temperature.

Photo 14-28. *UV strength index to warn patrons of the sun exposure risk.*

The midday hours between 10 a.m.–4 p.m. are the most hazardous for UV exposure. UV radiation is the greatest during the late spring and early summer. Ultraviolet (UV) rays are a part of sunlight that is invisible to the eyes. Ultraviolet rays penetrate and change the structure of skin cells.

Protective clothing, such as a widebrim

Photo 14-29. *Another issue for aquatic staff is that UV rays can reflect off virtually any surface and can reach them in the shade.*

hat, long-sleeved shirt, and long pants help protect people. For eye protection, wraparound sunglasses that provide 100 percent UVA & UVB ray protection are best. Lifeguards who may not be able to wear long-sleeved shirts or pants should always wear a broad-spectrum sunscreen, providing protection against both UVA and UVB rays, and lipscreen with a sun protection factor (SPF) of 15. Sunscreen has to be reapplied periodically as indicated by the sunscreen manufacturer's directions. If possible, the staff should work in the shade or have an umbrella on the lifeguard stand.

Although some sun exposure may yield positive benefits, excessive exposure can result in premature aging, undesirable changes in skin texture, and various types of skin cancer, including melanoma, one of the most serious and deadly cancers. UV rays have also been found to cause cataracts.

Another issue is that UV rays can reflect off virtually any surface, especially water, and can reach a person in the shade. The best bet for protecting skin and lips is to use sunscreen or wear protective clothing when outside, even when in the shade.

More information can be found on the CDC website at www.cdc.gov/healthyswimming.

© National Swimming Pool Foundation 2017

Notes

User Load

There are many formulas and guidelines for finding the maximum user load for a pool or spa. Some codes define circulation flow rates in gallons/minute per user; others have different maximum user loads for indoor pools and outdoor pools, or for the shallow and deep ends. The size of decks around the pool, and special equipment, such as slides and diving boards, may also be counted when finding the user load. Pool operators should consult local health codes for the formulas and standards for which the pool or spa was designed.

Photo 14-30. *Spa user loads are usually based on one user for each 10 square feet (0.93 meters squared) of surface area.*

Spa user loads are usually based on one user for each 10 square feet of surface area or one user per three linear feet of the seating area (1:3').

Example: A round spa is 12 feet in diameter. What is the user load?

$$\text{User load} = \text{surface area} \div 10 \text{ ft}^2/\text{user}$$
$$\text{Surface area} = 3.14 \times r \times r$$
$$\text{Surface area} = 3.14 \times 6 \times 6 = 113 \text{ ft}^2$$
$$\text{User load} = 113 \text{ ft}^2 \div 10 \text{ ft}^2/\text{user}$$
$$\text{User load} = 11 \text{ persons}$$

Metric: A spa is 3.66 meters in diameter:

$$\text{User load} = \text{surface area} \div 0.93 \text{ m}^2/\text{user}$$
$$\text{Surface area} = 3.14 \times r \times r$$
$$\text{Surface area} = 3.14 \times 1.83 \times 1.83 = 10.52 \text{ m}^2$$
$$\text{User load} = 10.52 \text{ m}^2 \div 0.93 \text{ m}^2/\text{user}$$
$$\text{User load} = 11 \text{ persons}$$

Notes

200

© National Swimming Pool Foundation 2017

Chapter 15:
Keeping Records

"If we could first know where we are, and whither we are tending, we could then better judge what to do, and how to do it."

–Abraham Lincoln

Keeping proper records is an important responsibility and takes the guesswork out of pool and spa operations. Good records are important because they show how the facility operates, helping to reduce wasteful spending, ensure employee and guest safety, and reduce liability to the facility. Records play a significant role in every management aspect of the facility. They are essential for protecting the facility, as well as possibly preventing or defending a lawsuit. Record keeping is an important part of a risk management plan (see NSPF® Aquatic Risk Management online course and handbook). Knowing what records to keep and how long to keep them is a vital part of the pool operator's job.

All pool operations must be accomplished on time. Some tasks are routine and are performed daily. Others, such as preventative maintenance, are performed infrequently.

As the size of the facility and staff grows, the number of reports and records increases. Documentation and written procedures are necessary for a successful pool/spa facility, and are part of good management practice.

Emergency response plans (ERP) are also part of a facility's records; they outline the steps taken by the staff during an emergency. ERPs increase in complexity with the size of the facility and as the number of staff increases. As such, ERPs need to be customized for each facility. See NSPF® Emergency Response Planning online course for more information.

Records

Records at an aquatic facility provide management personnel a way of evaluating and controlling how the facility is being operated. The types of records that should be kept include, but are not limited to

- Supervisors' Reports
- Incident Reports

Photo 15-1. *Safety checklists help ensure patron safety from injuries and illnesses.*

© National Swimming Pool Foundation 2017

- Staff Records
- Maintenance Records
- Training Reports
- Water Chemistry Logs
- User Load Logs
- Daily/Weekly/Monthly Inspection Records

Accumulating and maintaining good records of operation is a never-ending but important process. Maintaining proper records has become the standard of care in the industry, helping the owner maintain the facility safely and profitably. Pool records are helpful for assessing operating costs, including maintenance materials, hours, chemical consumption, the effects of weather, crowd size, and the distribution of staff hours. There should be sufficient information in the records to allow the owner or manager to evaluate the aquatic facility's performance.

Records are also critical to defend against legal actions and to assist in health department investigations. In reported disease outbreaks of *E.coli*, *Cryptosporidium* and other pathogens, records, and the lack thereof played heavily in the analysis of cause and solution. The length of time that records should be retained is usually determined by the health department, the facility's legal counsel, or the facility's insurance company.

Every aquatic facility should have a detailed process for recording key events with respect to pool and spa operations. Records should be maintained to document periodic inspection results and corrective action taken on defects, breakdowns, and repairs. Records should also be maintained regarding chemical additions, pool levels, treatment station chemical readings, time and amount of makeup water added, and daily consumption of bulk chemicals.

Records generated from any service provided by outside agencies or contractors, unplanned events, and pertinent notes are the records that will prove valuable to the operator. These records provide important information when it comes time to write budgets, evaluate chemical alternatives, troubleshoot problems, assess staff needs, and plan equipment replacement.

Daily inspections of the facility before it is opened should also be conducted. Daily water chemistry logs should be maintained as required by local codes. These logs will typically include chlorine levels, pH, total alkalinity, calcium hardness, cyanuric acid, and temperature.

The types of records kept should be well planned and blend into the workday system. They must be current in their recording and be preserved for a reasonable period of time. Water flow rates, pool levels, water quality, and communication systems should be verified to complete any inspection. More information regarding record keeping can be are found in the NSPF® Aquatic Risk Management online course and handbook.

Every record or report should include the name of the individual responsible for the report. When possible, the record should include the standard as well as the measured results.

Most codes and regulations require that daily operations records be maintained. These records are kept at the facility and made available to the enforcing agency. Local requirements vary as to what must be measured and recorded on a daily basis, as well as the frequency of recording. Engaging local health officials in developing proper measures and records for each facility will better ensure compliance.

Records and reports satisfy the following needs:
- To provide an effective legal defense if a lawsuit is ever filed. The absence of records will be used against the facility and their employees.
- To comply with all governmental

Photo 15-2. *Record keeping is an essential component to good pool management and operations.*

© National Swimming Pool Foundation 2017

Photo 15-3. *The types of records kept are well planned. They must be current and be kept for a reasonable period of time or as dictated by law.*

requirements concerning sanitation and maintenance

- To document any injury, to identify corrective management action, and to prevent further injuries
- To provide access to information about employee training, background, performance, procedures used to accomplish objectives, equipment operating and maintenance information, repair or renovation requirements, and more
- To help staff learn how best to achieve goals and to make the organization more effective

Records also play an important role in managing the business side of an aquatic facility. Maintenance records, opening and closing checklists, inventory, and training schedules all play an important part in establishing a budget. Understanding the budget helps the facility management run a financially stable facility.

NSPF® offers an all-weather Commercial Pool & Spa Log, a weatherproof six-month logbook with tables and chemistry guidelines for both pools and spas. In addition, the following sample forms and checklists are available in Appendix A1 to A9:

- Daily Opening & Closing Checklist
- Daily Pool Chemical Log
- Daily Locker Room Maintenance Checklist
- Aquatic Incident Report
- Seasonal Opening Checklist
- Seasonal Closing Checklist
- Preventative Maintenance Checklist
- New Plaster Start-Up Procedures
- Pool/Spa Inspection Checklist

Daily Operations Records

The most basic and necessary records are those kept on a daily basis. Pool water chemistry must meet the standard requirements before the pool is opened each day. All suction drain covers must be in place and intact. All safety and rescue gear must be in place and functional. The water must have the proper clarity and chemical levels, and the circulation flow must meet turnover requirements.

Often a manager will develop their own daily checklist. Most codes allow these customized reports as long as they contain the minimum required information; check with your local bathing codes should be consulted. It is important to record the date and time whenever checks are conducted. The following list may be considered as a foundation on which to build a daily record for any facility:

- Free chlorine or total bromine
- Combined chlorine
- pH
- Safety equipment in place and functional
- Suction drain covers visually observed and secured in place
- Barriers in place blocking unsupervised children from access to potentially dangerous parts of a facility
- Flow meter reading
- Filter pressure differential or pump vacuum
- Number of users daily
- Water temperature
- Air temperature
- Water clarity

Photo 15-4. *The opening checklist will assure all safety equipment is in place, such as a floating safety line.*

© National Swimming Pool Foundation 2017

- Filter backwashing
- Chemicals added
- Injury reports
- Skimmer and hair/lint baskets cleaned
- Deck waste containers emptied

Codes, regulations, and standard practice, as well as the type of facility, will determine exactly what the daily operations report should include. Water resistant log books and printer paper are available from NSPF®.

Opening and Closing Checklist

Unsafe conditions should be noted and corrected before the facility opens. If the correction cannot be completed before the facility opens, people should not be allowed access to the area. Signs, ropes, barriers, or cones may be necessary for this purpose. In severe cases, the facility may need to remain closed until the situation is resolved.

Photo 15-5. *Having the pool parameters and instructions on how to backwash the pool helps minimize mistakes.*

Upon closing, it is important that no patrons remain in the facility. All movable equipment should be returned to its normal locations, lights turned on or off as required, and the facility should be properly secured.

The following is a starting point to review when the facility is opened or closed:
- Pool and spa inspection checklist readily available
- Pool, bathrooms, and changing areas free of people

- Safety and rescue equipment in place and functional
- Suction drain covers securely in place and fully intact
- Ladders and handrails in place and secure
- All self-closing, self-locking gates operating as expected
- Lockers and restrooms clean and properly furnished with amenities
- Pool or spa rules are in place and easily seen
- Required deck clearance around pool or spa
- No settled debris in pool or spa
- All underwater lighting functional

Manufacturer's Equipment Manuals

Original documentation supplied by the facility designer and equipment manufacturer must be part of any facility's permanent records. This material provides the necessary instructions for installation as well as operation. Detailed instructions concerning routine and preventative maintenance are provided in these manuals, as are parts lists for repairs. These manuals should be kept as long as the equipment is online and operating. Manufacturer's manuals should also be kept if equipment has been disconnected and

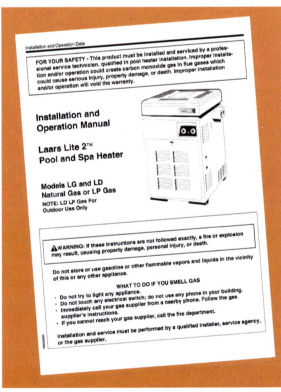

Illustration 15-1. *Many manufacturers provide installation and operation manuals online.*

© National Swimming Pool Foundation 2017

Photo 15-6. *The opening checklist will assure that proper clearance is maintained around the pool. Most states regulations require a clearance of 4 feet.*

remains on the premises in case the equipment needs to be reinstalled. All of the facility's equipment manuals should be readily available for reference purposes.

Data plates do not always survive the passage of time. Therefore, it may be useful to record and store photographs or digital images of the data plate information of all equipment. Should a piece of operating equipment require replacement, the exact specifications recorded in the photo can be used for reordering purposes. If a specific manual is missing, send a photograph of the data plate to the manufacturer and request a new copy of the manual. Many manuals are available at the manufacturers' websites.

Photo 15-7. *Digital photographs of motor data plates maybe useful to record in case the motor needs to be replaced.*

Routine Maintenance Schedules

Routine pool or spa maintenance is usually performed prior to the opening of the facility each day. This practice helps avoid conflicts between the operator and the program coordinators. Vacuuming the pool bottom is best accomplished after the pool has been closed for at least two hours. Pools are normally vacuumed in the morning prior to opening. Use of the facility for any reason should not be allowed while vacuuming the pool.

Cleaning and maintaining decks, locker rooms, showers and lavatories, and repositioning and cleaning deck furniture can be performed after the facility closes or before it opens; however, a plan should be in place to ensure that these areas are kept clean and operational throughout the day. Landscape maintenance and office and meeting room cleaning can be performed while the facility is open for use.

Routine maintenance of operating equipment and the delivery of chemicals to the facility have some risk involved. If possible, these tasks should be scheduled before the facility opens.

Preventative Maintenance Schedules

Long-term deterioration of the operating equipment and the physical pool or spa structure can be prevented or minimized by developing

Photo 15-8. *Staff training should be documented to verify the staff's skills and knowledge.*

and implementing a preventative maintenance program. The manufacturer's equipment manuals and the facility's suppliers can provide basic information on how to develop such a plan. Preventative maintenance usually requires that the facility be closed. To minimize down time, trained staff and proper materials and parts should be on hand.

Preventative maintenance also includes important items like painting, taking inventory, removing rust, pressure cleaning the deck, and inspecting and repairing pumps. As long as guests are not at risk, some of these items can be performed while the facility is open, preferably during slow use periods.

Training Schedules

Regular staff meetings should be held and documented. Topics to be discussed include how best to improve the staff's skills and knowledge, current issues, operating procedures, upcoming events, and lessons learned. The aquatic facility can rely on suppliers to provide professional support and training for these sessions.

Every full-time employee and seasonal employee should have a master plan for job-related training. This can include items such as the Certified Pool/Spa Operator® (CPO®) Certification Course, Certified Pool/Spa Inspector™ (CPI™) training, emergency response, first aid, CPR, and preventing sexual harassment. All training provided to an employee should be included in the employee's personnel record.

Hazard Communication Records

The federal Hazard Communication Standard requires management to maintain records of all chemicals used at an aquatic facility. Each chemical has a Safety Data Sheet (SDS) developed by the manufacturer. The SDS must be easily accessible to all employees.

Plan some time for every employee to be

Photo 15-9. *Along with operating instructions, SDS should be located at the job site for quick reference in case of an emergency.*

© National Swimming Pool Foundation 2017

Certified Pool / Spa Operator® Certification

Gregorio Isaias Naguas Yaguache

as an Operator of Aquatic Facilities
Issued by the

National Swimming Pool Foundation®

on

Certification Date: 15 July 2015
Certification Number: CPO-
Expires: 15 July 2020

NSPF® Instructors
Andrés Benjamín Encalada Celi
Moises Vinicio Encalada Ramírez

Thomas M. Lachocki
Chief Executive Officer

Illustration 15-2. *Certification is one of the most important records that should be maintained.*

trained with regard to the SDS and the handling of hazardous materials. Request that suppliers provide such training. SDS should be reviewed, and every employee should sign off that they understand and accept the information provided.

The SDS should be posted or readily accessible at the job site for immediate reference purposes. See the Regulations & Guidelines chapter for more information.

Proficiency Records

Many regulations require proof of proficiency for people who work in an aquatic facility. Lifeguards and swimming instructors are required to be certified by the American Red Cross®, the YMCA®, or another aquatic training agency. Individuals performing chemical treatment and routine maintenance at public pools may be required to have Certified Pool/Spa Operator® certification. In addition, hazardous material (HAZMAT) training is required; an online course is available at www.nspf.org.

Proficiency records should be part of the employee's permanent records. Any certificates should be either posted or filed at the appropriate site. It is important that these records are kept up to date because it becomes difficult to obtain proof that a qualified employee was on site if that employee leaves to work for another company, goes back to school, or moves. NSPF® maintains records and can provide replacement wallet cards or certificates to certified operators. In addition, public health officials and employers can request verification that an individual has obtained Certified Pool/Spa Operator® Certification.

Emergency Response Plans

Part of keeping patrons and staff safe at the aquatic facility is having an Emergency Response Plan (ERP) with procedures of how staff should respond in emergency situations. The plan must contain staff training requirements, alarm signals and their meanings, and the actions and procedures detailing how the facility expects the staff to respond to emergency situations. The pool operator may be part of the emergency response team of the aquatic facility. Being prepared to handle an emergency is key to

1. Pool & Spa Management
2. Regulations & Guidelines
3. Essential Calculations
4. Pool Water Contamination
5. Disinfection
6. Water Balance
7. Pool & Spa Water Problems
8. Chemical Testing
9. Chemical Feed & Control
10. Water Circulation
11. Pool & Spa Filtration
12. Heating & Air Circulation
13. Spa & Therapy Operations
14. Facility Safety
15. Keeping Records
16. Maintenance Systems
17. Troubleshooting
18. Facility Renovation & Design
References

minimizing injuries and administering care to a victim. The facility must have an ERP that the facility staff are familiar with. This ERP is a detailed plan of how everyone acts in emergencies. The ERP should be practiced often to ensure that everyone works together as a team during an emergency.

Developing Emergency Response Plans

The role that the pool operator plays in the development of the ERP will depend on the size and management structure for the facility. Consideration must be taken for the following:

- Types of emergencies: these include water emergencies, sudden illness, natural disaster, and facility emergencies, such as fire, chemical accident, etc.
- Layout of the facility: this includes the location of the rescue equipment, exits, telephones, etc.
- Available equipment: this includes the rescue equipment, first aid supplies, and protective equipment, such as gloves, etc.
- Emergency Medical Services (EMS): this includes the communication plan for notifying EMS and the facility access for them
- Chain of command: identifying who needs to be notified in an emergency. This determines who contacts the family members or parents, if needed.

Roles and Responsibilities of Staff

Preparation for an emergency includes knowing the roles and responsibilities that each staff member has. Responsibilities include:

- Covering the rescue area
- Clearing the facility, including the pool or spa
- Identifying the primary rescuer
- Calling EMS
- Performing crowd control
- Designating responsibilities after the emergency

After the Emergency

Completing reports, checking equipment, and replacing equipment are just three of the things that will need to be done after an emergency has been dealt with. These tasks may need to be done before the facility can be reopened. One report is the aquatic incident report. An example is found in Appendix A-4.

An emergency involving a serious injury or death is a very traumatic event. Rescuing a victim can be especially stressful for the staff if they feel they did something wrong or failed to do something. In these situations, professional counseling may be necessary to help the staff member cope with the stress.

A staff debriefing should take place after the emergency. This can help evaluate what happened and whether corrective steps can be taken to prevent it from happening in the future.

For more information on developing an ERP see the NSPF® Emergency Response Planning online course and handbook at www.nspf.org.

© National Swimming Pool Foundation 2017

Chapter 16:
Maintenance Systems

"A man too busy to take care of his health is like a mechanic too busy to take care of his tools."

—Spanish proverb

Many factors must be considered when establishing a maintenance system plan for an aquatics facility. Considerations may include:

- Design and type of facility
- Number and age of the pools and spas
- The length of the operating season
- The need to generate revenue
- Size and capabilities of staff
- Nature, purpose, goals or mission of the sponsoring agency

A manager of a small, seasonally operated, outdoor pool owned by a homeowner's association will not have the same responsibilities as the manager of an indoor multi-pool municipal natatorium. Both managers need to develop a systematic method of making sure their facility operates efficiently. The Pool & Spa Management chapter discussed the planning process, including details, such as forecasting, objectives, action steps, scheduling, budgeting, and policies and procedures. Developing a maintenance system plan for any aquatic facility involves all of these items. The operator should also be familiar with any local regulations that may pertain to maintenance.

First Steps

Before any maintenance plan can be developed, the scope of the plan must be defined. This can best be accomplished by obtaining a set of the original engineering drawings that were used to construct the facility. The professional engineer provided an equipment specification sheet giving the exact stipulations for equipment performance. The pool operator should maintain these construction drawings as part of the permanent file.

As discussed in the Keeping Records chapter,

Photo 16-1. *Maintenance systems can be simple or complex, depending on the design and use of the facility.*

© National Swimming Pool Foundation 2017

209

the installation and operation (I/O) manuals that are retained at the facility are useful resources in establishing a maintenance plan. They also supply specific information concerning the recommended installation requirements, operating instructions, troubleshooting, safety precautions, and routine and preventative maintenance requirements.

Maintenance Plan

There are three distinct categories of maintenance: routine, sometimes called daily; preventative; and seasonal, start-up and shut-down. Maintenance procedures involve inspection, servicing, and component replacement.

To properly develop a maintenance plan, the pool operator must first know what equipment or items will be included in the plan. An inventory of all items should be performed. After all equipment has been inventoried, then any equipment that requires periodic inspection, servicing, or component replacement should be categorized as to its function: i.e. deck equipment, pump room equipment, safety items, as well as office items. The certified operator should educate their supervisors that it is far better and usually less expensive to have an active and well-prepared maintenance plan than to wait until items break and need to be repaired or replaced.

Photo 16-2. *Water quality is one of the first considerations when opening a pool/spa facility for the day.*

Based on the manufacturer's I/O manuals, a calendar should be developed that covers what maintenance procedures should be done and the specific time interval.

Inventory Data Form

As the inventory is made, the following information should be recorded for each item:

- Equipment name, such as liquid feed pump
- Manufacturer
- Model number
- Cost
- Manufacturer's contact information
- Supplier/vendor contact information
- Specific weekly, quarterly, or annual maintenance procedures
- Warranty requirements, if any

Procedure Data

Once the inventory has been completed, then the necessary procedures for maintenance of each item can be developed.

Inspection Procedures

When conducting an inspection, use the senses of touch, smell, sight, and sound. Feel for vibration or heat. Take note of any strange odors. Look for missing or broken equipment. Listen for unusual sounds such as a pump cavitating. Using the information compiled on the inventory data forms, make a list of the mechanical equipment that must be inspected daily. Some items common to most daily inspection lists will verify

- Circulation outlets, including the main drain cover, are securely fastened and in good repair. The vacuum outlet cover is spring loaded and in place.
- All lights are operational and timers or photometric switches are operational
- All ladders, handrails, guard chairs, and other deck-related equipment are in place and securely anchored and in place
- For indoor pools, the ceiling above the pool shows no sign of deterioration or mold
- The flow meter is operational and providing accurate flow measurement
- The hair and lint strainer is free of debris
- The pump is securely fastened to its mounting and is not vibrating
- The vacuum and pressure gauges are in place, functional and providing accurate measurement

© National Swimming Pool Foundation 2017

- All chemical feed systems are functional and calibrated properly. There are no visible chemical leaks or unusual odors.
- Emergency eye-wash and drench showers are functional
- Automatic water level control devices are functional and maintaining accurate level conditions
- Filtration media or elements are clean. There is no evidence of bridging, channeling, or direct water pass-through. The influent and effluent pressure gauges (or vacuum) are within the normal operational ranges.
- All valves are properly tagged and are in the proper position for any specific water circulation requirement. There is a valve sequence chart laminated and posted in the filter room area for easy reference.
- All air pressure relief valves on pressurized systems are operational

If the circulation motor fails, then it is likely that the facility will remain closed until the problem is corrected. The following pump and motor items should be considered for installation and inspection:

- Install the pump/motor in a clean, dust-free area. Most pool and jet pump motors are open drip proof designs which circulate external air for cooling. Air contaminants, such as dust and grass clippings may clog internal air passages, leading to overheating.
- Verify the system total dynamic head to determine the system flow rate (see Appendix C-1)
- Protect the pump/motor from excess moisture. Don't hose down the area around the motor when it is running. Elevate the pump/motor if it is in an area that is prone to flooding.
- If an external motor cover is used, be certain it does not trap moisture or fail to allow cooling air to circulate
- Don't store or use chemicals close to the motor, or other hot surfaces
- A running motor that is too hot to touch is not necessarily overloaded. Some motors have a maximum operating temperature of 266°F (130°C).
- If pool or jet pump motors are removed from service at the end of a season, do not wrap them tightly in plastic. Temperature changes may cause condensation with negative effects.
- Thinner air at higher altitude has less cooling ability. As a rule of thumb, the next higher horsepower rating may be used at altitude above 3,300 feet (1,000 meters) to compensate.

The specifics listed in this section are just a few of the equipment-related daily inspection items. Other equipment items may be added depending on the complexity and sophistication of the system. This could include heaters, heat exchangers, blowers, air handling, vacuum systems, exhaust fans, system controllers, and supplemental equipment such as ozone generators.

The daily equipment inspection is just one part of the facility's daily opening and closing checklist discussed later in this chapter. Not all operating equipment requires daily inspection. Some items may require weekly, monthly, quarterly, or just seasonal or annual inspection. The I/O manuals will guide the operator concerning these matters, and the maintenance calendar can be adjusted as required.

Service Procedures

Servicing equipment can be as simple as moving valves through their entire range on an occasional basis, to as complicated as cleaning the soot blocking the primary air to gas-fired burners. In the first instance, facility staff members perform the task. The second instance requires the efforts of a qualified service technician or installer.

Servicing must be performed on a schedule as recommended in the equipment I/O manual. As an example, some disinfectant feed devices require lubrication of the lid on a monthly basis.

Photo 16-3. *Visual inspection can spot problems, such as improper bonding, before damage becomes excessive.*

© National Swimming Pool Foundation 2017

The manufacturer may recommend that the probes on an oxidation reduction potential controller be cleaned on a monthly basis.

Servicing equipment requires many items. The following are just a few examples:

- Non-petroleum, silicon-based lubricant
- Necessary tools
- Safety items, such as gloves and safety glasses
- Replacement materials, such as gaskets or O-rings

Replacement Procedures

Some equipment items will require component replacement on a scheduled basis, much like the oil and air filters in an automobile. The following is taken from an ozone generation I/O manual and is used only as an example of how a maintenance plan is detailed by a manufacturer: Yearly Service:

- Replace the cooling fan filters
- Replace the air inlet particulate filter
- Replace the Kynar® check valve and rebuild the stainless steel check valve
- Remove and clean the glass dielectric in the reaction chamber
- Rebuild the solenoid valve on the electrical interlock box
- Replace the flange gasket and clean the diffuser in the contact column
- Replace the desiccant in the air dryer and indicating chamber

Every three years:

- Replace the cooling fans
- Disassemble and hone the corona discharge reaction chamber

Photo 16-4. *Inspection of the grounds must include barriers and gates.*

- Clean glass dielectrics
- Replace O-rings

Every five years:

- Replace the glass dielectrics
- Replace O-rings

The preceding example shows the importance of maintaining the I/O manuals and how to use the information contained in them.

Component replacement of equipment requires many items; the following are just a few examples:

- Necessary tools
- Safety items, such as gloves, safety glasses
- Replacement materials, such as gaskets or O-rings
- Component parts that require special orders from the manufacturer or a local wholesale distributor

Routine Maintenance

Routine or daily maintenance is the work performed by the aquatics staff as an on-going responsibility. It begins and ends with unlocking/locking the facility and turning off/turning on any security system. In between, there may be a few tasks or dozens of tasks, depending on the size and complexity of the facility. A daily opening and closing checklist is provided in Appendix A-1.

Opening and Closing Checklist

Generally, the first area to be inspected is the pool/spa and deck followed by the pump and filter area. The bathhouse and restroom facilities are then checked, followed by the barriers, grounds and other general areas of the property. All of this must be performed before users are allowed into the facility.

Pool/Spa and Deck

The water quality and clarity must be tested. Any required corrections to pH and disinfectant level must be made before the pool or spa is opened to the users. The main drain cover must be observed to make sure it is firmly attached and is intact. The pool may require brushing or vacuuming before opening. The water level must allow for positive skimming. Water levels that are either too high or low can prevent proper skimming from taking place.

All suction openings in gutters and skimmers must be checked for debris. Any accumulation

© National Swimming Pool Foundation 2017

of scum must be removed from water-line tile. Return inlet fittings and vacuum line covers must be in place. All handrails, ladders, diving boards, slides and other equipment must be firmly attached and in good repair. Slides must be examined for any worn spots.

The deck area around the pool must be clear of any items. Deck furniture should be moved back from the pool to provide a minimum of four feet of clearance, or in accordance with local codes.

All signs, warnings and safety equipment must be in place. Waste receptacles must be emptied, and towel bins should be in their proper location.

Pump Room

The flow meter needs to be checked and the filters backwashed if necessary. Chemical reservoirs must be filled, and controller set-points observed. Vacuum and pressure gauges must be observed and readings recorded. The hair and lint strainer should be cleaned after the pump is turned off.

Brushing

All pools and spas need to be brushed on a regular basis. How often will depend upon the amount of soil and other debris that enters the water. Brushing removes the debris and biofilm from the pool and spa walls and allows for improved removal by means of the circulation flow. Debris brushes are made of nylon or polypropylene plastic.

Pool or spa surfaces that contain algae should be brushed to dislodge the algae and improve the disinfectant's or algicide's efficacy. Brushes have either stainless steel or plastic bristles for plaster or vinyl surfaces, respectively. A steel brush may damage the pool wall if used on a regular basis.

Vacuuming

Debris on the bottom of the pool is not only unsightly, but it may also provide a nutrient base for algae growth. This debris is removed by suction, utilizing a vacuum head, hose, and pole. The suction is provided by a separate vacuum pump, a vacuum line tied to the main circulation pump, or by a stand-alone portable vacuum pump and filter. Vacuuming is best done after debris has been allowed to settle after the pool has closed at the end of the day. A good rule of thumb is to allow at least two hours with no users

Photo 16-5. *Larger pools may benefit from the use of an automated vacuum system.*

present, or after all the dirt has settled. Therefore, it may be helpful to brush at closing and vacuum prior to opening.

Larger pools can benefit from the use of automated vacuuming systems. Many of these systems have a wireless remote control unit and control box with a timer. They are fully automatic and can completely clean a pool of several hundreds of thousands of gallons in a matter of hours. The facility must be closed and secured if these units are in operation.

Tile Cleaning

Cleaning the water-line and gutter tile must be done on a regular basis to maintain a clean, sanitary facility. The scum line is a collection of oils and dirt and can be a home to bacteria. Often algae growth starts in grout between tiles, with the oily material providing the nutrient base.

The tiles have a glazed, non-porous finish. A non-abrasive tile cleaner should be used to not harm this glaze. The cleaner should also be compatible with pool water chemistry: it should not cause foaming or contain phosphates. There are several commercial cleaners available on the market.

Preventative Maintenance

Preventative maintenance (PM) prevents long-term deterioration of the equipment and the facility. Some PM work must be done weekly. Other PM is scheduled monthly, quarterly, yearly, or on a longer time frame. PM work requires three things: time, materials, and labor. The specific equipment PM requirements are provided by the manufacturer in the I/O manual. Facility PM requirements are most easily determined by the inspection procedures described earlier in this

Photo 16-6. *Care must be taken not to damage the glaze on tiles. Always use a non-abrasive cleaner.*

Photo 16-7. *Preventative maintenance may also include making sure that the vent covers in the pump room are kept clean to ensure adequate ventilation.*

chapter. The Preventative Maintenance Checklist provided in Appendix A-7 may provide guidance in setting up the facility PM program.

Seasonal Maintenance

Weather becomes a factor in the management of pools and spa in many areas. Some areas require a full winterization program. Milder climates need only a partial winterization program. Seasonal maintenance programs should always be developed with a concern for the protection of the facility and the ease of start-up for the new season. Appendices A5 & A6 provide checklists for seasonal pools.

Winterizing

A good winterizing program prevents damage to the pool shell and mechanical equipment as well as to the buildings and grounds. Such a program will

- Prevent damage caused by hydrostatic pressure
- Prevent rust and general wear
- Reduce the chance for vandalism
- Use a checklist system for disassembling and assembling equipment
- Inventory and store equipment in a proper manner

In some areas, mild temperatures make it possible to leave the water in a pool to circulate occasionally. In more extreme climates, the pool may be drained and the circulation system winterized by using compressed air to blow all water out of the pipes and by the use of an antifreeze to prevent freezing in the pipes. The antifreeze must be designed for special use in pools. Never use automotive antifreeze, which contains ingredients that are toxic.

Hydrostatic Pressure

Hydrostatic pressure on the pool shell is a concern in all areas with high water tables. An empty pool can float out of the ground if the water table rises high enough.

Rising water exerts pressure on the underside of the pool shell, and this pressure must be relieved. This is accomplished by use of a hydrostatic relief valve. This valve, or valves in a large pool, is installed in the lowest part of the pool. When the ground water begins to exert

© National Swimming Pool Foundation 2017

Photo 16-8. *When ground water begins to exert pressure on the pool shell, the valve opens and allows the water to flow into the pool.*

pressure on the pool shell, the valve opens and allows the water to flow into the pool. This relieves the upward pressure on the pool shell and prevents the pool from floating out of the ground. Often, well points are installed around the pool or spa in the deck to further aid in the pressure release. These well points are tied into a suction pump that drains off the water surrounding the pool shell.

Pool Covers

There may be less damage to the pool structure by keeping the water in the pool during the off season. The decision is guided by how the facility is staffed and whether or not the pool can be checked on a weekly basis. Vandalism is also a consideration.

A pool cover can control staining, keep debris out, and help make it possible to keep water in the pool during the off season. The cover is not designed to prevent persons or animals from

Photo 16-9. *Most winter covers are fastened to the decks around the pool by a spring-loaded device.*

falling into the pool. Unauthorized access to the pool must be prevented.

Pool covers are designed to protect the pool from many winter problems. Most winter covers are fastened to the decks around the pool by a spring-loaded device. These fastening devices must be inspected every so often to see that they have not stretched or become loose. Tightening the springs will help keep the cover secure and prevent debris from getting into the water around the edges of a sagging cover.

Some covers are built to allow rainwater to drain through the cover into the pool rather than collect on top; others are not. Covers that do not allow water to drain through may need to have standing water pumped off the surface. The weight of standing water can cause the devices securing the cover to stretch and loosen, as well as become a drowning hazard. If the pool is being treated with any special chemicals such as algicides, the pool operator should check the warranty on the pool cover. Low pH or superchlorination may burn some covers and void the warranty. Local regulations may require pools remaining full during the off season be fully covered.

Deterioration

Damage to equipment and materials from rust, cold, dampness, condensation, weather conditions, UV rays, rodents, insects, and animal encroachment are some of the off-season problems a seasonal pool operation faces. These factors can reduce the life of a facility and its equipment. The operational costs of a seasonal facility can sometimes equal or exceed those of a year-round facility.

In unheated, moist areas, equipment should be brushed lightly or sprayed with an oil-based product or with a water displacement formula. Whenever possible, remove these items to a warm place for storage. If the item is too large to be removed or there isn't enough storage area, the item should be treated, covered, and secured for the winter.

Water lines to bathhouses, showers, and restrooms should all be disconnected and drained. Some facilities have lines that do not drain well due to their design. These lines should be blown clear using compressed air from a compressor or an air storage tank. If the pipes are small, a SCUBA tank can be used to clear the lines. Low pressure regulators must be used to control air flow since SCUBA tanks typically hold 3,000 psi or 200 bar of air.

To clear as much water as possible when blowing out lines, open and shut, after blowing out the water, all shower heads and valves, starting from the point closest to the air and working to the farthest away. In some cases, such as toilets, commodes, and traps, water may have to be removed by hand. A little non-toxic antifreeze should be added to these fixtures to prevent the small amount of remaining water from causing damage. If any pipes are taken apart and left open for the winter, be sure to plug the lines to prevent small animals, insects, or debris from entering.

Disassembling and Assembling

Equipment needing to be winterized falls into one of two categories:
- Items that need to be protected from vandals
- Items that need to be protected from weather, moisture, and freezing

All outdoor furniture, plumbing, and electrical fixtures should be stored indoors whenever possible. If no indoor storage space is available, these items should be covered and secured using cables or other locking devices. Smaller equipment, such as drinking fountains, clocks, speakers, light fixtures, cabinets, and program and instructional equipment should be stored and secured indoors to prevent vandalism and theft.

Pump houses, offices, staff rooms, and other indoor areas that may not be heated require special care as well. Chlorinators, feeders, boilers, office machines, and computers need to be protected from moisture and weather damage. Remove these to a warm and secure storage space. If no space is available, all equipment should be packed away. Mechanical devices should be lightly oiled and covered for protection. Electrical equipment, computers, and other office equipment should be tightly wrapped in plastic and stored in a locked area. Lastly, the entire building should be treated for pest and insect control before final closing.

The operator should compile a master list of all items, noting on the list exactly where each item is stored. A checklist of steps and parts required to reassemble each item should also be kept with this list. Taking photos of the installed equipment may help guide reassembly. All hardware for

Photo 16-10. *Chlorinators and feeders need to be protected from moisture and weather damage.*

each item should be placed in small plastic bags and attached to the equipment to which it belongs. Make at least three copies of the list and the reassembly instructions, storing one copy with each item, one in the pool office, and one in a safe place off site, in case of vandals, fire, or water damage at the pool site.

These checklist items are vital to the easy start-up of the pool in the spring and best for seasonal pools which have a large staff turnover from season to season.

Vandalism and Theft

Pool operators should think about ways to prevent damage to property and equipment by vandals. Remove as many attractive nuisances as possible to reduce the temptations. Also, if vandals are not attracted to the facility, there is less chance that someone will be injured while trying to vandalize equipment or property. Cover windows and doors with shutters or plywood.

Any item that is attractive to a thief or vandal, such as televisions, phones, computers, radios, must either be removed from the facility or stored in a locked, secure place. Such storage places should be checked regularly to see that they remain closed and secure. Overhead security lighting, alarms, security cameras, and time lapse video recorders are other methods that may help keep the facility secure during the offseason.

Pool Water Chemistry

Many health codes have few or no requirements during the offseason. The main concern during this period is to protect the pool from damage. In addition, the facility should be maintained so that it does not become a mosquito breeding ground to prevent spread of West Nile or Zika Virus.

© National Swimming Pool Foundation 2017

Photo 16-11. *A covered pool will acumulate less contaminants and debris.*

Most of the chemicals used during the offseason will be used to prevent algae and oxidize the small amounts of organic residue that may enter the water. A covered pool will accumulate fewer contaminants and debris. The lower winter temperatures will reduce the rate at which microorganisms grow.

Since only domestic water, rain water, or snow will get into the pool, the chemical demand in the winter will be low. Free chlorine, pH, and water balance should be maintained, although testing can be performed less frequently, such as weekly. In areas where freezing temperatures prevent the use of mechanical feeders, chemicals may be hand fed straight into the pool. Mechanical equipment should be drained and winterized.

Utilities

A decision must be made concerning shutting off water, electricity and gas service for the offseason. The local utility companies can assist in making this decision. In some cases, it may be costly to shut down and restart utilities. These costs must be balanced against the cost of maintaining minimal services during the offseason. The pool operator must be sure that power is available for the operation of any needed equipment or security devices.

Spring Start-up

Each facility has its own set of spring start up procedures. The challenge is to organize and schedule for the task of starting up the pool. This task, in fact, begins during the shutdown process. The operator should take care to store items in a logical sequence. Items that are needed first during the start-up process should be stored last for easy access. For example, brooms, cleaning supplies, and tools will likely be needed before cash registers, computers, and program supplies. By thoughtfully closing the facility, the start-up process is simple and efficient (see Appendix A-5).

More detailed information and training about the routine maintenance of swimming pool and spa equipment is available at www.nspf.org.

Photo 16-12. *Routine maintenance, such as regular filter cleaning, is important to help ensure correct operation and extend the life of pool/spa components.*

© National Swimming Pool Foundation 2017

Chapter 17:
Troubleshooting

"Become a fixer not just a fixture."

—Anthony J. D'Angelo

When equipment fails, there is a tendency to try to fix the problem as soon as possible to avoid closing the facility. A pool operator should never attempt to perform a task for which he or she is not qualified. This also applies to other members of the staff. Always have a qualified service technician or contractor perform repair and replacement work unless there is a staff member that has the qualifications and proper license. This applies to all types of situations, and, in particular, it is most important for electrical equipment and gas heaters, which pose unique and substantial risks.

Every pool and spa facility will have its own unique set of problems. A pool operator has a well-defined plan in place to take care of common problems. These plans or corrective steps should be laminated and placed at the appropriate sites around the facility for easy reference.

There are several troubleshooting tips

> ### Warning
> The information provided in the following troubleshooting discussion should only be used by individuals with proper qualifications, licenses, and the necessary equipment and tools.

throughout this book, especially as it concerns water-related problems. Please use the index to find specific topics.

The Maintenance Systems chapter discusses the need to obtain the manufacturer's installation and operating (I/O) manual for every equipment item at the facility. Most I/O manuals provide an expanded view of the equipment, a detailed parts list, and a troubleshooting guide. The Facility Safety chapter provides many safety precautions. In particular, understanding the principles of Lock Out/Tag Out to ensure that equipment is not only turned off, but also makes sure another person does not turn something on while the equipment is being serviced. It is important that all local codes and laws be followed, as well as recommended safety guidelines provided by the manufacturer.

Pumps & Motors

Nothing can cause a pool/spa facility to close faster than having a pump or motor failure. When troubleshooting pumps and motors, operators should only perform work for which they have the proper qualifications.

Motor Fails to Start

If the motor hums or attempts to start, then:
- Check the voltage at the motor line terminals. If the voltage is inadequate to start the motor, then check for loose connections, undersized wiring, an overloaded circuit, or any other causes for a voltage drop.

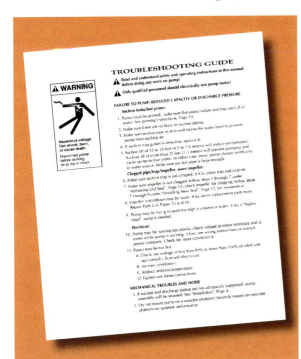

Illustration 17-1. *Manufacturers' installation and operating manuals usually contain troubleshooting guides.*

- Check the power, breakers, switches, etc. If there is a timer on the system, make sure it is working properly
- Check the capacitor when used to see if it is shorted or open
- Check motor windings for shorts or open wires

Turn the motor shaft by hand to get the feel of the motor. If the shaft feels tight or doesn't turn smoothly, then:
- Check the bearings for smooth operation
- See if there is any evidence of the rotor striking the stator
- Check for internal corrosion, cracked end frames, a clogged fan, or other obstruction within the motor
- Check the pump for obstructions, such as debris in the impeller or a bent shaft

Photo 17-1. *Chemicals that emit corrosive fumes and D.E. should never be stored near motors.*

Motor Overheats

With all motor applications, excess heat is very damaging to the motor operation and life. Over time, heat breaks down motor insulation and leads to failure. The relationship of temperature to motor life is most important. As the temperature goes up, the winding life is shortened at an increasing rate.

A continuously running pump motor may be hot to the touch; this by itself does not mean the motor is overheating. Motors have a thermal overload that will shut the motor off when it gets too hot, and it will restart itself once it has cooled down. Excess heat has many possible causes:
- Insufficient power due to undersized or very long power wires
- Improper wiring that fails to fulfill code requirements and the motor manufacturer's recommendations

Photo 17-2. *All repairs should be done in a professional manner to protect people and equipment.*

- Low voltage. The voltage may be low at the source or there may be excessive voltage drop when the load is applied because a wire is too small.
- Over voltage. This needs to be corrected by the power supply company.
- High ambient temperature. Pool motors are normally designed to operate in higher ambient temperatures (122°F/50°C) than spa jet pump motors which usually have short duty cycles. Artificially high ambient temperatures may be created if the motor operates in a confined space and circulates the air.
- Protect the motor from excess heat by shading it from the sun with a motor cover. When using a motor cover, it is important to provide fresh air circulation. Air heated by the motor should not be allowed to circulate.
- In cases of flooded suction or positive pressure on the inlet to the pump, flow may be increased, overloading the motor
- Specific motor and impeller combinations are sized to do a specific job. In most cases, the impeller loads the motor to the service factor horsepower. A replacement motor must be able to develop the same total horsepower, or nameplate horsepower times the service factor, as the motor being replaced. Larger motors should not be used because they increase the risk of suction entrapment. Smaller pumps may provide inadequate flow.

© National Swimming Pool Foundation 2017

Photo 17-3. *Clogged hair and lint strainers may be a blockage in the suction line, causing the motor to be noisy.*

Motor is Noisy

If the motor is noisy, there are several factors that may contribute:

- Sounds can be caused by vibrations between the pump base and the base or concrete pad it is sitting on. Make sure the pump is properly secured.
- The bearings may be noisy due to normal wear. Feeding high concentrations of chemicals on the suction side of the pump may cause corrosive damage to the pump seal, which can leak and damage the motor bearings.
- Cavitation as a result of improper suction line sizing, leaks in the piping, a blockage in the suction line, or a low level of pool water will cause higher than normal sound

Bubbles in The Return Flow

If bubbles are detected in the return flow, several factors may contribute:

- If there is a strainer with a loose cover or a damaged gasket, check and replace the cover or gasket as necessary
- The pool water level may be too low, allowing air to mix with water through the skimmer. In this case, raise the water level.
- The skimmer weir, sometimes called the flapper, may be stuck in the up position, allowing air to mix with water in the suction line
- There can be a leak at any connection in the suction piping or a leak inside any suction side valve at the stem O-ring
- There may be a leak in the suction side underground piping caused by a loose joint, tree roots damaging plumbing, or pests, such as termites or ants, that chew into flexible piping

> **Caution**
> If the pump and/or motor are replaced, make sure you verify the total dynamic head (TDH) and determine the flow rate to ensure VGB Act compliance.
> (See Appendix C-1)

No Line Pressure

No line pressure is caused by a dirty or clogged filter, a blocked return line, or a valve that is shut off or partially shut on the return piping.

- The pump's impeller may be clogged with debris. Check by first shutting off the pump. Remove the basket and check the impeller.
- The seal may be broken. For seal replacement instructions, refer to the I/O manual supplied by the manufacturer of the pump.
- The handles on most ball valves are perpendicular to the line when there is no flow. In contrast, the handles on other ball valves are parallel to the line when there is no flow.

Pump Fails to Prime

If the pump fails to prime, the following conditions should be checked:

- There may be a suction leak if there is not enough water in the strainer housing
- There may be a leak at any joint, especially at the first fitting that is screwed into the strainer housing
- The strainer cover may be loose, or an O-ring under the strainer housing cover may be worn
- There may be a clogged suction pipe
- Debris may have bypassed the pump basket, causing damage to the impeller
- The pump may be located above the pool water level or may be too far from the pool, requiring longer time to prime

Water Loss

It is not unusual for a pool to lose ¼ inch (6 mm) or more of water in 24 hours. It is worthwhile to tape a ruler to the side of the pool or spa during different times of year to gauge how much water evaporates under typical conditions. Losses of any greater amount usually indicate a leak in the system. Additional signs of a pool leak are

- Unexplained increase in water bill
- Difficulty in maintaining water balance

- Air in the pool water
- Loose or popping tiles
- A settling of the pool and/or deck cracks
- Differences in surrounding vegetation like plants dying due to excess water at an outdoor pool
- Leaking multi-port valve gasket

To determine if there is a leak, the first step is to perform a bucket test. This must be performed during periods of non-use. The procedure is as follows:

- Place a five-gallon (20 liter) bucket on the second step, and fill it with water to the exact level of the surrounding pool water. The water should be as close to the top of the bucket as possible. If necessary, use a lower step and place some form of spacer under the bucket.
- Mark the outside and inside of the bucket with a permanent marker at the water level

Allow the bucket to remain in place for 24 hours, with the circulation system running. If the level in the bucket and the level of the pool remain the same, there is no leak. If the pool level is below the level in the bucket, there is a leak. Repeat the test with the circulation system turned off.

- If the two levels remain even, then the leak is most likely in the circulation system
- If the pool level drops with the circulation off, the leak is most likely in the pool structure

A leak detection company can perform more sophisticated testing. Leaks may be found in piping under the decking of the pool or spa, for example.

Photo 17-4. *Pool water level losses greater than ¼ inch (6 mm) of water in 24 hours may be due to a leak.*

Gas-Fired Heaters

Troubleshooting gas-fired heaters must only be performed by qualified personnel:

Photo 17-5. *Troubleshooting gas-fired heaters must only be performed by qualified personnel.*

- Do not operate the heater if any part has been under water. Immediately call a qualified service technician to inspect the heater and replace any part of the control system and any gas control which has been under water.
- Should overheating occur or the gas supply fail to shut off, turn off the manual gas control valve to the heater
- Keep all objects off the top of the heater. Blocking air flow could damage the heater and may void the warranty or start a fire.
- Vent pipes, draft-hoods, and heater tops get hot! These surfaces can cause serious burns. Do not touch these surfaces while the heater is in operation. Adding a vent cap reduces the temperature on the top.

Heater Will Not Ignite

If the heater will not ignite, check the following:
- Is the system switch on?
- Is the thermostat up to temperature?
- Is the pump running with sufficient flow to keep the low-flow switch from activating?
- Is the gas valve in the on position?
- Is the pilot lit?
- Is the gas supply valve open?
- Are all plumbing and filter valves open?
- If a bypass is installed, is it properly adjusted?

> **Warning**
> Many items that could cause a gas-fired heater to malfunction must be corrected only by a qualified service technician. Use the manufacturer's I/O manual for specific instructions. If you do not follow these instructions exactly, a fire or explosion may result, causing property damage, personal injury or loss of life.

© National Swimming Pool Foundation 2017

Photo 17-6. *Gas-fired pool/spa heaters must be installed so as to not be affected by water run-off from roofs.*

- If you hear clicking or sparking, but the heater will not ignite, contact a qualified technician

Pilot Light Problems

Troubleshoot pilot light issues in the following ways:

- If the pilot light won't light, it could be due to low gas pressure, inadequate air supply, or improper venting. Make sure gas is turned on; with propane, make sure the tank has fuel. Also check for water run-off from roof or sprinklers.
- If the pilot light needs to be frequently relit, check for water run off from above, or sprinklers directed at the heater that could extinguish the pilot light. A high wind stack may be needed due to heater location. Further troubleshooting will require a service technician.

Water Temperature Too Low

When troubleshooting low water temperature, consider the following:

- The thermostat may be set too low. If the heat loss is greater than the heater input, the heater may be too small. If outside air temperatures are too low, a solar cover will slow heat loss, helping an undersized heater.
- If the heater cycles on and off before it reaches the desired temperature, it could be the result of inadequate water flow due to a dirty filter, closed valve, external bypass out of adjustment, reversed water

connections, or the pressure switch out of adjustment. It is also possible that the thermostat is out of calibration or needs replacing.

Heater Is Leaking Water

If the heater is leaking water, check the following:

- The heat exchanger may be leaking because a low pH may have corroded plumbing lines or the heat exchanger. Alternatively, the damage may be from winter freezing. Leaks usually appear during spring start-up.
- If the heater appears to leak only when the burner is lit, this may be caused by condensation occurring when heating very cold water, a missing or damaged bypass, or excessive water flow through the heater from an oversized pump

Black or Dark Heater Exhaust

If the heater is black on top, or if the heater exhaust is dark, it could be due to low gas pressure and/or inadequate air supply and venting. In both cases, review the installation requirements in the owner's manual. Both conditions may need to be evaluated by a qualified service technician.

Heater Has Excessive Heat Damage

If the heater has excessive heat damage, a warped or buckled finish, it might be due to

Photo 17-7. *Troubleshooting filters usually does not involve electricity or moving parts, unless there is an automatic backwashing system.*

low gas pressure, a down-draft, improper air supply, or a venting problem. The heater may need a high wind stack if installed near a vertical wall or windy area. Contact a qualified service professional.

Copper or Iron Stains In The Pool

All chemicals should be fed into the circulation line after all equipment, especially heaters. Disinfectants or improper water balance can deteriorate protective coatings on heater components and create rust. Rebalance the chemicals and replace damaged components.

Filters

Troubleshooting filters does not involve electricity or moving parts unless there is an automatic backwashing system installed. It may, however, necessitate the release of air pressure in a pressure system. These warnings are repeated on the following pages

> **Caution**
> If the heater and/or filter are replaced, make sure you verify the total dynamic head (TDH) and determine the flow rate to ensure VGB Act compliance.
> (See Appendix C-1)

More training on troubleshooting pool and spa equipment maintenance, installation and repair can be gained from the NSPF® Advanced Service Technician™ training program. In addition, operators should maintain qualifications that are in compliance with jurisdictional requirements.

© National Swimming Pool Foundation 2017

Troubleshooting Pressure Sand Filters

PROBLEM	CAUSE	SOLUTION
Pool water is not clear or clean	1. Backwash cycle too frequent	Backwash according to pressure and not time. See manufacturer's I/O instructions for proper pressure differential (usually 7 to 10 psi above starting pressure)
	2. Freeboard not sufficient or improper sand was used for replacement purposes	Check freeboard and sand depth. Make sure of sand specifications.
	3. Insufficient turnover rate as compared to total user load	Check flow meter and determine if there are any hydraulic restrictions. Limit user load if necessary.
	4. Algae growth	Maintain proper pool chemistry and treat algae as necessary. Test water for total and free chlorine.
Short filter cycles	1. Improper backwash procedures	Follow manufacturer's I/O instructions. Watch sight gauge and backwash until effluent is clear.
	2. Sand bed blocked	Remove top 1 to 2 inches of sand and replace. Chemically soak sand bed with commercial sand cleaner and flush to waste.
	3. Algae growth	Maintain proper pool chemistry and treat algae as necessary. Test water for total and free chlorine.
	4. High flow rate exceeds Filter Media Rate (FMR)	Use flow meter to manage and restrict water flow through filter
	5. Pool chemicals being fed into circulation prior to the filter	Relocate chemical input lines to feed after all equipment, including filters and heaters
High filter pressure	1. Insufficient backwashing	Follow manufacturer's I/O instructions. Watch sight gauge and backwash until effluent is clear.
	2. Sand bed blocked with mineral deposits	Chemically soak sand bed with commercial sand cleaner, and flush to waste
	3. Blocked return line or partially closed valve	Remove line obstruction or open valve
Sand in pool	1. Broken under-drain lateral	Replace damaged laterals. Examine sand to determine if high filter pressure caused damage to laterals.
Sand in waste water	1. Damaged distributor or air strainer	Replace damaged items
	2. Backwash rate too high	Reduce backwash flow rate
	3. Improper size sand	Replace sand with new sand having the specifications required by the filter manufacturer
Flow rate to pool below minimum required and low influent pressure	1. Blockage in suction line to the pump	Check the hair and lint basket. Check the skimmer strainer. Open valves on the suction line.
	2. Impeller damaged or broken	Disassemble the pump and repair

Warning: Pressure filters operate under high pressure. Always open all air bleed valves and turn off the pump before changing valve positions or removing any clamps or fittings. Failure to follow proper procedures could result in violent separation of the equipment, causing possible serious injury or death.

225

© National Swimming Pool Foundation 2017

Troubleshooting Pressure Cartridge Filters

PROBLEM	CAUSE	SOLUTION
Pool water is not clear or clean	1. Cartridge filter dirty	Hose cartridge filter, soak in commercial cleaner, and rinse. Acid wash only if necessary to remove minerals
	2. Media element is torn or punctured	Replace element
	3. Insufficient turnover rate as compared to total user load	Check flow meter and determine if there are any hydraulic restrictions. Limit user load if necessary.
	4. Algae growth	Maintain proper pool chemistry and treat algae as necessary. Test water for total and free chlorine.
Short filter cycles	1. Cartridge filter dirty	Hose cartridge filter, soak in filter cleaner, and rinse. Acid wash if necessary.
	2. Algae growth	Maintain proper pool chemistry and treat algae as necessary. Test water for total and free chlorine.
	3. High flow rate exceeds Filter Media Rate (FMR)	Use flow meter to manage and restrict water flow through filter
	4. Pool chemicals being fed into circulation prior to the filter	Relocate chemical input lines to feed after all equipment, including filters and heaters
High filter pressure	1. Cartridge filter dirty	Hose cartridge filter, soak in filter cleaner, and rinse. Acid wash if necessary.
	2. Blocked return line or partially closed valve	Remove line obstruction or open valve
Unfiltered water returning to pool	1. Damaged cartridge filter element	Replace element
	2. Flow rate too high	Reduce flow rate
	3. Cartridge filter element not properly seated or located on center pipe	Re-seat element
	4. Air strainer is damaged or missing	Replace air strainer.
Flow rate to pool below minimum required and low influent pressure	1. Blockage in suction line to the pump	Check the hair and lint basket. Check the skimmer strainer. Open valves on the suction line.
	2. Impeller damaged or broken	Disassemble the pump and repair
	3. Obstruction in impeller	Remove obstruction, disassemble pump if necessary

Warning: Pressure filters operate under high pressure. Always open all air bleed valves and turn off the pump before changing valve positions or removing any clamps or fittings. Failure to follow proper procedures could result in violent separation of the equipment, causing possible serious injury or death.

Troubleshooting

© National Swimming Pool Foundation 2017

Troubleshooting Pressure D.E. Filters

PROBLEM	CAUSE	SOLUTION
Pool water is not clear or clean	1. Filter covering is plugged	Oils, dirt, and minerals have clogged the fabric openings. Remove oils and grease with commercial cleaner. Acid wash only if necessary to remove minerals. Follow the manufacturer's instructions in the I/O manual.
	2. No D.E. powder on filter grids	Follow the manufacturer's recommendations in the I/O manual regarding the proper amount of new D.E. to add. The usual amount is 2 ounces per square foot of filter area.
Air bubbles in water returning to pool	1. Excessive air build-up in pump housing	Use air relief valve to discharge air. Check pool water level, clogged skimmer basket, and O-ring on hair and lint basket. Correct, repair, or replace as necessary.
Short filter cycles	1. Filter covering is plugged	Oils, dirt, and minerals have clogged the fabric openings. Remove oils and grease with commercial cleaner. Acid wash only if necessary to remove minerals. Follow the manufacturer's instructions in the I/O manual.
	2. Pool chemicals being fed into circulation prior to the filter	Relocate chemical input lines to feed after all equipment, including filters and heaters
	3. Too little D.E. being added during the pre-coat cycle	Follow the manufacturer's recommendations in the I/O manual regarding the proper amount of new D.E. to add. The usual amount is 2 ounces per square foot of filter area.
High filter pressure	1. Filter covering is plugged	Oils, dirt, and minerals have clogged the fabric openings. Remove oils and grease with commercial cleaner. Acid wash only if necessary to remove minerals. Follow the manufacturer's instructions in the I/O manual.
	2. Dirty D.E. powder has accumulated at the bottom of the filter housing	Open the tank drain and hose out interior of tank to remove all settled debris
	3. Pool chemicals being fed into circulation prior to the filter	Relocate chemical input lines to feed after all equipment, including filters and heaters
D.E. in pool	1. Damaged filter element(s)	Inspect elements for any tears or holes. Inspect internal air bleed sock for tears and proper installation.
Unfiltered water returning to pool	1. Damaged filter element(s)	Inspect elements for any tears or holes. Inspect internal air bleed sock for tears and proper installation.
	2. Damaged manifold	Inspect manifold for chips and cracks. Inspect manifold joints. Replace as necessary.
Flow rate to pool below minimum required and low influent pressure	1. Blockage in suction line to the pump	Check the hair and lint basket. Check the skimmer strainer. Open valves on the suction line.
	2. Impeller damaged or broken	Disassemble the pump and repair
	3. Obstruction in impeller	Remove obstruction and disassemble pump if necessary

Warning: Pressure filters operate under high pressure. Always open all air bleed valves and turn off the pump before changing valve positions or removing any clamps or fittings. Failure to follow proper procedures could result in violent separation of the equipment, causing possible serious injury or death.

© National Swimming Pool Foundation 2017

Troubleshooting

Troubleshooting Vacuum D.E. Filters		
PROBLEM	**CAUSE**	**SOLUTION**
Pool water is not clear or clean	1. Filter covering is plugged	Oils, dirt, and minerals have clogged the fabric openings. Remove oils and grease with commercial cleaner. Acid wash only if necessary to remove minerals. Follow the manufacturer's instructions in the I/O manual.
	2. Unfiltered water is returning to pool	See unfiltered water instructions below
	3. No D.E. powder on filter grids	Follow the manufacturer's recommendations in the I/O manual regarding the proper amount of new D.E. to add. The usual amount is 2 ounces per square foot of filter area.
Air bubbles in pool return flow	1. Filter covering is plugged, causing the pump to pull air from the weakest point in the system above water level	Oils, dirt, and minerals have clogged the fabric openings. Remove oils and grease with commercial cleaner. Acid wash only if necessary to remove minerals. Follow the manufacturer's instructions in the I/O manual.
	2. Damaged manifold or vacuum piping connections	Inspect manifold, connections and piping for cracks. Inspect all joints. Replace or repair as necessary.
	3. Blockage in suction line to the pump	Check the hair and lint basket. Check the skimmer strainer. Open valves on the suction line.
Short filter cycles	1. Filter covering is plugged	See item 1 under Troubleshooting Sand Filters
	2. Pool chemicals being fed into circulation prior to the filter	Relocate chemical input lines to feed after all equipment, – including filters and heaters
	3. Too little D.E. being added during the pre-coat cycle	Follow the manufacturer's recommendations in the I/O manual regarding the proper amount of new D.E. to add. The usual amount is 2 ounces per square foot of filter area.
High filter pressure	1. Filter covering is plugged	See item 1 under Troubleshooting Sand Filters
	2. Pool chemicals being fed into circulation prior to the filter	Relocate chemical input lines to feed after all equipment, including filters and heaters
D.E. in pool	1. Damaged filter element(s)	Inspect elements for any tears or holes
Unfiltered water returning to pool	1. Damaged filter element(s)	Inspect elements for any tears or holes
	2. Damaged manifold or vacuum piping connections.	Inspect manifold, connections and piping for cracks. Inspect all joints. Replace or repair as necessary.
Flow rate to pool below minimum required and low influent pressure	1. Blockage in suction line to the pump	Check the hair and lint basket. Check the skimmer strainer. Open valves on the suction line.
	2. Impeller damaged or broken	Disassemble the pump and repair
	3. Obstruction in impeller	Remove obstruction and disassemble pump if necessary

© National Swimming Pool Foundation 2017

Chapter 18:
Facility Renovation & Design

"The engineer's first problem in any design situation is to discover what the problem really is."

–Author Unknown

Expert assistance is required to ensure that new swimming pools and spas are not out-of-date as soon as the water begins to circulate. The rapid introduction of new technologies and building techniques can create many choices. Whether an existing aquatic facility needs renovation or a new facility is being contemplated, it is important to seek outside professional help.

The first step in any existing facility renovation or new aquatic facility is to develop a plan. The foundation for this plan is the program use expected for the facility. The community of users for pools and spas may change over time. Population growth and the demographics of age and culture may change. When renovating a pool, consideration should be given to the program use for the next 20 years. The expected programs should be compared to the needs of the community. This should be repeated on an annual basis, and must be done before undertaking any renovation or new facility project.

Photo 18-1. *New pools and attractions require several considerations that are beyond the scope of responsibility of most pool operators.*

Design, Construction, and Renovation Considerations

While many engineers and architects have obtained Certified Pool/Spa Operator® certification, construction of a new facility, renovation, or the modernization of an existing facility, is not a responsibility that can be categorized as part of the swimming pool or spa operation. Therefore, these jobs fall outside of the scope of a pool operator. But there are cases where a pool operator may be involved in planning a renovation, modernization, or even a new facility. In any case, the facility operator will take responsibility to direct the facility once it is done, and it is advisable that the designer/constructor provide start-up training to the operator and staff prior to hand-off. This section includes factors that relate to these considerations in the event the pool operator is involved.

Photo 18-2. *The planning process is very involved and requires professional help.*

Before construction begins, permits must be obtained. To receive a permit, building departments require plans to be submitted. In many cases, the plans must be certified by a professional engineer and comply with accepted engineering practices.

The owner/operator must develop clear and concise goals and objectives for the facility. These objectives must take into account the demographics of the community that the facility will serve. Local government can assist in forecasting expected changes over the next 20 years. Any new facility should be designed with the future in mind and not just the requirements of today.

Photo 18-3. *Multi-use pool facilities require specialized design and program planning to meet the needs of the community.*

The facility could be as simple as a condominium pool and spa or as complex as a local parks and recreation facility with interactive water features, slides, and competitive swimming and diving. In either extreme, a licensed professional engineer must be involved in the development of the design engineering. To locate a certified design, build, and/or renovation professional, or to learn more about related certification programs, visit www.genesis3.com.

Facility design and renovation include many important decisions that ultimately affect operators, program managers, and users. The designs that are implemented must consider how the design will reduce any risk of injury and please the facility's users.

At some point in time, all swimming pools or spas need to be renovated or modernized. The project can be as simple as a new pool finish or as complicated as a reconfiguration. There may be changes to the circulation and filtration systems. New methods of disinfecting the water may be employed. New amenities such as interactive water play areas may be added. Simple or complex, the first consideration has to be potential liabilities and the need for the facility to meet the key program objectives.

The costs to renovate often become an impediment to proper decision-making. A pool surface that is not intact can result in pool water leaks, algae growth, or even injury. For hotels, motels, apartments, and condominium facilities, a swimming pool or spa renovation can be a management nightmare. Roofs, parking lots, balconies, and other common areas often have reserves set aside for renovation purposes. This is not always the case with swimming pools.

Modernization can start the very day a new pool is commissioned for use. Modernizing a pool in small increments can greatly reduce the cost of a major renovation. New pools always lack some item that could reduce operational cost, provide better safety, or improve overall quality of service conditions. The improvement could be an automatic pool vacuum system or improved storage for chemicals and equipment.

Photo 18-4. *Indoor air quality is an example of a complex technical consideration requiring expert advice.*

To assist in identifying modernization opportunities, a facility audit by an outside consultant is recommended every five years. Items such as automated chemical control, chlorine generation, variable speed pumps, or LED lights can be incorporated into the facility annual budget process. Improved signage, relocation of safety equipment, the installation of emergency telephones, and other repairs can often be accomplished with no down time.

As codes are updated, they often require new design features. Usually, these new design features are required for new facilities and not for existing facilities until that facility undergoes a renovation. Even if it is not required by code, it is often wise to upgrade the pool or spa facility to the new requirements as they are implemented.

© National Swimming Pool Foundation 2017

This proactive approach spreads renovation costs over a longer time and avoids very expensive renovations when several upgrades must be performed at one time.

Photo 18-5. *Automatic chemical feed control can be made part of any modernization project.*

Professional Help

The swimming pool or spa facility is an integrated system involving water treatment and circulation, structural and environmental considerations, and program use. Every aquatic facility is unique. Any successful renovation or new facility project requires a full understanding of design and construction as well as regulatory concerns and program requirements. The design and construction phases require engineering knowledge. The pool owner/operator is often faced with making technical decisions for which they do not have the expertise or background. Outside assistance is recommended. Any major project will involve a consultant, an architect, and a contractor. With the facility owner or manager and staff, these outside individuals become the design team.

A consultant has the expertise to avoid design errors that result in facilities quickly becoming obsolete and making the facility difficult to manage and operate. New materials and equipment can be evaluated. Cost effectiveness of new technologies can be determined. Equipment specifications must meet operational and program requirements. The consultant shares the responsibility to assure that the facility will comply with all federal, state, and local regulations upon completion of the project.

Some contractors offer consulting or architectural and engineering services. The owner or manager of an aquatic facility must

Photo 18-6. *All pool projects will require professional help for engineering and architectural considerations.*

be careful of the all-inclusive design-build approach. In some cases this type of contractor has little background in risk management or operational requirements of the aquatic facility. Before choosing a design-build contractor, make sure there is a competent professional on the contractor's staff who is knowledgeable about the type of programs offered by the facility and any specialized equipment that will be utilized.

The pool/spa contractor is responsible for the materials supply, construction, and start-up of the facility. The contractor will install all equipment according to approved specifications. Selecting the right contractor can be a major contribution to a successful aquatic program. Here are some considerations:

- Membership in professional and trade organizations
- Design and operation warranties
- References concerning contract performance, operational reliability, staff training, operating and maintenance manuals, and customer service
- Length of time in the industry
- Current licensing and certification
- Percent of work done in-house as compared to being sub-contracted

Design, Construction, and Renovation Guidelines

In addition to the considerations of cost and intended use of the facility, the following material addresses factors that must be considered during facility design, construction, and renovation.

Materials

The materials chosen for construction affect the life and utilization of the facility. Some of the considerations are

- Materials should be durable and long lasting
- Materials as constructed should not be toxic to users or the environment
- Surfaces within the pool should be watertight, slip resistant, and withstand design stresses
- Pool wall finishes should not reduce the ability of an observer to see objects and surfaces within the water
- There should be no protrusions or features that can entangle users and cause injury
- Construction tolerances should comply with customary practices or codes

Safety

To help protect the safety of users, several design features should be considered:

- Proper hydraulic design and the inclusion of features like dual main drains or gravity feed balancing tanks, etc., that significantly decrease the potential for suction entrapment
- Drain covers that comply with the appropriate standard to prevent entrapment (VGB 2008)
- If an over the rim spout is used, the design should consider a location and design to ensure it does not introduce a hazard
- The design to dictate the number and the location of hand holds and locations to enter and exit the pool
- The location and number of lifeguard station. If users have access in the absence of lifeguards, designers should consider additional appropriate signage.

Safety Equipment

Designers should review codes and plan to incorporate lifesaving equipment. The equipment should be clearly visible. Some frequently used equipment includes an accessory pole with a hook typically 12 feet (3.66 m) long and a throwing rope, usually about 1.5 times longer than the widest part of the pool, connected to a ring buoy. This allows the buoy to be thrown to swimmers in distress. Many codes commonly

Photo 18-7. *Suitable barriers should be designed to prevent unauthorized access.*

require first aid kits, phones, posted emergency numbers, and signs describing the location of emergency shut off switches.

Suitable **barriers** should be designed to prevent unauthorized access and potential injury or death due to drowning. The barrier acts as an additional level of protection in the event there is a gap in parental supervision for small children or non-swimmers. It is best if the perimeter fence does not block the view of the pool. External handholds, footholds, or horizontal members that facilitate climbing are undesirable since they act as a means for a person to climb over the fence.

The design should consider other objects, such as walls, trees, or other building structures that can become a means for gaining unauthorized access to the pool area. The space between the bottom of the barrier and the pool deck or ground and between vertical members should be small enough to prevent a child from passing under or through it.

If the barrier is composed of diagonal members, such as a lattice or chain link fence, the maximum opening formed by the diagonal is typically no more than 1¾ inches (4.45 cm)

© National Swimming Pool Foundation 2017

to prevent a child from stepping in the holes. Similarly when the barrier is composed of horizontal and vertical members, the horizontal members should not be step locations to allow a child to scale the fence. Decorative cutouts in fences should be small enough to prevent a child's foot from entering.

Gates for pool enclosures are designed to open outward away from the pool, are self-closing, and are self-latching. According to the Consumer Product Safety Commission (CPSC), when the release mechanism of the self-latching device is less than 54 inches (137 cm) from the bottom of the gate, the release mechanism for the gate should be at least three inches (7.62 cm) below the top of the gate on the side facing the pool. Placing the release mechanism at this height prevents a young child from reaching over the top of a gate and releasing the latch.

Plumbing

The plumbing used to release backwash water and the sewer lines that accept that water should have sufficient capacity. The local water district can provide information on the capacity and water quality that can be discharged in the sewer.

Fill and make-up water for a swimming pool and spa is potable/drinking water. Most codes require that the water distribution system serving the pool or spa be protected against backflow and back-siphonage. As such, there should be an air gap to prevent pool or spa water from contaminating the drinking water system.

General Use Considerations

The specific use of the pool must be considered during planning. In the event that people have access in the evening, deck lighting and underwater lighting sufficient for patrons or security personnel should be considered. Water depths should be considered for the intended use like swimming, wading, diving, activity pools, catch pools, leisure rivers, vortex pools, spas, therapy pools, etc. The use of controllers, probes, and automatic feeders should be considered, especially for high use small volume pools like spas and wading pools.

Decks

There are many options to consider for decks and deck equipment. Federal, state, and local regulations often establish guidelines for decks. Some deck considerations are

- Deck drains around the pool should be included and all deck floors should mildly slope to the drains to minimize stagnant water
- The deck and the areas within the deck area, such as copings, markers, ramps, steps, etc., should be slip resistant to prevent slips and falls
- Deck surfaces or transitions to adjoining surfaces should be constructed in a way to avoid creating a tripping hazard
- Decks should be designed with control joints to limit cracks. Expansion joints should be used to protect against slab movement.
- Access covers should be designed into the deck to allow access to valves
- Hose bibs should be designed to prevent back flow into the potable water system
- Warning signs concerning diving are often recessed into the deck

Climate

Different regions have unique requirements due to the climate. The potential for freezing and damage to plumbing and surfaces should be considered in cold environments. In other regions, the height of the water table must be considered, and the pool design should include hydrostatic relief valves to avoid major damage due to the pool structure lifting/floating if water within the pool is drained too low. The design around the pool and the inclusion of water features should account for increasing or decreasing loss of heat from the water as either a desirable or an undesirable feature.

Other Equipment and Amenities

Often ancillary equipment is installed around the pool. If a diving board is installed, the guidelines from Federation Internationale de Natation (FINA), the board manufacturer, or other sanctioning body should be consulted to establish appropriate water envelope beneath the board. Designers also should consult guidance documents from the CPSC if a slide is in the plan.

Dressing facilities and restrooms are usually required with a public pool or spa unless they are easily available within the general facility. Codes and standards dictate the design of this portion of the facility. There are several factors that should be considered in the design phase including lighting, plumbing, the number of toilets, sinks, trash receptacles location and number, soap dispensers, shatter-resistant mirrors, shower fixture numbers and types, drainage, baby changing stations, drinking water fountains, partitions, materials of construction, slip resistance of flooring, floor slopes, floor drain locations, and compliance with the Americans with Disabilities Act.

Depending on the use of the facility, there are further factors to consider. For larger facilities, visitor and spectator areas may be included in the design. Eating and drinking in the pool area is usually prohibited unless the facility is appropriately designed and unbreakable containers are used.

Pool Resurfacing

Some pool or spa interior surfaces need replacement every year. Others have advertised life claims and warranties of 30 years. Most pools or spas, however, need to have the interior surface replaced every five to eight years. Pools or spas must be resurfaced when the condition of the surface becomes a danger to the facility users. Regulations may require that pools be refinished when the pool surfaces cannot be maintained in a safe and sanitary condition. The pool operator should consult the applicable regulations.

Most commercial pools have a plaster surface. This surface material is on top of a mixture of aggregate, cement, and sand, which is often called gunite. This gunite is sprayed to form the pool shell. When the plaster surface is applied, the majority of the hydration takes place within the first 28 days. It is during this period that the surface is susceptible to staining, scaling, and discoloration. Proper start-up procedures including timely brushing and constant monitoring and adjustment of water balance is recommended to ensure that the plaster surface does not deteriorate. For the recommended start-up procedures, see Appendix A-8. For more information about new plaster surface swimming pool start-up procedure contact the National Plasters Council or visit their website at www. npconline.org.

The Water Balance chapter gives guidance on how to help protect the surface and avoid the need to resurface a pool or spa. Properly balanced water helps preserve the surface so that it does not slowly corrode or dissolve into the water, and it prevents abrasive scale from forming on the surface. In addition, the Pool & Spa Water Problems chapter describes the use of scale inhibitors that help prevent the formation of scale on the wall surfaces.

Other Resurfacing Considerations

Pool or spa resurfacing is a minor renovation that occurs on a periodic basis. Certain key items should be reviewed, and made part of the resurfacing project as necessary. Correcting these items at the time of resurfacing is an excellent way to comply with current codes. These items are

- Ladder: remove and reinstall the ladder(s) so that it is secure and a child cannot become entrapped behind the ladder. Typically, a gap of 3 to 6 inches (7.5–15 cm) is used. Often the decorative flat metal plates, or escutcheons, encircling the place where the ladder is mounted to the floor would be repaired or replaced. Ladder manufacturers or local codes can help define the ladder specifications for height above the deck and handhold diameter.
- Handrail: jurisdictional codes provide guidance on the handrail design and installation. The rails are normally securely mounted in the deck and on the bottom step. A Figure 4 handrail extends laterally to a point vertically above the bottom step.

Photo 18-8. *Dual handrails may not be sufficient to meet ADA guidelines.*

Often the escutcheon plates on a handrail would be repaired or replaced. Handrails have historically been 1.90 inches (4.8 cm), outside diameter (O.D.). New ADA guidelines (ADAAG 4.26, 2002) specify a 1.25 to 1.50 inch (3.17 to 3.8 cm) O.D. Seek professional assistance in selecting the proper O.D. handrail.
- Steps and Benches: there are several

© National Swimming Pool Foundation 2017

design features for stairs and benches that should be considered. It is important that they be visible by people above the water or entering the water. To improve visibility, a continuous dark color and permanent contrasting step markings (i.e. bullnose tile) are often used. To help ensure people don't slip, glazed tiles are not typically used on the horizontal portion. The underwater markings should be permanent and not be degraded by footsteps, sunlight, or oxidizer.

- Slope Break: many pools have a change in their floor slope. A milder slope is usually used in the shallow areas. To allow for deeper water, the slope increases. Codes use a combination of features to protect against people venturing into deep water including markings, safety ropes, and depth markers. It is important that there be markings at the location prior to the slope increasing.

- Safety Line: the safety lines are installed in a recessed anchor cup that does not protrude into the pool area. The recessed cup prevents injury to people who pass by that area. Certain codes allow the safety line to be removed under certain conditions like the presence of lifeguards or swim coaches.

Photo 18-9. *Safety lines need to be installed according to regulations.*

- Depth Markings: codes define the location, size, and placement of depth markers to help people see that there is shallow and deep water. Most codes require depth markings that are permanent slip-resistant tile on horizontal surfaces.

- Gutter: jurisdictional codes may require gutters to be returned to new construction standards. When the pool is being resurfaced, there is an opportunity to repair broken gutter drain grates. To help

ensure that the drains can be cleaned and maintained, it is better to have removable drain grates. Overflow to waste systems shall be operated as originally designed.

- Inlets: replace mushroom inlets with flush-style inlets to prevent contact and possible injury to users

- Suction Outlets: the trend among public health departments is to pay careful attention to the suction outlets. The motivation is to prevent suction entrapment that causes injury or death. Fortunately, suction entrapment is "entirely preventable through proper covers or grates, split drains, specified suction side flow rates, and maintenance." Federal law requires suction outlets to comply with the Pool & Spa Safety Act. See Appendix C-1 for more information.

- Barrier Fence and Gates: it is wise to evaluate barriers and gates during any renovation process. This topic is discussed in greater depth in the Design, Construction, and Renovation Guidelines section earlier in this chapter.

- Pool Deck: when the pool or spa is being resurfaced, it is worthwhile to evaluate and repair damage in the deck area. For example, the evaluation should look for holes, trip hazards, chipped or broken tiles, non-slip surfaces, and lighting and consider disabled access.

Photo 18-10. *Deck repair or replacement is often part of a pool resurfacing project.*

Disability Access

Before undertaking any renovation or new construction of an aquatic facility, a written opinion should be obtained from an outside legal counsel concerning the need to comply with The Americans with Disabilities Act (ADA) as administered by the Department of Justice (DOJ). See Appendix C-2 for more information.

If it is determined that accessibility is required, the Americans with Disabilities Act Accessibility Guidelines (36 CFR Part 1191) should be followed. The National Center on Accessibility conducted a research study on access to swimming pools for people with disabilities. This study identified and evaluated methods and standards related to enabling access to swimming pools by people with disabilities.

The study found nearly unanimous agreement that at least one accessible means of entry and exit should be provided at all pools, and most believed that more than one accessible means should be provided. Study participants also indicated that the ability to use a design or device independently, without help or assistance, was important to them. Although no single means of access was preferred by a majority of subjects, the methods of access most often preferred were lifts, ramps, stairs, and zero depth entry. Stairs, however, were only preferred by those who were ambulatory. Similarly, ramps, zero depth entry, moveable floors, and lifts were the means of access most non-ambulatory users would be willing to use at a pool.

Entry

When designing and renovating a facility, there are many factors to consider. Pools are often required to have at least one accessible means of water entry/exit for people with disabilities. The location of that entry and exit point should be located on an accessible route. Larger swimming pools with over 300 linear feet (100 m) of pool wall may require additional accessible means of water entry/exit.

When only one accessible means of water entry is provided, it is most common that the entry is via a pool lift, wet ramp, or zero depth entry. When a second accessible means of water entry/exit is provided, a different type of entry/exit is preferred. There are several options available: transfer wall, transfer steps, moveable floor, stairs, swimming pool lift, wet ramp, or zero depth entry. When a second accessible means of water entry/exit is provided, designers should consider serving both ends or both sides of the pool.

Lifts

Pool lifts are a helpful feature for people with disabilities. Designers should consult with equipment manufacturers to ensure that lifts comply with the current requirements. The lifts

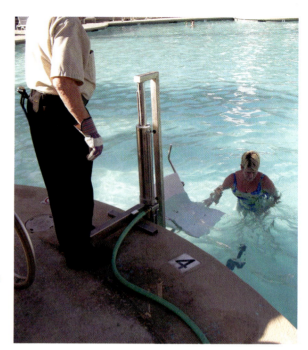

Photo 18-11. *Pool lifts should be user-operated and not require the assistance of others.*

should be mounted with sufficient deck space beside, beneath, and in front of the lift to allow people to access and use the lift. The seat location should be sufficiently above the deck to prevent a person falling into the water as they get into the seat. Seats are typically 17 inches (43 cm) above the deck, 19 inches (48 cm) wide, and include a footrest and armrests. They usually submerge to 20 inches (51 cm) below the water. The controls are mounted on the front of the seat and can be operated from the deck or water and do not require excessive force by the user. The lift's capacity should exceed 300 lb (136 kg).

Ramps

When pool ramps are present on a pool, they should be designed and maintained to consider disabled patrons. For example, the ramp should be firm, stable, and slip resistant. In addition, the slope should not be too steep. For example, for every one foot (30 cm) of vertical drop, there should be 12 feet (3.7 meters) of horizontal distance (1:12 slope). Risers should not be too high and are usually less than 30 inches (76 cm). To allow for wheelchair passage, ramps are typically more on the top and bottom of the ramp. The landing under water is usually between 24 and 30 inches (61–76 cm) below the water's surface and has a length and width of 60 inches (152 cm). All ramps should have hand rails designed and spaced appropriately for people with disabilities.

© National Swimming Pool Foundation 2017

Photo 18-12. *Professional help is necessary to insure that ramps are designed to meet ADA guidelines.*

Zero Depth

A zero depth or beach entry is an alternative way to allow people with disabilities to access the water. Surfaces should be stable, firm, and slip resistant, and not exceed a 1:12 slope to a depth of 30 inches (76 cm). The degree of the slope can affect other design features. For example, the guidance for ramps should be considered. Applicable codes should be reviewed to ensure that hand rails, platforms, and aquatic chairs are included if required.

Photo 18-13. *Zero depth or beach entry is an alternative way to allow people with disabilities to access the water, even in a wheelchair.*

Transfer Walls/Moveable Floors

A transfer wall is another means to provide disabled access to a pool. A transfer wall allows a bather to leave their mobility device and transfer onto the wall and then into the water. When designing a transfer wall the deck should have sufficient space at the transfer wall to allow access. The wall heights are typically 17 inches (43 cm) and about 12–15 inches (30–38 cm) wide. The walls should be non-abrasive without sharp edges. Properly designed handrails are also required with transfer walls.

Another option to provide access is a moveable floor. It is important that the pool coping be no greater than 0.5 inches (1.3 cm)

different in height than the movable floor. This is to insure that no tripping hazard exists nor an impediment to smooth movement for a wheelchair. A nearby sign should indicate change in depth. A clearly visible gauge should provide a measurement of the depth at all times.

Transfer Steps

Transfer steps are positioned poolside to allow the bather to move from a mobility device onto the upper step, and then lower themselves into the water step by step. Transfer step design has some similar features to other access methods. For example the surface should be firm and non-abrasive and should have no sharp edges. They require clear deck space adjacent to the transfer steps. The highest step should be no more than 17 inches (43 cm) above the pool deck. The step risers should be about five to seven inches (13–18 cm) high and should go at least 18 inches (46 cm) below the water's surface. The steps are typically 12 inches (30 cm) deep to allow ample space for foot placement and about 22 inches (56 cm) wide. At least one handrail should be properly installed.

Sometimes stairs are provided to allow exit and entry to the disabled. The steps should be firm, stable, and slip resistant and have uniform riser heights and tread widths. The widths are usually at least 11 inches (28 cm). Steps should have two handrails at different levels above the surface. One rail is about 36 inches (91 cm) and the second rail is about 21 inches (53 cm) above the stairs. The rails should be designed so they don't extend into the pool's programmable area to avoid collisions.

To provide access to a wading pool, a transfer wall, transfer steps, a pool lift, a wet ramp, or a zero depth entry can provide the means of entry/exit. To provide access to a spa, the most common means of water entry/exit are a transfer wall, transfer steps, or lifts. If the spa is unattended, it is a good design criterion to have a means of emergency notification, and the spa should be adjacent to the accessible means of egress and within reach of someone seated in the spa.

Removable Devices

Often pools include a device that is removable. When using a removable device, it is important that the device remain in place until all users of the device have exited the pool. These devices should be on-site, readily available, maintained, and operable at all times. If a removable device is not in place, it is helpful to have a sign posted to instruct users how to request the device be installed.

Aquatic Play Features

Facilities with Aquatic Play Features (APF) are the fastest growing segment of the aquatic industry. Aquatic Play Features (APFs) are designed for play and recreation, such as body slides, raft rides, wave pools, and more. These types of pools require a different approach to operating them compared to the traditional swimming pool.

In order for the facility to provide these attractions for guests, APFs often have greater vertical distances from the deck to the water. These features may have vast areas of shallow water. In addition, there is a lot of water and users moving at high velocities, water surging and pulsating, vehicles conveying passengers, and pressurized air projecting water.

These features are used to produce special effects and recreational activities, such as water falls, sprays, river rides, or water being pushed uphill to create a water roller coaster effect. If one operates an APF by applying the same rules used for traditional swimming pools, failure may result. Some common failures can include cloudy water, high water bills for replacement water, high use of disinfectant/oxidizer chemicals, and short filter runs.

The growth in number, complexity, and popularity of facilities with APFs, including waterparks, is a clear sign of innovation in recreational aquatics. As stated earlier, it is not part of the pool operator's responsibility to design and renovate facilities. However, the operator should be familiar with some of the unique features and be able to contribute to a design team. In this way, the design will better consider how the facility will operate once construction is complete.

There are many unique features, just a few of which are listed here, that must be addressed by the design team for any waterpark:

- The ability to maintain sanitary water with heavy use
- Design and safety features of wave action pools
- Design of vortex pools
- Additional barriers to prevent children being separated from family or their supervisors
- Handling food and drink in and around the water features
- Design and safety parameters for slides
- Circulation and turnover for heavy use pools
- Circulation and turnover to propel water in lazy rivers
- Safety barrier to prevent access in wave pools
- Deck areas suitable for users to queue in lines

For more information about APFs and their unique consideration, see the NSPF® Aquatic Play Feature™ Handbook and online training course at www.nspf.org.

Photo 18-14. *There are many unique features that must be addressed by the design team for any waterpark.*

© National Swimming Pool Foundation 2017

Reference:
Appendix A

Sample Checklists & Logs

These checklists contain suggestions and are provided as reference only. Not all items apply for every facility. Some locales may require items that are not listed in these checklists. The checklists may be customized to meet the specific needs of a facility. Please follow all applicable laws and regulations and comply with all manufacturer's directions.

© National Swimming Pool Foundation 2017

A-1 Daily Opening & Closing Checklist

Pool_____   Date_____

Opening

Initials*

____1. Enter the pool area, and lock the gate or door behind you to prevent unauthorized entry. Turn off the pool and deck lights and security alarms. Turn on the bathhouse and office lights.

____2. Inspect the grounds, barriers and gates, safety equipment, handrails, ladders, deck, bathhouse, office area, pump and chemical rooms, and auxiliary areas for broken or malfunctioning equipment, minor maintenance needs, or vandalism which may have occurred since the previous day.

____3. Remove the pool cover. Make sure there are no people or items in the pool. Check for pool wall stains and algae.

____4. Make sure main drain cover is visibly attached and fully intact. (See Appendix C-1)

____5. Inspect all inlets and outlet fittings.

____6. Perform the tests on the Daily Pool Chemical Log sheet and record. Adjust disinfectant and pH if needed. Check readout of controller if used.

____7. Vacuum the pool. Clean the vacuum.

____8. Scrub off the scum line.

____9. Empty and clean the skimmer baskets or gutters.

____10.Sweep, rinse, and disinfect the decks. Clean the deck drains.

____11.Clean the hair and lint strainer.

____12.Check the Flow Rate and backwash the filters if needed.

____13.Check disinfectant reservoir level.

____14.Record pressure and vacuum gauge readings.

____15.Check the pool water level for proper skimming.

____16.Wash down and arrange the deck furniture.

____17.Place program equipment in needed locations.

____18.Check to see that safety equipment is in place.

____19.Check water temperature.

____20.Insert new garbage bags, and put the garbage cans back out on the deck.

____21.List all maintenance jobs that need to be done during the day. Report any repair needs to the proper supervisor.

____22.Clean up the guard room, pool office, first aid room, pump room, chemical room, storage rooms, and bathhouse.

____23.Unlock the entrance doors to the pool immediately before opening to the public.

Closing

Initials*

____1. Pick up the refuse and debris on the deck.

____2. Empty towel bins.

____3. Straighten or put away deck furniture.

____4. Empty the garbage cans, rinse and store off the deck.

____5. Take the final chemical readings. Make water balance adjustments. Add chemicals if necessary.

____6. Check the pool water level for proper skimming.

____7. Make sure main drain is visibly attached and fully intact.

____8. Secure the program equipment.

____9. Check to see that safety equipment is in place.

____10. Record pressure and vacuum gauge readings.

____11.Check disinfectant reservoir level.

____12.Clean the locker rooms or bathhouse.

____13.Make sure that all running water (hose bibs) on deck and in the bath house is turned off.

____14.Compile a list of maintenance jobs or repairs that need to be done prior to reopening.

____15.Check all areas of the facility to make sure all patrons have left the premises.

____16.Make sure there are no people or items in the pool. Place cover on pool.

____17.Turn on/off deck, security, and pool lights.

____18.Lock all doors and gates.

____19.Turn on the security alarm system to warn of unauthorized entry onto the premises overnight.

*The person actually completing the maintenance job should initial the log

All maintenance duties have been satisfactorily completed as indicated.

_____
Maintenance Supervisor

© National Swimming Pool Foundation 2017

References

A-2 Daily Pool/Spa Chemical Log

Pool_____   Date_____

Check with local codes to see which tests must be conducted and the testing frequency.

Item	1st	2nd	3rd	4th	Standard (Min | Max | Ideal)
Time	___	___	___	___	
FAC	___	___	___	___	1 | 5 | 2–4 ppm (mg/L)
CAC	___	___	___	___	0 | 0.2 pools (0.5 spas) | 0
pH	___	___	___	___	7.2 | 7.8 | 7.4–7.6
ORP	___	___	___	___	650 or code compliance
Total Alkalinity	___				60 | 180 ppm | 80–120
Cyanuric Acid	___				30-50, 150 ppm (mg/L)
Calcium Hardness	___				150 | 1000 ppm (mg/L) | 200–400
Water Temperature°F	___	___	___	___	NA | 104°F | 78–82°F
Water Temperature°C	___	___	___	___	NA | 40°C | 25.5–27.8°C,
TDS	___				1,500 ppm (mg/L) over starting
Saturation Index	___				- 0.3 to + 0.3
Water Clarity	___				Main drain clearly visible
Water Level	___	___	___	___	$\frac{1}{8}$ - $\frac{1}{4}$ inch (3-6 mm) above gutter
User Load	___	___	___	___	
Flow Rate	___	___	___	___	
Turnover	___	___	___	___	
Influent Pressure	___	___	___	___	
Effluent Pressure	___	___	___	___	
Pressure Differential	___	___	___	___	
Air Temperature	___	___	___	___	
Certified Operator ID(s)#	___	___	___	___	

Initialed by: ___   ___   ___   ___

Notes: _____

_____

Chemicals and Amounts Added:

Opening: _____

_____

Closing: _____

_____

1. Pool & Spa Management
2. Regulations & Guidelines
3. Essential Calculations
4. Pool Water Contamination
5. Disinfection
6. Water Balance
7. Pool & Spa Water Problems
8. Chemical Testing
9. Chemical Feed & Control
10. Water Circulation
11. Pool & Spa Filtration
12. Heating & Air Circulation
13. Spa & Therapy Operations
14. Facility Safety
15. Keeping Records
16. Maintenance Systems
17. Troubleshooting
18. Facility Renovation & Design

References

241

© National Swimming Pool Foundation 2017

A-3 Daily Locker Room Maintenance Checklist

Pool_____   Date_____

Initials*

_____1.   Trash containers emptied

_____2.   Litter, debris, clothes, or misplaced articles picked up

_____3.   Area checked for unpleasant odors, algae, mold, or mildew

_____4.   Mirrors cleaned

_____5.   Toilet bowls and urinals cleaned and disinfected

_____6.   Sink basins cleaned and disinfected

_____7.   Toilet paper and disposable hand towels available

_____8.   Soap and other amenities available and containers filled

_____9.   Suit dryer operational and in good repair

_____10.   Hair dryers operational

_____11.   Diaper changing area clean and disinfected; sanitary bed liners available

_____12.   Markings and graffiti removed

_____13.   All lights operational; burnt out light bulbs replaced

_____14.   Floor drains cleaned

_____15.   Floors swept, rinsed and disinfected

_____16.   Walls and ceilings cleaned

_____17.   Non-slip flooring and removable mats rinsed and disinfected

_____18.   Lockers opened and checked for items left behind by users

_____19.   Interior and exterior of lockers cleaned and disinfected

_____20.   Showers, faucets, and toilets working and in good repair

_____21.   Plumbing checked for dripping water or leaks

_____22.   Benches or seating secure and in good repair

* The person actually completing the maintenance job should initial the log

All maintenance duties have been satisfactorily completed as indicated.

_____
Maintenance Supervisor

© National Swimming Pool Foundation 2017

A-4 Aquatic Incident Report

Pool_____   Date_____

Instructions: Record factual information. Do not judge, or state opinions from witnesses or yourself, or admit fault.

Injured person's name: _____

Address: _____

Phone number (home): _____   (work): _____

Sex:_____   Age:_____

Class or activity in which enrolled: _____

Date of accident:_____   Time of accident: _____

Where did the accident occur? _____

What was the injured party doing when he/she was injured? _____

What piece of equipment, if any, was involved? _____

Name and location of supervisor(s), lifeguards, other personnel at the time of the accident:

_____

_____

_____

_____

What part of the body was injured? _____

Type of injury sustained: _____

Type of first aid administered: _____

Did the injured party seek medical assistance? _____

Was EMS called? _____

Describe what happened: _____

_____

_____

_____

Take digital images of incident location for clarification. Do not photograph individuals without their signed consent.

Witness 1   Witness 2

_____   _____
Signature   Signature

_____   _____
Name   Name

_____   _____
Address   Address

Witness 3   Witness 4

_____   _____
Signature   Signature

_____   _____
Name   Name

_____   _____
Address   Address

Report filed by (name): _____

Signature: _____

Position: _____   Date:_____

© National Swimming Pool Foundation 2017

A-5 Seasonal Opening Checklist

Review current local health codes to identify any changes since the facility was closed. If a pre-season inspection is required by the health department, or if you are outsourcing any opening tasks to a vendor, contact them months in advance to schedule and to allow sufficient time to correct issues prior to the opening date. Date Initiated:_____

_____ 1. Start seasonal opening procedures at least one month prior to the scheduled opening day.

_____ 2. Hire the pool staff. Plan pre-season training programs.

_____ 3. Conduct a complete inventory.

_____ 4. Check for winter damage and vandalism.

_____ 5. Make sure that chemical and maintenance contracts are in effect.

_____ 6. Check to see that repairs and/or renovations scheduled during the off-season were completed.

_____ 7. Order staff uniforms. Purchase sunscreen products and personal protective gear.

_____ 8. Replace worn or missing rescue equipment.

_____ 9. Restock the first aid kit.

_____ 10. Prepare all record forms and logs. Revise the staff, policy and operating manuals.

_____ 11. Pump any accumulated water and debris off the top of the winterizing pool cover.

_____ 12. Remove the winter pool cover. Clean and store it away for the season.

_____ 13. Turn the water supply back on.

_____ 14. Have the phone company restart service.

_____ 15. Empty all debris from the pool. Don't try to pump out dead or decaying leaves and animals.

_____ 16. Check for proper operation of the hydrostatic relief valve.

_____ 17. Drain the pool with a trash pump, after verifying hydrostatic relief valve operations.

_____ 18. Pump remaining liquid from the pool using a sump pump with an auto shut-off.

_____ 19. Rinse down the pool using a high pressure nozzle and hose. Flush out the gutters or skimmers.

_____ 20. Sandblast, acid wash, chlorine wash, recoat, repaint, replaster, fiberglass, and/or patch liner tears, or otherwise prepare the pool surface.

_____ 21. Paint or touch-up depth markings, drop-off lines, lane lines and targets, step edges, and graphics before refilling the pool.

_____ 22. Clean all pool and deck equipment.

_____ 23. Remove the winterizing plugs and expansion blocks. Uncap the inlets.

_____ 24. Lubricate all metal parts and hardware.

_____ 25. Replace gutter drain grates, bolts, gaskets, inlets, and plugs.

_____ 26. Verify main drain grates and sumps are VGB Act compliant, not expired, and installed in accordance with the manufacturer's instructions. Confirm proper operation of any secondary suction safety systems.

_____ 27. Clean and replace skimmer baskets, weirs, and lids.

_____ 28. Reassemble circulation pipes, the pump, and the motor. Drain anti-freeze from all piping and flush with fresh water.

_____ 29. Pressure test all circulation lines to make sure the pipes have not broken during the off-season. Repair broken pipes to prevent leaks from developing.

© National Swimming Pool Foundation 2017

_____30. Service and reinstall flow meters, pressure and vacuum gauges, thermometers, and humidity meters.

_____31. Reinstall the hair and lint skimmer basket. Replace gaskets or o-rings. Make sure the lid seals tightly.

_____32. Replace cracked or chipped tile.

_____33. Replace broken or burnt out pool lights, lenses and seals. Lubricate and tighten bolts and reinsert in the pool wall.

_____34. Check that all ground wires are connected.

_____35. Service the heater, replace elements, turn on the gas and relight the pilot, or check electrical connections.

_____36. Clean the filter media or elements. Repair or replace filter elements or cartridges if necessary. Close and re-plug the filter tank.

_____37. Test the manual air pressure relief valves on pressurized filter tanks.

_____38. Drain and clean the surge chamber. Check that valves, overflow, and water level devices are in operating order.

_____39. Obtain the maintenance and start-up chemicals.

_____40. Reinstall the chemical feeders, controllers, probes, and other feed pumps.

_____41. Begin filling the pool with water at least seven to ten days prior to the anticipated opening day.

_____42. Start circulating and filtering the water as soon as possible after the water level covers the inlets. Remember to temporarily shut off the skimmer lines to prevent air from entering the system.

_____43. Adjust the pressure inlets to maximize circulation. Perform a dye test if needed.

_____44. Treat the water to prevent the growth of algae or bacteria.

_____45. Add chemicals to achieve water balance, obtain acceptable water clarity, prevent damage (sequestering agents or chelating agents), or prevent chlorine loss (stabilizer).

_____46. Restock the test kit with fresh reagents. Calibrate testing instruments.

_____47. Vacuum the pool and backwash as needed until the water clears.

_____48. Turn on the water heater and begin to raise the water temperature to desired levels.

_____49. Cover the pool with a solar or insulating pool blanket to help prevent heat loss and reduce energy costs.

_____50. Reinstall ladders, rails, guard chairs, backstroke flags, and stanchions.

_____51. Replace handles on hose bibs and fill spouts.

_____52. Clean and disinfect the decks. Inspect for cracks or deterioration. Resurface if necessary.

_____53. Clean and arrange the deck furniture.

_____54. Repaint, spruce up, and clean the pool building, locker rooms, and auxiliary areas.

_____55. Replace vandalized or missing signs. Check that all signage required by code is posted.

_____56. Stock supplies.

_____57. Continue regular grounds maintenance.

_____58. Conduct a pre-opening inspection and facility safety audit.

_____59. Run mandatory pre-season training for the facility staff.

© National Swimming Pool Foundation 2017

A-6 Seasonal Closing Checklist

____1. Adjust the chemical balance of the pool water to recommended levels.

____2. Treat facility water with appropriate products to minimize algae, bacteria, or damage to surfaces.

____3. Clean and vacuum the pool.

____4. Empty and store skimmer baskets and hair and lint traps for the winter.

____5. Backwash the filter thoroughly and clean the filter media or elements.

____6. Drain sand filters. Remove cartridges or D.E. filter elements, inspect for tears or excessive wear, and store.

____7. Lower the water level to below the skimmers and return lines for plaster pools. If needed, remove the remaining water from the circulation lines using an air compressor or industrial type tank vacuum cleaner.

____8. Open all pump room valves and loosen the lid from the hair and lint skimmer. However, if the filter is below pool water level, close the valves leading from the pool to the filter.

____9. Grease all plugs and threads.

____10. Add antifreeze formulated specifically for recreational water applications to the pipes to prevent bursting. Do not use automotive antifreeze.

____11. Plug the skimmer or gutter lines. Winterize with antifreeze and expansion blocks. Secure the skimmer lids to the deck to prevent their loss. Plug vacuum and wall return lines and the main drain

____12. Make sure the hydrostatic relief valve is operational.

____13. Drain and protect pumps. If a pump and motor will be exposed to severe weather, disconnect, lubricate, perform seasonal maintenance of the pump, and store. Add antifreeze to help protect pumps and seals from any residual water left after draining.

____14. Clean surge pits or balancing tanks.

____15. Disconnect all fuses and open circuit breakers.

____16. If underwater wet niche lights are exposed to the elements, remove them from their niches and lower them to the bottom of the pool.

____17. Drain the pool water heater. Grease the drain plugs and store for the winter.

____18. Turn off the heater gas supply, gas valves, and pilot lights.

____19. Install the winter safety cover.

____20. Properly store any unused chemicals as described on their labels to prevent containers from breaking and the mixing of potentially incompatible chemicals. Dispose of test reagents, disinfectants, and other chemicals that will lose their potency over the winter.

____21. Disconnect, clean and store the chemical feeder, controllers, and other chemical feed pumps. Store controller electrodes in liquid.

____22. Clean and protect pressure gauges, flow meters, thermometers and humidity meters.

____23. Store all deck furniture (chairs, lounges, tables, umbrellas, etc.). Identify and separate all furniture in need of repair.

References

© National Swimming Pool Foundation 2017

A-6 Seasonal Closing Checklist (Continued)

_____24. Remove deck equipment, hardware, and non-permanent objects such as ladders, rails, slides, guard chairs, starting blocks, drinking fountains, handicapped lifts, portable ramps, clocks, weirs, and safety equipment to prevent vandalism. Store in a clearly-marked, identifiable, weather-protected location. Cap all exposed deck sockets.

_____25. Remove the diving boards. Store the boards indoors, upside down and flat so they will not warp.

_____26. Turn off the water supply to restroom showers, sinks, and toilets. Drain the pipes and add antifreeze. Remove shower heads and drinking fountain handles. Open hose bibs and fill spouts.

_____27. Have the phone company disconnect the pool telephone and discontinue service for the winter.

_____28. Install a pool deck alarm system.

_____29. Inventory all supplies and equipment. Make suggestions for preventative maintenance and repair, upgrading, and needed equipment purchases.

_____30. Confirm security of facility to prevent unauthorized access.

_____31. Agree to a periodic facility inspection procedure during the offseason.

_____32. Store ADA compliant pool lift.

A-7 Preventative Maintenance Checklist

There are many items for which preventative maintenance can help prevent costly and untimely equipment failures. This list includes many items that may be included in maintenance checklists.

1. Air pressure relief valve
2. Automatic chemical controller
3. Automatic fill valve
4. Backboard
5. Backstroke flags
6. Buoyed life lines
7. Centrifugal force circulation pump
8. Chemical containment dikes
9. Chemical metering pumps, chemical injection
10. Chemical room storage cabinets and shelving
11. Chemical spill clean-up equipment
12. Chemical storage barrels and containers
13. Color coding and labeling of pump room
14. Competitive timing equipment
15. Coping
16. Coven wall bases
17. D.E. separation tanks
18. Deck
19. Deck chairs, kickboards, exercise equipment, etc.
20. Deck drains
21. Dehumidification system
22. Depth markings
23. Diaper changing stations
24. Diving boards, towers, rails, and hardware
25. Diving well bubbler
26. Drinking fountain
27. Emergency alarms
28. Emergency exit doors, crash bars
29. Emergency eye wash and drench shower station
30. Emergency telephone
31. Extension poles
32. Eye bolts for lane lines and lifelines
33. Fencing, gates, latches, locks
34. Fill spout
35. Filter
36. First aid kit
37. Floating lane lines, reels, and covers
38. Flow meter
39. Grab rails, safety rails, handrails
40. Gutters
41. Hair and lint trap
42. Hair dryers
43. Handicap accessibility lift
44. Heaving lines
45. HVAC system
46. Humidity meter
47. Inlets and outlet covers
48. Ladders
49. Lights: deck, security, under water
50. Locker room benches, components, and flooring
51. Lockers
52. Main drains and suction outlets
53. Motor
54. Moveable bulkhead
55. Personal protective gear
56. Pipes, circulation lines
57. Pool blankets
58. Pool finish or coating
59. Pressure gauges: filter and pump discharge
60. Ramps
61. Rescue tubes
62. Ring buoys
63. Safety Data Sheet station
64. Sauna equipment
65. Shepherd's crook
66. Showers
67. Sight glass
68. Signage: pool rules, warning signs - code compliant
69. Skimmers
70. Spa aerators
71. Spectator bleachers
72. Stanchions, anchors, caps
73. Starting blocks
74. Storage rooms
75. Suit dryers
76. Sump pit, backwash holding tank
77. Surge chamber
78. Test kits and reagents
79. Thermometers
80. Toilets, urinals, and sinks
81. Towel and equipment hooks
82. Underwater sound system
83. Vacuum
84. Vacuum gauges
85. Valves
86. Water heater (domestic water supply)
87. Water heater (pool)
88. Water polo goals
89. Windows and skylights

References

© National Swimming Pool Foundation 2017

A-8 New Plaster Start-Up Procedures

The pool finish will start to hydrate immediately after mixing, with the majority of hydration taking place within the first 28 days. This critical time period is when a finish is most susceptible to staining, scaling and discoloration. Proper start-up procedures including timely brushing and constant monitoring and adjusting of the pool water are mandatory. The following recommended start-up method is based on procedures shown to produce the best aesthetic results. Due to unique local water conditions and environmental factors, parts of these recommended start-up procedures may need to be modified to protect the pool finish. For example: filling the pool with water that exhibits extremely low calcium hardness, low pH or low total alkalinity levels may necessitate changes to these procedures. Brushing and monitored chemical adjustments will be mandatory by the homeowner or a trained pool technician during the service life of any pool surface. It is best to dilute or dissolve any chemical before adding to the pool water. **ALWAYS ADD A CHEMICAL TO WATER, NEVER WATER TO THE CHEMICAL. Use appropriate personal protective equipment.**

Pool Filling Day

- **Step 1:** Make sure the filtration equipment is operational.
- **Step 2:** Remove all floor return heads and directional eyeballs (if appropriate and recommended in your geographical area).
- **Step 3:** Based on temperature and type of finish, fill the pool to the middle of the skimmer or specified water level without interruption as rapidly as possible with clean potable water to help prevent a bowl ring. Place a clean rag on the end of the hose, always placed in the deepest area, to prevent damage to the surface material. If a water truck is required, 24 inches (60 cm) of water should be placed at the deepest area for a water cushion. Wheeled devices should not be used in the pool until after 28 days.
- **Step 4:** At no time should any person or pets be allowed in the pool during the fill. Do not allow any external sources of water to enter the pool to help prevent streaking. It is recommended that you do not swim in the pool until the water is properly balanced.
- **Step 5:** Test fill water for pH, alkalinity, calcium hardness and metals. Record test results.
- **Step 6:** Start the filtration system immediately when the pool is full to the middle of the skimmer or specified water level.

1ST Day, Following Pool Filling Day (It is vital to follow these steps in order.)

- **Step 1:** Test pH, alkalinity, calcium hardness and metals. Record test results.
- **Step 2:** High alkalinity should be adjusted to 80 ppm (mg/L) using pre-diluted muriatic acid (31-33% hydrochloric acid). Always pre-dilute the acid by adding it to a five gallon (19 liter) bucket of pool water.
- **Step 3:** Low alkalinity should be adjusted to 80 ppm (mg/L) using sodium bicarbonate (baking soda).
- **Step 4:** pH should be reduced to 7.2 to 7.6 adding pre-diluted muriatic acid if the alkalinity is already 80-100 ppm (mg/L).
- **Step 5:** Once the alkalinity is adjusted to 80 ppm (mg/L) and the pH is adjusted to 7.2 to 7.6, then adjust calcium hardness levels to a minimum of 150 ppm (mg/L).
- **Step 6:** Brush the entire pool surface thoroughly at least twice daily to remove all plaster dust.
- **Step 7:** Although optional, it is highly recommended to pre-dilute and add a quality sequestering agent using the recommended initial start-up dosage and then the recommended maintenance dosage per the sequestering agent's manufacturer.
- **Step 8:** Operate filtration system continuously for a minimum of 72 hours.
- **Step 9:** DO NOT add chlorine for 48 hours. DO NOT turn on pool heater until there is no plaster dust in the pool.

© National Swimming Pool Foundation 2017

A-8 New Plaster Start-Up Procedures (Continued)

2ND Day

- Follow steps of 1st Day

3RD Day

- **Step 1:** Test pH, alkalinity and calcium hardness and repeat 1st Day Steps 1 through 6.
- **Step 2:** Pre-diluted chlorine may now be added to achieve 1.5 to 3 ppm (mg/L). NO SALT SHOULD BE ADDED FOR 28 DAYS.
- **Step 3:** Brush the entire pool surface thoroughly at least twice daily to remove all plaster dust.

4TH Through the 28TH Day

- **Step 1:** Test pH, carbonate alkalinity and calcium hardness and repeat 1st Day Steps 1 through 5 every day for 14 days to help prevent the scaling of the pool surface.
- **Step 2:** On the 7th day, if there is any plaster dust remaining - remove it using a brush pool vacuum.
- **Step 3:** After the 4th Day - calcium levels should be adjusted slowly over the 28 day period not to exceed 200 ppm (mg/L).
- **Step 4:** After the 4th Day - adjust cyanuric acid levels to 30 to 50 ppm (mg/L) based on the primary disinfectant of the pool (pre-dissolve and add through the skimmer).

**For more information contact the National Plasterers Council
www.npconline.org or call (847) 416-7272**

© National Swimming Pool Foundation 2017

A-9 Pool/Spa Inspection Checklist

This pool/spa inspection checklist is an example of a guideline that can be used to audit or evaluate a facility. All items do not apply to every facility. Many items do not fall under the direct responsibility of a pool operator. Additional training and resources for conducting self-audits and inspections are available through the Certified Pool/Spa Inspector™ certification course and the Aquatic Facility Audits course from NSPF.

Pool_____ Date_____

Address:_____
City / State / Zip:_____
Phone: (   )_____ Year Built:_____
Maintenance Director / Manager / Supervisor:_____

❏ 1. Main drain grates are bolted securely to the pool bottom.

❏ 2. A six-inch black disk or the main drain grates are clearly visible from any point on the deck.

❏ 3. Drain covers are VGB Act certified, not expired, and installed according to manufacturer's instructions; and the suction system has a flow rating equal to or greater than 100% of circulation system flow rate.

❏ 4. The circulation system is properly plumbed to provide uniform distribution of water throughout the pool and prevent hazards.
Inlet type_____
Inlet number and spacing_____
Inlet location_____

❏ 5. The pool is vacuumed daily or as needed. No settled debris is visible.
Vacuum type_____ _____

❏ 6. A hydrostatic relief valve has been installed on in-ground pools in areas where the ground freezes or where high ground water tables may pose a problem.

❏ 7. Algae growth is not visible in the pool. The water is not discolored from an algae bloom.

❏ 8. Coping stones and tile lines are not chipped, cracked, or loose.

❏ 9. The pool shell is finished in a smooth but slip resistant, easily cleaned, and water tight surface material, white or off-white in color. There are no cracks in the shell except structural expansion joints.
Pool construction material_____
Surface type_____

❏ 10. The presence of minerals or dissolved metals has not caused surface staining or water discoloration.

❏ 11. Correct water level is maintained to allow for the removal of floating debris and for the continuous overflow of water into the pool gutters or skimmers.

❏ 12. Type of perimeter overflow system:
_____Skimmers: Number_____
_____Gutters
_____Prefabricated
_____Water-to-waste
_____Fully recessed
_____Partially recessed
_____Rim flow
_____Roll-out

❏ 13. Skimmer weirs, equalizer lines, skimmer baskets, deck covers, and flow adjustment or anti-entrapment drain covers are all present and in good repair.

❏ 14. A current license or permit to operate a public pool is posted in a conspicuous place in the facility.

❏ 15. Certified operator certifications are conspicuously posted.

© National Swimming Pool Foundation 2017

A-9 Pool/Spa Inspection Checklist (Continued)

☐16. Adequate storage space has been provided for wet, dry and secure storage of equipment. Decks are uncluttered. They are not used for storage of teaching or maintenance equipment.

☐17. The pool is covered with an insulating or safety pool cover when not in use.

☐18. Pool equipment is not being improperly used or misused.

☐19. Emergency exit doors are unlocked, and crash bars are operational. An alarm sounds when an emergency door is opened.

☐20. All lights are operational and installed in compliance with National Electrical Code Article 680.

☐21. The pool area is well lit and sufficient overhead and/or pool lighting is provided.
Type of deck lighting_____
Number of deck lights_____
Wattage of each light_____
Type of underwater lighting_____
Number of underwater lights_____
Wattage of each light_____
Illumination level_____
Footcandles (day)_____
Footcandles (night)_____

☐22. A security lighting system is installed in indoor facilities that require light for patrons to exit safely. Lights are tested on a regular basis.

☐23. Glare from natural lighting does not interfere with the ability to see below the surface of the water.

☐24. Glare from artificial lighting does not interfere with the ability to see below the surface of the water.

☐25. Ground fault circuit interrupters (GFCI) have been installed on all electrical outlets in the pool, locker rooms, and other wet areas of the facility.

☐26. The deck and all floors leading to the pool are slip resistant.
Deck surface material
_____

☐27. Deck mats, raised grid interlocking tiles, or anti-bactericide runners, if used, are removed for cleaning and disinfection.

☐28. Decks are clean and disinfected.
Number of hose bibs_____
Hose bib location_____
Backflow prevention_____

☐29. Decks on all four sides of the pool must meet the minimum regulations regarding unobstructed clearance. The minimum required unobstructed deck space is provided where diving boards or starting blocks are installed. The required deck space separates the swimming pool from the wading pool, spa, or other pools.

☐30. Decks are sloped properly to drain and do not collect pools of standing water.
Number of deck drains_____
Max. distance between drains_____
Coven wall bases present _____

☐31. All ladders, backstroke flag stanchions, guard chairs, rails and treads, deck plates, and other deck equipment are tightly secured in place.

☐32. When stanchions, starting blocks or other pieces of deck equipment are removed, anchor sockets are capped.

☐33. The fresh water fill spout is located so as not to be a tripping hazard. An air gap of at least 6 inches (14.25 cm) has been provided between the spout and the pool as a means of backflow protection.
Water supply source_____
Drought restrictions_____

☐34. A drinking fountain has been provided within the pool enclosure.

☐35. Backstroke flags and support stanchions are placed 15 feet (4.57 m) (USS short course, NCAA, NFSHSA) or 16'5" (5 m)

References

© National Swimming Pool Foundation 2017

A-9 Pool/Spa Inspection Checklist (Continued)

(USS long course, FINA) from each pool edge.

☐36. Underwater observation windows are mounted flush with the pool wall. Hardware securing the window frame to the pool wall does not protrude or otherwise pose a hazard to users.

☐37. Spectator seating areas are physically separated from the pool deck.

☐38. Electrical wiring does not pass directly over the pool.

☐39. Towel and equipment hooks are installed on the walls in a way that does not present a hazard to users.

☐40. Swim lanes are a minimum of seven and preferably ten feet wide.

☐41. Targets have been provided and are in alignment with swim lanes.

☐42. Floating lane lines are secured to the pool with recessed hooks. Lines are stored on a reel when not in use, and the lane line reel is covered and stored off deck.

☐43. An adequate means of egress from the pool is provided.

☐44. The pool is handicapped accessible and in compliance with the ADA and barrier-free design requirements.

☐45. Rescue equipment, including rescue tubes, ring buoys, extension poles, and shepherd's crooks are all in good repair and immediately available for use.

☐46. Elevated lifeguard chairs are placed at appropriate locations around the pool deck.

☐47. The first aid kit is well stocked and instantly accessible. (Minimum: 24-unit first aid kit) A first aid room is provided.

☐48. A backboard, rigid cervical collars, head immobilizer, and straps are in good repair and immediately available for use. Guards are trained and practiced in current spinal management techniques.

☐49. An emergency telephone is located on the pool deck.

☐50. Emergency phone numbers are posted. Directions to the facility and other pertinent information to be conveyed to the 911 operator is posted next to the phone.

☐51. An established procedure is in place to ensure that employees who make direct contact with minors do not have a criminal record as sex offenders.

☐52. Pool rules, methods of enforcement, safety literature, and meaningful warning signs are posted.

☐53. Pool capacity (user load) signs are posted. Capacity limits are not exceeded. Method of determining user load

_____

Maximum user load _____

☐54. Depth markings are plainly and conspicuously marked at or above the water surface on the vertical wall of the pool and on the edge of the deck. Markings conform to local and state code as to size, color, and spacing. Depth is marked to indicate feet and inches. Numbers other than those indicating depth have been removed.

☐55. Depth or drop-off lines and/or buoyed life lines are correctly positioned in the pool to indicate sudden changes in slope.

☐56. A contour depth chart is posted next to the pool to help users judge the depth and shape of the pool.
Slope ratio (shallow)_____

☐57. Steps, treads, ramps, ledges or any other protrusion into the pool are marked with a contrasting color coating or tile on both the top and vertical rise.

© National Swimming Pool Foundation 2017

❏58. Diving board is in compliance with manufacturer specifications regarding installation, structural features, and pool water depth configuration.

❏59. Starting blocks are located in a depth of water that meets the minimum requirement of state or local regulations or the standards established by the sanctioning competitive body(s). Warning labels are affixed. Blocks are removed from the deck except during competition or training for competition. Use of starting blocks is prohibited unless swimmers are under the direct supervision of an instructor or coach.

❏60. Adequate fencing, gates, barriers, alarms or other protective devices are installed to prevent entry, or alert staff to the unauthorized entry of a trespasser into the pool area.

❏61. The pool manager or operator is certified by the NSPF® Certified Pool/Spa Operator® certification Program, and is knowledgeable in all aspects of pool operation, water chemistry and maintenance.

❏62. Pool water is tested at the frequency required by the code or at a frequency to ensure the water is disinfected and balanced.

❏63. Test kits are properly stored and reagents fresh.
Brand(s) of test kits_____

❏64. A system of regular testing, recording of findings, and chemical adjustment of pool water has been implemented. A daily pool water analysis log is posted. Capability of testing or calculating:
_____FAC
_____TAC
_____CAC
_____Cyanuric acid
_____pH

_____Acid/base demand
_____Total alkalinity
_____Calcium hardness
_____TDS
_____Sodium chloride
_____Water temperature
_____Air temperature
_____Relative humidity
_____Saturation index
_____ORP

❏65. All water quality and chemicals levels are within acceptable ranges.

❏66. Detailed maintenance checklists for daily opening and closing procedures and seasonal and long term maintenance are maintained, completed daily and available for inspection.
_____Daily checklists
_____Preventative maintenance checklists

❏67. Trash containers are covered and emptied as needed.

❏68. Markings and graffiti have been removed.

❏69. Water temperature is maintained within acceptable levels and is appropriate for the primary activities being conducted in the pool.
Water temperature_____ °F (°C)

❏70. Air quality is monitored. No unpleasant odors or irritating fumes are discernible.
Air temperature_____°F (°C)

❏71. Fresh air is introduced into the pool area consistent with ASHRAE standards.
Type of air handling system_____
Humidity level (pool)_____%

❏72. Upon visual inspection, the ceiling over the pool does not show any obvious signs of deterioration.

❏73. Lifeguards have suitable training and certification.

© National Swimming Pool Foundation 2017

References

A-9 Pool/Spa Inspection Checklist (Continued)

❑74. The doors leading to the equipment and chemical rooms are locked and only accessible to authorized personnel.

❑75. Appropriate signage and warnings are affixed to the outside of the equipment and chemical room doors.

❑76. The pool chemical room has at least two exits, and does not open out on to the pool deck or to other heavily traveled areas.

❑77. The surge chamber is properly sized.
Surge tank volume_____gal (liters)
Type:
_____Surge chamber
_____Balancing tank
_____Surge trench
_____In-pool surge capacity
_____Vacuum filter tank

❑78. The flow meter is operational, accurate and properly located on a return line at operator eye level.
Meter type:
_____Digital
_____Mercury manometer
_____Analog
_____Variable area
Straight length of pipe prior to the flow meter _____ inches (cm)
Straight length of pipe after the flow meter _____ inches (cm)
Pipe diameter _____ inches (cm)

❑79. Rate of circulation is appropriate to meet minimum turnover requirements and to accommodate peak user loads.
Volume = _____ gallons (liters)
Flow rate = _____ gpm (lpm)
Required flow rate = _____ gpm (lpm) for _____ hour turnover
Turnover = _____ hours

❑80. The hair and lint strainer basket is clean of debris. Additional baskets and gaskets or o-rings are available.

❑81. The centrifugal force pump is properly secured to its base, located so as to avoid cavitation, and is operating quietly.

❑82. The pump is self-priming or located so as to eliminate the need for priming.

❑83. The circulation pump is properly sized according to the manufacturer's pump curve.
Influent pressure
_____(psi) x 2.31 = _____ feet of head
Vacuum reading
_____(in. Hg) x 1.13 = _____ feet of water
Feet of head + feet of water = _____TDH
Minimum flow rate = _____ gpm (lpm)
Pump horsepower = _____ hp

❑84. Pipes are not leaking, are properly supported, and do not show obvious external signs of calcification, corrosion or deterioration.
Pipe type:
_____PVC 40
_____Copper
_____CPVC 80
_____Stainless steel
_____Cast iron
_____Galvanized steel

❑85. Air pressure relief valves have been installed on all pressure filter tanks.
_____ Manual _____ Automatic

❑86. Valves and piping have been provided on multi-filter systems to isolate individual filter tanks for maintenance or repair.

❑87. The filter tanks are positioned to allow for accessibility and proper air circulation.

❑88. Total filter surface area is adequate to meet recommended design flow rates.
Filter type:
_____ Rapid sand
_____ Pressure D.E.
_____ Vacuum sand
_____ Vacuum D.E.
_____ High rate sand
_____ Regenerative D.E.

© National Swimming Pool Foundation 2017

A-9 Pool/Spa Inspection Checklist (Continued)

_____ Pressure cartridge

_____ Vacuum cartridge

Filter brand_____

Design flow rate = _____ gpm/ft² (m³/m²/hr)

Required filter size = _____ ft² (m²)

Number of filter tanks (elements)

_____ x ft² (m²) of filter surface area = _____ ft² (m²)

Actual filter size = _____ ft² (m²)

☐89. Diatomaceous earth, chemicals or discharged pool water are neutralized, separated, settled or otherwise properly disposed of.

☐90. A clean sight glass or visual outfall of at least three feet has been provided.

☐91. A sump pit or backwash holding tank has been installed and has been properly sized to prevent water discharged during the backwash process from flooding the filter room.

☐92. Adequate drainage has been provided in the pump room.

☐93. Filter media or elements are clean. No channeling, mud ball formation or bridging is evident.

☐94. Pressurized filter tanks and hair and lint traps are properly sealed.

☐95. All influent and effluent pressure gauges and vacuum gauges are operational and accurate.

Vacuum _____ Hg

Influent pressure _____ psi (kPa)

Effluent pressure _____ psi (kPa)

☐96. The pool auxiliary rooms are clean, maintained in a safe and acceptable manner, well lit and ventilated.

☐97. Diagrams and operating instructions are posted in the pump rooms. Operating manuals have been obtained from the manufacturers.

☐98. Chemical feed pumps are interlocked to the circulation pump to ensure chemicals are not fed if circulation is off.

☐99. All piping, filters, and components which are part of the mechanical operating system are labeled, tagged, or color coded.

☐100. The heater is properly sized and maintained.

Type of heater_____

Fossil fuel_____

Efficiency rating_____%

Variables reducing heater efficiency

_____

☐101. Pool chemicals and other flammable materials are stored a safe distance from the heater or in a flammable storage cabinet.

☐102. Adequate clearances have been established between the heater and the equipment room walls.

☐103. The heater is installed on a level, non-combustible base.

☐104. Safety devices have been installed on the heater to prevent improper operation and to eliminate the possibility of patrons being accidentally burned by excessively high water temperatures.

_____ High temperature limit switch

_____ Thermostat

_____ Low voltage fireman's switch (if a timer is installed)

_____ Check valves between the filter and heater

_____ Check valves between the heater and chemical injection equipment

_____ Bonded and grounded

_____ Flow or pressure switch

_____ Gas pressure regulator

☐105. The heater is installed downstream of the pump and filter and upstream of chemical injection equipment.

© National Swimming Pool Foundation 2017

A-9 Pool/Spa Inspection Checklist (Continued)

❑106. A copper, stainless steel, or CPVC heat sink has been installed between the heater and piping.

❑107. Compensation has been made for variables which reduce heater efficiency.
_____Altitude
_____Wind breaks erected near outdoor installations
_____Properly vented to insure combustion and adequate exhaustion
_____Heater is installed close to the pool to minimize heat loss

❑108. An active solar heating system has been installed and is operating effectively.
Solar Heating Type:
_____ Open loop (water)
_____ Closed loop (antifreeze)
Panels:
_____Flat plate _____Flexible plastic
_____Glazed _____Unglazed
Collector location_____

❑109. SDS are posted for all chemicals stored on the premises. SDS stations and a master file have been created.

❑110. Chemicals are properly stored, contained, labeled, transported, and handled in compliance with safe chemical storage practices.
_____Primary disinfectant
_____Supplemental chemicals
_____pH adjustment chemical
Chemical inventory:
_____
_____
_____

❑111. Chemicals are correctly dispensed into the pool.
Injection:
_____ Peristaltic pump
_____ Gas chlorinator
_____ Piston pump
_____ Brominator
_____ Diaphragm pump
_____ Erosion feeder
_____ Slurry pot
_____ Hand feeding

❑112. Automated chemical controllers are calibrated and operating properly.
Controller brand_____
Paper print-out or remote read-out
_____
Automatic probe cleaner_____
Frequency of probe cleaning_____
Chemical spills_____

❑113. Empty or used chemical storage containers are rinsed and disposed of in accordance with manufacturers' recommendations.

❑114. Equipment for containing and cleaning up chemical spills is available. Containment dikes, overpacks, and chemical clean-up gear have been provided.

❑115. Emergency fresh water drench showers and eye washes are available for use by all persons required to handle chemicals.

❑116. Personal protective equipment, such as goggles, full-face shields, splash guard aprons, neoprene gloves, boots, respirators, gas masks, SCBAs, disposable latex gloves, and 1-way CPR pocket masks, are available and staff members have been instructed in their proper use.

❑117. The facility is in compliance with all bathing codes. (Contact your department of health for a copy of the health and safety, building, general industry safety, and administrative codes that pertain to the design, construction, maintenance and operation of pools in your state.)

© National Swimming Pool Foundation 2017

A-9 Pool/Spa Inspection Checklist (Continued)

❏118. The facility is in compliance with all applicable codes, such as the Uniform Fire Code, Emergency Planning and Community Right-to-Know Act, Hazard Communication Standard, Safe Drinking Water and Toxic Enforcement Act, and Occupational Exposure to Bloodborne Pathogens.

❏119. Fire extinguishers are charged and are located throughout the facility.
_____Type A
_____Type B
_____Type BC

❏120. Locker rooms are adequately sized to provide patrons with a desired level of privacy.
Locker rooms:
_____Men
_____Women
_____Boys
_____Girls
_____Staff
_____Family or transgender changing room

❏121. Lockers are provided in adequate numbers.

❏122. The locker rooms are adequately illuminated and ventilated.

❏123. Locker room maintenance is completed as needed. Sink basins, floors, mirrors, toilet bowls and urinals are cleaned and disinfected.

❏124. The locker room plumbing has been checked for dripping water or leaks. Showers, faucets and toilets are working and in good repair.
Showers:
_____ Group
_____ Private
_____ Handicap

❏125. Toilet paper, paper hand-towels, soap and other amenities are available and containers filled.
Amenities:
_____ Toilet paper

_____ Paper towels
_____ Soap
_____ Suit dryers
_____ Hair dryers
_____ Scales
_____ Diaper changing
_____ Baby seats in stalls
_____ Other_____

❏126. The suit dryer is operational and in good repair.

❏127. A diaper changing area, sanitary bed liners, and a disposal can for soiled diapers has been provided.

❏128. Benches, chairs, and tables are secure and in good repair.

❏129. The locker rooms are aesthetically pleasing and provide a comfortable and pleasant environment.

❏130. The spa 15 minute timer is operational and suitably located so it cannot be reached by a user sitting in the spa.

❏131. An emergency spa pump shut-off switch is installed on the spa deck. The switch is clearly labeled.

❏132. Sauna timers are suitably located on the outside of the rooms and operational.

❏133. Steam room timers are suitably located on the outside of the rooms and operational.

❏134. Signs are posted instructing users on the proper use of saunas, steam rooms, and spas and warning users of the hazards associated with their use.

❏135. An adequate number of nearby parking spaces have been provided in anticipation of maximum user loads.

❏136. Measures are being taken to prevent infestation by roaches and other unwanted pests without contaminating pool water.

© National Swimming Pool Foundation 2017

Reference:
Appendix B

Water Chemistry Guidelines & Worksheets

1. Pool & Spa Management
2. Regulations & Guidelines
3. Essential Calculations
4. Pool Water Contamination
5. Disinfection
6. Water Balance
7. Pool & Spa Water Problems
8. Chemical Testing
9. Chemical Feed & Control
10. Water Circulation
11. Pool & Spa Filtration
12. Heating & Air Circulation
13. Spa & Therapy Operations
14. Facility Safety
15. Keeping Records
16. Maintenance Systems
17. Troubleshooting
18. Facility Renovation & Design

References

B-1 Water Chemistry Guidelines

These commonly accepted chemical parameters do not supersede local or state codes and regulations.

Parameter	Min.	Ideal	Max	Pool Type
Free Chlorine (ppm or mg/L)	1.0	2.0 – 4.0	5.0	Pools, Waterparks
	2.0	3.0 – 5.0	10.0	Spas
Combined Chlorine (ppm or mg/L)	0	0	0.4	Pools, Waterparks
	0	0	0.5	Spas
Total Bromine (ppm or mg/L)	2.0	4.0 – 6.0	10.0	All Types
PHMB (ppm or mg/L)	30	30 – 50	50	All Types
pH	7.2	7.4 – 7.6	7.8	All Types
Total Alkalinity as $CaCO_3$ (ppm or mg/L)	60	80 – 100* 100 – 120**	180	All Types
Total Dissolved Solids (ppm or mg/L)	NA	NA	1500 over start-up	All Types
Calcium Hardness as $CaCO_3$ (ppm or mg/L)	150	200 – 400	1,000	Pools, Waterparks
	100	150 – 250	800	Spas
Heavy Metals	None	None	None	All Types
Visible Algae	None	None	None	All Types
Bacteria	None	None	Local Code	All Types
Cyanuric Acid (ppm or mg/L)	****	30 – 50	****	All Types
Temperature °F/°C	78°F (25.5°C)	80.5°F (26.9°C)	82°F (27.8°C)	Competition Pools
	–	–	104°F	Spas
	–	Personal Preference	104°F	Other Pools
Ozone (ppm or mg/L)	–	–	0.1 over 8-hr. time wtd. avg.	All Types
ORP	Calibrate to Disinfectant Level*****			All Types

*	For calcium hyphchlorite, lithium hypochlorite, or sodium hypochlorite
**	For sodium dichlor, trichlor, chlorine, gas, BCDMH
***	Start-up includes the TDS contribution of salt found in chlorine generating systems
****	Dictated by local codes. Typically 100 ppm (mg/L). Some codes are higher, some are lower
*****	Some local codes may dictate a minimum and maximum

© National Swimming Pool Foundation 2017

Notes

261

© National Swimming Pool Foundation 2017

B-2 Water Chemistry Adjustment Guide

These commonly accepted chemical parameters do not supersede manufacturers' instructions. Smart phone apps can help calculate associated pool volume and dosage.

Dosages to Treat	10,000 Gallons			40,000 Liters		
Chemical	**Desired Change**			**Desired Change**		
Increase Chlorine	1 ppm	5 ppm	10 ppm	1 mg/L	5 mg/L	10 mg/L
Chlorine Gas	1.3 oz	6.7 oz	13 oz	40 g	200 g	390 g
Calcium Hypochlorite (67%)*	2 oz	10 oz	1.25 lbs	63 g	315 g	630 g
Sodium Hypochlorite (12%)	10.7 fl.oz.	1.7 qts	3.3 qts	330 mL	1.36 L	3.3 L
Lithium Hypochlorite	3.8 oz	1.2 lbs	2.4 lbs	110 g	570 g	1.1 kg
Dichlor (62%)	2.1 oz	10.75 oz	1.3 lbs	65 g	320 g	650 g
Dichlor (56%)	2.4 oz	12 oz	1.4 lbs	72 g	360 g	720 g
Trichlor	1.5 oz	7.5 oz	14 oz	44 g	220 g	440 g
Increase Total Alkalinity	10 ppm	30 ppm	50 ppm	10 mg/L	30 mg/L	50 mg/L
Sodium Bicarbonate	1.4 lbs	4.2 lbs	7.0 lbs	670 g	2.0 kg	3.4 kg
Sodium Carbonate	14 oz	2.6 lbs	4.4 lbs	400 g	1.2 kg	2.0 kg
Sodium Sesquicarbonate	1.25 lbs	3.75 lbs	6.25 lbs	600 g	1.8 kg	3.0 kg
Decrease Total Alkalinity	10 ppm	30 ppm	50 ppm	10 mg/L	30 mg/L	50 mg/L
Muriatic Acid (31.4%)	26 fl.oz.	2.4 qts	1 gal	800 mL	2.4 L	4.0 L
Sodium Bisulfate	2.1 lbs	6.4 lbs	10.5 lbs	1.03 kg	3.1 kg	5.15 kg
Increase/Decrease pH	For more information on pH adjustments, see the pH Adjustment Testing section in the Chemical Testing chapter					
Increase Calcium Hardness	10 ppm	30 ppm	50 ppm	10 mg/L	30 mg/L	50 mg/L
Calcium Chloride (100%)	0.9 lbs	2.8 lbs	4.6 lbs	402 g	1.2 kg	2.0 kg
Calcium Chloride (77%)	1.2 lbs	3.6 lbs	6.0 lbs	575 g	1.7 kg	2.9 kg
Increase Stabilizer	10 ppm	30 ppm	50 ppm	10 mg/L	30 mg/L	50 mg/L
Cyanuric Acid	13 oz	2.5 lbs	4.1 lbs	400 g	1.2 kg	2.0 kg
Neutralize Chlorine	1 ppm	5 ppm	10 ppm	1 mg/L	5 mg/L	10 mg/L
Sodium Thiosulfate	2.6 oz	13 oz	26 oz	79 g	395 g	790 g
Sodium Sulfite	2.4 oz	12 oz	1.5 lbs	71 g	356 g	711 g

Chemical amounts have been rounded off for convienience. Always follow the instructions on the manufacturer's label for exact dosage amounts.

*Other calcium hypochlorite products are available from 47% to 78%. Follow the label directions for dosage amounts.

© National Swimming Pool Foundation 2017

B-3 Water Chemistry Adjustment Worksheets

Use the following blank chemical adjustment worksheets to perform your own calculations.

Amount of Chemical (from appendix B-2 or product label)	Actual Pool Volume in Gallons	Desired Chemical Change	Total
	÷ 10,000 Gallons (From appendix B-2 or product label)	÷ ppm (From appendix B-2 or product label)	
	X	X	=

Notes:

Metric

Amount of Chemical (from appendix B-2 or product label)	Actual Pool Volume in Liters	Desired Chemical Change	Total
	÷ 40,000 Liters (From appendix B-2 or product label)	÷ mg/L (From appendix B-2 or product label)	
	X	X	=

Notes:

© National Swimming Pool Foundation 2017

B-4 Conversion & Calculation Guide

Liquid Conversions

	Tea Spoon	Table Spoon	Fluid Ounce	Cup	Pint	Quart	Gallon (US)
Teaspoon (tsp.)	1.0	3.0	6.0	48	96	192	768
Tablespoon (TBS.)	0.33	1.0	2.0	16	32	64	256
Fluid Ounce (fl.oz.)	0.16	0.5	1.0	8.0	16	32	128
Cup	0.02	0.06	0.125	1.0	2.0	4.0	16
Pint (pt.)	0.01	0.03	0.06	0.5	1.0	2.0	8.0
Quart (qt.)	0.005	0.02	0.03	0.25	0.5	1.0	4.0
Gallon (gal.) (US)	0.001	0.004	0.008	0.06	0.15	0.25	1.0
Liter	0.005	0.015	0.0296	0.237	0.473	0.946	3.785

Formulas and Conversions

Feet		Formula	Gallons	x 3.785 =	Liters
Yards	3	Yards x 3 = feet	Liters	x 0.264 =	Gallons
Meters	3.28	Meters x 3.28 = feet	Pounds	x 0.454 =	Kilograms
Pounds		Formula	Kilograms	x 2.205 =	Pounds
Ounces	16	Ounces ÷ 16 = Pounds	Ounces	x 28.35 =	Grams
Temperature		Conversion	Grams	x 0.0353 =	Ounces
°F to °C		°C = (°F − 32) x 0.555	U.S. Gallon	x 0.832 =	Imp. Gallon
°C to °F		°F = (°C x 1.8) + 32	Imp. Gallon	x 1.202 =	U.S. Gallon

Additional Calculations and Conversions

BTU	BTU = 8.33 x gallons x °F temperature rise
1 ppm	= 1 mg/L (milligram per liter)
1 Cubic Foot Water	= 7.5 gallons
1 Cubic Meter Water	= 1000 liters
1 Gallon Water	= 8.33 pounds
1 Square Foot	= 144 square inches
Area Circle	= 3.14 x r x r (r is the radius, or 1/2 of the diameter)
Area Rectangle	= Length (L) x Width (W) or L x W
Average Depth	= (Shallow Depth + Deep Depth) ÷ 2
Volume Rectangle (gallons)	= Length x Width x Avg. Depth x 7.5
Volume Circle (gallons)	= 3.14 x radius x radius x Avg. Depth x 7.5
Volume Oval (gallons)	= Short Radius x Long Radius x 3.14 x Average Depth x 7.5*
Volume Kidney (gallons)	= (Width$_A$ + Width$_B$) x Length x 0.45 x Average Depth x 7.5*

*See Figure 3-3 in the Essential Calculations chapter

© National Swimming Pool Foundation 2017

Appendix C

Legislation & Regulation Information

© National Swimming Pool Foundation 2017

C-1 The Virginia Graeme Baker Pool & Spa Safety Act

The Virginia Graeme Baker Pool & Spa Safety Act (VGB Act) was enacted by Congress and signed by President Bush on December 19, 2007, with the goal of preventing drownings in pools and spas. It addresses fencing, alarms, and the hazard of suction entrapment, by mandating all suction outlets (main drain covers, mounting hardware and sumps) to be 3rd party certified, and that the drain covers have not exceeded their installed service life. It also requires public pools and spas with single, blockable drains to be equipped with a secondary system designed to prevent suction entrapment. Compliance with the law was mandatory as of December 19, 2008.

The law addresses private and public pools. Residential drain covers must comply when they are replaced, and public pools require retroactive upgrades. The VGB Act provides financial incentives to jurisdictions that adopt and enforce VGB Act policies for all private pools and spas.

All drain covers, fasteners, and mounting assemblies must be tested and 3rd party certified to ASME/ANSI A112.19.8-2007. In mid-2008, the Association of Mechanical Engineers (ASME) requested the standard be transferred, and the name changed to ANSI/APSP 16-2011. During the transition, manufacturers were instructed to mark newly certified products with VGB-2008. As a result, compliant drain covers are identified by any of the following: ASME/ANSI A112.19.8-2007, VGB-2008, or ANSI/APSP 16-2011.

Not all drain covers require one of these marks, as the standard provides for a non-manufactured type of unblockable suction outlet called Field Fabricated Outlets. These are designed and certified by a Registered Design Professional (RDP) using conventional building materials, products, or custom fabrication (i.e., weldments). For any Field Fabricated Outlet, the RDP is the 3rd party certifier and VGB Act compliance is demonstrated through a written report that must be kept at the facility to show proof of full compliance.

Understanding the legal difference between between blockable and unblockable suction outlets is important for compliance, as blockable drains cannot be used alone. The difference is defined by the size of the sump, or opening, under/behind any drain cover. When used in new construction, both public and private, at least two are required; and existing single, blockable drain systems must be upgraded for VGB Act compliance. Several options are available: permanently disabling the single, blockable drain; adding a secondary system designed to prevent suction entrapment; or installing another suction outlet to convert the single suction outlet system into a multiple outlet system.

This important child safety law strives to:

- Enhance the safety of public and private pools and spas
- Reduce child drownings in pools and spas (each year nearly 300 children younger than five)
- Reduce the number of suction entrapment incidents, injuries and deaths
- Educate the public on the importance of

Photo C1-1: *Visit www.poolsafely.gov for the latest updates and resources on the Virginia Graeme Baker Pool and Spa Safety Act.*

© National Swimming Pool Foundation 2017

References

C-1 The Virginia Graeme Baker Pool & Spa Safety Act (Cont'd)

constant supervision of children in and around water

- Encourage the use of multiple safety steps at all pools and spas

In its role as the lead agency implementing and enforcing the VGB Act, the U.S. Consumer Product Safety Commission (CPSC) is working with the pool and spa safety community to encourage the use of multiple safety steps, such as fencing around pools, constant supervision of children and a requirement for the installation of anti-entrapment drain covers and other safety devices as needed, on all public pools and spas.

> ### Warning
> Under the law, all public pools and spas must have ANSI/APSP-16 or subsequent compliant suction fittings installed. No pool or spa is safe if a drain cover is broken, missing, or cracked, and the pool should be closed until repairs can be made.

The VGB Act mandated the following changes in federal pool and spa regulations for public pools and spa:

- All pool drain covers manufactured, distributed or entered into commerce on or after December 19, 2008, must meet the ANSI/APSP 16-2011 standard
- All public pools and spas must be equipped with new ANSI/APSP 16-2011 compliant drain covers, with flow rating higher than the circulation system flow rate; which must be installed in accordance with the manufacturer's installation instructions; and which must not be expired

It is common to use the terms drain, main drain, outlets, and drain covers interchangeably. One important cautionary note: the ANSI/APSP 16-2011 standard referenced by the VGB Act has a very specific definition of suction fittings. They are defined as all components, including minimum sump size, pipe attachment fitting, mounting frame, cover/grate, and mounting hardware. In most cases, swapping covers will not assure compliance with the VGB Act.

Additional Requirements for Safety Devices or Systems

The VGB Act requires all public pools and spas with a single main drain, or multiple drains less than three feet apart, to add one or more additional anti-entrapment devices or systems. The CPSC ruled in September 2011 that even unblockable covers/grates installed over blockable sumps must also have one of the following devices or systems:

1. **Safety vacuum release system (SVRS)**—a safety vacuum release system ceases operation of the pump, reverses the circulation flow or otherwise provides a vacuum release at a suction outlet when a blockage is detected. The SVRS must conform to the ANSI/PSPS/ICC-7-2013 or ASTM F2387 standard.

2. **Suction-limiting vent system**—a suction-limiting vent system with a tamper-resistant atmospheric opening, also called an atmospheric vent, is a pipe teed to the suction side of the circulation system on one end and open to the atmosphere on the opposite end. When a blockage occurs at the main drain, air is introduced into the suction line causing the pump to lose prime and relieving the suction forces at the main drain.

3. **Gravity drainage system**—a gravity drainage system uses a collector tank and has a separate water storage vessel from which the pool circulation pump draws water. Water moves from the pool to the collector

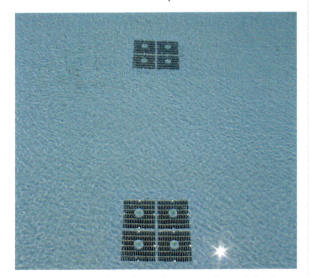

Photo C1-2: *Dual main drains more than 3 feet apart*

© National Swimming Pool Foundation 2017

tank depending on atmospheric pressure, gravity and the displacement of water by bathers, which removes the need for direct suction at the pool. This type of system is also referred to as a reservoir, surge tank or surge pit. Not all gravity drainage safety systems will serve as surge tanks. Some new systems are designed simply to eliminate direct suction.

4. **Automatic pump shut-off system**—an automatic pump shut-off system is a device that would sense a drain blockage and automatically shut off the pump system. There is no current standard for this category and the CPSC is requiring conformance to the ANSI/PSPS/ICC-7-2013 or ASTM F2387 standard.

5. **Drain disablement**—this is the only option that eliminates rather than mitigates the hazard. To satisfy the definition of drain disablement, the drain/outlet would need to be physically removed from the system by filling the sump with concrete, cutting and capping the piping in the equipment room or re-plumbing the suction line to create a return line and reverse flow.

6. **Other systems**—any other system that is determined by CPSC to be equally effective as, or better than, the safety systems listed here.

Note: States are permitted to limit these options or even specify which of the options are allowed as long as they do not make compliance with the act an impossibility.

Pools and spas that have more than one drain, or those with unblockable drains with covers that are properly sized for the maximum system flow rate and are installed in accordance with the manufacturer's instructions, do not need the additional measures or backup systems listed above.

Five Forms of Entrapment

The VGB Act is designed to reduce the risk of five forms of entrapment. The following entrapment categories are the result of analysis of all reported cases of entrapment to CPSC. It is important to note that not all entrapments are caused by suction. Excessive water flow through a cover (certified or not) can entangle and knot hair. Alternatively the entrapment can be the result of physically becoming stuck in an outlet or submerged pipe. In this case flow is not required, such as in the case of mechanical entrapment. The entrapment categories are:

1. **Body:** a body part, often the torso or bottom, covers a drain and is held down by the force of the suction
2. **Hair:** long hair is caught or entangled in a cover with excessive flow
3. **Limbs:** arms, legs, feet or fingers are lodged in a pipe, equalizer, vacuum port or uncovered sump
4. **Mechanical:** jewelry, bathing suits or other materials are entangled in a drain cover
5. **Evisceration/disembowelment:** when suction draws out the intestines and organs

Turnover and Flow Rates

To understand entrapment and ways in which it can be minimized, flow rates must be studied. Approved drain covers have specific flow rates that must not be exceeded. The current industry standards of a six hour turnover rate for public swimming pools are based on sequential dilution studies. A faster turnover rate results in a greater flow rate measured in gallons per minute (gpm). Other, non-circulation suction outlets (e.g. for spa therapy jets) must also be properly sized to handle the full flow rate of the attached pump.

Approved drain covers are rated in gallons per minute. Once the true flow rate of a pool system

RELATIONSHIP BETWEEN FLOW RATE AND TURNOVER RATE
Flow Rate
Pool volume ÷ turnover rate in hours ÷ 60 min/hr = flow rate in gpm
Turnover Rate
Pool volume ÷ flow rate ÷ 60 min/hr = turnover rate in hours

© National Swimming Pool Foundation 2017

is known, the drain cover can be properly sized. Flow rate can be determined by

- Flow meters installed on the return line back to the pool
- Total dynamic head measurement and pump curve

Flow Meters

Flow meters must be installed correctly and also be calibrated. Flow meters come in a variety of types, digital or analog. It can be a device mounted on return line back to the pool with a metered reading on the side of the flow meter. This type of flow meter should be properly sized for the design flow rate and must be capable of measuring from ½ to at least 1½ times the design flow rate. The clearances upstream and downstream from the flow meter must comply with the manufacturer's installation specifications. Pipe fittings, such as tees, elbows, etc., can interfere with flow and result in inaccurate flow measurements. Because of this, flow meter manufacturers specify the flow meter be installed with a minimum amount of straight pipe before and after the meter. Typically the requirement is ten times the pipe diameter of equivalent straight pipe before the flow meter and four or five times the pipe diameter of equivalent straight pipe after the flow meter. Some

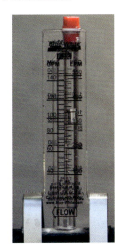

Photo C1-3: *Flow meters must be installed correctly and calibrated regularly.*

flow meters do not have these straight pipe requirements.

Health departments are accepting the use of magnetic flow meters to determine the maximum flow rate for the pumping system. With all circulation valves fully opened and with a clean filter, strainer and skimmer baskets, the maximum flow can be determined. If the maximum flow exceeds the flow rating on the drain cover, it may be possible to adjust valves that will limit flow through a pipe to a certain level. The flow rating of the cover must exceed the maximum achievable flow by the pump, as installed.

Total Dynamic Head

Total Dynamic Head (TDH) is a measure of a system's resistance to flow. Each pool will have its own unique flow rate based on the piping and fittings used. The same pump, on different pools, can produce significantly different flow rates. It is the resistance to flow in circulation systems that dictate the flow rate, not just the pump size. Particular caution should be used with pool codes that specify requirements in horse power ratings. Each circulation system is unique based on pipe length and diameter, number of fittings, filters, heaters, bypasses, and feeders. The resistance in the circulation system impacts the flow rate so measuring the TDH can prove valuable. The best time to measure the TDH is when the pool is filled with water and the filter media is clean.

Historically, TDH was used to properly size the circulation system's turnover. Many state health and building codes specify a TDH and the pump needs to meet turnover at that TDH. Today with the increased focus on energy efficiency, systems are being built with much lower TDH

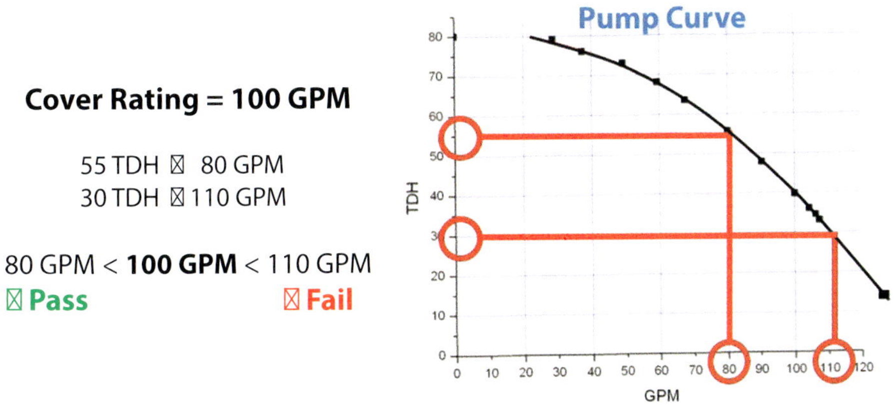

Cover Rating = 100 GPM

55 TDH ⊠ 80 GPM
30 TDH ⊠ 110 GPM

80 GPM < **100 GPM** < 110 GPM
⊠ **Pass**　　　　　⊠ **Fail**

Pump Curve

Illustration C1-1: *Hypothetical pump performance curve. For illustration purposes only.*

© National Swimming Pool Foundation 2017

(less resistance). Lower TDH (as built) would result in more flow than the specified higher number. For this reason, specified TDH should never be used to size suction outlet covers. TDH can be measured directly with a gauge or using the pressure and vacuum gauges on either side of the pump. The vacuum gauge is found on suction side of the pump and measures vacuum in **inches of mercury (in. Hg)**. The pressure gauge is found on the discharge side of the pump and is measured in **pounds per square inch (psi)**. Both of these measurements are converted to feet of head. Pressure head is calculated by multiplying psi by 2.31; pressure and vacuum head are calculated by multiplying Hg by 1.13. These two values are then added together to give total feet of head.

For example:

1. 21 psi X 2.31 = 48.5 feet of head
2. 6 Hg X 1.13 = 6.8 feet of head
3. Total TDH = 48.5 + 6.8 = 55 feet of head

The TDH value of 55 feet of head can now be used to determine flow rate. Feet of head can be converted to flow rate by going to the pump performance curve supplied by the manufacturer. As the resistance to flow increases, flow rate decreases.

Take your calculated TDH of 55 on the vertical scale of the graph and move horizontally across until it intersects with the pump curve. From there follow vertically down to the horizontal axis to determine the flow rate. In this example the flow rate is 80 gpm (see Illustration C1-1).

If the cover was rated at 100 GPM, then this flow rate of 80 GPM would be below the rating of the cover and compliant. If pressure was measured at 10 psi instead of 21 psi, this, for example, could be the difference between a clean and dirty filter. Now, when calculating TDH, using 10 psi in place of 21 psi, TDH has dropped to 30 feet of head. Using the same pump/pump curve, the flow rate is now 110 GPM and the cover would not be sufficiently rated. This example also serves to illustrate the difference between a health code specified TDH (55) and field verified TDH (30). Some newer systems can be even lower in measured TDH.

If flow rate is less than the flow rate specified on the suction drain cover, then the pool and cover would be in compliance with the VGB Act. However, if the measured TDH or flow rate gives you a higher flow rate than the cover specifies, then this would not be in compliance. In the design phase of a swimming pool the TDH estimated is based on pipe and fitting size and dimensions. The flow is typically underestimated so that you will still have enough flow to meet the desired turnover rate, which is typically six hours. If flow ends up being greater than desired, there is a faster turnover rate, or, the flow can be regulated by using the valves of the pool system. Because the design calculated TDH usually underestimates flow, it is not recommended that it be used to determine flow for cover sizing. The suction fitting should be sufficiently sized for the maximum flow rate and any valve position. Alternatively, a permanently installed flow restriction plate can be used to bring excessive flow into compliance with the installed suction fittings. The measured TDH, pump curve, and flow meter readings should all have comparable flow rates and should be used to size the drain cover.

Total Dynamic Head Measuring Meter

Gauges are now available on the market and can directly measure the pool or spa circulation system's exact TDH. Once the TDH is known, use the pump's performance curve to determine to flow rate.

VGB Act Compliance and Inspection

Compliance with the VGB Act, which references the ANSI/APSP 16-2011 standard, requires that suction fittings be tested and that they be installed in accordance to the standard, i.e. the manufacturer's instructions. The manufacturer's instructions should be retained per the ANSI/APSP 16-2011 standard.

Suction fitting labeling should include:
- Flow rate in gallons per minute (gpm)
- Lifespan or number of years
- Whether it is a wall and/or floor mount drain cover
- Whether it is designed to be used as a single or multiple drain cover

© National Swimming Pool Foundation 2017

C-1 The Virginia Graeme Baker Pool & Spa Safety Act (Cont'd)

- Manufacturer's name
- Model number
- The drain cover can be certified, in writing, by a registered design professional
- ANSI/APSP 16-2011 or VGB 2008 label (drain covers manufactured after November 12, 2008, must have the VGB 2008 marking)

Photo C1-4: *Example of compliant drain cover markings*

Proper installation: when inspecting any suction fittings, make sure they are installed correctly. This includes the drain covers (floor and wall), vacuum fittings, and skimmer equalizer line fittings. The CPSC has ruled that the skimmer equalizer lines, usually located beneath the skimmer openings, are submerged suction outlets and must be covered with covers or grates meeting ANSI/APSP 16-2011 standard.

Unblockable Drains

An unblockable drain includes a suction outlet defined as all components, including the sump and/or body, cover/grate, and hardware, such that its perforated (open) area cannot be shadowed by the area of the 18" x 23" Body Blocking Element of ANSI/APSP 16-2011 and that the rated flow through the remaining open area (beyond the shadowed portion) cannot create a suction force in excess of the removal force values in Table 1 of the ANSI/APSP 16-2011 standard.

A drain cover that is larger than 18"x 23" may be placed over a smaller sump to replace a smaller cover of a blockable size, if allowed by the manufacturer. This replacement cover must be compliant with the ANSI/APSP 16-2011 standard and must be secured as directed by the manufacturer.

All suction outlet covers, manufactured or field-fabricated, shall be certified as meeting the applicable requirements of the ANSI/APSP 16-2011 standard. The cover manufacturer should be consulted to confirm 3rd party certification to the VGB Act, and to determine the maximum flow rating and the product specific sump depth requirements. Placing an unblockable cover

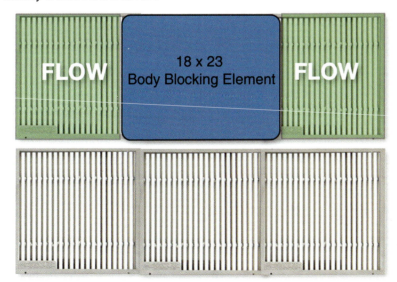

Illustration C1-2: *This photo shows an unblockable drain with and without an 18 x 23 body blocking element. Flow through the remaining open area (beyond the shadowed portion) cannot create a suction force in excess of the removal force values in Table 1 of the ANSI/APSP 16-2011 standard.*

© National Swimming Pool Foundation 2017

over a blockable size sump will not render it unblockable. Single main drains of a blockable size need to be equipped with one of the six anti-entrapment devices or systems.

Sumps

CPSC recognizes and supports the technical requirement of the ANSI/APSP 16-2011 standard, which requires manufacturers to specify the sump onto which the cover/grate is to be attached. When manufacturers do not specify the sump, they must specify depth, when measured from the bottom of the cover to the top of the outlet piping, of 1.5 times the diameter of the piping. While the VGB Act does not require pool owners to replace existing sumps, the cover/grate must be compatible, including size, attachment method, and depth.

It is important to have the manufacturer's instructions when conducting an inspection to ensure that the installation was carried out as per the instructions. Instructions should also be retained by the facility. The drain fasteners (screws) should be observed before each use of the facility. The inspector should also verify the separation between outermost drains in a multiple drain system to ensure they are at least three feet apart, center to center.

Retrofitting new covers on old sumps and frames that do not match means the facility is not in compliance. You must not drill new holes in the old frame to attach a new cover, unless it is part of a manufacturer's supplied kit. It may require that the old sump or mounting frame be removed and the new one for the new cover be cemented

> **Warning**
> Under the law, all public pools and spas must have ANSI/APSP 16-2011 or subsequent compliant drain covers installed. No pool or spa is safe if a drain cover is broken, missing, or cracked and should be closed until repairs can be made.

in place before the new cover can be installed. A proper inspection and installation requires verification of the cover, attachment hardware, and sump/frame.

When inspecting a pool that is filled with water it may be very difficult to see the drain to verify that the drain covers and sump are both compliant. It may also be difficult to see that the drain cover is secured in place with the recommended fasteners. This is especially the case in deep pools. Getting a close up view of the underwater suction outlet is ideal, which would eliminate any glare and reflections. Diving down to inspect the drain cover and sump is certainly an option, but be certain that the pump has been turned off before any underwater inspection begins. Alternately, a waterproof video camera attached to the end of a pole can be used to record the outlet and for later viewing.

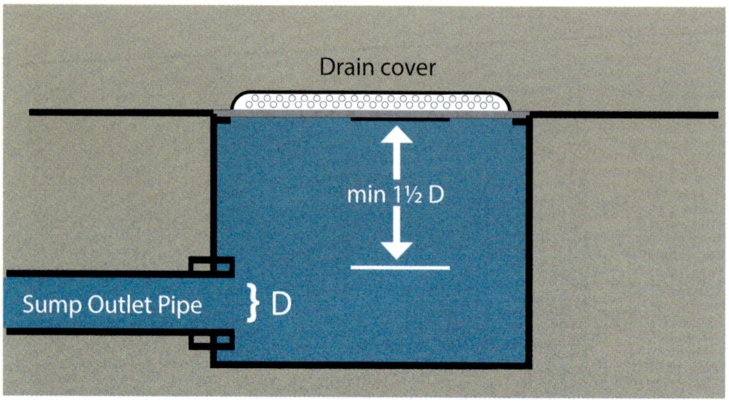

Enforcement of the VGB Act

The VGB Act also strengthened the CPSC's civil and criminal penalty authority, giving the agency the ability to shut down pools or spas that are not in compliance with the law. Visit www.poolsafely.gov/pool-spa-safety-act to download the entire Pool & Spa Safety Act.

Both CPSC and state attorneys general are empowered to enforce the VGB Act. The CPSC is looking to state health and building officials to assist in enforcing the VGB Act. State law can be more restrictive than the federal law as long as the state does not make compliance a physical impossibility.

Illustration C1-3: *Field-built sumps must have a depth, when measured from the bottom of the cover to the top of the outlet piping, a minimum of 1.5 times the diameter of the piping.*

© National Swimming Pool Foundation 2017

**Virginia Graeme Baker Pool and Spa Safety Act
Compliance Inspection Form**

PART I - Pool Management Information

INSPECTOR NAME		INSPECTION DATE
FACILITY NAME		POOL LICENSE / PERMIT NUMBER
ADDRESS	PHONE NUMBER	
CITY	STATE	ZIP CODE
CONTACT NAME	TITLE	
CONTACT ADDRESS		
CITY	STATE	ZIP CODE
EMAIL ADDRESS	FAX #	

PART II - POOL / SPA Information

POOL LOCATION	INDOOR	OUTDOOR	WATER PARK	OTHER
POOL TYPE	SWIMMING POOL	WADING POOL	SPA ☐ / HOT TUB ☐	OTHER
WATER FEATURES (If any)	SPRAY	SLIDE	HYDRO-JET	OTHER
VOLUME OF POOL (Gallons)	MFGR, MAKE, MODEL NUMBER, HORSE POWER OF PUMP			

PART III - Inspection Check List

DESCRIPTION	DATA	COMPLIANT	NON-COMPLIANT	COMMENTS
Determine if the pool has suction outlets (If it does not, the inspection is complete)				
Measured TDH:				
Drain sump measurements:				
Drain cover data: Check the manufacturer's instructions and certification paperwork; look for markings such as the standard, lifespan, flowrate, wall or floor mount, etc.				
If there are suction outlets, main drains, vacuum fittings, etc, determine the total flow rate generated by all pumps in the system				
Do the suction outlets need a secondary anti-entrapment device and is one present?				
If there are multiple floor drains, are they at least three feet apart, center to center? If not, is there a secondary anti-entrapment device or system?				

273

© National Swimming Pool Foundation 2017

PART III - Inspection Check List (Continued)

DESCRIPTION	DATA	COMPLIANT	NON-COMPLIANT	COMMENTS
Are the drain cover flow rate specifications equal to or greater than the flow rate of the system?				
Is the drain cover secure and attached to the sump according to the manufacturer's instructions?				
If there is a vacuum line present with a compliant cover, CPSC recommends that it be covered whenever the pool is in use.				
Do the skimmer equalizer fittings have compliant covers?				

PART IV - Comments

If pool is not in full compliance, provide a description of actions or steps needed to bring pool or spa into compliance with the Virginia Graeme Baker Pool and Spa Safety Act.

COMMENTS

_____

_____

_____

_____

_____

_____

_____

Inspector - Print Name	Inspector - Signature	Inspection Date

© National Swimming Pool Foundation 2017

C-2 Revised Americans with Disabilities Act Regulations

On Friday, July 23, 2010, new Americans with Disability (ADA) regulations were signed into law, including its ADA Standards for Accessible Design. The official text was published in the Federal Register on September 15, 2010. The revised regulations amend the Department's Title II regulation, 28 C.F.R. Part 35, and the Title III regulation, 28 C.F.R. Part 36. These final rules will take effect March 15, 2011. Compliance with the 2010 Standards for Accessible Design was permitted as of September 15, 2010, but not required until March 15, 2012.

Introduction

The Americans with Disabilities Act (ADA) is a comprehensive civil rights law that prohibits discrimination on the basis of disability. The ADA requires that local government facilities, places of public accommodation, and commercial facilities be readily accessible to, and usable by, individuals with disabilities. The ADA Accessibility Guidelines (ADAAG) is the standard applied to buildings and facilities. Recreational facilities, including swimming pools, wading pools, and spas, are among the facilities required to comply with the ADA.

The Access Board issued accessibility guidelines for newly constructed and altered recreation facilities in 2003. These recreation facility guidelines are now a component of the revised ADA Regulaltions. All recreation facilities, including swimming pools, covered by the ADA were required to comply with these guidelines by March 15, 2012. To view the ADA Accessibility Guidelines, visit https://www.access-board.gov/guidelines-and-standards/buildings-and-sites/about-the-ada-standards/background/adaag#15.8.

Summary of Swimming Pool and Spa Changes

ADA Standards Chapter 2, Section 242: Swimming Pools, Wading Pools, and Spas

242.1 General. Swimming pools, wading pools, and spas shall comply with 242.

242.2 Swimming Pools. At least two accessible means of entry shall be provided for swimming pools. Accessible means of entry shall be swimming pool lifts complying with 1009.2; sloped entries complying with 1009.3; transfer walls complying with 1009.4; transfer systems complying with 1009.5; and pool stairs complying with 1009.6. At least one accessible means of entry provided shall comply with 1009.2 or 1009.3.

Photo C2-1: *A swimming pool with two accesible points of entry.*

EXCEPTIONS:

1. Where a swimming pool has less than 300 linear feet (91 m) of swimming pool wall, no more than one accessible means of entry shall be required provided that the accessible means of entry is a swimming pool lift complying with 1009.2 or sloped entry complying with 1009.3.

2. Wave action pools, leisure rivers, sand bottom pools, and other pools where user access is limited to one area shall not be required to provide more than one accessible means of entry provided that the accessible means of entry is a swimming pool lift complying with 1009.2, a sloped entry complying with 1009.3, or a transfer system complying with 1009.5.

3. Catch pools shall not be required to provide an accessible means of entry provided that the catch pool edge is on an accessible route.

Advisory 242.2 Swimming Pools. Where more than one means of access is provided into the water, it is recommended that the means be different. Providing different means of access will better serve the varying needs of people with disabilities in getting into and out of a swimming pool. It is also recommended that where two or more means of access are provided, they not be provided in the same location in the pool. Different locations will provide increased options for entry and exit, especially in larger pools.

Advisory 242.2 Swimming Pools Exception Pool walls at diving areas and areas along pool walls where there is no pool entry because of landscaping or adjacent structures are to be counted when determining the number of accessible means of entry required.

242.3 Wading Pools. At least one accessible means of entry shall be provided for wading pools. Accessible means of entry shall comply with sloped entries complying with 1009.3.

Note: The ADAAG states that a wading pool is a pool designed for shallow depth and is used for wading. Each wading pool must provide at least one sloped entry into the deepest part. Other forms of entry may be provided as long as a sloped entry is provided. The sloped entries for wading pools are not required to have handrails.

242.4 Spas. At least one accessible means of entry shall be provided for spas. Accessible means of entry shall comply with swimming

Photo C2-2. *Each wading pool must provide at least one sloped entry into the deepest part.*

© National Swimming Pool Foundation 2017

pool lifts complying with 1009.2; transfer walls complying with 1009.4; or transfer systems complying with 1009.5.

EXCEPTION: Where spas are provided in a cluster, no more than 5%, but no fewer than one, spa in each cluster shall be required to comply with 242.4.

Where provided, pool lifts, sloped entries, transfer walls, transfer systems, and pool stairs shall comply with 1009.

To view the ADA Standards, visit https://www.access-board.gov/attachments/ article/983/ADAstandards.pdf.

Who is Affected by the ADA Law?

Entities affected by the revised regulations generally fall under either Title II or Title III of the Act. Title II outlines regulations for any public entity. A public entity is any activity, service, program or facility owned by any governmental agency. Title III regulates places of public accommodation, commercial facilities, and private companies that offer courses and examinations related to educational and occupational certification.

The ADA does not affect any type of residential dwelling, such as a private residence, an apartment complex, a condominium, or a home owner's association. However, if any of these residential facilities operate an element of public accommodation within their premises, these elements would be subject to ADA regulations.

Here are some examples of situations where a residential entity would fall under ADA regulations with respect to swimming pools:

- A private residential apartment complex sells memberships to their swimming facilities. This situation would be considered providing a public accommodation.
- A Home Owner's Association pool is used for swimming competitions that are open to competitors from outside the association. This situation would also be considered offering a public accommodation.
- A condominium actively rents out their units when owners are absent, including advertising, taking reservations over the phone, and providing either meals or housekeeping services. In this instance, the condominium would be considered a hotel.

- A vacation timeshare that operates as a hotel. This facility would be considered a hotel.

If any residential entity strictly limits use of their facilities to residents and their guests, they would not be subject to ADA regulations. Although residential facilities are not required to comply with ADA regulations for swimming pools, they must comply with the Fair Housing Act. Under this legislation, a privately owned residential community must provide a barrier free pathway up to the edge of a pool. In addition, they cannot prevent a resident from using their own apparatus to gain access to the pool, providing it does not provide a hazard for other residents. In other words, if a resident has a portable pool lift and keeps it in storage when not in use, the facility cannot prevent that resident from using the lift to gain access to the pool.

Private clubs are also excluded from ADA regulations in some cases. Final determination would be based on the control of operations, membership requirements, and the amount of fees involved. Operations that have limited or no membership requirements and minimal dues charges do not fall under the private club exclusion. If a private club limits use of their facilities strictly to members and their guests, then the club would not be subject to ADA regulations. However, if that club hosts swimming competitions or any other type of activity that opens the pool to nonmembers, the club would be required to follow ADA regulations for their pool.

For more information visit http://www.ada.gov. For additional information or to order copies of any documents, call the ADA Information Line (800) 514-0301 (voice) or (800) 514-0383 (TTY).

For technical assistance on the guidelines for swimming pools, wading pools, and spas is available from the Access Board at (800) 872-2253 (voice), (800) 993-2822 (TTY) or email ta@access-board.gov

C-3 Model Aquatic Health Code Summary

The The Centers for Disease Control and Prevention (CDC) works with public health, academia, and aquatics industry representatives across the United States on guidance to prevent drowning, injuries, and the spread of recreational water illnesses at public swimming pools and spas. The MAHC 1st Edition Code and Annex were posted in 2014, followed by the 2nd Edition in 2016.

The Model Aquatic Health Code (MAHC) is voluntary guidance based on science and best practices that can help local and state authorities make swimming and other water activities healthier and safer. The MAHC serves as a voluntary model and guide for local and state agencies needing to update or implement swimming pool and spa code, rules, regulations, guidance, law, or standards governing the design, construction, operation, and maintenance of public swimming pools, spas, hot tubs, and other disinfected aquatic facilities.

Background

In the United States, there is no federal regulatory authority responsible for public disinfected aquatic facilities like pools, waterparks, and spas. As a result, the health and safety at public disinfected aquatic facilities is regulated by state and local jurisdictions. About 68% of local health departments have public pool inspection programs. All public pool codes are developed, reviewed, and approved by state and/or local public health officials or legislatures. Consequently, there is no uniform national guidance informing the design, construction, operation, and maintenance of public swimming pools and other disinfected aquatic facilities. As a result, the code requirements for preventing and responding to recreational water illnesses (RWIs), drowning, and injuries can vary significantly among local and state agencies. State and local jurisdictions spend a great deal of time, personnel, and resources creating and updating their individual codes on a periodic basis.

The effort to create the MAHC stems from a CDC-sponsored national workshop called "Recreational Water Illness Prevention at Disinfected Swimming Venues" that was convened on February 15-17, 2005, in Atlanta, Georgia. The workshop assembled persons from different disciplines working in state, local, and federal public health agencies, the aquatics industry, and academia to discuss ways to minimize the spread of recreational water illnesses at disinfected swimming venues. The major recommendation from this workshop was that CDC lead a national partnership to create an open-access model guidance document that helps local and state agencies incorporate science-based practices into their swimming pool codes and programs without having to reinvent the wheel each time they create or revise their pool codes. The attendees also recommended that this effort be all-encompassing so that it covered the spread of illness but also included drowning and injury prevention. Such an effort was intended to increase the evidence base for aquatic facility design, construction, and operation while reducing the time, personnel, and resources needed to create or improve pool codes across the country.

Beginning in 2007, CDC worked with public health, industry, and academic representatives from across the United States to create this guidance document called the Model Aquatic Health Code (MAHC). Although, the initial workshop was responding to the significant increases in disease outbreaks at swimming pools, the MAHC is a complete aquatic facility guidance document developed with the goal of reducing the spread of disease and occurrence of drowning and injuries at public disinfected aquatic facilities.

MAHC Vision, Mission, and Anticipated Health Outcomes

The Model Aquatic Health Code's (MAHC) vision is "Healthy and Safe Aquatic Experiences for Everyone." The MAHC's mission is to provide guidance on how state and local officials can transform a typical health department pool program into a data-driven, knowledge-based, risk reduction effort to prevent disease and injuries and promote healthy recreational water experiences. The MAHC provides local and state agencies with uniform guidelines and wording covering design and construction, operation and maintenance, and policies and management

© National Swimming Pool Foundation 2017

C-3 Model Aquatic Health Code Summary (Cont'd)

of swimming pools and other public disinfected aquatic facilities. The availability of the MAHC provides state and local agencies with the best available guidance for protecting public health so they can use it to create or update their swimming pool codes while conserving valuable time and resources previously used to write or update code language. The guidance will be regularly updated using input from a national stakeholder partnership called the **Council for the Model Aquatic Health Code (CMAHC)** to keep the MAHC up to date and current with the latest advances in the aquatics industry while also responding to public health reports of disease and injury.

Short-term Outcomes: use of the MAHC should help reduce the risk of diseases and injuries and promote healthy and safe swimming. It is anticipated that the practices promoted in the MAHC will initially lead to the following system improvements:

- Fewer pool and facility closures
- More-meaningful inspection and tracking/ surveillance data
- An established research agenda to drive future iterations of the MAHC
- Enhanced collaboration among stakeholders

Long-term Outcomes: by adopting the practices outlined in the MAHC, jurisdictions should also be able to improve the long-term health and safety of aquatic facilities. This should include a reduced risk of the following:

- Outbreaks of waterborne illnesses
- Drowning incidents
- Injuries from pool chemicals and disinfection by-products
- Swimming-related emergency department visits
- Redundant spending on separately updating numerous codes in various jurisdictions

CDC is developing systems to track the impact and potential health improvements related to this national public health effort.

NSPF encourages public pool facilities to become members of the Council for the Model Aquatic Health Code, to engage in Model Aquatic Health Code updates, and to adopt Model Aquatic Health Code language. Attending the World Aquatic Health™ Conference will keep

facility operators informed of scientific advances related to the Model Aquatic Health Code and further information can be found at http://www.cdc.gov/mahc/index.html.

279

© National Swimming Pool Foundation 2017

C-4 Float Tanks

While there are many similarities between pool/spa operation and float tank operation, differences must be kept in mind in order to run a float tank safely and effectively.

Float Tank Equipment

Components used on float tanks are chosen to accommodate the high quantity of Epsom salt (usually about 800-1200 lbs) that is present in the water. The entire float system needs to be able to withstand this saline solution. As a result, metals are rarely used in a float system, with the exception of metals such as titanium and high-grade stainless steel.

Magnetically Driven Pumps

A float tank's filtration system commonly uses a magnetically driven pump, since salt crystallizes on the seals of traditional mechanically driven pumps. A magnetically driven pump is seal-less, relying on a magnet connected to the motor that spins another magnet connected to the impeller.

Cartridge and Bag Filters

Most float tanks are self-contained systems in regard to their plumbing; they do not plumb into the building. As a result, a filter that requires backwashing is not often seen on a float tank. The most commonly used filter is a cartridge filter, but some float tanks use a bag filter instead.

Float Tank Disinfection

Because of the way commercial float centers are operated, the level of contaminants that is introduced into a float tank differs from pools and spas in the following ways:

- Risk of cross-contamination is greatly reduced, since most float tanks are single user, with a filtration cycle between each user
- Users shower both before and after using the float tank
- Users float without a bathing suit, so much of the dirt and bacteria that are harbored in a suit are eliminated
- Users produce much less sweat than in a swimming pool, since floating requires no vigorous movement and the water is maintained at skin-temperature

- Children rarely use float tanks; children are ordinarily some of the highest contributors to bacteria in pools and spas
- Users float with their mouth, nose, and eyes above the water; this leads to much lower ingestion of the solution than is typical of pool/spa users

High Salt Effect

The amount of Epsom salt (25% or 250,000ppm) in a float tank can have an impact on how well certain bacteria can survive. A study done through NSF International shows that *Pseudomonas aeruginosa* placed in an Epsom salt solution with no additional chemicals or disinfectants added had a 5.54 $\log_{10}$ reduction after 24 hours, while the same dose of *Pseudomonas aeruginosa* in a control sample of distilled water showed a 0.96 $\log_{10}$ growth. Use of disinfectant is necessary in a float tank, however, as Epsom salt is not able to achieve a 3 $\log_{10}$ reduction in the 15–30 minute duration that most float centers schedule between users.

Types of Disinfectants Used

Due to the low level of airflow in float tank environments, leading to potentially high levels of disinfectant by-products, most commercial float centers avoid using chlorine or bromine as disinfectants. Float centers more commonly prefer a Hydrogen Peroxide / UV system or an Ozone / UV system.

Float Tank Water Testing

Testing float tank water proves challenging, as many test kits and devices that are designed for pool and spa water encounter interference with the high levels of Epsom salt. It is not certain whether most pH testers give accurate results in the float water, and very unlikely that most pool alkalinity test kits give accurate readings. Total Hardness tests reveal high levels of magnesium, ORP meters often give unpredictable readings, and even flow meters are generally calibrated for the density of regular water. In addition to the interference, many test kits that involve electronics are susceptible to damage from the high levels of salt.

© National Swimming Pool Foundation 2017

C-4 Float Tanks (Cont'd)

Float Tank Operation

Day to day operational considerations of running a commercial float tank are as follows:

Non-continuous filtration

In order to achieve the quiet and stillness that is essential to the float experience, the pump is not run while a user is in the float tank. Instead, the filtration system is turned on in between users, achieving 3–5 turnovers in the 15–30 minutes generally allotted between float sessions.

Cost of solution

Because of the high volume of Epsom salt in the water, the cost of the float tank solution is considerably higher than that of pool water. This can make chemistry-correcting methods such as draining and refilling much more cost-prohibitive.

Saltproofing

Salt in the float solution can be extremely corrosive and detrimental to the float tank surroundings and facility, often requiring the use of very specific construction materials to protect against salt damage.

Soundproofing

Careful consideration is taken to prohibit noise entering the float tank. Without adequate soundproofing, scheduling of activities in the vicinity of the float tank becomes important.

Float Tank Regulation

Lack of data surrounding float tank operation, and the differences between pool/spa and float tank operation, cause regulations to vary significantly. Some health departments may decide to leave float tanks unregulated, while others subscribe float tanks to pool/spa code, usually with a great number of variances. Some jurisdictions have created float tank-specific code. Operators should regularly reference jurisdictional codes, as float tank regulations are developing and changing very quickly.

© National Swimming Pool Foundation 2017

C-5 Listing of Pool Industry Regulations & Standards

Below is a listing of pool & spa industry regulations and standards that were mentioned in this handbook with the web address for the agency or organization responsible.

Federal and State Regulation Setting Agencies

California Energy Commission
www.energy.ca.gov
- Title 20 California Code of Regulations and Rules of Practice and Procedure Relating to Power Plant Site Certification

Centers for Disease Control and Prevention (CDC)*
www.cdc.gov
- Model Aquatic Health Code www.cmahc.org
- National Center for Environmental Health, Vessel Sanitation Program Operations Manual, 2000

Consumer Product Safety Commission (CPSC)
www.cpsc.gov
- HR6-303 to 309 Title XIV Pool and Spa Safety-Virginia Graeme Baker Pool and Spa Safety Act (VGB Act)
- Safety Barrier Guidelines for Home Pools (Publication 362)
- Guidelines for Entrapment Hazards
- An Evaluation of Swimming Pool Alarms

Department of Justice
www.justice.gov
- Americans with Disabilities Act (ADA)
- 36 CFR Part 1191 Americans With Disabilities Act (ADA) Accessibility Guidelines For Buildings And Facilities; Architectural Barriers Act (ABA) Accessibility Guidelines

Environmental Protection Agency (EPA)
www.epa.gov
- Federal Insecticide, Fungicide, Rodenticide Act (FIFRA)
- Emergency Planning & Community Right-to-Know Act (EPCRA)
- Superfund Amendments and Reauthorization Act of 1986 (SARA) (SARA Title III)
- Food Quality Protection Act of 1996 (FQPA)

Occupational Safety & Health Administration (OSHA)
www.osha.gov
- Hazard Communication Standard (HCS)
- 29 CFR 1910.134 Respiratory Protection
- OSHA Regulation 29 CFR 1910.147 The Control of Hazardous Energy

The CDC, although a government agency, is not a regulatory agency, but rather sets standards.

© National Swimming Pool Foundation 2017

References

Standard Setting Agencies

American National Standards Institute (ANSI)
www.ansi.org
- ANSI/NSF Standard 14: Plastics Piping Components and Related Materials
- ANSI Z535: Safety Alerting Standards
- ANSI Standard 2223.1: National Fuel Gas Code

American Society of Heating, Refrigerating and Air-Conditioning Engineers (ASHRAE)
www.ashrae.org
- ANSI/ASHRAE Standard 62.1-2007: Ventilation for Acceptable Indoor Air Quality
- ASHRAE Standard 55-1992: Thermal Environmental Conditions for Human Occupancy

American Society of Mechanical Engineers (ASME)
www.asme.org
- ASME/ANSI Standard A112.19.8M Suction Fittings for Use in Swimming Pools and Wading Pools, Spas, Hot Tubs and Whirlpool Bathtub Appliances
- ASME/ANSI A112.199.17-2002 Safety Vacuum Release Systems for Swimming Pool SuctionFittings and Drains

Association of Pool and Spa Professionals (APSP)
www.apsp.org
- ANSI/APSP-16 2011 Suction Fittings for Use in Swimming Pools, Wading Pools, Spas, and Hot Tubs

ASTM International (ASTM)
www.astm.org
- F2049-03 Standard Guide for Fences/Barriers for Public, Commercial, and Multi-Family Residential Use Outdoor Play Areas
- F2409-10 Standard Guide for Fences for Non-Residential Outdoor Swimming Pools, Hot Tubs, and Spas
- F1346-91 (2003) Standard Performance Specification for Safety Covers and Labeling Requirements for All Covers for Swimming Pools, Spas and Hot Tubs
- F2518-06 Standard Guide for Use of a Residential Swimming Pool, Spa, and Hot Tub Safety Audit to Prevent Unintentional Drowning
- F2208-08 Standard Safety Specification for Residential Pool Alarms
- F2387-04 Standard Specification for Manufactured Safety Vacuum Release Systems (SVRS) for Swimming Pools, Spas and Hot Tubs
- F2461-09 Standard Practice for Manufacture, Construction, Operation, and Maintenance of Aquatic Play Equipment

Chlorine Institute
www.chlorineinstitute.org
- Pamphlet 1 The Chlorine Manual
- Pamphlet 63 First Aid and Medical Management of Chlorine Exposures
- Pamphlet 82 Recommendations for Using 100 and 150-Pound Chlorine Cylinders at Swimming Pools
- Pamphlet 96 Sodium Hypochlorite Manual

International Code Council (ICC)
www.iccsafe.org
- International Swimming Pool & Spa Code (ISPSC)

National Fire Protection Association (NFPA)
www.nfpa.org
- NFPA 400 Hazardous Materials Code
- NFPA 704 Standard System For The Identification Of The Hazards Of Materials For Emergency Response
- NFPA 70 National Electrical Code (NEC)
- NFPA 780 Standard for the Installation of Lightning Protection Systems

© National Swimming Pool Foundation 2017

NSF International (NSF)
www.nsf.org

- NSF/ANSI Standard 50 Equipment for Swimming Pools, Spas, Hot Tubs, and Other Recreational Water Facilities (2010)

World Health Organization (WHO)
www.who.int

- Guidelines for Safe Recreational Waters Volume 2 Swimming Pools and Similar Recreational Water Environments

© National Swimming Pool Foundation 2017

Reference:
Glossary

Acid - A chemical compound that lowers pH by contributing hydrogen ions to a water solution. The opposite of a base.

Acid Demand - The amount of acid needed to bring the water pH to a specific level.

Aggressive Water - Water with corrosive properties due to low pH, calcium hardness, and/or total alkalinity.

Algae - A general class of microscopic plant life that includes many species. It enters water by rain, wind, dust, storms, or tap water. Some float freely in the water; others grow on surfaces.

Algicide (a.k.a. Algaecide) **-** Any chemical that kills algae.

Algaestat - A chemical that inhibits the growth of algae.

Alkali - See Base.

Alkalinity - See Total Alkalinity.

Alum - See Aluminum Sulfate.

Aluminum Sulfate (a.k.a. Alum) ($Al_2SO_4 \cdot 18 H_2O$) - A white solid chemical that brings together fine particles in water to form larger particles that can be filtered (Flocculant).

Ammonium Hydroxide (NH_4OH) **-** An ammonia and water mixture used for detecting chlorine gas leaks.

Ammonia (NH_3) **-** A chemical compound of hydrogen and nitrogen that combines with free chlorine in pools to form inorganic chloramines (Combined Chlorine).

Amperometric Probe - An electrode that measures changes in current within the probe due to changes in concentrations of specific chemicals in water.

Anion - An ion that has a negative charge.

Atom - The smallest particle into which matter can be broken by ordinary means. Atoms combine with other atoms to form molecules or chemical compounds.

Automatic Feeders - A chemical feeder that has valves controlled by electronic equipment to deliver needed chemicals. The electronic device (controller) receives signals from electrodes (probes) that monitor the water's properties.

Available Chlorine Content - The relative strength of a chlorine-releasing chemical compared to elemental chlorine gas (Cl_2), which is arbitrarily assigned an available chlorine content of 100%.

Backwash - The process of cleaning a swimming pool filter by reversing the flow of water through the filter.

Backwash Rate - The rate of flow required for efficient filter cleaning. Typically measured as the volume of water (gallons or liters) per minute per filter surface area.

Bacteria - Single-celled microorganisms that lack chlorophyll and reproduce by fission. They play many important positive roles in human life, but some are also pathogenic (disease causing).

Bactericide - Any chemical that kills bacteria.

Balanced Water - The correct ratio of hardness, alkalinity, temperature, dissolved solids, and pH that prevents pool water from being either corrosive or scale forming.

Barrier - A device or system of devices that control access to a pool, spa, or other recreational water. Barriers may include fencing or walls, pool or spa covers, surrounding buildings, etc.

Base (a.k.a. Alkaline) **-** A chemical that neutralizes acids, usually by furnishing hydroxyl ions (OH-). The opposite of an acid.

Base Demand - The amount of alkaline material needed to achieve a specific pH level.

Bather Load - See User Load.

Bicarbonate Alkalinity - That portion of the total alkalinity composed of bicarbonate (HCO_3^-) and carbonate (CO_3^{2-}).

Bleach - see Sodium Hypochlorite.

Bluestone - see Copper Sulfate.

© National Swimming Pool Foundation 2017

Body Coat - A layer of filter medium like diatomaceous earth or another material on a filter element.

Body Feed (a.k.a. Slurry Feed) - Diatomaceous earth fed constantly or intermittently during a filter run to produce a layer of material over the filter elements.

Borax ($Na_2B_4O_7 \cdot 5H_2O$) - A naturally occurring mineral in the form of a white powder that is used to soften water, add buffering capacity, or inhibit the growth of algae.

Breakpoint Chlorination - Elimination of inorganic chloramines by adding enough Free Chlorine to destroy the inorganic chloramines that contribute to combined chlorine. Ten times the Combined Chlorine minus the existing Free Chlorine is used.

Bridging - An excessive buildup of a body coat on diatomaceous earth filter elements to the point where the body coats of two adjacent elements touch.

Broadcasting - A method of distributing chemicals broadly over a water surface.

Bromide (Br-) - A salt that contains the bromide anion.

Bromine (a.k.a. 1-bromo-3-chloro-5,5-dimethylhydantoin or BCDMH; 1,3-dibromo-5,5-dimethylhydantoin or DBDMH; bromide/oxidizer) - A generic term used to describe any chemical that releases hypobromous acid when dissolved in water. Elemental bromine (Br_2), a brown liquid, is no longer used to treat recreational water.

Bromine Feeder - A chemical feeder designed specifically to dissolve chemicals that release hypobromous acid into water.

1-Bromo-3-chloro-5,5-dimethylhydantoin (a.k.a. BCDMH) - See Bromine.

Buffer - A mixture of chemicals added to water that causes the solution to resist pH change. The amount of buffer in the water is measured by the total alkalinity.

Calcification - Formation of calcium carbonate scale on pool walls or the surface of circulation system components due to the precipitation of calcium carbonate.

Calcium Carbonate ($CaCO_3$) (a.k.a. Scale) - A water-insoluble white solid that is the major component of scale.

Calcium Chloride ($CaCl_2$) - A soluble white salt used to raise the calcium hardness level.

Calcium Hardness - The calcium portion of the total hardness. The level of calcium determines whether water is overly soft (too little) or hard (too much). Excessively high hardness levels may cause cloudy water and scale. Excessively low levels may harm the pool.

Calcium Hypochlorite ($Ca(OCl)_2$) (a.k.a. Cal Hypo) - A white solid disinfectant and oxidizer that releases chlorine (Hypochlorous Acid) when dissolved in water. It is available as granules, briquettes, and tablets. It contains from 65-78% available chlorine content in the industrial grade, or less in formulated products.

Calibration - the process of checking or adjusting (by comparison with a standard) the accuracy of a measuring instrument.

Carbon Dioxide (CO_2) - A gas that is used to lower pH in water.

Cation - An ion with a positive charge.

Cartridge Filter - A filter that uses a replaceable and disposable porous element as the filter medium.

Caustic Soda - See Sodium Hydroxide.

Cavitation - Formation of partial vacuums when the pump volume exceeds the water supply.

Centrifugal Force - The outward force exhibited by anything in circular motion. The principle by which water is propelled through a circulation system by a pump impeller.

Certified Pool/Spa Operator® (a.k.a. CPO®) Certification - A certification for an individual who has satisfied the classwork requirements and demonstrated knowledge of course material by passing the examination administered by National Swimming Pool Foundation® certified instructors.

Channeling - The creation of paths through a sand media bed caused by water hardness or organic load. This allows water to bypass the filter medium and not remove solids from the water.

Check Valve - A device that limits flow in a pipe to a single direction.

Chelating Agent (a.k.a. Sequestering Agent or Complexing Agent) - An organic chemical that forms more than one bond to metal ions in solution, forming complexes that have different properties than the metal ion.

© National Swimming Pool Foundation 2017

Chemical Feeder - A device that dispenses chemicals into water at a predictable rate. May be controlled automatically or manually.

Chloramines (a.k.a. Combined Chlorine) - The chemical species that forms when chlorine chemically bonds to ammonia from urine and perspiration, chloramine-treated potable fill water, and fertilizers. Chloramines can irritate the eyes and skin of users. They have a strong chlorine-like odor.

Chlorinator - Any chemical feeder used to dispense any form of chlorine; often used conversationally to refer specifically to gas chlorinators.

Chlorine (Cl_2) - A heavy, green, highly poisonous gas compressed in liquid form and stored in heavy steel tanks. Used in swimming pools as a disinfectant and algicide. Extreme caution must be used in handling.

Chlorine Demand - The amount of free chlorine that is consumed by the contaminants that are readily oxidized by chlorine.

Chlorine Generator - A device that uses electrolysis to convert sodium chloride (salt) or sodium bromide into free chlorine or total bromine.

Chlorine Residual - See Residual.

Circulation - The flow or movement of water through a given area or volume including the pool or spa vessel and through the pump, filter, heaters, feeders, and any other system components.

Clarifier - A chemical that causes small particles to combine into larger particles that can be removed by a filter.

Clarity - The degree of transparency of pool water. Characterized by the ease with which an object can be seen through a given depth of water or by use of a turbidity meter.

Coagulation (a.k.a. Flocculation) - The process of separating or precipitating solids suspended in a liquid as a result of the particle's growth.

Coliform Bacteria - A family of bacteria common in soils, plants, and animals. The coliform family is made up of several groups, one of which is the fecal coliform group found in the intestinal tracts of warm-blooded animals including humans. May cause gastroenteritis in humans.

Combined Chlorine (a.k.a. Combined Available Chlorine or Chloramine) - The chemical species that forms when chlorine chemically bonds to nitrogen-containing compounds like urine, perspiration, dead algae, etc. Combined chlorine can cause eye and skin irritation and has a strong chlorine-like odor.

Contaminant (a.k.a. Impurity) - A substance that makes another substance impure.

Coping - The deck edge around a pool or spa water surface.

Copper Sulfate ($CuSO_4$) (a.k.a. Blue Stone or Cupric Sulfate) - A blue water-soluble solid used on its own or in formulated products to kill algae.

Corona Discharge - A discharge of electricity that creates a bluish glow adjacent to a conductor when the voltage gradient exceeds a certain critical value. A method used to generate ozone.

Corrosion - A state of deterioration in metals or pool surfaces caused by oxidation or chemical action.

Cove - The curved transition from wall to floor in a pool or spa.

Cross Connection - An unprotected connection between a domestic water supply and a pool or other non-potable water where a contamination of the domestic system could occur. Protective devices must be used to eliminate possible contamination.

Cyanuric Acid ($C_3N_3O_3H_3$) (a.k.a. Stabilizer, Conditioner, or 2,4,6-trihydroxy-s-triazine) - A white, granular solid chemical that reduces the loss of chlorine due to the ultraviolet rays from sunlight.

Deck - The area immediately surrounding or next to a pool or spa, giving users room for sitting, standing, or accessing the water.

Degreaser - A product designed to remove grease from filters.

Defoamer - A product designed to remove foam from pool and spa water typically containing silicone emulsions.

Dermal - Skin

Design Rate of Flow - The average rate of flow used for design calculations in a system.

Diaphragm Pump - A positive displacement metering pump in which a diaphragm isolates the operating parts of the pump from the liquid. Used in conjunction with one-way suction and discharge check valves to provide a constant and adjustable feed rate regardless

© National Swimming Pool Foundation 2017

of varying injection pressures, flow rates, and liquid levels.

Diatomaceous Earth (D.E.) **-** A white powder composed of fossilized skeletons containing microscopic pores from one-celled organisms called diatoms. Used as a replaceable filter medium for D.E. swimming pool filters.

Diatomaceous Earth Filter (a.k.a. D.E. Filter) **-** A filter designed to use diatomaceous earth, cellulose fiber, volcanic ash, or other such specially formulated filter medium on a filter element. May be either a pressure or a vacuum type.

Dichlor - see sodium Dichloro-s-triazinetrione.

Diethyl-p-phenylenediamine (DPD) **-** A reagent used in test kits or strips to measure and indicate either total or free available chlorine. The presence of chlorine turns the reagent pink.

Dilution - Process of reducing the concentration of a substance or chemical in solution, usually simply by mixing with more water.

Disinfectant (a.k.a. Sanitizer) **-** An agent that destroys microorganisms that might carry disease.

Disinfection (a.k.a. Sanitization) **-** The process of destroying microorganisms that might cause disease.

Dry Acid - See Sodium Bisulfate.

Dry Feeder - A device consisting of a small, electrically operated, revolving auger in the bottom of a hopper that feeds solids into water.

Effluent - The outflow of water from a filter, pump, or pool.

Electrode (a.k.a. Probe) **-** A device placed in a liquid or mounted in a liquid stream that measures specific water properties based on conductance of electricity within the device. Usually linked to an automatic controller.

Electrolysis - A method by which chemical reactions are carried out by passing an electrical current through a substance. Examples include chlorine generation or ionizers.

Emissivity - The relative ability of a surface to emit radiant energy.

Enzyme - Proteins that are produced by living cells that catalyze (cause) chemical reactions to take place without the enzyme itself being altered or destroyed.

Equalizer Line - A flow line from below the pool surface to the body of a skimmer, designed to prevent air being drawn into the filter when the water level drops below the skimmer inlet.

Erosion - The process of wearing away a solid substance by running water.

Erosion Feeder - A chemical feed device in which powder, tablets, sticks, or briquettes are placed in a container and through which a water stream is passed, eroding and dissolving the chemical.

Feet of Head - A basic measurement of pressure or resistance in a hydraulic system that is equivalent to the height of a column of water that would cause the same resistance. The dynamic head is the sum of all the resistance in a complete system when in operation. The principle factors of head are vertical distances and resistance due to friction of the flow against the walls of the pipe, fittings, or vessel.

Ferric Iron (a.k.a. Fe_3+ or Fe(III)) **-** A brown water-insoluble iron ion precipitate.

Ferrous Iron (a.k.a. Fe_2+ or Fe(II)) **-** A green water-soluble iron ion. When exposed to an oxidizer, it will convert to ferric ion, which can precipitate from water.

Filter - A mechanical device for separating suspended particles from water. Refers to the complete mechanism including all component parts.

Filter Cartridge - A disposable element, usually of fibrous material, used as a filter septum in some pool filters. May filter dirt from the water at the cartridge surface or allow penetration of smaller suspended particles within the matrix of fibers.

Filter Cycle (a.k.a. Filter Run Time) **-** The amount of time of filter operation between backwash and cleaning procedures.

Filter Element - A filter cartridge, or that part of a D.E filter on which the filter aid is deposited.

Filter Medium - The portion of the filter that performs the separation of solids from liquid including sand, cartridge, or diatomaceous earth.

Filter Media Rate - The rate of flow of water through a filter during a set period of time expressed in U.S. gallons per minute per square foot of effective filter area.

© National Swimming Pool Foundation 2017

Filter Sand - A type of filter media composed of hard, sharp silica, quartz, or similar particles with proper grading for size and uniformity.

Filter Septum - That part of a filter on which diatomaceous earth or similar filter media is deposited. Usually consists of cloth, wire screen, or other fine mesh material.

Flocculant - A chemical that brings together fine particles in water to form larger particles. A compound usually used with sand-type filters to form a thin layer of gelatinous substance on the top of the sand. Aids in trapping fine suspended particles that might have passed through the sand.

Floc - A gelatinous substance resulting from the use of a flocculant.

Flow Meter - A device that measures pressure differential across a calibrated orifice and indicates the rate of flow at that point, usually given in gallons per minute or liters per minute.

Foot Spray - A device for spraying user's feet with water or a disinfectant. Usually a shower head at knee height to rinse sand, soil, and grass from feet before entry into the pool.

Free Chlorine (a.k.a. FC or Free Available Chlorine) **-** The portion of total chlorine that is not combined chlorine and is available as disinfectant (HOCl, and OCl-). The portion of total chlorine that reacts with DPD.

Friction Head - The head lost by flow in a stream due to friction between water and the piping and by friction between water molecules.

Galvanic Corrosion - Corrosion of metals that occurs when two or more dissimilar metals are immersed in an electrolyte (including pool water).

Gallons per Minute (gpm) **-** A measurement of water flow rate.

Gastroenteritis - Inflammation of the stomach and intestines.

Gutter - Overflow trough at the edge of a pool.

Hair & Lint Strainer - See Pump Strainer.

Hardness (water) **-** Refers to the quantity of dissolved minerals, chiefly calcium and magnesium compounds in the water. May be measured as Total Hardness (TH), which includes both calcium and magnesium hardness, or as Calcium Hardness (CH), which isolates only the calcium portion of the Total Hardness. Improper water balance may lead to these minerals being deposited as scale in pipes, pools and heaters.

Head - See Feet of Head.

Horsepower (hp) **-** A method for quantifying the power of a pump motor. Equal to 550 foot pounds per second and 746 watts.

Hose Bib - A valve with a threaded connection used to connect a hose.

Hydrochloric Acid (HCl) (a.k.a. Muriatic Acid) **-** A strong acid used to reduce the pH and total alkalinity and to clean scale or acid wash surfaces. It is also generated in the reaction of chlorine gas and water.

Hydrogen - A colorless, odorless, tasteless gaseous chemical element. High concentrations in air can detonate if ignited.

Hydrogen Ion (H+) **-** The positively charged ion of a hydrogen atom. Its presence in water solution is used as a measure of acidity of the solution (see pH).

Hydrogen Peroxide (H_2O_2) **- A** liquid oxidizer used with polyhexamethylene biguanide (PHMB) systems. Sold as 27.5 % and 7.5% in pool and spa applications. Reacts with and neutralizes chlorine and bromine.

Hydrotherapy Jet - A fitting that creates a high velocity stream of air in water.

Hydroxide Ion (OH-) **-** A negatively charged ion composed of one hydrogen atom and one oxygen atom.

Hypochlorinator - A chemical feeder through which liquid solutions of chlorine-bearing chemicals are fed into the pool water at a controllable rate.

Hypochlorite - Refers to any compound containing a metal ion and the (OCl-) anion. Most commonly refers to calcium, sodium, or lithium hypochlorite in pool usage.

Hypochlorous Acid (HOCl) **-** An unstable acid with excellent bactericidal and algicidal properties. The active agent by which chlorine serves as a disinfectant. Formed by dissolving chlorine gas, hypochlorites, chlorinated isocyanurates, or any other chlorinating agent in water. It is in dynamic equilibrium with hypochlorite ion (OCl-), dependant on the pH of the water.

Impeller - The rotating part of a centrifugal pump.

Impurity - See Contaminant.

Influent - Water flowing into a pool, pump, filter, chemical feeder, or other space.

Iodine - A blue-black crystalline chemical

© National Swimming Pool Foundation 2017

element of the same chemical family as chlorine and bromine. No longer used to treat pool or spa water.

Ion - An isolated atom or molecule that has gained or lost an electron and has acquired a negative or positive charge, respectively.

Ionizer - A device that releases heavy metal ions, such as copper or silver, into water. Used in conjunction with a residual disinfectant such as chlorine or bromine.

Isocyanurate - See Chlorinated Isocyanurates.

Lifeguard - An individual with the proper training and skills designed to keep patrons of aquatic facilities safe in and around the water.

Lifeline - A rope line across a pool to designate a change in slope in the pool bottom or the beginning of deep water. Usually supported by regularly spaced floats.

Lint Strainer - See Pump Strainer.

Lithium Hypochlorite (LiOCl) - A white granular solid disinfectant that contains 35% available chlorine content.

Logarithm - A mathematical term. The number that represents the power to which a given number must be raised to obtain another number. In pool usage, the power to which 10 must be raised to equal the reciprocal of the hydrogen ion concentration of the pool water. It is represented by the term pH.

Makeup Water - Potable water used to fill or refill a pool or spa.

Manometer - An instrument that measures pressure differential across an orifice by means of a column of liquid, usually mercury.

Marcite - A regional term used to describe pool plaster, specifically plaster containing a marble (calcium carbonate) aggregate.

Melamine - The reagent used to test for cyanuric acid and cyanurate concentrations in pool or spa water.

Micron - A unit of measure representing one millionth of a meter, or one thousandth of a millimeter.

Microorganism - A microscopic plant or animal.

Milligrams Per Liter (mg/L) - See Parts Per Million.

Molecule - A group of atoms bound together in a specific arrangement.

Monopersulfate - see Potassium Monopersulfate and Non-Chlorine Oxidizers.

Multiple Filter Control Valve (Multi-port Valve) - A special switching valve with a separate position for each of various filter operations such as normal filtration, backwash, drain, circulation, etc. Combines in one unit the functions of several direct-flow valves.

Muriatic Acid - See Hydrochloric Acid.

Non-Chlorine Oxidizers - Products other than chlorine that oxidize body wastes, organic matter, or reduce combined chlorine or chloramines. These products may not kill bacteria or algae. Many non-chlorine oxidizers are sold for pool and spa use, including potassium monopersulfate, hydrogen peroxide (H_2O_2), and sodium percarbonate ($NaHCO_4$).

NSPF® (a.k.a. National Swimming Pool Foundation®) - A non-profit foundation focused on improving public health by attracting more people to get exercise in the water and protecting people who go into the water with research and education programs.

Orifice - An opening, usually calibrated in size, through which liquid or gas flows.

Orifice Plate - A disc with a sharp edged, circular opening in the center. When placed in a water flow line, it creates a pressure differential to operate a rate of flow indicator, chemical feeder or other hydraulic mechanism.

Organic Waste - The portion of several contaminants in water (perspiration, body oils, urine, saliva, suntan oil, cosmetics, and/or contaminants) that contain carbon atoms. Other sources of organics in the water may include spilled food, animal wastes, soil, pollen, remnants of plants, etc.

Organisms - Plant or animal life. Usually refers to algae (plant), bacteria, viruses, or protozoa in pool water.

Orthotolidine (a.k.a. OTO) - A test reagent that turns yellow in the presence of total chlorine or total bromine. At higher concentrations, OTO darkens to gold and brown. OTO is a suspected carcinogen and banned by some health departments.

Overflow Gutter (a.k.a. Overflow Trough or Scum Gutter) - Trough around the top perimeter of a pool. Used to remove the water on the surface either to waste or to a filter.

Oxalic Acid - A weak organic acid, usually contained within products designed to remove metal stains from pool walls and floors or to clean rust from filter septa.

Oxidation - The process of changing the chemical structure of water contaminants

© National Swimming Pool Foundation 2017

by increasing the number of oxygen atoms or reducing the number of electrons in the contaminant.

Oxidation Reduction Potential (a.k.a. ORP) - A method of measuring the potential, which often relates to the concentration of an oxidizer in the water. ORP probes send signals to electrical controllers that can open valves on chemical feeders to dissolve and release disinfectants into the water.

Oxidizer - A substance capable of increasing the number of oxygen atoms or reducing the number of electrons in another chemical.

Ozone (O_3) - A gaseous oxidizer and supplemental disinfectant that is generated on-site, and then dissolved into water to oxidize contaminants and disinfect the water containing the ozone. Ozone is generated either by UV light or by a corona-discharge generator.

Parts per Million (a.k.a. ppm) - The amount of item being measured in one million units. In dilute water solutions, the weight volume relationship of milligrams per liter (mg/L) may be substituted.

Pathogen - A microorganism that causes disease in humans.

pH - The negative logarithm of the hydrogen-ion concentration of a water solution. A measure of the degree of acidity or alkalinity of a solution. A pH below 7.0 is considered acid. A pH above 7.0 is considered alkaline.

Phenol Red - An organic dye that is yellow at a pH of 6.8 and then turns progressively deeper red and purple in color as the pH increases to 8.4. The most commonly used test reagent for pH in pools.

Polymeric Clarification - The process of using a large organic chemical to flocculate contaminants and clear cloudy or colored water.

Potable - Water that is safe and suitable for drinking.

Potassium Alum (a.k.a. Potassium Aluminum Sulfate) - A flocculant in sand filter operation.

Potassium Monopersulfate (KHSO$_5$) (a.k.a. Potassium Peroxymonopersulfate) - A non-chlorine oxidizer used to reduce contaminants or to activate bromide ions to produce hypobromous acid.

Polyhexamethylene Biguanide (a.k.a PHMB) - A disinfectant used largely in residential pools or spas as part of a program that includes an oxidizer (hydrogen peroxide) and an algaecide that is compatible with biguanide.

ppm - See Parts per Million.

Pounds per Square Inch (a.k.a. psi) - A U.S. unit of measure for pressure or head.

Precipitate - A solid substance separating from a liquid as a result of a chemical or physical change to the environment. For example, the formation of scale or a scum line.

Precoat - The layer of diatomaceous earth deposited on the filter septa at the start of a filter run with D.E. filters.

Precoat Feeder - A chemical feeder designed to inject diatomaceous earth into a filter in sufficient quantity to coat the filter septa at the start of a filter run.

Pressure Differential - The difference in pressure between two points in a hydraulic system, such as the difference in pressure between the influent and the effluent points of a filter, a pump, a venturi tube, or an orifice plate.

Pressure Filter - A filter through which dirty water is pushed by a pump mounted on the influent side of the filter.

Probe - See Electrode.

Protozoa - A single celled parasite that causes gastroenteritis (stomach diseases) and release oocysts, which are resistant to disinfectants, in the feces of the victim. These oocysts can then infect other users. The most common pool-related protozoa are *Giardia* and *Cryptosporidium*.

Pump Curve - A graph of performance characteristics of a given pump under varying power, flow, and resistance factors. Used in checking and choosing a pump.

Pump Strainer (a.k.a. Lint Strainer, Pump Pot, or Hair and Lint Trap) - A container installed in the pump suction line with a removable basket, designed to protect the pump from debris in the water flow.

Quaternary Ammonium Compounds (a.k.a. Quat) - A family of chemicals used in various mixtures and concentrations to kill and prevent algae growth.

Rate of Flow Indicator - See Flow Meter.

Recirculating System - The entire system of pipes, pumps, and filters that allows water to be taken from the pool, filtered, treated, and then returned to the pool.

Reducing Agent - A substance capable of neutralizing oxidizers.

Residual - The concentration of a chemical (typically the disinfectant) in water.

Return Inlet - A fixture through which water is returned to the pool or spa from the circulation system.

Reverse Circulation - The name given to a pool water circulation system setting in which water is taken from the surface of the pool and returned through inlets at the bottom of the pool. Usually done to affect the water temperature.

Ring Buoy - A ring-shaped floating object capable of supporting a drowning person. Usually attached to a rope and kept at poolside for rescue use.

Sand Filter - A device that uses sand, or sand and gravel as the filter medium.

Sanitizer - See Disinfectant.

Saturation Index - A mathematical calculation based on the water temperature, calcium hardness, total alkalinity, pH, and dissolved solids that predicts if water has a tendency to deposit calcium carbonate (scale) or has a tendency to be corrosive.

Scale - Calcium carbonate ($CaCO_3$) deposits that can be found deposited in the filter, heater, or on the pool tile and wall. Generally caused by high calcium hardness, total alkalinity, temperature, and/or pH.

Septum - The plastic skeleton and cloth covering that holds the filter medium in a D.E. filter.

Sequestering Agent (a.k.a. Chelating Agent or Complexing Agent) **-** A chemical that binds to metal ions forming a complex with different properties than the metal ion. The sequestering agent is often used to form a complex that will precipitate from solution to remove the metal from water.

Service Factor - The degree to which an electric motor can be operated above its rated horsepower without danger of overload failure.

Skimmer - A device other than an overflow trough for continuous removal of surface water and floating debris from a pool. Water drawn through the skimmer goes to the filter.

Skimmer Weir - See Weir.

Slurry Feed - A suspension of solid in water that is easily pumpable.

Sodium Bicarbonate ($NaHCO_3$) (a.k.a. Baking Soda) **-** A powder used to raise the total alkalinity content of a pool with a small change in pH.

Sodium Bisulfate ($NaHSO_4$) (a.k.a. Dry Acid) **-** A white powder that lowers pH and alkalinity.

Sodium Carbonate (Na_2CO_3) (a.k.a. Soda Ash) **-** A white, water soluble solid used to raise the pH and alkalinity of pool water.

Sodium dichloro-s-triazinetrione ($C_3N_3O_3Cl_2Na$) (a.k.a. Dichlor or Dichloroisocyanuric acid) **-** A white solid disinfectant and oxidizer that releases chlorine (hypochlorous acid) and cyanuric acid (stabilizer) when dissolved in water. It is available in tablet or granular products. It contains about 56%-63% available chlorine content in the industrial grade, or less in formulated products.

Sodium Hydroxide ($NaOH$) (a.k.a. Caustic Soda or Lye) **-** A corrosive solid with a very high pH (14) that is usually sold in a liquid form to raise pH and alkalinity.

Sodium Hypochlorite ($NaOCl$) (a.k.a. Bleach or Liquid Chlorine) **-** A liquid disinfectant and oxidizer that releases chlorine (hypochlorous acid) when added to water. It contains between 10% to 15% available chlorine for swimming pool products and about 5% for household products.

Sodium Percarbonate ($NaHCO_4$) **-** A white solid oxidizer that generates hydrogen peroxide when dissolved in water.

Sodium Sesquicarbonate ($Na_2CO_3 \bullet NaHCO_3 \bullet 2H_2O$) **-** A solid white chemical used to raise the pH and alkalinity of pool water. This chemical has properties similar to a 50:50 blend of sodium carbonate and sodium bicarbonate.

Sodium Sulfite - A chemical used to neutralize oxidizers in water including disinfectants like chlorine and bromine.

Sodium Thiosulfate ($Na_2S_2O_3$) **-** A chemical used to remove chlorine from water. Used to remove chlorine from a test sample to avoid false pH test readings or false bacteria test results. It is also used in larger quantities to dechlorinate swimming pools.

Spa (a.k.a. hot tub, hydrotherapy pool, whirlpool, or swim spa) **-** A small recreational water vessel, usually designed for soaking as opposed to swimming. Spas are usually equipped with features and devices such as benches for sitting, venturi jets, air

© National Swimming Pool Foundation 2017

bubble bars, heated water, etc. Because of the smaller water volume, use, and water temperature, spas must be treated differently than pools.

Stabilizer - see Cyanuric Acid.

Sterilize - To kill all microorganisms.

Suction Head - The distance in feet a pump on the inlet side must raise the water from the pool or spa to the level of the pump.

Suction Outlet - A location within a pool or spa through which water is drawn by a pump through the circulation system.

Suction Piping - The piping or tube that feeds into the inlet side of a pump.

Superchlorination - The practice of adding large quantities of a chlorinating chemical to kill algae and microorganisms, eliminate slime, destroy odors, or improve the ability to maintain a disinfectant residual.

Supplemental Disinfectant - A chemical that kills pathogens, but does not maintain an adequate residual to maintain a sanitary state in pool or spa water.

Surface Area - a. The amount of water exposed to the air in a pool or spa, usually measured in square feet or square meters. b. The amount of plaster (or other interior pool coating material) exposed to the water, usually measured in square feet or square meters. c. The area of filter medium available to filter water, usually measured in square feet or square meters.

Surge - The displacement of water in a system, such as by users in a pool.

Surge Tank - A holding tank, pit, or vessel designed to offset surge displacement in a pool.

Swimmer Load - See User Load.

Titrant - A standard solution of known concentration used for titration.

Titration - A method of analyzing the composition of a water solution by adding known amounts of a standardized solution until a given reaction and color change occurs.

Total Alkalinity - A measure of the ability of the water to maintain a desirable pH when acid is added to the water. This value is usually expressed as the equivalent amount of calcium carbonate ($CaCO_3$) in either mg/L or ppm.

Total Chlorine (a.k.a. TC or Total Available Chlorine) **-** The total of all free available chlorine and combined chlorine in the water.

Total Dissolved Solids (TDS) **-** The amount of residue that would remain if all the water evaporated or was removed. Expressed as the mass of solid per the total initial volume of water (ppm or mg/L). Typically measured by electrical conductance.

Total Dynamic Head - A measure of a system's resistance to flow.

Total Hardness (TH) **-** The total of all calcium hardness and magnesium hardness in water.

Trichloro - See Trichloro-s-triazinetrione.

Trichloro-s-triazinetrione ($C_3N_3O_3Cl_3$) (a.k.a. **Trichlor or Trichloroisocyanuric acid) -** A disinfectant that releases chlorine (hypochlorous acid) and cyanuric acid (stabilizer) when dissolved in water. It is available as an active ingredient in tablet or granular products.

Trihalomethane (CHX_3) **-** A potentially carcinogenic chemical produced by the reaction between either chlorine or bromine with organic contaminants in water. One carbon atom (methane) with three halogen (X) atoms (chlorine or bromine) bound to the carbon.

Turbidity - A measure of the cloudiness or haziness of an otherwise clear liquid due to the presence of small liquid or solid particles in the liquid. Turbidity is measured in Nephelometer Turbidity Units (NTUs).

Turnover Rate - The time it takes (in hours) to circulate an amount of water equivalent to the volume of the pool or spa.

Ultraviolet Light (UV) **-** Electromagnetic radiation with a shorter wavelength (higher frequency) than visible light that is part of the spectrum of light emitted by the sun or can be generated artificially. Subdivided into three wavelengths: UV-A (315-400 nanometers), UV-B (290-315 nanometers), and UV-C (220-290 nanometers). A method used to generate ozone (see ozone). Used as a supplemental disinfectant to inactivate microorganisms. Exposure to UV light can lead to sun burn and ultimately skin cancer.

Underwater Light - A fixture designed to illuminate a pool from beneath the water's surface. May be wet-niche located in the pool water, or dry-niche located in the pool sidewall

© National Swimming Pool Foundation 2017

behind a waterproof window and serviced from outside the pool.

User Load (a.k.a. Swimmer Load) **-** The number of users in the water at a given moment or during a specific period of time. Maximum allowable user loads are often regulated in public pools and spas.

Vacuum Cleaner - One of several types of suction devices designed to collect dirt from the bottom of the pool. Some vacuums discharge dirt from the bottom of the pool, some discharge dirt and water into the filter, some discharge to waste, and some collect debris in a porous container, allowing water to return to the pool. Some vacuums are self-propelled; others must be manually pushed or pulled across the pool.

Vacuum Filter - A filter through which dirty water is pulled by a pump mounted on the effluent side of the filter.

Valve - A device used to control, restrict, or redirect the flow of water through the circulation system. Includes, backwash, multi-port, gate, ball, bleeder, and other types of valves.

Velocity - The distance water travels in a unit of time expressed in feet per second or meters per second.

Venturi Tube - A tube mounted in a water line that causes restriction of flow. The restriction causes a pressure differential that can be used to draw a liquid or a gas into the water line.

Virus - A microscopic infectious agent that replicates itself within living cells; many are pathogenic (disease-causing). They are carried and passed from infected people or animals. The most common pool-related viruses are Norwalk, Hepatitis A, and Adenovirus.

Voids - Spaces in or between particles or fibers of a filtering medium. These spaces determine the permeability and the dirt-holding capacity of the filter.

Volume - A measure of the size of a three-dimensional space. Typically the amount of water that occupies that space measured in gallons, cubic feet, or liters. One U.S. gallon is equivalent to 3.79 liters. One cubic foot is equivalent to 28.3 liters.

Weir - A flap within a skimmer that adjusts automatically to small changes in water level and assures a continuous water flow to the skimmer.

Winterizing - A method of closing a pool for the off-season. This may include preparing for cold or freezing conditions with both chemical and mechanical strategies for the pool and the facility.

Zeolite - A family of minerals containing hydrated aluminum silicates formed in cavities in lava flows and in plutonic rocks. Used as a filter medium that may be used in place of sand in sand filters.

© National Swimming Pool Foundation 2017

Reference:
Index

1. Pool & Spa Management
2. Regulations & Guidelines
3. Essential Calculations
4. Pool Water Contamination
5. Disinfection
6. Water Balance
7. Pool & Spa Water Problems
8. Chemical Testing
9. Chemical Feed & Control
10. Water Circulation
11. Pool & Spa Filtration
12. Heating & Air Circulation
13. Spa & Therapy Operations
14. Facility Safety
15. Keeping Records
16. Maintenance Systems
17. Troubleshooting
18. Facility Renovation & Design

References

References

© National Swimming Pool Foundation 2017

References

© National Swimming Pool Foundation 2017

1. Pool & Spa Management
2. Regulations & Guidelines
3. Essential Calculations
4. Pool Water Contamination
5. Disinfection
6. Water Balance
7. Pool & Spa Water Problems
8. Chemical Testing
9. Chemical Feed & Control
10. Water Circulation
11. Pool & Spa Filtration
12. Heating & Air Circulation
13. Spa & Therapy Operations
14. Facility Safety
15. Keeping Records
16. Maintenance Systems
17. Troubleshooting
18. Facility Renovation & Design
References
299

© National Swimming Pool Foundation 2017

Notes

© National Swimming Pool Foundation 2017

Notes

.

301

© National Swimming Pool Foundation 2017

Notes

© National Swimming Pool Foundation 2017

Notes

303

© National Swimming Pool Foundation 2017

Facility Manager Web App

FM

Special facilities demand exceptional care *and* a customizable tool to record it all. Meet **Facility Manager**, your time-saving solution!

- Pool testing and reporting
- Customizable checklists
- In-service records
- Pool closure reports
- Illness and injury reports
- MAHC & local code compliance

The Facility Manager App simplifies **risk management**, **daily documentation**, and **code compliance** all in one package.

Ready to make your record keeping and risk management reporting the easiest part of your day?
Contact **Michelle Kavanaugh**: **719.203.3531** | **michelle.kavanaugh@nspf.org**

Keeping Pools Safer.
Keeping Pools Open.

Counsilman·Hunsaker
AQUATICS FOR LIFE

Earn CEUs Through NSPF® Courses

ACCREDITED
IACET
PROVIDER

Upon completion of each NSPF® course, students receive information about how to acquire CEUs for the completed course. For a list of NSPF® CEU-approved courses, visit www.nspf.org, and click on the CEU icon at the bottom of the page.

NSPF® is accredited as an Authorized Provider of Continuing Education Units (CEUs) by the International Association for Continuing Education and Training (IACET). IACET provides a standard framework for learning and educational development through accreditation, and developed the original concept of CEUs as a unit of measure of educational training.

Earning CEUs indicates a student's commitment to best practices and professional training. Many organizations and employers require professionals to earn CEUs in order to maintain their licensure, certification, or employment status. NSPF courses meet this requirement and equip operators and service professionals with education to enhance their day-to-day operations.

CEU

© National Swimming Pool Foundation 2017